King, Kaiser, Tsar

Also by Catrine Clay

Master Race, 1993
Princess to Queen, 1996

King, Kaiser, Tsar

Three Royal Cousins Who Led
the World to War

CATRINE CLAY

WALKER & COMPANY

Copyright © 2006 by Catrine Clay

All rights reserved. No part of this book may be used or reproduced in any manner
whatsoever without written permission from the publisher except in the case of brief
quotations embodied in critical articles or reviews.
For information address Walker & Company, 104 Fifth Avenue, New York, New York 10011.

Published by Walker Publishing Company, Inc., New York
Distributed to the trade by Holtzbrinck Publishers

All papers used by Walker & Company are natural, recyclable products made from wood
grown in well-managed forests. The manufacturing processes conform to the environmental
regulations of the country of origin.

LIBRARY OF CONGRESS CATALOGING-IN-PUBLICATION DATA HAS BEEN APPLIED FOR.

ISBN-10: 0-8027-1623-7
ISBN-13: 978-0-8027-1623-1

Visit Walker & Company's Web site at www.walkerbooks.com

First published in Great Britain by John Murray, a division of Hodder Headline
First U.S. Edition 2007

1 3 5 7 9 10 8 6 4 2

Typeset by Servis Filmsetting Ltd, Manchester, UK
Printed in the United States of America by Quebecor World Fairfield

For John, naturally

Contents

Illustrations

The author and publishers wish to thank the following for permission to reproduce illustrations: 1, 2, 3, 5, 8, 11, 13, 14, 15, 19, 21, 22, 23, 27, 29, and 32, Her Majesty Queen Elizabeth II; 4, 12, 16, 18, 24, 25 and 33, GARF; 6, 7, 17, 28 and 31, Getty Images; 9, John Murray; 26 and 35, private; 10, Donaueschingen; 20, Bulow; 30, Grabbe.

Acknowledgements

I am most grateful to Her Majesty Queen Elizabeth II for permission to quote from the letters of King George V, Kaiser Wilhelm II and Tsar Nicholas II, as well as the diaries of George V, both before and after he became King. The three cousins, Georgie, Willy and Nicky, wrote to one another regularly right up to and including the First World War, freely mixing political comment with the usual gossip of family life; indeed, it is often hard to tell the difference. Without this special access to their private letters this book could not have been written in the form it now takes. I am equally indebted to Her Majesty for allowing me to reproduce a selection of photographs from the Royal Collection, and examples of the actual letters from one royal cousin to the other, allowing us to study handwritings and signatures. I would like to take this opportunity to thank the staff at the Royal Archives. Pamela Clark, the Registrar, Jill Kelsey, who had the arduous task of checking my numerous quotes, and Lisa Heighway, who helped to locate the many illustrations, were all unfailingly generous with their expert help.

My thanks otherwise can best be expressed in chronological order. Without the constant encouragement and advice of Anthony Sheil, my esteemed literary agent, this book would never have been written at all. It was Anthony Sheil who suggested it in the first place, after seeing the BBC documentary I made of the same title in early 2003, and then placed it with John Murray. It was my luck that Roland Philipps not only took the book on, but took on the task of editing it. I would describe Roland as the ideal editor. He makes his incisive comments with the most engaging good humour. His best advice was characteristically succinct: 'Slash away!' His team at John Murray, including Rowan Yapp who oversaw the production, Liz Robinson who copy edited, Edward Bettison who designed the fine jacket, Nikki Barrow, the whiz publicist, Amanda Jones, the Production

Manager, and Douglas Matthews who did the index, share Roland's excellent way of doing business. I thank them all.

Research in Germany was relatively unproblematic since I speak the language. Not so in Russia, nor in Denmark. In Russia I have Sergei Podbolotov to thank for help with document research, and Lena Yakovleva for picture research, at the State Archives of the Russian Federation, GARF. For help with the Danish princesses, Alexandra and Minny, I have Liselotte Sykes to thank. The two sisters, mothers of George V and Tsar Nicholas II respectively, played a crucial but little-known role in royal family alignments. They hated Prussia with a vengeance. Without Liselotte Sykes's translations of relevant sections of Inger-Lise Klausen's book on the Tsarina, I would not have been able to give a full account of this, or of the influence the sisters had on Georgie and Nicky, their two sons.

I have been extremely fortunate in my informal advisers. Kenneth Rose offered me many good tips, usually over lunch in some congenial spot. His fine biography of George V makes regular appearances in this book. John Röhl, Emeritus Professor of History at the University of Sussex, has given me the benefit of forty years of scholarship on the Kaiser. His three-volume collection *Philipp Eulenburgs Politische Korrespondenz* pinpoints once and for all the central importance to Wilhelm of his relationship with the homosexual Count Philipp zu Eulenburg. I thank John Röhl very much for taking time from writing the third volume of his biography of Wilhelm II to talk to me on the subject, and offer some extra details of research.

John van der Kiste read and checked the manuscript of the book. Kevin Brownlow pointed me in the direction of fascinating archive film of the period, an under-used source of historical research. Robert Lacey kindly gave me the transcript of his Radio 4 series on George V's 1914 diary. Hugo Vickers introduced me to *Royalty Digest*, a magazine filled with unexpected bits of information about Georgie, Willy and Nicky, as well as their various brothers, sisters, mothers, fathers and aunts.

My friends, who have listened patiently as I talked on about the three cousins, know who they are. I thank them all 'from my heart', to quote George V. But most of all I thank John, my husband, who has helped and advised me throughout, and to whom this book, naturally, is dedicated.

Note on Dates and Spellings

Russian dates in this book follow the Western calendar, which was twelve days ahead of the Russian calendar in the nineteenth century and thirteen days in the twentieth, until February 1918 when the two were standardised. Names were spelt in a confusing variety of ways within the European royal family. Nicknames also varied, as with Alix, the Tsarina, who was also known as Alicky. I have tried to make them as consistent as possible, as I have place-names.

The European royals loved exclamation marks, capital letters and underlinings. For the purpose of this book. I have used capital letters.

The families of the King, the Kaiser and the Tsar

Only the main characters who feature in the book are named here.

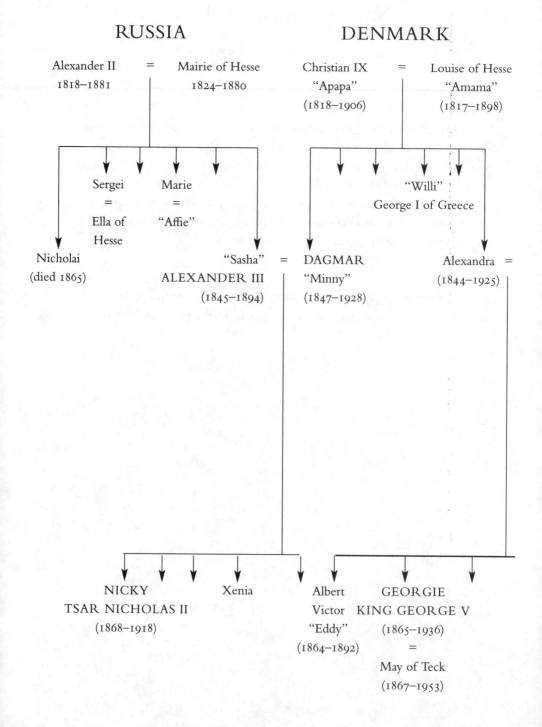

RUSSIA

Alexander II = Mairie of Hesse
1818–1881   1824–1880

Sergei
=
Ella of
Hesse

Marie
=
"Affie"

Nicholai
(died 1865)

"Sasha" =
ALEXANDER III
(1845–1894)

DENMARK

Christian IX = Louise of Hesse
"Apapa"   "Amama"
(1818–1906)   (1817–1898)

"Willi"
George I of Greece

DAGMAR
"Minny"
(1847–1928)

Alexandra =
(1844–1925)

NICKY
TSAR NICHOLAS II
(1868–1918)

Xenia

Albert
Victor
"Eddy"
(1864–1892)

GEORGIE
KING GEORGE V
(1865–1936)
=
May of Teck
(1867–1953)

BRITAIN

GERMANY

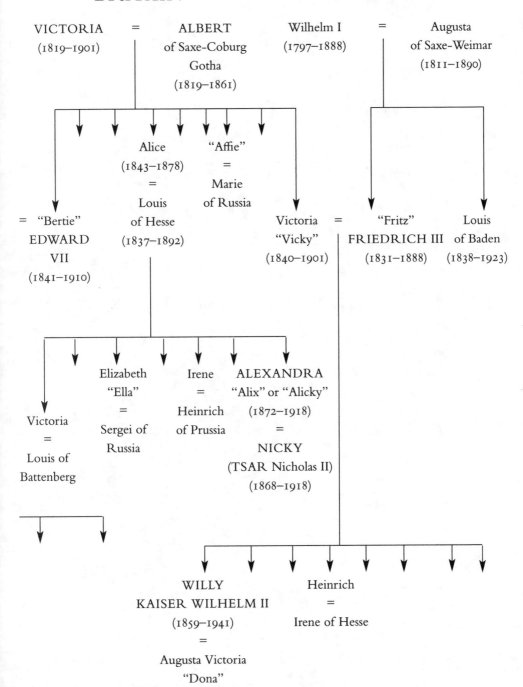

VICTORIA = ALBERT
(1819–1901) of Saxe-Coburg
Gotha
(1819–1861)

Wilhelm I = Augusta
(1797–1888) of Saxe-Weimar
(1811–1890)

Alice
(1843–1878)
=
Louis
of Hesse
(1837–1892)

"Affie"
=
Marie
of Russia

= "Bertie"
EDWARD
VII
(1841–1910)

Victoria =
"Vicky"
(1840–1901)

"Fritz"
FRIEDRICH III
(1831–1888)

Louis
of Baden
(1838–1923)

Elizabeth
"Ella"
=
Sergei of
Russia

Irene
=
Heinrich
of Prussia

ALEXANDRA
"Alix" or "Alicky"
(1872–1918)
=
NICKY
(TSAR Nicholas II)
(1868–1918)

Victoria
=
Louis of
Battenberg

WILLY
KAISER WILHELM II
(1859–1941)
=
Augusta Victoria
"Dona"

Heinrich
=
Irene of Hesse

Introduction

~

O N 21 MAY 1913 dockworkers were standing about on the quayside at Flushing in Holland when the Royal Yacht *Victoria and Albert* came alongside. Her hull was black, decorated with a double gold line. She had a full-time crew of a hundred and twenty and she could carry fifty guests. The dockworkers watched as George V, dapper in bowler hat and carrying a tightly furled umbrella, came down the gangplank, followed by his Private Secretary Lord Stamfordham and Frederick Ponsonby, his Equerry-in-Waiting. Queen Mary had preceded him and was already seated in the automobile which would take them the short distance to the railway station where the Kaiser's Imperial train awaited them. They were on their way to Berlin to attend the wedding of the Kaiser's only daughter, Princess Victoria Louise. George V decided to walk to the station, accompanied by his courtiers. A couple of urchins ran alongside this august group, curious to see a real King.

In the train George V changed into his German Field Marshal's uniform. 'We reached Berlin at 11.30 & were received by William, Victoria & all the Princes & Princesses, Generals, Adm[ira]ls etc. and a G[uar]d of H[onour] of the 1st Regt of the Guards which marched past. I drove to the Schloss with William in an open carriage with escort, streets lined by the whole garrison of Berlin, very fine sight,' wrote George that evening in the comfort of his own rooms in the royal palace at Potsdam. Kaiser Wilhelm II was George V's first cousin. George called him William or Willy, just as their grandmother Queen Victoria had. Tsar Nicholas II, the third royal cousin, known in the family as Nicky, would arrive from Russia the next day. Between them Georgie, Willy and Nicky ruled more than half the world.

'May and I have accepted William's kind invitation to be present at his daughter's wedding next month,' Georgie had telegraphed Nicky, his cousin on his mother's side. 'I also understand he has invited you and I trust that you may be able to come as it would give me the greatest pleasure to meet you there. I hope nothing will prevent this. Our best love to Alix and the children. Georgie.' 'I'll go if you go,' Nicky telegraphed back.

It looked like just another family outing, one of a series of weddings, funerals and christenings which punctuated the royal calendar. But beneath the friendly exchange of invitations and telegrams, and almost obscured by the pomp and ceremony of a royal event, lay a long history of personal jealousies and rivalries. Years later George V recalled that he was rarely able to be alone in a room with the Tsar during that Berlin visit without the Kaiser hovering outside the door, spying on them. Though they did not know it, the Berlin wedding was to be the last occasion on which the three royal cousins were together before the First World War, the last time any of them would ever see each other. By 1918 Nicky was dead, assassinated along with his family by the Bolsheviks at Ekaterinburg, and Willy was in exile in Holland, there to live on in obscurity for another twenty-three years. Georgie was the only one of the three to survive the war with his monarchy intact – more than intact: flourishing.

The three cousins had known one another since childhood. They had shared holidays, visited each other's homes, played together, celebrated each other's birthdays, danced with each other's sisters, and later attended each other's weddings. They were tied to one another by history, and history would tear them apart. Queen Victoria – Georgie and Willy's grandmother, Nicky's grandmother by marriage – was the lynchpin of the family, having her say on everything. 'I fear I cannot admire the names you propose to give the Baby. George only came over with the Hanoverian family,' she wrote to Georgie's father, the Prince of Wales, on 13 June 1865. 'However, if the dear child grows up good and wise, I shall not mind what his name is. Of course you will add Albert at the end, like your brothers, as you know we settled long ago that all dearest Papa's male English descendants should bear that name, to mark our line, just as I wish all the girls to have Victoria at the end of theirs!' She minded less about Georgie because he was only the second son, not the eventual heir to the throne.

The story of the three royal cousins begins lightly, but ends in the dark of the First World War. And the question which runs through it, right up to the last moment of hope before the outbreak of war, is to what extent they – the King, the Kaiser and the Tsar – through their own personalities and their relationships to one another contributed to the political developments and failures which finally made that war inevitable. The answer forms the subject of this book, an answer filled with contradictions and complications but one which leads ineluctably to the conclusion that the relationships between the three, their personal likes and dislikes, did indeed contribute to the outbreak of hostilities.

At the end of the nineteenth and the beginning of the twentieth century the monarchs of Europe, principally those of England, Germany and Russia, still enjoyed great power, especially in Russia and Germany, where the Tsar and the Kaiser were autocrats. But at the same time these monarchs were also plain Georgie, Willy and Nicky, three cousins affected by the usual ups and downs of family life. But whereas in any ordinary family the inevitable quarrels and clashes of personality could play themselves out with little damage to anyone else, any private quarrels and rivalries between Georgie, Willy and Nicky were played out in public, on the dangerous stage of international politics. The homosexual scandals surrounding the Kaiser, the power exerted by Alix, the Tsarina, over her vacillating husband Nicky, the snubs regularly meted out to Willy by his English relations – none of these would have had any impact on world events but for the fact that the three cousins were also the King, the Kaiser and the Tsar.

'What a strange spectacle Europe is presenting, a perfectly unknown future depending upon the will of three or four men,' wrote the Prime Minister Lord Salisbury to his friend Canon Gordon in August 1896. 'It is very remarkable that in spite of the progress of democratic ideas, the weight of individual personalities, for good or evil, is greater than ever. Now every turn in the humours of the Emperor Nicholas or the Emperor William, or the Sultan of Turkey is watched and interpreted – the fate of many thousands of lives depends on them.' Salisbury did not mention his own sovereign, Queen Victoria, because England was a constitutional monarchy, and the Queen was answerable to Parliament.

Power in the wrong hands is a constant theme, as pressing then as it is today. At the turn of the century the systems of power were beginning to shift as the old regimes were forced to give way to the new. The Ottoman Empire was fading, the nation states were rising. The people were on the march, fuelled by industrial progress. In hindsight it is easy enough to see that the monarchies of Europe were under threat; but the King, the Kaiser and the Tsar were not the only ones who failed to read the signs.

For all three royal cousins the monarchy was what mattered most, the one thing for which all else might be sacrificed. This was what they unquestionably shared, the thing they understood like no one else. Monarchs stood shoulder to shoulder, and together they faced the problems of obstreperous parliaments, rising Socialism, a critical press, and threatening Republicanism, writing each other long letters of commiseration and support. Paradoxically, however, once it came to national interests and defending their own crowns, the Trade Union of Kings, as Edward VII liked to call it, fell apart and the King, the Kaiser and the Tsar, instead of helping to maintain the peace, contributed to its destruction and to the outbreak of a war more terrible than anyone could ever have imagined.

I

Willy's Bad Start

~

JUST BEFORE MIDNIGHT on 26 January 1859 Vicky, Crown Princess of Prussia and eldest daughter of Queen Victoria and Prince Albert, went into labour in the Royal Palace in Berlin. She was attended by a team of German doctors, led by the court physician Dr Wegner. Standing by were Sir James Clark, Queen Victoria's personal physician, and Mrs Innocent, the midwife, sent from England by the Queen, oblivious to the resentment this would inevitably cause in Prussia. Fourteen long hours later the child was born. He was named Friedrich Wilhelm Viktor Albrecht von Hohenzollern, Willy for short.

During the fourteen hours of labour it became increasingly clear that something was amiss. At ten o'clock next morning Dr Éduard Martin, Professor of Obstetrics at Berlin University, was summoned to assist Dr Wegner. Sir James Clark had brought some of the newly invented chloroform from England, but had confined himself diplomatically to the sidelines. After an internal examination, the alarmed Dr Martin was forced to administer chloroform to the mother and use forceps to lever out the child. It was a breech birth and there was little hope, for babies rarely survived breech births at that time. The mother was half dead from exhaustion and pain. The Berlin newspapers had her obituary ready and prepared for publication. But at last, early that afternoon, Willy emerged, rump first, with his left arm wrapped awkwardly round his neck. He was quite lifeless and badly bruised, 'seemingly dead to a high degree' as Dr Martin later reported. But after being slapped hard many times, Willy finally began to breathe.

The initial reaction was one of relief. The mother was safe, the child was born and, last but by no means least, it was a boy. Once tidied up, the baby was joyfully presented to his German grandparents and attendant courtiers. Outside the palace a large crowd had gathered in the snow, waiting for news. At three o'clock in the afternoon a hundred-and-one-gun salute told them what they hoped to hear:

there was a son and heir for the Prussian throne. Sir James Clark sent word to Queen Victoria, assuring her that all was well. 'God be praised for all his mercies, and for bringing you through this awful time!' the Queen wrote on 29 January from Windsor Castle. 'My precious darling, you suffered much more than I ever did . . . Poor dear Fritz – how he will have suffered for you! I think and feel much for him. The dear little boy if I could but see him for one minute, give you one kiss. It is hard, very hard.'

Vicky was confined to her bed for a month. On 28 February she wrote back to her mother: 'I am so thankful, so happy, he is a boy. I longed for one more than I can describe, my whole heart was set upon a boy and therefore I did not expect one . . . I feel very proud of him and very proud of being a Mama.' Queen Victoria was now able to turn her attention to less pressing matters. 'I am shocked to hear baby leaves off his cap so soon,' she wrote. 'I hope however only in the nursery, for they look so frightful to be seen without caps. In the nursery it is wholesome but it is not pretty.' Willy had a wet nurse for the first eight months, while Mrs Innocent oversaw the nursery. 'Quite between ourselves,' Vicky confided to her mother, 'I would not have had a German nurse come close to him for all the world.'

Unusually for a royal marriage, Vicky and Fritz's had been a love match, if a most convenient one. It enabled Vicky's parents, Queen Victoria and Prince Albert, to fulfil a dream they had cherished ever since they themselves were married: to see the English model of monarchy adopted throughout Europe. 'English' meant constitutional and liberal, and neither Victoria nor Albert was troubled by a single doubt that this was the right model to unite Europe, foster peace and stave off revolution. Being related to most of the other monarchs was helpful, but the best way to secure real influence was, as it had always been, through marriage. Queen Victoria's letters and journals are filled with accounts of match-making, both significant and insignificant. The insignificant were permitted to be purely romantic, the significant were always supposed to be in 'our' interest. If any of the relations disagreed, which from time to time they did, they were treated to Queen Victoria's famous disdain.

But of all the European Crowns, the one Victoria and Albert minded about most was the Crown of Prussia and, later, of Imperial Germany. After all, they were more than half German themselves, Queen Victoria having German grandparents, and Albert having arrived in England from the small and impoverished German state of Coburg in 1840, to marry the young Queen and Empress of the most powerful nation in the world.

Vicky, or Pussy as a family obsessed with nicknames liked to call her, was the eldest of their nine children and determined to hold on to her pre-eminent position, a feat she was clever and attractive enough to achieve with ease. It did not hurt that the second child, Bertie, the future Edward VII, was considered very ordinary, neither very bright nor very ambitious. Vicky referred to him haughtily as 'the boy', and the boy accepted his inferiority without much of a fight. Her father, with little official work to do while his wife attended to affairs of state, spent hours talking to Vicky, his undisputed favourite. Prince Albert of Saxe-Coburg-Gotha was serious and high-minded, and loved nothing better than educating his precocious daughter. Vicky for her part was a most receptive pupil who loved and admired her father, perhaps excessively.

From the age of six Vicky's mornings were spent with her governess doing arithmetic, dictation, poetry and history (mostly royal) and in the afternoons, geography, more history, scripture, music, art and dancing. She was irritatingly good at everything. Bertie quickly transferred his affections to his younger and gratifyingly average sister, Alice. While the proud parents smiled on Pussy, they shook their heads and frowned on Bertie. As for Alfred or Affie, the fourth and again disappointingly unpromising child, he was educated from the start to become the heir to the Coburg throne, 'that dear small country' as Queen Victoria liked to call it. Affie would be German whether he liked it or not.

'I must write down at once WHAT has happened – what I FEEL and how grateful I am to God for one of the happiest days of my life!' Queen Victoria wrote ecstatically in her journal on 29 September 1855, referring to the day Crown Prince Friedrich of Prussia came to Balmoral to propose to Vicky. Vicky was barely fifteen, but already extremely confident, not to say opinionated. Prince Friedrich, or Fritz, was handsome enough to be known as 'Siegfried' in his own country, but certainly not as intelligent or as determined as his betrothed. From the start there were rumours that Fritz loved Vicky too much, and was too much in her power, but Victoria and Albert's dream of a 'Prussian marriage' was secure. They were sublimely unconcerned that the Prussian aristocracy was offended by what they in turn called the 'English marriage', that the Tsar of Russia was less than pleased with this new alliance, even that *The Times* referred to Prussia as that 'wretched state'.

From the moment of the betrothal, Prince Albert spent two hours every evening preparing his daughter Vicky for her future role as Crown Princess of Prussia, bearer of those liberal ideas which would shape the new Germany. And Vicky, quick on the uptake and believing her father could do no wrong, happily absorbed the lessons, eager to put them into practice as soon as possible. Nevertheless, her parents insisted she wait till she was eighteen before she married and could embark on her mission, one which did not, in the event, evolve quite as planned.

The Prussians expected the marriage to take place in Berlin. Queen Victoria was pleased to disagree. 'Whatever may be the usual practice of Prussian Princes,' she wrote sharply to Lord Clarendon, who was to inform the Prussians otherwise, 'it is not every day that one marries the eldest daughter of the Queen of England. The question therefore must be considered as settled and closed.' The couple were married on 25 January 1858, in the Chapel Royal at St James's Palace. After a short honeymoon at Windsor, they set off for Berlin. 'My Beloved Papa,' Vicky wrote from the Royal Yacht *Victoria and Albert*, crossing the North Sea to Germany, 'The pain of parting from you yesterday was more than I can describe; I thought my heart was going to break when you shut the cabin door and were gone . . . I should have liked to have thanked you for all that you have done for me, for all your kindness. All your love . . . To you, dear Papa, I owe most in this world. I shall never forget the advice it has been my privilege to hear from you at different times. I treasure your words in my heart, they will have with God's help an influence on my whole life.' Now that she had to part from everything that was familiar and dear to her, she was broken-hearted.

The Crown Prince and Princess's triumphal procession through Northern Germany took almost a week. Everywhere there were speeches, deputations of welcome and gala banquets. First they stopped at Cologne, then at Magdeburg. At Hanover there was an awkward moment when Vicky saw that the King of Hanover had inadvertently (or perhaps advertently) ordered that the gold plate service be used for the gala dinner. Queen Victoria claimed the plate belonged to her, the King, her cousin, disputed it, and they were currently embroiled in a legal battle to decide the outcome. Vicky sensibly pretended not to notice. On Monday 8 February they finally made their grand entry into Berlin to pealing church bells and thundering cannon. In a true spirit of welcome the crowds lining the royal route waved English as well as Prussian flags as the state coach, drawn by eight horses with postilions and outriders, made its way through the Brandenburg Gate down Unter Den Linden to the Royal Palace. Vicky, wearing a coronet of diamonds, waved and smiled, though the state coach, made largely of glass, was freezing cold, and she only had a short ermine cape over her thin silken gown. 'She shivered from head to foot,' recalled a German Court official, 'and I was told that after the first greetings at the Schloss were over she broke down and cried.'

The festivities lasted a fortnight. The same Court official reveals that the German people were delighted that this royal wedding was a love match. But the future Chancellor, Otto von Bismarck, was not so pleased. On 8 April 1858 Bismarck wrote to General von Gerlach, the Prussian delegate at Frankfurt: 'You ask me in your letter what I think of the English marriage. I must separate the two words to give you my opinion. The 'English' in it does not please me, the 'marriage' may be quite good, for the Princess has the reputation of a lady of brain and heart. If the Princess can leave the Englishwoman at home and become a Prussian, then she may be a blessing to the country.' That, unfortunately, was precisely what Vicky could not do without betraying her parents' dearest wish. Prussia was to become English, hardly the other way round.

Meanwhile she was trying to accustom herself to her new life and the strange ways of the Prussian Court. Everything was reported back in long letters to her mother. The Berlin Court was provincial, the etiquette stiff and old-fashioned; the men excessively military, always in uniform, the women extremely boring, it not being the Prussian way for women to have opinions. Vicky herself naturally held opinions on everything and was used to expressing them in a forthright manner. And she expected to be taken seriously. Perhaps because her dazzled husband fully agreed, she never managed to curb this tendency, and in all the years ahead, she never managed to think of Prussia as home. 'She certainly was a little tyrant,' wrote Countess Walburga von Hohenthal, one of her ladies-in-waiting, 'and with a less chivalrous and devoted husband there might have been difficulties.' Vicky was soon being referred to not as the Crown Princess of Prussia, but as 'the English Princess'.

Her mother did not help. She demanded letters almost daily, and in return gave endless advice. 'Promise me faithfully dear not to keep your rooms too hot – or let the fire catch your face, and also to get fresh air as much as you can. I know that you are quite aware of the necessity of it, but you are lazy, my good child, often, and may neglect looking at thermometers and to open windows.' She was by no means pleased to hear that Vicky was pregnant. She thought her much too young at nineteen, and Fritz a typically selfish man to place his wife in such a position hardly a year after their marriage. 'What you say of the pride of giving life to an immortal soul is very fine, dear,' she wrote, 'but I own I cannot enter into that; I think much more of our being like a cow or a dog at such moments.'

Within a few days of Willy's birth the nurses noticed that his left arm hung limp and useless at his side. Later it was discovered that he was unable to sit up properly. The neck muscles and ligaments had been so badly torn by Dr Martin's brutal wielding of the forceps that Willy's head drooped to one side, unbalancing him. Later still it was found that his right ear and hearing had also been seriously damaged. As Willy grew older the ear developed inflammations, with growths and excretions affecting the delicate inner ear which, as the medical specialists warned, was dangerously close to the brain.

At first his parents were not too alarmed. The doctors suggested that Willy's right arm be strapped to his side to make him use the left one. When there was no improvement he was subjected to a series of treatments. First came animal baths, when the limp arm was wrapped in the still-warm skin of a freshly killed hare. Next the arm was treated with primitive electric shocks. When he was four Willy was strapped into an iron machine for an hour every day to straighten him out. The child seemed to bear it all with remarkable cheerfulness and forbearance, but Willy himself put it slightly differently in his memoirs: 'Medical science was not as advanced in those days as it is now,' he wrote. 'So I was subjected to various treatments which one could nowadays only describe as amateur, the only result being that I was painfully tortured.'

The crippled arm, which eventually was some five inches shorter than the other, with the hand half-size and quite useless, caused Vicky increasing distress. 'The ARM makes hardly any progress,' she wrote to her father when Willy was one. 'The idea of his remaining a cripple haunts me . . . I long to have a child with everything perfect about it like EVERY BODY ELSE . . .' She blamed herself because she had tripped over a chair on a slippery palace floor when she was five months pregnant. She asked her parents not to tell the others at home about Willy's deformity.

When her next child Charlotte was born eighteen months after Willy, Vicky wrote unfeelingly: 'She is 1000 times nicer because she is always good and a great deal prettier then he ever was and takes twice as much notice now, as he did when he was twice the age she is . . . I am so proud of her and like to show her off, which I never did with him as he was so thin and pale and fretful at her age.' 'The ARM' was the reason Vicky felt Willy wasn't 'pretty', because otherwise he was a good-looking child.

The science of psychology was not advanced in the 1860s, and Willy was mishandled from the start. Medical specialists completely missed the most important symptom of all: the child's extreme restlessness and lack of concentration, which became a distinguishing feature of the mature man, causing endless problems for his courtiers and political advisers. In a later, post-Freudian period, Willy's strange behaviour as a child might have been seen for what it was, an emotional disturbance which needed careful handling. As it is, he was surrounded by ignorance and empty flattery, which only made his condition worse. He longed for affection, the one thing his mother found it almost impossible to give. His father, less complicated than Vicky, refused to acknowledge any problems, blindly believing that everything would come right in time, and was often seen carrying his over-lively child around the palace, proudly showing him off to anyone who might come their way.

Willy's greatest problem was unavoidable: the hopes and expectations of Prussia rested on his shoulders. But at the same time he was expected to fulfil Victoria and Albert's dream of a united Germany ruled along English democratic lines. So Wilhelm, future German Kaiser, was split from the start, Prussian on one hand, English on the other. Even his name was split. Friedrich Wilhelm Viktor Albrecht arrived into this world festooned with the names of his German father, German grandfather, English grandmother and English (albeit originally German) grandfather, in that order. If he was Wilhelm in Germany, in England he was always William. Luckily Willy worked in both languages, though Queen Victoria persisted in spelling it 'Willie'. The liberal English model represented by his mother came into daily conflict with the autocratic Prussian one represented by his grandfather King Wilhelm, and by Bismarck. And Willy, bright and ambitious but emotionally confused, jumped first this way then that, with only one certain outcome: if he pleased one side, he offended the other.

The rift between Vicky and Bismarck was apparent early on. As soon as her father-in-law inherited the Prussian crown in 1861 Bismarck was at his side, guiding him to put his own stamp on Germany. The stamp was purely Prussian – militaristic, and most certainly not liberal – and was bound to come into conflict with the democratic forces beginning to flourish in Germany as a result of rapid industrial expansion. The first confrontation with Parliament was over King Wilhelm's planned reform of the Prussian army, which he intended to enlarge massively. When the Reichstag refused to fund it he dismissed his ministers, dissolved the Reichstag and called in Bismarck, who was at that time the Prussian Ambassador in Paris. Bismarck became Minister-President in 1862, and together he and King Wilhelm embarked on their vision of a militaristic state ruled by a monarchy which told Parliament what to do, and not the other way round. The fact that the Liberals were gaining ground in the Reichstag did not bother Bismarck, the Iron Chancellor. 'Germany does not look to Prussia's liberalism, but to Prussia's might,' he said in a speech almost designed to offend Vicky. 'The great questions of the times will not be solved by speeches and majority decisions, but by iron and blood.'

The antipathy between the two was cast in stone a year later when Bismarck set about curtailing the freedom of the press. Vicky and Fritz were appalled. Not used to holding her peace, Vicky persuaded Fritz to condemn the act as unconstitutional during a speech he was giving in Danzig. It caused an awful row between father and son, and permanent hostility between Vicky and Bismarck. In her letters home to her mother she calls Bismarck false, dangerous, unprincipled, and an Anglophobe.

In fact Bismarck never forgot Danzig, and began a secret campaign to undermine the Crown Prince and Princess. The Court official who reported on their wedding had a particular liking for Vicky, but was forced to admit that her obstinacy and lack of diplomacy had created serious problems. He felt that Vicky 'idolised' her father and that at the heart of the problem lay the discussions she had had with him before ever coming to the Berlin Court. 'These discussions', he sadly reflected, 'were injudicious and sometimes detrimental to harmony later on . . . Her education, in fact, had been, for Prussian ideas, on a quite unnecessary scale for a woman.'

Willy's own memories of his early years began with England. 'The earliest memories I can recall are connected with Osborne on the Isle of Wight,' he wrote in his memoirs, *Aus Meinem Leben*, published in 1922 from his exile in Holland after the First World War. 'I have an exact memory of my grandfather, Prince Consort Albert, husband of Queen Victoria. He spent a lot of time with his eldest little grand-child, and liked to put me in a napkin and swing me around . . . I was two and a half years old.' The grandparents had in fact met Willy for the first time at Coburg the previous summer. 'Such a little love!' Queen Victoria wrote in her Journal.

The Prussian Crown Prince and his small family were in England for three months in 1861, from June to August. For Vicky it was the first visit home since her marriage, and it is not difficult to imagine her joy. Father and daughter had plenty of time to pick up the threads of their political discussions, happy again to agree on everything. Once Vicky was back in Berlin, Prince Albert wrote urging her, a touch ponderously, to keep up the good work: 'May your life, which has begun beautifully, expand still further to the good of others and the contentment of your own mind! True inward happiness is to be sought only in the internal consciousness of effort systematically directed to good and useful ends.' It was a letter to celebrate her twenty-first birthday. A month later Prince Albert was dead, struck down by typhoid after visiting wayward Bertie in Cambridge. Queen Victoria's grief is well known; Vicky's was almost as bad.

Willy remembered much more of their next visit to England, in 1863 for his uncle Bertie's wedding in St George's Chapel, Windsor on 10 March. The ceremony was long for four-year-old William (as he was for the time being), attending in full Highland costume. Although he loved the pageantry and the music, he soon grew rest-less. When one of his uncles ticked him off, he bit him in the leg. Queen Victoria watched the proceedings with a certain detachment from the Royal Closet above the chapel. For her the real ceremony had already taken place privately the day before. 'Drove with Alix, Lenchen [her third daughter] and Bertie to the Mausoleum where Vicky and Fritz met us. I opened the shrine and took them in. Alix was much moved and so was I. I said "He gives you his blessing," and joined Alix and Bertie's hands, taking them both in my arms and kissing them. It was a very touching moment and we all felt it.' Alix might not have been clever, but she knew how to reach Queen Victoria's heart.

On Willy's sixth birthday Queen Victoria sent him a present of a writing case. 'That beloved and promising child was adored Papa's great favourite; he took (and he takes I am sure) so deep an interest in him and in his physical and moral well-doing,' she wrote to Vicky. 'But bring him up simply, plainly, not with that terrible Prussian pride and ambition, which grieved dear Papa so much and which he always said would stand in the way of Prussia taking that lead in Germany which he ever wished her to do!' Vicky wrote back about the 'important task' of Willy's education: 'I shall endeavour to make him feel that pride and devotion for his country and ambition to serve it that will make sacrifices and difficulties seem easy to him. And may I be able to instil our British feeling of independence into him, together with our brand of English common sense, so rare on this side of the water.'

From September 1866, when he was seven, Willy began lessons with Dr Georg Hinzpeter, who had a greater influence on his upbringing than anyone else. Hinzpeter was a 39-year-old bachelor, aesthetic in habit and appearance, and extremely Spartan in his tastes. He was a strict Calvinist who believed in duty, self-sacrifice and the value of hard work. He had absolutely no sense of humour. The future monarch must not be spoilt and he must learn duty and self-discipline. The regime should be simple and strict, for this child would sooner or later be surrounded by flattery. These are notions which crop up again and again in the education of all three royal cousins, and it is easy now to see how misguided it was, and how useless as a defence against the corroding power of flattery. Vicky was additionally determined that Willy's education be civil in character, not military. Or to put it another way, English not Prussian.

To Willy's parents Hinzpeter seemed the perfect choice. He was not a noble, a fact much appreciated by both of them, but the son of an ordinary grammar school teacher, and an ordinary grammar school teacher himself before entering the service of an acquaintance of theirs. The Crown Prince and Princess were impressed by his seriousness of purpose and his cleverness, because Hinzpeter was a Doctor of Philosophy. Hinzpeter, for his part, was perhaps a little more ambitious than his extremely respectful demeanour implied. To Vicky and Fritz's delight he appeared to agree with them on everything, even sharing their own liberal views and keen interest in social matters. They were increasingly worried by Willy's restlessness and lack of concentration, and thought Hinzpeter just the man to curb this dangerous tendency and to mould their son into the responsible ruler he would one day have to become. Hinzpeter could only agree, and keenly set about his task.

Willy's day started at 6 a.m. in summer and 7 a.m. in winter, ending at 6 or 7 p.m., again depending on the season, with just two breaks, the first for breakfast and the second for the midday meal, which never lasted more than three-quarters of an hour. Breakfast consisted of plain bread. Occasionally someone came to tea. Willy had to offer them cake, but was not allowed any himself. Lessons consisted of Latin, history, arithmetic, religious instruction, geography and later Greek, as well as English with a Miss Archer, and French with a Mme Darcourt who subsequently married Dr Hinzpeter. Hinzpeter never gave praise, as a matter of principle. Everything was done as an exercise in duty. 'It was hard for a seven-year-old,' Willy wrote. 'One can think what one likes about Hinzpeter's method, but it seems certain to me that lessons with no joy to them start out from the wrong psychological standpoint.' In good hands, Willy might have shaped up into an intelligent, if always difficult, ruler.

Lessons were shared with his younger brother Heinrich. While everyone could agree that Willy was bright, with an exceptional memory and a natural talent for languages, Heinrich, though perfectly agreeable, was distinctly dull. Hinzpeter did his pious best with Heinrich, but soon gave up to concentrate all his efforts on his main charge, the future Kaiser. Willy repaid Hinzpeter by applying himself conscientiously to his studies and working hard, always hoping to please his tutor and gain some small praise. History was his favourite subject, especially Ancient and German. The pages were filled with stories of heroes which the handicapped boy especially loved, with the added pleasure that many were his own ancestors. Frederick the Great was Willy's favourite, referred to again and again throughout his life, in conversations, speeches and memos.

But the education of a Prince required more than school work. There were dancing, gymnastics, fencing, shooting, swimming, rowing, sailing and, most important of all, riding. All presented difficulties to Willy with his crippled arm. His strenuous exercise regime had corrected his posture, but had made no difference to the arm. 'The poor arm is no better,' wrote Vicky to Queen Victoria when he was ten. 'William begins to feel being behind much smaller boys in every exercise of the body – he cannot run fast, because he has no balance, nor ride, nor climb, nor cut his food . . . I wonder he is as good tempered about it. His tutor thinks he will feel it much more, and be much unhappier about it, as he grows older, and feels himself debarred from everything which others enjoy, and particularly so as he is so strong and lively and healthy.' They obviously had not reckoned with Willy's character and his own keen sense of what was required of him for his future position. By the time he was fourteen, when he easily passed all his exams to go to grammar school, he could join in virtually everything his classmates did. Only eating still presented a problem, though a clever gadget combining a knife, fork and spoon helped. A friend, Prince Heinrich von Schönburg-Waldenburg, noted that Willy never made an issue of his handicap, simply saying 'With my arm, I can't do this or that'. Nor did he try to hide it, except in public, when the sleeve of the left arm might be folded into his pocket, or his small hand rested on a sword or a saddle.

In time Willy mastered all the sports: only riding remained. With his useless arm and his uncertain balance, riding was a torture for him, and yet it was the one thing a future Kaiser had to be able to do. Prussia's pride was her army, the largest and most powerful army in Europe; a Prussian army without the Kaiser riding at its head in parades, on military manoeuvres and, if necessary, to war was unthinkable. But Willy at nine still could not ride, only sit on his pony, being led on a lead. Riding was terrifying because he could not get his balance, a problem at the time put down to his crippled arm, rather than his damaged ear. No one in the royal stables had the heart to force the weeping child to ride without support. Finally Hinzpeter stepped in. In the memoirs written when he was nearly sixty the exiled Kaiser still vividly recalled the sheer terror of it, quoting Hinzpeter's own account: 'In spite of all his begging and pleading and crying, he was mercilessly put back on his horse every time he fell off, until eventually, after weeks and weeks of torture, he finally found his sense of balance.' Even Hinzpeter was moved, admitting that these morning exercises were a horror for everyone involved. Prince Heinrich was regularly reduced to tears, just watching. But Wilhelm always graciously accepted that Hinzpeter did what had to be done, and even thanked him for it.

As it happened, Willy's parents had totally misunderstood one crucial aspect of Hinzpeter's character. They had chosen him because he shared their views on the training required for a future monarch and also on the importance of establishing in Germany a liberal society which paid humane attention to the social problems of the lower classes. Vicky herself spent many hours on her various charities, hospital work and educational schemes, particularly for women. Without proper consideration for the lower orders, society itself was in danger, Willy's parents and Hinzpeter agreed. As did Queen Victoria, who on 18 December 1867 wrote to Vicky: 'I wished to answer what you said about the bar between high and low. What you said about it is most true . . . The higher classes – especially the aristocracy (with of course exceptions and honourable ones) – are so frivolous, pleasure-seeking, heartless, selfish, immoral and gambling that it makes one think (just as the Dean of Windsor said to me the other evening) of the days of the French Revolution . . . The lower classes are becoming so well informed, are so intelligent and earn their bread and riches so deservedly – that they cannot and ought not be kept back – to be abused by the wretched, ignorant, high-born beings who live only to kill time. They must be warned and frightened or some dreadful crash will take place.' With this in mind, and encouraged by the Crown Prince and Princess, Hinzpeter took his two young charges on frequent visits to the factories and workshops of the lower classes, engaging the workers in polite conversation, the princes always remembering to doff their caps to their bewildered hosts before they left.

Hinzpeter was not, however, a liberal. He dedicated his life to preserving the system of absolute, not constitutional, monarchy. The lot of the labouring poor had to be improved only so that it should not become a threat to the system. The Crown Prince and Princess would have been extremely surprised to learn that Hinzpeter's great hero was Bismarck. They entrusted their son to Hinzpeter's care for twelve hours every day for eleven years, even taking him on holiday with them, and whether through Hinzpeter's powerful influence or through his own choice and temperament, Willy emerged wholeheartedly sharing his tutor's views. Next to Frederick the Great there now stood two contemporary heroes: his grandfather Wilhelm I of Prussia, and Otto von Bismarck.

Bismarck himself lost no time putting his political beliefs into practice. His aim was to make Willy's grandfather, currently the King of Prussia, Kaiser of a united Germany, ruling as an absolute monarch and avoiding the democratic English model which they both considered weak and dangerous. Wilhelm I was a military man with simple tastes and simple political views. He was happy for Bismarck to wield the power behind the throne, applying his 'iron and blood' policy to both internal and foreign affairs alike.

In all, Bismarck launched three wars of German unification; the first, with the help of Austria, was in 1864 against Denmark, to gain the duchies of Schleswig and Holstein, which had the misfortune to straddle the border between Germany and Denmark. Bismarck was determined to gain the territory for Prussia, and as soon as possible build a canal through them to join the North and the Baltic seas. Willy never forgot the sight of the soldiers, German, Austrian and Hungarian, marching up Unter Den Linden in Berlin, off to war. He was just five as he looked down on the scene from the window of the Royal Palace as his grandfather, splendidly uniformed and standing on a dais, took the march-past. 'A born Berliner naturally has childhood memories which are military in nature,' he wrote later. The war was won within six months by Prussia and Austria and the victory parade, again along Unter Den Linden, with row upon row of marching Prussian soldiers, regimental flags flying, bands playing and wildly cheering crowds, left an indelible mark on Willy, not least because his own father was one of the returning heroes.

But the war caused a deep rift with the English side of the family. Queen Victoria's early misgivings about Bertie's marriage to the Danish Princess Alexandra now became a pressing reality. Alexandra's father, who had only recently gained the Danish throne as King Christian IX, was forced to give up almost half his kingdom and pay a heavy compensation which as a poor ruler of a poor country he could not afford. Princess Alexandra never forgave the Prussians. Queen Victoria, remembering beloved Albert's dream of a united Germany, supported the Prussian claim in spite of the fact that her own son and daughter-in-law as well as her Government and her people sympathised with the Danes. Bertie, pulled both ways, at first tried to take a balanced view, but Alexandra's distress was so great that he was soon openly and not always discreetly abusing Prussia. Queen

Victoria was not pleased. Bertie took no notice, accusing his sister Vicky of having become a thorough Prussian.

If only it were that simple. 'My position is not an easy one,' Vicky had written to Fritz, fighting at the front. 'They reprove me here for being too English, at home I am too Prussian. It seems I cannot do anything right.' Things weren't much easier for Fritz. The victory parade down Unter Den Linden was a confusing mixture of pride and pain. The crowd was hailing him as their hero, but the war had been against a small, poor and defenceless country, and it had been unprovoked. 'I feel ashamed,' he wrote in his diary. On 18 December, the day his father the King had decreed as a day of thanksgiving for the Prussian victory, the church bells of Berlin rang out all day long. But that evening at the grand banquet, when Bismarck's health was proposed Fritz did not raise his glass. It was a foolishly provocative act, not lost on Bismarck.

In England Vicky and Fritz's dilemma went unnoticed, especially by the Prussian-hating Prince and Princess of Wales. On 21 June 1865 Queen Victoria was obliged to write a painful letter in reply to Vicky's request that she and her family should come to England for Christmas. They were effectively banished from Windsor that year, and Vicky even had to subscribe to the idea that it was for her own sake, as she 'would not be happy' in the company. The truth was that Queen Victoria was changing her mind about the Prussians, who seemed determined to maintain a military and aggressive stance in their foreign policy quite unlike what dear Albert had envisaged. Poor Vicky, groomed into the Prussian marriage by her parents, now had to suffer the role of the outcast, both at home in England and at home in Prussia.

Bismarck was meanwhile planning his next war of German unification, this time against his ally Austria in order to acquire the whole of Schleswig and Holstein for Prussia, a plan he had made as soon as the first war was won. In June 1866 the Seven Weeks' War broke out, ending with Austria's quick defeat. The smaller German states which had sided with Austria were shown no mercy, in accordance with Bismarck's 'iron and blood' policy. Frankfurt was given twenty-four hours to pay 25 million guilders in war reparations. The wealthy King of Hanover (the one with the gold dinner service) lost everything and fled to England. Worst of all for the English Royal family was the fate of the small state of Hesse-Darmstadt. Vicky's sister

Alice, the quiet, average sister who was Bertie's favourite, had married Louis of Hesse in 1862. When war broke out in 1866 they sent their two children, Victoria and Ella, to England for safety, to stay with their grandmother Queen Victoria. Alice was expecting their third child, but she busied herself helping to organise a hospital for the wounded. There were 40,000 dead on the Austrian side in one day alone at the decisive battle of Königgratz, commanded on the Prussian side by Crown Prince Friedrich. Louis was still away fighting on the other side when the Prussians entered Darmstadt, and Alice had to watch helplessly while they marched arrogantly about, looting whatever took their fancy. Hesse, already poor, was made virtually bankrupt. Louis III (Louis' uncle) was only allowed to keep his throne because his sister was married to Tsar Alexander II of Russia. The fact that Alice's brother-in-law was the Commander of the Prussian army only made matters worse.

Queen Victoria and English public opinion were outraged by this further manifestation of Prussian aggression. It was impossible for Vicky and Fritz, again torn between the two countries and the two Royal families, to know where to place their loyalties. During the war there had been an additional tragedy for Vicky, made much worse because Fritz was away fighting. Their fourth and favourite child, Sigismund, known as Sigi, not yet two years old, caught meningitis and died within days. Vicky wrote to her mother in despair: 'Your suffering child turns to you in her grief . . . My little darling graciously lent me for a short time, to be my pride, my joy, my hope, is gone, gone . . . Oh HOW I loved that little thing, from the first moment of its birth, it was more to me than its brothers and sisters, it was so fair, so loving, so bright and merry.' Willy, Charlotte and Henry between them could never make up for the loss of the child Vicky called 'her own happy secret'. In letters home she referred to Henry as 'dull and idle', Charlotte as 'fat' and Willy as 'loud and rough'. Even the new baby, Victoria, could not help. From then on, every Sunday after church the family made their way to the Friedrichskirche and the chapel where Sigi was buried.

As for Willy, his anxious parents could not help noticing that this second Prussian victory was increasing his tendency, eagerly encouraged by his grandfather, to a certain Prussian pride. On 27 January 1869 he celebrated his birthday. 'My tenth birthday was an extremely significant one for me,' he wrote later, 'in the sense that on this day, according to the customs of our royal house, I was enlisted in the renowned Prussian army. Thus it happened that my grandfather awarded me the highest Order of the Black Eagle and at the same time I acquired my uniform of the First Foot Guards Regiment. The ceremony took place in our most intimate family circle. My father handed the Order to my grandfather in a gold vessel, and I had already put on my uniform in order to pronounce my oath to his Majesty.'

On the same day he was allowed to accompany his grandfather to the parade ground at Potsdam, where in front of the whole family he fell into line with his regiment and practised marching for the first time. He had trouble keeping up and had to run and dodge about to keep his place. It was a charming sight, but not everyone was amused. 'Poor Willy in his uniform looks like some unfortunate little monkey dressed up standing on top of an organ,' Vicky wrote to Queen Victoria.

Bismarck and Willy's grandfather would seem to have won that particular round. Willy was a real Hohenzollern now, and nothing would change that. His grandfather began to request his presence on the parade ground, not caring that this meant interrupting lessons: the old King not only disliked books, but was proud of it. Wilhelm I held the opinion that in order to be a good Prussian officer, books were not required. This all went down extremely well with Willy, happy to escape the schoolroom and delighted with military parades. Willy's parents were less happy, recognising this as part of Bismarck's plan to wean the boy away from their influence. In the same way, Bismarck continued his secret campaign to turn the King against his son the Crown Prince. At that time father and son still felt an affection for one another, despite having little in common, but Bismarck found it easy enough to sow suspicion in the King's mind about his son and his daughter-in-law, the 'English princess'.

In 1870 Bismarck instigated his third and final war of German unification, this time against France. The Franco-Prussian war was by far the most ambitious, bitterly fought over nine months to gain Alsace-Lorraine and Metz. For Willy the Franco-Prussian war was, and for the rest of his life remained, Prussia's finest hour. This time the triumphant victory parade down Unter Den Linden was preceded by a ceremony in the Hall of Mirrors at the Palace of Versailles on 18 January 1871 at which his grandfather was pronounced Kaiser Wilhelm I of the new German Empire. The young and impressionable Prince Wilhelm gloried in the idea that his grandfather was now the ruler of a great Empire, just like his grandmother Queen Victoria in England. When the troops returned to Berlin from France he was allowed to accompany his father and mother riding out to meet them. 'My mother wore the uniform of her Hussar regiment. I was naturally in the uniform of the First Foot Regiment,' he recalled in his memoirs. 'The ecstatic cheering of the crowds knew no bounds, the soldiers being bedecked with laurel wreaths again and again.'

Now Germany was a nation, albeit under Prussia's iron leadership. The next two decades brought a period of rapid expansion to the young Reich, buoyed up by this new identity and power, propelling the country from a largely rural to a modern industrial society. Germany was soon looking across the globe for new markets for its trade. Russian diplomats and businessmen returned home from this thrusting country in some alarm. The English maintained their superior air, but kept a careful eye on developments. As for the French, humiliated by the war and the loss of Alsace-Lorraine, they hated the new German Empire with a Gallic hatred which lasted till the First World War.

2

Georgie, the Second Son

~

GEORGE V, COUSIN of Kaiser Wilhelm II of Germany on his father's side and of Tsar Nicholas II of Russia on his mother's, differed from them in one important respect: he was the second son. As such, he was spared the excessive expectations lavished on the other two cousins from the moment of their birth. His, which took place at home at Marlborough House in London on 3 July 1865, was relatively easy, leaving his parents, the Prince and Princess of Wales, relieved as well as happy, though not his grandmother Queen Victoria, who was most put out. 'It seems that IT IS NOT TO BE that I am to be present at the birth of your children, which I am very sorry for,' she wrote to Bertie in her best capital letters. Somehow Bertie and Alexandra always managed to get the date wrong. Affie, Bertie's younger brother, the one destined to inherit 'that dear small country' Coburg, smelled a rat: 'I am sure you said it was later on purpose.'

The same thing had happened eighteen months earlier when their first son Prince Albert Victor was born. This too had been an easy birth, which was just as well, since everything else within the royal clan was about to become extremely complicated, not to say bitter. At the same time as Princess Alexandra was producing Albert Victor in England, the Prussians and their Austrian allies were crossing the border to make war on Denmark in Bismarck's first war of German unification. Poor and defenceless, Denmark was easily crushed, and Alexandra spent night after night weeping over the loss of Schleswig-Holstein, and the crippling compensation her father King Christian IX was then forced to pay the Prussians for a war Denmark had not provoked. Queen Victoria was most displeased, having always maintained that this Danish marriage was diplomatically awkward, the matter of Schleswig-Holstein being complicated, in the way of border disputes, with merit on both sides. She had chosen to favour Prussia, as her dear Albert would have wished, but public opinion in England sided with Denmark out of habitual love of the underdog, and because the people already adored their 'Danish Princess'.

Alexandra had captured their hearts from the moment she set foot on English soil in March 1863, arriving at Gravesend on the Royal Yacht *Victoria and Albert*, accompanied by her father, mother, two sisters and three brothers, to marry the Prince of Wales. She was eighteen and, as Queen Victoria had to admit, 'outrageously beautiful'. The Prince of Wales, in love and typically impetuous, ran up the gangplank and kissed his bride in full view of the wildly cheering crowd. They had never seen anything like it.

The match-making had been difficult, and Bertie's parents had frequently consulted their daughter Vicky in Berlin. Choice was limited by the fact that the bride had to be not only royal, but Protestant. In addition, as Vicky and her parents agreed, she had to be sensible, because Bertie was not. Compared to Vicky he was dull and lazy, and much too easily distracted; the unpromising child had grown into an equally unpromising young man. He had done badly at his schooling, and no better at Cambridge. As an adult Bertie liked to spend his time in dubious company engaged in various undesirable pursuits: gambling, horse-racing, women, anything that counted as having 'fun' – not a word either of his parents appreciated, or even wholly understood. This would have mattered less were he not heir to the greatest throne on earth. 'Oh dear, what would happen if I were to die next winter!' Queen Victoria wrote to Vicky in Berlin in April 1859. 'One trembles to think of it. It is too awful a contemplation . . . His only safety – and the country's – is his implicit reliance in everything on dearest Papa, that perfection of human beings!'

Bertie needed a good wife, but typically made the already difficult task of finding one more difficult by insisting that he would only marry for love. Rejecting all the help he was offered, he chose Princess Alexandra Caroline Marie Charlotte Louise Julie of Schleswig-Holstein-Sonderburg-Glucksburg – a long name for a family who were minor royals, and poor. Added to which, the mother, Queen Louise, was disapproved of. She came from the Hesse-Cassel line of the European royals, known for their frivolous style of life, which they pursued at every opportunity at the castle of Rumpenheim near Frankfurt, gossiping, gambling and playing practical jokes on one another.

Bertie completely saw the point of Rumpenheim, even if his parents did not. And he had no intention of giving up Princess Alexandra, who was sweet-natured as well as 'outrageously beautiful', though perhaps not clever like his sister Vicky, which was a blessing. It was only when news reached Queen Victoria that Tsar Alexander II of Russia was interested in the Danish Princess on behalf of his own son and heir that the matter was suddenly and quickly settled.

When Alexandra arrived in England to marry Bertie, Prince Albert had been dead for two years. Fortunately Bertie, always short of money, had inherited £600,000 from him, which was now added to his income of £50,000 a year as Prince of Wales from the Duchy of Cornwall. Since the average wage in England at the time was little more than £50 a year, this was a lot of money, though not enough for Bertie. He immediately spent £220,000 on 7,000 acres at Sandringham in Norfolk, in emulation of friends like the Duke of Buccleuch and the Duke of Devonshire, landed aristocracy with great estates on which they shot and hunted for large parts of each year. Before the First World War less than half a per cent of the population owned four-fifths of the land and, taxation being negligible, their wealth was enormous; their town houses and country estates were serviced by dozens of indoor and outdoor servants who were lucky if they had half a day off a week. The new barons of industry who had made their fortunes from coal and steel or shipping or the railways were equally wealthy, barely hampered by a slowly emerging Trade Union movement which was trying to improve the conditions of the working classes.

In comparison with these fabulously wealthy men, Bertie spent quite modestly. Another £100,000 went on carriages and furniture for Marlborough House in London, and a further amount on jewellery. The rest of the capital sum was invested, bringing his income up to £65,000 a year – still not enough to cover his necessary expenditure. Encouraged by Gladstone as Chancellor of the Exchequer, Parliament agreed to stump up another £40,000 a year, and additionally voted £10,000 per annum for the Princess of Wales's personal use, she having absolutely no money of her own. It was a shabby sum in some people's eyes, but to the Princess and to her father the King of Denmark, who made do on £2,000 a year, it was a magnificent sum. Nevertheless, for the next few years, until Parliament could again be persuaded to step in, the Prince of Wales was always some £20,000 overspent.

Having kissed Alexandra in full view of the crowds, Bertie presented the members of his Household: Sir William Knollys, his Comptroller and Treasurer, then Lord Spencer, Groom of the Stole, followed by two Lords and two Grooms of the Bedchamber, and Francis Knollys, Sir William's son and Bertie's Private Secretary. For a young woman brought up simply and modestly, it must have been overwhelming. The royal party formed up into a carriage procession to make their way from Gravesend through London to Paddington station, where the royal train waited, bound for Windsor. The streets along the route were lined with cheering crowds straining to catch a glimpse of the famed beauty of the 'Danish Princess', and to admire the clothes she was wearing, a gown in grey silk with a violet jacket trimmed with sable, set off by a white bonnet decorated with red rosebuds. Everything pleased. The crowds took her forever to their hearts.

Queen Victoria, reconciled, was waiting at Windsor. 'I went down nearly to the bottom of the staircase, and Bertie appeared, leading dear Alix, looking like a rose. I embraced her warmly,' she wrote in her Journal. After a few minutes spent with all the Danes in the White Drawing Room, Queen Victoria retreated to her own room, 'desolate and sad'. She was still there, grieving for Prince Albert, when there was a quiet knock on the door. 'Alix peeped in, and came and knelt before me, with that sweet, loving expression which spoke volumes. I was much moved and kissed her again and again. She said the crowd in London had been quite fearful, and the enthusiasm very great, no end of decorations etc., but the crush in the City had been quite alarming. Bertie came in for a moment whilst Alix was there. There was a family dinner, I dining alone.'

At the wedding three days later the Queen was again sad. 'At one moment, when I first heard the flourish of trumpets, which brought back to my mind my whole life of twenty years at his dear side, safe, proud, secure, and happy, I felt as if I should faint.' Bertie, Prince of Wales, waited at the altar, attended by his brother-in-law Friedrich, Crown Prince of Prussia and his uncle the Duke of Coburg. He wore his Garter robes and gold collar, looking pale and nervous. Finally the bride arrived. Her dress of silver thread was trimmed with orange blossom and with roses, shamrocks and thistles of Honiton lace, with yards of white tulle and a long silver train. 'She was trembling and very pale,' noted Queen Victoria, 'looking very lovely.' She entered to Handel's Processional March, and was given away by her father. There were six bishops in attendance and eight bridesmaids, 'eight as ugly girls as you could wish to meet', wrote one spiteful wedding guest. Another agreed: 'the bridesmaids looked well – when their backs were turned.'

After a week's honeymoon at Osborne on the Isle of Wight, the Prince and Princess of Wales went first to Sandringham, which was being completely rebuilt at the greatest expense, and then, at the beginning of April, to their new London home, Marlborough House. Now began the most brilliant Season London had witnessed in years, led by the most fashionable royal couple in living memory. The Marlborough House set, as it was soon known, intended to be amused and amusing, more or less all the time. The rules were relaxed. Its members minded less about the social standing of those in their set than that they should be good company and, essentially, rich enough to afford the life. A man might be a *nouveau riche* industrialist or a Jewish banker; a woman might be a famous actress. They were all part of what Queen Victoria disapprovingly called 'the fast set'. They went racing and yachting and hunting, depending on the season. In the evenings there were balls and dinners and theatres. After dinner they danced, played cards and gambled. Kaiser Wilhelm's Court in Berlin was shocked. While appearing to mind about nothing much, the Marlborough House set did mind very much about some things: manners mattered, and discretion. And, like the Prince of Wales, they minded very much about the way they were dressed.

The Princess of Wales was soon the leader of fashion, and the Prince of Wales was soon in debt. The British public was enchanted. They had hardly glimpsed their Queen for years, and when they did she appeared dour, dressed in black. Now they had a properly glamorous Royal Couple, out to have fun in ways which they themselves understood, and in a small way tried to emulate. They too loved to go to the races on a rare day off, or to a music hall in the evenings. They lined the streets to catch a glimpse of the *toilette* the Princess of Wales was wearing, or the Homburg hat the Prince of Wales had, single-handedly, made fashionable. And when the Royal Couple transgressed, they forgave them, because they were only human. Not until later, when the Prince of Wales was seen to upset the Princess with his infidelities, did they object, and even then not for long. Public opinion, so essential an element in a constitutional monarchy, was something Bertie and Alexandra understood in their bones, even if Queen Victoria did not.

At first the Queen was gratified by Alexandra's effect on her wayward son. 'The dear young couple are here and I must again say that I am quite astonished at Bertie's improvement,' she wrote to Vicky on 25 March 1863. 'Dear Alix felt the parting from her parents very much, but she is always calm and sweet and gentle and lovely. Very clever I don't think she is, but she is right-minded and sensible and straightforward.' It did not last long. News soon reached the Queen that 'the dear young couple' were gadding about every night, and not by any means with all the right people. She was particularly concerned that Alexandra was becoming 'a little grand'. Nor was she proving strong-minded enough to restrain her husband from gambling, or from going out '*en garçon*' as and when it suited him. In May, only two months after the wedding, Queen Victoria was already looking anxiously for signs of a pregnancy, at the same time worried as to the quality of the stock of the future heir. 'Are you aware', she wrote to Vicky in Berlin, 'that Alix has the smallest head ever seen? I dread that – with his small empty brain – very much for future children.'

As it happened, the Princess of Wales was indeed already pregnant. Albert Victor was born prematurely, weighing less than four pounds. But he was healthy and well, and Princess Alexandra, desperately worried about her parents during the Prusso-Danish war, was determined to visit them as soon as possible. Happy in her own childhood, throughout her life the Princess always put family first. Now she longed to show off her baby son and heir, and was keen to see her sister Dagmar. Known as Minny, Dagmar was being courted by Grand Duke Nicholai, eldest son and heir of Tsar Alexander II of Russia, the other great Empire, and he was arriving in Copenhagen at the end of September.

Queen Victoria was not pleased with the planned visit. It was highly inconvenient politically, and she gave her consent only reluctantly, and on certain conditions. First, the Prince and Princess of Wales were to stay in Stockholm, incognito in a hotel, during the time Grand Duke Nicholai was in Copenhagen wooing Princess Dagmar. Secondly, they must visit Prussia on the way home, to avoid causing offence and to make peace with Vicky and Fritz. Thirdly, they were commanded to send the infant Prince back on the Royal Yacht as soon as they left Denmark for Germany.

Bertie's solution was to agree in principle but loosen the terms in practice. They went to Stockholm as bidden, but not to stay in a hotel, and not incognito. They stayed with King Charles XV of Sweden in his palace, and caused a great stir. 'I have not the intention of letting Alix be uncomfortably lodged if I can help it,' Bertie wrote to his mother with a new firmness on 7 October. When they arrived in Copenhagen they were openly delighted to receive a delirious welcome from the Danish people. Humiliated by the Prussians, the Danes celebrated their Princess who was married to the heir to the most powerful nation on earth. Alexandra refused point-blank to go to Berlin on the way home, forcing the two royal couples to meet instead in more neutral Cologne. It took Vicky many days to arrange the meeting, because Bertie never answered her letters. Queen Victoria was shocked, and declared that he had become quite unmanageable. Bertie let it be known that he and Alix found it extremely disagreeable that Fritz was always in Prussian uniform, flaunting his medals 'for his DEEDS OF VALOUR??? against the unhappy Danes.'

There had been a great to-do about Albert Victor's name. Queen Victoria had definite opinions on the names of all her grandchildren, and since the child was a son and eventual heir she assumed the right to take full charge. 'I felt rather annoyed', Bertie wrote to her in futile remonstration, 'when Beatrice told Lady Macclesfield that you had settled what our little boy was to be called before I had spoken to you about it.' Beatrice was Queen Victoria's youngest daughter, and only six. The baby was duly christened Albert Victor Christian Edward: Albert after his deceased grandfather, Victor after his grandmother, Christian after his Danish grandfather and, lastly, Edward after his father. But Bertie and Alexandra got their way in the end: he was always known as plain 'Eddy'. Only Queen Victoria persisted in calling him Albert Victor, and let it be known that once he became King, he would take the name Albert, as would Bertie himself. Bertie let this pass, a tactic he was perfecting, and took the name Edward when his time came, with the perfect excuse. In an affecting impromptu speech at his Accession, he announced that there could only ever be one Albert – his father, Albert the Good.

Bertie decided on a pre-emptive strike when it came to naming their second son. 'As to the names of the young gentleman,' he wrote to his mother, 'we had both for some time settled that, if we had another boy, he should be called GEORGE, as we like the name and it is an English one.' They also wanted Frederick, a name which conveniently featured on both sides of the family. Neither went down well. 'I fear I cannot admire the names you propose to give the Baby,' countered Queen Victoria. 'I had hoped for some fine old name. Frederick is, however, the best of the two, and I hope you will CALL him so. GEORGE only came in with the Hanoverian family. However, if the dear child grows up good and wise, I shall not mind what his name is. Of course you will add ALBERT at the end . . .' The parents settled on a compromise, and the baby was christened George Frederick Ernest Albert on 7 July 1865 in St George's Chapel, Windsor; but in the family he was always known as Georgie.

In August everyone was in Coburg for the grand unveiling of a statue of Prince Albert. It was another family gathering edgy with ill-feeling. Princess Alexandra had already caused a stir one evening in London when, strikingly dressed in pink satin, she ostentatiously cut Count Bernsdorff, the Prussian Ambassador. Now she refused to speak to Prince Christian of Schleswig-Holstein-Sonderburg-Augustenburg, recently married to Princess Helen, 'Lenchen', Bertie's younger sister, and whose family had supported the Prussians in the war. Bertie had threatened to boycott the wedding. Matters deteriorated further on the way home from Coburg. Bertie and Alix, travelling by train, passed through Coblenz where the Queen of Prussia, Willy's grandmother, held her Court. The Queen graciously came to the railway station to greet the Prince and Princess of Wales, but Alix refused to leave the train. Bertie had to find some excuse, but no one was fooled. 'Alix is by no means what she ought to be. It will be long, if ever, before she regains my confidence,' Queen Victoria confided to her Journal.

By the following spring Princess Alexandra was pregnant again. It meant that she could not attend the greatest royal event of the year, her sister Dagmar's wedding to the Tsarevich in St Petersburg that November. Bertie, however, was determined to go. He had never been to Russia and he was keen to see for himself the fantastic splendour of the Russian Court. Lord Derby, the Prime Minister, was happy for the Prince to represent his country, though essentially he was there in a private role. Disraeli, then Chancellor, agreed to contribute a thousand pounds of Government money towards his expenses. Delighted, Bertie wrote to Lord Derby that he would be 'only too happy to be the means in any way of promoting the "entente cordiale" between Russia and our own country.' It was an early indication of Bertie's interest, spurred on by his wife and her sister

Dagmar, in furthering a more formal Entente between England and Russia, and against Germany.

The semi-diplomatic role was particularly gratifying to the Prince of Wales because Queen Victoria was never willing to give him any real responsibility, instructing that he 'UPON NO ACCOUNT be put at the head of any of those Societies or Commissions'. Knowing this, Bertie put it to his mother that Princess Dagmar had personally requested his presence as so few of her relations, including her own parents, could afford the expense of attending an Imperial wedding. On 16 October he received Queen Victoria's reply. First, it was a bad time of year; secondly, the private visit should not be attached to a public event; thirdly, the Government overrated the importance of it, from a political point of view. 'These are my reasons against it, and to that I may add another, which, dear Child, you know I have often already alluded to, viz: your remaining so little quiet at home, and always running about. The country, and all of us, would like to see you a little more stationary, and therefore I was in hopes that this autumn and winter this would have been the case. However, if you are still very desirous to go now, I will not object to it.' The only condition she appended was that her son should break his journey in Berlin to see Vicky and Fritz.

Bertie was away for six weeks. Princess Alexandra, missing her husband, went to visit her mother-in-law at Windsor with Eddy, aged three, and Georgie, one and a half. They took walks and drives together, and had many tête-à-têtes, past irritations quite forgotten. 'Dear Alix arrived here yesterday with the tiny little boys,' the Queen wrote to Vicky. 'She is dear and good and gentle but looking very thin and pale.' Conversations included reference to the tiny boys' education, the Queen always observing that this was a matter for the Nation and the Sovereign as much as a personal one. But in this Bertie and Alexandra remained politely if resolutely independent, quite failing to live up to Vicky's fine example in always thinking of 'dear Papa' when she made decisions about Willy's upbringing and education. On 21 November Vicky herself arrived to visit her mother, but without Willy who, now aged seven, was busy with his studies, supervised by Dr Hinzpeter.

When the Prince of Wales returned from St Petersburg, preceded by rumours of his flirtations with various Russian beauties, the Princess, heavily pregnant, was feeling low and unwell. By February she was seriously ill with rheumatic fever. On 20 February 1867, still ill with the fever, she gave birth to a daughter, Princess Louise, named after her Danish grandmother. Lady Macclesfield, her Lady of the Bedchamber, was indignant because the Prince of Wales left London to attend a steeplechase and a dinner at Windsor just days before the birth. Bertie was not deliberately unkind, but he needed constant distraction. He was still only twenty-five, easily bored, always restless, and incapable of staying in one place for any length of time. The company he kept included the beautiful and clever Duchess of Manchester whose liaison with Lord Hartington was an open secret, so open that Queen Victoria wrote to Alix, equally charmed by her: 'Believe me, dearest child, the Duchess of Manchester IS NOT A FIT COMPANION FOR YOU.' When the Conservatives returned to power in 1867 poor Sir William Knollys, trying to cope with the Prince of Wales's rising debts, was obliged to ask Disraeli for more money. Although promised in principle, it was not immediately forthcoming.

Improvement in Princess Alexandra's health was slow, but by 10 May she was well enough to attend the baby's christening, albeit in a wheelchair. That same evening Bertie was off to Paris for the opening of the Paris Exhibition. Sir William Knollys, left behind in London, was not happy about the rumours he heard of Bertie's activities there, and the British public, catching a whiff of them, began to feel disenchanted with their Prince of Wales. At Ascot that year he received a cool reception from the racing crowd, usually his exuberant champions. When Queen Victoria visited Marlborough House at the beginning of July she found Alexandra sitting in the wheelchair looking lovely but, as she noted in her Journal, and in capital letters, 'ALTERED'. It was a perceptive remark, covering many things. The illness had left Alexandra with a permanently stiff knee and a slight limp. It is some indication of the oddness of Court life that some society ladies soon began to imitate her walk, affecting what became known as the 'Alexandra limp'. But the limp was not the worst effect of the illness, and fun-loving Alexandra was soon dancing again, even riding and skating. Much worse was the onset of otosclerosis, a form of deafness brought on by illness, inherited from her mother. At first not serious, with time it became more pronounced, leaving her in later years almost totally deaf. These physical disabilities, combined with her unhappiness at Bertie's behaviour, probably lay behind Queen Victoria's description of her as 'altered'.

As far as Georgie, the future King George V, was concerned, it meant that he had a doting mother. Princess Alexandra never lost her gaiety and love of life, but as her hearing worsened and her husband, loving and indulgent as he was, increasingly led his own life, she lavished her love on her children. During the Season in London she was often seen driving out in her barouche, sitting between her two little boys. 'She was in her glory when she could run up to the Nursery,' related the head nurse, Mrs Blackburn, 'put on a flannel apron, wash her children, and see them asleep in their little beds.' Even when George was a grown man and a naval officer she might end a letter to him 'With a great big kiss for your lovely little face', and he might write to 'My own darling sweet little beloved Motherdear', signing himself 'Your loving little Georgy'.

By the summer Princess Alexandra was fit enough to travel, and doctors agreed that a cure at a spa would do her good. On 18 August 1867 therefore the Prince and Princess of Wales, their three children, their Household (headed by Sir William Knollys), two doctors and twenty-five servants set off on the Royal Yacht *Osborne* for Dordrecht in Holland and thence by river-steamer down the Rhine to Wiesbaden in Germany. There they were to stay for two months, long enough for Alexandra's sister Dagmar and her husband the Tsarevich to visit them from Russia, as well as her parents from Denmark, and from Greece her brother Willi, who in 1863 had unexpectedly been nominated to the Greek throne by the Great Powers, becoming, in the odd logic of European royals, King George I of the Hellenes.

By an unfortunate coincidence the Prince of Wales was away on the day a telegram arrived at Wiesbaden from the King of Prussia, as he still was in 1867, asking whether that evening or the next day would be the most convenient time for him to pay a visit. Alexandra refused to receive him, so on his return Bertie was forced to send the King a telegram reversing the arrangements: he himself would be delighted to call on the King, but unhappily the Princess of Wales was not well enough to accompany him. The altered plan was diplomatically accepted.

The Princess of Wales promptly set off for Rumpenheim, making it perfectly clear that she was well enough to travel. When the King of Prussia arrived some days later to return Bertie's visit, Princess Alexandra was barely polite. Vicky, Crown Princess of Prussia, called Alexandra's behaviour 'neither wise nor kind'. The Queen of Prussia complained to Queen Victoria, adding that Alexandra's sister Dagmar shared the Princess of Wales's views and was busy poisoning her husband the Tsarevich against the Prussians. Queen Victoria complained to Bertie. But Bertie, loyal and indulgent, defended his wife. 'A lady may have feelings which she CANNOT repress, while a man MUST overcome them,' he told his mother. 'If Coburg had been taken away as Hanover, Hesse and Nassau have been, I don't think you would much care to see the King either. You will not, I hope, be angry, dear Mama, at my last sentence; but it is the only way that I can express what dear Alix feels.' Queen Victoria turned to Lord Derby, the Prime Minister. 'The Queen trusts that Lord Derby will take an opportunity of expressing BOTH to the Prince and Princess of Wales the IMPORTANCE of NOT letting any private feelings interfere with what are their public duties.' The theory was right, but in practice it never happened. In the inner circles of European royalty, where everyone was related to everyone else, private and public were constantly confused.

Family troubles were not the only ones besetting Queen Victoria in 1867. All that year the great political issue was the Reform Bill. After opening Parliament the Queen wrote to Vicky that there had been ' a good deal of hissing, some groans and calls for Reform, which I – in my present forlorn position – ought not to be exposed to. There were many, nasty faces – and I felt it painfully.' The Queen's main fears centred on the nascent Republican movement, which wanted to do away with the monarchy altogether. Bismarck in Germany, applying his 'iron and blood' method to the agitators, had no such problems. Queen Victoria knew where at least part of the problem lay. 'Regarding the higher classes, the way in which their sins and immoralities are overlooked, indulged, forgiven – when the third part in lower orders would be highly punished, is enough to cause democratic feelings and resentment,' she wrote to Vicky in Berlin. The following year the Conservative Government was replaced by the Liberals led by Gladstone, one of Queen Victoria's least favourite politicians. When Knollys and the Queen requested that the House of Commons vote the Prince of Wales a larger income, Gladstone replied he had 'no intention, or disposition, to give him any addition.'

In 1868 it was decided that the Prince and Princess of Wales should go on a royal tour of Europe and the Near East. They would be away for six months in all, leaving the children behind in the care of their nannies. They set out for Paris in November, with thirty-three servants and a suite of six courtiers, Princess Alexandra cheered by the fact that Bertie had agreed to spend Christmas in Denmark. There had been persistent rumours about his flirtations, and he was keen to please his wife, but it was a considerable sacrifice. Life at the Danish Court was extremely dull. The rooms were uncomfortable, the company limited, the food mediocre. The King liked to dine at six, and there was little in the way of amusement to fill the long winter evenings. But Bertie could not have enjoyed the usual family Christmas in any case, for Sandringham was being rebuilt, complete with an indoor bowling alley.

There was no question of the children accompanying their parents. Queen Victoria never approved of 'the Children of the Country' travelling abroad. But after an affecting letter from Princess Alexandra in which she called Queen Victoria 'my angel mother', the Queen agreed to let Eddy and Georgie, now aged almost five and three, go to Denmark for Christmas. But she insisted that Princess Louise and the new baby, suitably named Victoria, were altogether too young, and stung Alexandra by calling her selfish for wanting to have them with her in Denmark. Bertie grasped the nettle. 'Alix has made herself nearly quite ill with the worry about this but what she felt most are the words which you have used concerning her . . . None of us are perfect – she may have her faults – but she certainly is not selfish – and her whole life is wrapt up in her children.' Vicky and her sister Alice of Hesse came to England nearly every year with their children, he pointed out, so it seemed 'rather inconsistent' that Alexandra could not travel with hers. In this he missed the point: as far as Queen Victoria was concerned, England was not 'abroad'.

The Queen relented about Louise, but the baby stayed at home. And when the time came for the Prince and Princess of Wales to leave Denmark on 15 January to continue their tour, the three children were smartly despatched back to England in the Royal Yacht. Bertie and Alexandra travelled on for a three-day visit to Vicky and Fritz in Berlin, where their nephew Willy was celebrating his tenth birthday, Alexandra this time taking care not to give offence to the King and Queen of Prussia. From Berlin they travelled to Vienna for a week of balls and theatres and race meetings, and thence to Egypt. Queen Victoria held her peace about some of Bertie's disreputable friends who joined the royal party in Cairo, and about the size of his entourage. Six blue-and-gold steamers travelled up the Nile towing barges filled with horses, a white donkey for the Princess, three thousand bottles of champagne and four French chefs. They returned to Cairo five weeks later with 32 mummy cases and a ten-year-old Arab orphan named Ali Achmet, who was despatched to Sandringham where, later, dressed in his native costume, he served coffee to the guests.

By May 1869 the Prince and Princess of Wales were on their way home by way of Turkey and Greece. Queen Victoria had written broaching the subject of the education of the children again, describing them as extremely ill-disciplined. Perhaps remembering his own childhood, Bertie wrote a sharp reply: 'If children of their age are too strictly, or perhaps too severely treated, they get shy, and only fear those whom they ought to love; and we should naturally wish them to be very fond of you, as they were in Denmark of dear Alix's Parents. I quite agree with you that the question of a governess being appointed must be considered on our return.' This elicited a conciliatory reply. 'The dear little children are very well, and I shall be very sorry to lose them,' Queen Victoria wrote from Windsor. 'They have been very well with me and are very fond of Grandmama. You must let me see them often, and sometimes let one or other of them come and stay with me for a little while.'

In July 1870 the older children again went to stay with their Danish grandparents in Copenhagen, leaving Princess Victoria and the newest baby, Princess Maud, behind. Alexandra's sister Dagmar, or Minny, came home from Russia for the summer with her new baby, Nicky, the son and heir. It was therefore in Denmark that the future King George V first met his Russian cousin, the future Tsar Nicholas II. Georgie was five, Nicky was two.

The Prince of Wales came to pick up his wife and children. He had not been invited to stay that summer because of a nasty scandal, the Mordaunt divorce case, which had broken out in London, forcing him to appear in the witness box, though not as a co-respondant. The British public was disenchanted, and there were times when the Prince of Wales was hissed in the streets as he passed. 'Now that Ascot Races are approaching, I wish to repeat earnestly and seriously', wrote his mother, 'that I trust you will . . . as my uncle William IV and Aunt, and we ourselves did, confine your visits to the Races, to the two days, Tuesday and Thursday and not go on Wednesday and Friday, to which William IV never went, and nor did we.' The Prince of Wales had a bad reception from the crowd when he arrived at the meeting, but when his horse won the last race a great cheer went up. Bertie, quick to note the change, lit a fat cigar and raised his hat. The crowd responded by cheering even louder.

But Gladstone was worried. 'For our time as a Government, and my time as a politician, Royalty will do well enough in this country, because it has a large fund to draw on,' he wrote to Lord Granville, his Foreign Secretary. 'But the fund of credit is diminishing, and I do not see from whence it is to be replenished as matters now go. To speak in rude and general terms, the Queen is invisible and the Prince of Wales not respected.' He knew very well that there were some fifty Republican clubs in England at the time. However, a stroke of luck was on the way. In November 1871 the Prince of Wales caught typhoid fever. Queen Victoria rushed to Sandringham to be at his side. His sister Alice had already arrived from Darmstadt, as well as his brother Affie. For some days Bertie's life hung in the balance, and it was not until the New Year that he was out of danger. Public opinion swung dramatically back in his favour. Hundreds of letters and telegrams poured in, and many fulsome articles appeared in the press, which only recently had been extremely critical.

The Prince of Wales's popularity was fully restored. A thanksgiving service was arranged for 27 February. The royal family drove in procession in open carriages to St Paul's Cathedral, Georgie travelling in the seventh carriage with his three uncles, Eddy following behind with his parents and grandmother in the State Landau with six horses and three postilions. Troops lined the route and there were fifteen military bands along the way playing 'God Save the Queen' and 'God Bless the Prince of Wales'. The Lord Mayor came up to present the sword at Temple Bar, dressed in his crimson velvet and ermine robes. Bertie, pale but recovered, was continually doffing his hat to the cheering crowds. The people went on celebrating in the streets late into the night, and the Republican movement died a quiet death.

As Bertie grew older his confidence increased. He became ever more adept at circumventing his mother's wishes, only giving way on those matters about which he minded not very much. One choice he made at this time concerned a man who was to have an enormous influence on his life, and on Georgie's in his turn, once he became King. When his Private Secretary resigned in June 1870 Bertie decided on Francis Knollys, son of Sir William Knollys, to replace him. Queen Victoria disputed his choice, finding Francis too young and inexperienced. Bertie replied, unperturbed: 'He has had so much to do for me lately that I am convinced he will suit me in every way; and I have already told him of my intention.' Francis Knollys, young and inexperienced perhaps, but clever and essentially liberal in outlook, served the Prince of Wales with devotion for the rest of Bertie's life.

The boys' education was another case where Bertie held his own counsel. Although he had promised to address this vexed subject, he and Alexandra failed to do anything about it until Eddy was eight and Georgie six. Only then did they come to an agreement with Queen Victoria, appointing the Reverend John Neale Dalton as the boys' tutor. Dalton had been spotted by Queen Victoria at Whippingham parish church near Osborne, where he was the curate. He was a bachelor of thirty-two, with a First Class Honours degree in Theology from Cambridge, and although not in the same league as Willy's tutor Dr Hinzpeter when it came to pedantic instruction, he nevertheless believed in the Victorian virtues of self-discipline and hard work. He was the boys' tutor for fourteen years, spending a good ten hours a day in their company. But unlike Hinzpeter, he not only attempted to teach his two charges, he also played with them. When George V looked back on those years he remembered games of bows-and-arrows with Dalton running around in the bushes pretending to be a deer. In the afternoons they went riding, in winter skating, and in summer they played cricket or lawn tennis. Dalton was a kind man, and fair, but strict enough to keep the two 'ill-bred, ill-trained children', as Queen Victoria described them, at their work. When he was away on his holidays he wrote to the boys regularly, and the letters always included some amusement along with comments about their spelling or their grammar. In later years Georgie kept in touch with him, writing to him often, and always expressing a real affection for his former tutor.

Having been chosen by the Queen, Dalton sent her regular progress reports. 'The two little Princes ride on ponies for an hour each alternate morning in the week, and take a walk on the other three days, in the afternoon also their Royal Highnesses take exercise on foot,' he reported dutifully from Sandringham in 1874. 'As regards the studies, the writing, reading and arithmetic are all progressing favourably; the music, spelling, English history, Latin, geography, and French all occupy a due share of their Royal Highnesses' attention.'

This might have been putting a gloss on things: neither of the princes was very bright. Prince Eddy was the worse, with great problems of concentration and an odd lethargy which combined to make him distinctly backward. Georgie in comparison was happily average, 'always merry and rosy' as his grandmother put it. It was generally agreed that the only thing which helped Eddy was working alongside Georgie – though Georgie himself could be difficult at times, as Dalton noted in his Journal of Weekly Work in September 1876: 'Prince G. this week has been much troubled by silly fretfulness of temper and general spirit of contradiction. Otherwise work with me has been up to the usual average.' The boys were not Dalton's only problem: he had trouble stopping the Prince and Princess of Wales from interrupting lessons. Being entirely un-academic themselves, they found it hard to take the business of education seriously.

Georgie's early years were spent mostly at Sandringham, and always with Eddy. The boys joined the rest of the family for short periods at Marlborough House, and at Osborne Cottage on the Isle of Wight during the summer, where they sailed, swam and caught crabs, spending more time than usual with their mother, all of which they related with delight in letters to Dalton. In mid August they moved on to Scotland and Abergeldie near Balmoral, then back to London in November. Christmas was always spent at Sandringham. Many summers included a visit to their grandparents in Denmark. They also visited their English grandmother at Windsor or Osborne, since she had specially requested it, but the visits were always short.

During these years their father was often away, mostly on the business of private pleasure. Every spring he spent three weeks on the Riviera, and at least twice a year he went *en garçon* to Paris. It is one of the more amusing aspects of these travels that the Prince of Wales often liked to go incognito, fondly believing that no one recognised him, despite the luxury of his luggage and the size of his entourage. It was a sport he shared with many royals who grandly felt they were entitled to some free time and some privacy, just like ordinary people. Even Queen Victoria liked to slip away to the French Riviera from time to time, calling herself the Countess of Lancaster. Her favourite haunt was the Excelsior-Regina Hotel, perched high on the cliffs above Nice, which she took over in its entirety for the duration for her stay, bringing her own best-loved pieces of furniture with her as well as a quantity of servants and Royal Household staff.

Official duties rarely took up more than thirty days a year of the Prince of Wales's time. Then he opened hospitals, visited factories, attended ceremonies and committee meetings and unveiled statues and plaques with a charm and good humour which were his great talent and ensured his continuing popularity. Although the Queen allowed him no proper role or influence, he was finally appointed to two Royal Commissions on subjects close to his heart, the first inquiring into the improvement of housing for the working classes, the second into the needs of the aged poor.

Perhaps because they were grand enough not to mind, neither the Prince of Wales nor Queen Victoria, nor King George V after them, had any real sense of class or colour distinction. When he went to India Bertie thought it 'disgraceful' that British officers referred to the natives as 'niggers' and wrote to complain about it to Lord Salisbury, the Secretary for India. 'Because a man has a black face and a different religion from our own,' he additionally wrote to his friend Lord Granville, 'there is no reason why he should be treated as a brute.' In this the British royal family differed fundamentally from the German Kaisers, who were obsessed with ideas of racial purity long before the Nazis institutionalised it. Even liberal Vicky and Fritz were shocked when, at a ball given by the Prince of Wales at Marlborough House in 1881 in honour of King Kalakana of the Sandwich Islands, the Princess of Wales danced an opening quadrille with the very black King. The Germans complained that the King had been given precedence over their own Crown Prince and Princess. But as far as the Prince of Wales was concerned, a King was a King, and that was the end of it.

3

Nicky, the Third Cousin

~

IN MARCH 1868, a few weeks before Minny gave birth to her first child Nicky at Tsarskoe Selo, thirteen miles south-west of St Petersburg, her sister Princess Alexandra wrote to her from Marlborough House in London, offering medical advice, wishing she could send her 'my good Mrs Clarke' and reminding her of what happened to poor Vicky's little son in Berlin 'who came out wrongly'. Even before they were born, the three cousins Georgie, Willy and Nicky, the King, the Kaiser and the Tsar, were inextricably linked in a private familial relationship destined to have its final outcome in the full public glare of international politics.

Minny's parents, the King and Queen of Denmark, liked to refer to their three daughters as 'the beautiful, the clever and the good'. Princess Alexandra, who married the Prince of Wales, was the beautiful one; Princess Dagmar, who married the Tsarevich, was the clever one; which left poor Princess Thyra to content herself with being 'good'. The three brothers were Freddi, the Crown Prince; Willi, who became King George I of the Hellenes in 1863: and Waldemar, who remained plain Waldy.

'The mother's family are bad, the father's foolish' was Queen Victoria's sharp assessment of the Danish royal family. Acting on her convictions, she forbade Bertie and Alexandra, during the first summer after their wedding, from going to Rumpenheim. 'I found, as I heard that I should, a most rabid anti-Prussian feeling at Rumpenheim,' Sir William Knollys recorded when he accompanied the Prince and Princess of Wales there in September 1867. 'They all seemed to have been bit by some Prussian mad dog, and the slightest allusions set the whole party – and we were 36 at dinner – into agitation.'

The Danish royal family's hatred of Prussia was extremely awkward, but not hard to understand. Bismarck's coldly calculated war against the Austrians in 1866 had gained the whole of Schleswig-Holstein for

Germany and signalled a permanent shift of power away from the fast-declining Austrian Hapsburgs in favour of the seemingly unstoppable Prussians and the emerging German nation. 'Prussia is hereby empowered to construct a canal from the North to the Baltic Seas' stated Article 7 of the Convention of Gastein, revealing Bismarck's motive in acquiring Schleswig-Holstein: a German fleet was to be established, based at Kiel. With each loss, the Danish royal family hated the Prussians more. Their hatred was deep and lasting and, with Alexandra and Minny married to the future King of England and the future Tsar of all the Russias, extremely significant.

In May 1866 the extended Danish family was gathering as usual at their summer residence of Fredensborg, outside Copenhagen. Willi, soon to be married to Olga of Russia, Tsar Alexander II's niece, was arriving from Greece, Olga's cousin Alexander, the Tsarevich, from Russia. Only two years earlier his elder brother Nicholai had arrived in the same manner and for the same purpose: to ask the King of Denmark for the hand in marriage of his second daughter, Princess Dagmar. Minny and Nicholai had become engaged before Nicholai returned to Russia, and preparations for the wedding were under way the following year when Nicholai caught tuberculosis and died. It was a personal tragedy for Minny, and a political tragedy for Denmark. But now, after a suitable period of Court mourning, Nicholai's brother Alexander, known as Sasha, was coming, as it were, to replace him. He arrived at the beginning of June.

First impressions were perhaps discouraging. Instead of the elegant, intelligent and liberal-minded Nicholai, so like their father Alexander II, Sasha was large and bear-like and not in the least bit elegant, intellectual or, as it turned out, liberal. His tastes were simple – high society and Court life were not to his liking – but he did have a certain amount in common with the Danish royal family. He liked a good practical joke, and his interest in books was limited, which must have pleased most of them, though not necessarily Minny, the clever one.

At 9 a.m. on 23 June the family gathered for tea in the usual way. However, when Sasha entered the room it was instantly clear to everyone that this was not a day like any other, because he was wearing his Danish tie. Royal circles were sharply attuned to the coded significance of dress: he might as well have been wearing a sign round his neck saying 'this is the day'. After tea they all went for a walk and some sketching. Later the group made their way to Minny's room.

Soon 'everyone went and we were left alone,' wrote Sasha in his diary that evening, for he shared the royal habit of keeping a daily record. Thyra 'the good' shut the door behind her, so no one could see what was going on. 'I was thinking about when I could start my conversation with Minny,' he continued. 'My hands began to tremble and I felt a great excitement. I said: "Has the King talked to you about our conversation and my suggestion?" Then I added, "I asked for your hand in marriage." She threw herself towards me and put her arms around me . . . and she kissed me passionately. The tears were running down our cheeks, both hers and mine.'

It is possible that Minny was able to transfer her affections swiftly from the elegant, intelligent elder brother to the shy and shambling younger one, but it is hard not to construe the matter differently. Minny, the princess from small, defeated and impoverished Denmark, was marrying the man who would one day be Tsar of All the Russias, an Empire so vast that when the sun rose on the eastern border, it was already setting on the western.

For Minny there were only two months left to be with her family in Denmark before embarking on her new life at the Russian Court. She was just nineteen. She spoke almost no Russian. She knew Sasha only slightly, from meeting him occasionally at Rumpenheim when they were children, because their mothers were sisters. After the modest provincial Danish Court, the medieval and labyrinthine ways of Russian Court life were incomprehensible to her, though she had the small advantage of having visited St Petersburg once, two years earlier, when she was still betrothed to Nicholai.

On that occasion she had been met by Nicholai at the Russian frontier in the Imperial train, she herself having arrived on an ordinary passenger train. It was January, and elegant Nicholai stood waiting for her on the platform, wrapped in furs. The Imperial train alone was more sumptuous than any Danish royal palace. There were saloons furnished in velvet and gilt, bedrooms, bathrooms and dining rooms. Pages and footmen hovered about, attending to every wish. But it was hardly comfortable, as the train shook and rattled along the tracks belching out clouds of steam, travelling across mile upon mile of flat, white, featureless terrain, with clusters of peasants gathered along the tracks in the cold to watch them pass, paying their respects.

St Petersburg was buried under deep snow, the Neva river frozen over, but inside the Winter Palace the air was hot and heavily perfumed. Accompanied by the entire Imperial family, Minny proceeded through one vast hall after another, passing row upon row of Guard Cossacks, Guard Lancers, Guard Hussars, gigantic Abyssinian Guards in scarlet and Guards aux Chevaux dressed in white. At the Court Ball two evenings later there were several thousand guests. It opened as always with the Imperial Polonaise, led by Tsar Alexander II and the Tsarina, Minny's aunt. Nicholai had meanwhile succumbed to a cold and lay in bed, so it was Sasha in his red Hussar uniform who shuffled along beside Minny, dancing through hall after hall, avidly scrutinised by all St Petersburg society. Sasha was no dancer, and he was clearly hating it. His carefree younger brother Vladimir laughingly told Minny that their father called Sasha 'the bullock' because of the way he lumbered along, head pushed forward, shoulders hunched. The soldiers in his regiment called him 'the Bull'. Sasha, six foot two and massively built, was certainly strong as an ox. After the dancing he sprawled at the table, surrounded by elegant courtiers and ladies of Russian high society, and did the thing he knew best: he reached out for a large silver platter and crushed it in half, using only one hand.

By September 1866 Minny was on her way to St Petersburg again, this time for good. From the train she wrote her first letter home to her distraught parents. Weeping, they read it again and again, and fought over who might keep it under their pillow that night. Arriving in St Petersburg for the second time, Minny had only a few short weeks to acclimatise herself and prepare for the wedding, which took place on 9 November in the Chapel of the Winter Palace. Her trousseau, given her by the Tsar as was the custom, filled an entire hall. There were winter furs, coats, jackets, hats and headdresses, handfuls of jewels and gems, silk stockings by the hundred, gloves, lingerie, shawls, day shoes, evening shoes, boots, and piles of lace handkerchiefs. It took three hours in the Malachite Drawing Room, supervised by her aunt the Tsarina and assisted by the Mistress of the Robes and other ladies of the Russian Court, to prepare the bride for the wedding ceremony. When she finally emerged Minny could hardly move, so stiff was the antique wedding gown of silver thread, made heavy with clusters of diamonds, and with the ermine train which spread out far behind her.

The air in the Chapel was hot and laden with incense, the elaborate ritual of the Russian Orthodox Church long and largely incomprehensible to Danish Dagmar, though she had by now converted to the Orthodox faith. The reception which followed was interminable, and Minny had to drag her ermine train around from group to group by herself. Unaccountably, train-bearers were not allowed for this. Everyone did their utmost to speak French, the official language of the Court, but conversation was stilted. Nevertheless, Minny managed. She more than managed. She was borne forward on a wave of popularity which had began two years earlier when St Petersburg Society first caught sight of her dancing elegantly next to lumbering Sasha and spontaneously broke out clapping – a popularity which never left her throughout her life at the Russian Court. Finally, as night fell on her wedding day, she found herself in a covered sledge, wrapped in furs, Sasha monosyllabic at her side, travelling swiftly through the countryside to Ropsha, the small palace where the Romanovs spent their honeymoons. When Sasha appeared in the bridal chamber, bashful and sporting the huge traditional silver turban decorated with fat cavorting cupids, she burst into peals of laughter. Perhaps it reminded her of nothing so much as one of the practical jokes back home at the Danish court.

Minny's main sorrow was that her parents could not afford to attend her wedding. The 60,000 Danish crowns demanded by tradition as a dowry almost bankrupted them. They could afford to send only one member of the family and that was Frederick, the Crown Prince. It was humiliating, but by now the King and Queen of Denmark were quite used to humiliation. The only other familiar face at the wedding belonged to Minny's brother-in-law Bertie, the Prince of Wales.

The Prince of Wales arrived in St Petersburg some days in advance of the marriage, and in the highest of spirits. He, used to grandeur and sophistication, nevertheless found the fabulous splendours of the Russian Court beyond his imagination. These splendours included the Russian Court beauties, and further delights were revealed when he visited various low spots and haunts of St Petersburg with some of Sasha's brothers, and Sasha himself. Bertie flirted openly with the Court ladies and indiscreetly with the others, and the news soon spread across the courts of Europe to Vicky in Berlin, and thence to Queen Victoria in England. In every other respect the Prince of Wales's natural charm, keen curiosity and developing diplomatic skills ensured that his visit was the greatest success. At the end of his stay, at the ball given in St Petersburg by the English Ambassador Sir Andrew Buchanan and attended by the entire Imperial family, Bertie wore

Highland dress and danced every dance. In his speech that evening he made a point of stressing his satisfaction at the marriage as a means of strengthening the friendly relations between Great Britain and the Russian Empire.

The following May, 1867, Minny was able to return home to Denmark in triumph with her new husband the Tsarevich for her parents' silver wedding anniversary. The Imperial couple received a delirious welcome from the Danish people, who crowded the streets as they made their way to the royal palace and refused to go home till Minny and Sasha had appeared again and again on the balcony. After two weeks Sasha reluctantly left Copenhagen to attend the Paris Exhibition. He found the simple life at the Danish court very much to his taste, and he already disliked being without Minny, who was to stay behind with her parents.

In St Petersburg, people had soon noticed a change in the Tsarevich. His wife the Tsarevna, now known as the Grand Duchess Marie Feodorovna, was taking him in hand, apparently able to cope with his strange moods and manners with ease and good humour. He was seen to spend more and more of his time in her company, less and less with his more dubious friends, and he seemed a far happier man. That summer Sasha and Minny, accompanied by Queen Louise, went to England to stay with Alexandra and Bertie at Marlborough House. 'My own angel Minny,' Alexandra wrote once Minny and Sasha had left, 'It is painful for me that we are once again separated and I can hardly believe that we have SEEN each other as it now appears just like a dream!! How terrible our parting, I DESPAIRED as I looked on your angel face for the last time!!' By the time the Imperial couple returned to St Petersburg it was evident that Minny was pregnant with their first child.

Nicholai Alexandrovitch Romanov, the future Tsar Nicholas II and last of the three royal cousins, was born on 18 May 1868 and named after his deceased uncle, once betrothed to his mother. His father Sascha was present at the birth and recorded in his diary: 'The pangs were stronger and stronger, and Minnie suffered a lot. Papa helped me hold my darling all the time. At last, at half past two, came the last minute and all the suffering stopped at once. God sent us a son whom we gave the name Nikolai. What joy it was, it is not to be described. I rushed to embrace my darling wife who cheered up at once and was terrifically happy. I was crying like a baby . . . We embraced with Papa and Mama wholeheartedly. We drank tea and talked with Minnie till 11, and I went several times to admire our little angel.'

His diary reveals a different Sasha, one hidden from people who met him in everyday life and found him shambling and inarticulate. It reveals an emotional man, easily given to tears, and very much in love with his wife. Unlike his father Alexander II who openly kept his mistress and their children in an apartment in the Winter Palace on the floor above the one he inhabited with his wife, Sasha, once given the chance, became a devoted family man, spending all his free time with his children and joining in all their games, just like one of them.

Nicky's maternal grandparents, the King and Queen of Denmark, came to Russia for the first time in August 1868, for Nicky's christening. In their wake followed a flood of Danish businessmen hoping to find a new market for their goods. The King and Queen found the Tsarevich and their daughter the Tsarevna living in the Anitchkoff Palace on the Nevski Prospect, the most fashionable area in St Petersburg, itself the most fashionable and westernised city in Russia. Sasha and Minny were surrounded by an army of servants, pages, footmen and guards, with a further army of secret police to secure their safety. In Russia the Tsar and his family were never safe, in spite of the fact that Alexander II was a liberal and in 1861 had taken the critical political decision to end slavery by freeing the serfs.

Minny was soon the acknowledged leader of St Petersburg society, famed for her wit and cleverness as well as her expensive fashion sense. At Court functions it was noticed that the Tsarevna had the knack of talking to anyone, from whatever background, in the same charming and natural manner, the perfect opposite of her husband, who remained awkward and monosyllabic. It was also noticed that the Tsarevna was using her cleverness to influence her husband. To those who knew her well, the area of her influence came as no surprise: she was educating him. As the second son and certainly not academically gifted, Sasha had been all but neglected by Pobedonostsev, the tutor who had educated and disciplined the four sons of Alexander II. Pobedonostsev had been a hard task-master who much preferred the elegant and charming first-born, Grand Duke Nicholai, and the third-born, Grand Duke Vladimir, who shared Nicholai's charm. He even preferred Alexei, the youngest, to lumbering and increasingly unconfident Sasha. Nevertheless he had a profound influence on Sasha, who respected him, even feared him.

When Nicholai died Pobedonostsev at first held back, as rumours at Court suggested Alexander II meant to bypass his hopeless second son in favour of his third, Vladimir. But they were quite wrong about that, and as soon as Pobedonostsev was sure of Sasha's succession, he began courting him. He was soon a regular visitor to the Anitchkoff Palace, though he cannot have enjoyed the company very much. The Tsarevna, brought up in liberal Denmark, naturally tended towards the more progressive in St Petersburg society, writers, musicians and liberal politicians. Pobedonostsev by contrast was a convinced reactionary, believing that a country as vast and unmanageable as Russia could only be ruled by a powerful and autocratic monarchy.

The majority of Tsar Alexander II's subjects were illiterate peasants, living in extreme poverty. By the 1870s they numbered almost a hundred million, only half of them Russian. There were Armenians, Georgians, Latvians, Estonians, and Muslims in central Asia and the Caucasus. Many were nomads. Because of the distances involved, the cost of building roads and bridges to rural communities and then providing them with schools and hospitals was excessive. Yet if Russia were to survive internationally, she had to modernise. Russian businessmen returned home from newly united Germany alarmed at the rapid industrialisation and expansion, aware that Germany was fast becoming the most successful economy in Europe. But in Russia, industrialisation meant millions of peasants leaving their villages and swamping the towns, where living and working conditions were appalling. Modernisation only increased Russia's instability, and threats to her internal as well as her external security increased. The Ministry of Finance and the Ministry of the Interior disagreed as to the solution, the Ministry of Finance favouring an increase in free enterprise and a loosening of restraints, the Ministry of the Interior favouring forceful repression.

Paradoxically, Alexander II's liberal initiatives had led to more unrest, not less. Already in the 1860s Russia had an underground revolutionary movement, led by disillusioned young radicals from the educated classes, which was active in the cities though less so in the rural areas. They plotted mutinies in the Army and rebellion among the peasantry, and in 1863 they made their first attempt to assassinate the Tsar. For all these reasons, Pobedonostsev was convinced that a powerful and repressive system was the only solution. Minny, the young Tsarevna from provincial Denmark, could hardly be expected to understand the full complexities of a country like Russia. But she did understand that her husband would one day have to rule this unruly Empire, and she sensed that, apart from herself, the only man Sasha would listen to was his old tutor.

Minny herself educated Sasha in a hatred of Prussia, and the hope she shared with her sister Alexandra of a special *entente* with England. It was not long before people noticed that the Tsarevich, much like the Prince of Wales in England, was abusing Prussia loudly and indiscreetly. It sat oddly at the Court of St Petersburg, where Alexander II was known to like the Germans – had, indeed, a German wife – and where many of the Court officials and top administrators were Russians of German descent from the Baltic states, with German names. Things became awkward as Sasha got into his stride. He took to turning his back on German visitors at Court, walking off in the opposite direction when they were about to be introduced. When Friedrich, Crown Prince of Prussia came to visit, Sasha flatly refused to meet him, and Alexander II, exasperated but unable to influence his son 'the bullock', had to content himself with an agreement that Sasha keep to his quarters. Fritz was told the Tsarevich was in bed with a severe cold, which he politely accepted.

The Tsarevich's young wife, meanwhile, thrived. She oversaw every detail of the care of Nicky, their son and heir, and as soon as she could she took him to Denmark to see her parents and show him off to the adoring crowds. It was in the summer of 1870, as the Franco-Prussian war – Bismarck's third and final war of German unification – broke out, destroying relations between France and Germany for good. Princess Alexandra arrived from England in July with her three eldest children, Eddy, Georgie and Louise Victoria, but without her husband, and without Princess Victoria and the baby Princess Maud, born the previous November to complete the family. 'My naughty little man', as Alexandra referred to her husband, suitably chastened after the Mordaunt divorce case, only arrived to collect his family at the end of their stay.

Minny also came without her husband. Sasha was away on military manoeuvres, and wrote to her complaining about the Prussians. He wrote mostly in French, since that was the only language they had in common. He hoped to come at least for a day or two, because he hated to be without her. He added that he regretted not seeing his sister-in-law Alexandra, but 'The French-German war has ruined all my chances of coming.' When Minny wrote back she told him Nicky was being admired by everyone and enclosed a drawing done for him by the child using a feather pen. 'We had glorious times in Denmark with my cousins,' Nicky recalled years later when he was Tsar, those carefree days far behind him. 'There were such a lot of us staying with my grandfather, King Christian IX, that some of my Greek cousins as boys used to sleep on sofas in the reception rooms when our elders had retired. We bathed in the sea. I remember once as a tiny boy Mother swimming out far into the Sound with me sitting astride on her shoulders.'

For Minny, staying in her own old room, this homely family gathering conducted in the usual simple style must have made a strange contrast to life at the Russian Court. A gushing official at the Danish Court observed the scene as two-year-old Nicholai was being admired by the whole family. 'With cautious tenderness have the noble ladies passed the little Grand Duke from arm to arm, from lap to lap. The little innocent smiles happily at everyone and has cried only a little this evening, when he was put to bed. How can this tender infant who now sleeps so soundly possibly know what the Fates now guarding his cradle have in store for him? The tiny soft hand which perhaps will some day grasp the world's mightiest sceptre in its manly grip may well now, in his sleep, be grasping a rattle.' If this sounds excessive, it is as well to remember that all three royal cousins were surrounded by obsequiousness and flattery from the moment of their birth, but particularly Nicky and Willy, the first-born, the ones destined to grasp the sceptre.

Alexandra had spent only two weeks at Fredensborg before naughty Bertie arrived. The Franco-Prussian war was a great deal closer to England than to Denmark or Russia, and it was thought wiser that she and the children should return to the safety of home. From Marlborough House Alexandra wrote to Minny, 'It could be interesting if France beat Prussia.' And then, getting to the heart of the matter, 'It is to be hoped France will win and return the conquered provinces to Denmark.' The Prince of Wales was indiscreet enough to tell Bernsdorff that he believed the Prussians would at last be taught a lesson. The Prussian Ambassador promptly made an official complaint that this was not a neutral comment. Queen Victoria was disconcerted but Bertie, writing to her, merely commented that 'Bernsdorff is an ill-conditioned man, and I only long for the day when he will be removed from here.' By September the war was over, the Prussians again the victors, and the Paris Commune, set up during the siege of Paris, collapsed. 'Heard that the mob at Paris had rushed into the Senate and proclaimed the downfall of the dynasty, proclaiming a Republic!' the Queen noted with distaste.

During the war Vicky busied herself organising field hospitals for the wounded, provocatively making no distinction between German and French soldiers. Bismarck was furious. He sharply commented that Fritz was foolish enough to behave 'as though Germany had never possessed a hospital before the Crown Princess arrived on the scene' and insisted that she be recalled to Berlin. Next he fiercely criticised the Crown Prince who, having already offended by objecting to the bombardment of Paris, now urged Bismarck not to humiliate the French at the Armistice. Although Fritz was again a war hero, he was less and less a man who gloried in war. Once again Bismarck put Fritz's weakness down to Vicky's influence.

Vilified or not, now that Germany was unified Vicky busied herself with one of the royal family's favourite pastimes: titles. She telegraphed the good news to Queen Victoria, followed by a letter: 'We are called Kaiserliche und Königliche Hoheit Kronprinz des Deutschen Reichs und von Preussen,' she wrote, unable to hide her pleasure. 'I am always spoken to as Imperial Highness (I own I liked the other better) but as it reminds one of the great political fact of Germany's being gathered under one head, I am proud to bear this title.' The subject inevitably led to Willy, who had just celebrated his twelfth birthday and had enjoyed the presents sent to him by his grandmother. 'I am sure you would be pleased with William if you were to see him – he has Bertie's pleasant, amiable ways – and can be very winning. He is not possessed of brilliant abilities, nor of any strengths of character or talents, but he is a dear boy, and I hope and trust will grow up a useful man.' With fateful misjudgement she added, 'I watch over him myself, over every detail, even the minutest, of his education, as his Papa has never had the time to occupy himself with the children. These next few years will be very critical and important for him, as they are the passage from childhood to manhood. I am happy to say that between him and me there is a bond of love and confidence, which I feel sure nothing can destroy.'

There is a whiff of anxiety in the claim. Vicky knew well enough that Bismarck and the Kaiser were bent on destroying that bond, Willy's link with liberal England. And although the tone of her comments about William, or Wilhelm, is affectionate, it is evident that they refer to the education of a future Kaiser as much as that of a son. Vicky's obsessive watching over Willy, down to the last detail, was in preparation for his future role. Willy was the recipient of any amount of attention, but try as Vicky might, she could never feel the same love for him as she had felt for Sigi. Nevertheless, in these early years there were still times when they were happy together and Vicky was able to feel some pride in her son. For his part, Willy longed for his mother's love and approval. Some of his happiest times, he recalled in his memoirs, were spent when he was allowed to join his mother in her studio, reading aloud to her while she was painting. The language was English, the thrilling tales of Sir Walter Scott some of their favourites.

But the problem of the crippled arm remained. 'He has very strong health,' Vicky's letter to her mother continued, still on the same subject, 'and would be a very pretty boy were it not for that wretched unhappy arm which shows more and more, spoils his face (for it is on one side), his carriage, walk and figure, makes him awkward in all his movements, and gives him a feeling of shyness, as he feels his complete dependence, not being able to do a single thing for himself. It is a great additional difficulty in his education, and is not without its effect on his character. To me it remains an inexpressible source of sorrow!' It is a telling description. There is no doubt the crippled arm played its part in Willy's life and character, and his later erratic behaviour when Kaiser. At the same time, the extreme pessimism reveals his mother's sorrow. It is extraordinary that she should describe Willy as not being able to do 'a single thing' for himself, since by now he had mastered everything except feeding himself, including many sports, and riding.

As soon as the war was over the Crown Prince and Princess asked the Kaiser's permission to go with their children to England for the summer. To their surprise the request was granted without the usual protests. When they returned to Potsdam at the end of the summer it became clear why. Having unified Germany, Bismarck set about consolidating his position, and took advantage of the Crown Prince's absence to remove him from the Council of State. It is possible that Bismarck was finally pushed into it by an article in *The Times* which praised Fritz extravagantly, describing the Crown Prince, somewhat naively and provocatively, as 'the constant friend of all mild and Liberal administration. When he succeeds the main obstacle to friendship with England will disappear.'

Wilhelm, or William as he was in England, remembered that summer with fondness in his memoirs. First they stayed at Buckingham Palace, then moved on to Windsor and later to Osborne: the usual round, in fact. He noted that his grandmother never played down her German origins but expressed herself proud of her title of Duchess of Saxony, and included the arms in her Royal Standard. He also noted that she spoke German without an accent. He remembered playing soldiers with his Aunt Beatrice, who was only a few years older than himself, and being taken round London by his favourite uncle, Prince Arthur, Duke of Connaught. He, Willy noted, was an excellent soldier, who loved to wear his German Hussar uniform whenever he went on manoeuvres there. Most of all Willy remembered his favourite aunt, Princess Louise, later Marchioness of Lorne, who let him play in her room and gave him sweets. Aunt Louise was fun-loving, with the same sense of humour, he felt, as her mother Queen Victoria. 'I adored her,' he wrote, 'and have continued to adore her for the rest of my life.'

Willy's best memory of that summer was of the day on the Isle of Wight when he attended a parade of the 103rd Royal Bombay Fusiliers. He was profoundly impressed by the solemnity of the ceremony as the Regimental Colours were handed first to his mother, their Commander-in-Chief, who then solemnly passed them on to his uncle, the Duke of Connaught. This was only outdone by trips in the Queen's royal paddle steamer from Cowes to Portsmouth, where they saw many towering English battleships anchored alongside Nelson's famous *Victory*. When he returned home to Germany Queen Victoria sent Willy a replica of a British man-of-war, complete with mast and rigging, which was duly erected for him on the lawn at the Neues Palais in Potsdam. It was another example of a seemingly innocent act behind which lay a serious purpose. Queen Victoria and Vicky thought it a good idea to encourage his interest in the British Navy as an antidote to all the Prussian militarism. They could hardly have guessed that Willy's enthusiasm, thus fostered by them, would later lead to a bitter naval race between England and Germany.

In the summer of 1872 Minny was again in Denmark, this time with one-year-old Georgei as well as Nicky, but again without her husband. Sasha wrote to her from the Dom area, where he was once again on military manoeuvres: 'For this insane militarism you can blame the Prussians.' No one knew where Bismarck might roam next.

Sasha was longing to join Minny in Copenhagen, but his father had written bluntly to tell him that it did not matter how much he longed for it, 'military matters are military matters'. Sasha, complaining to Minny about life in the military camp and the lack of post, ended, 'I hold you in my arms and I embrace you with all my heart and long fearfully to kiss you again and be with you in nature's costume, like Adam and Eve.'

By 1873 Alexandra and Minny were busy with a small coup designed to help the Anglo-Russian *entente*. It was planned that the Tsarevich and his family should make a semi-official visit to the Prince and Princess of Wales in England for two months, beginning in June. Secretly the two sisters made a plan. In letters from London to St Petersburg and back again they exchanged sketches and patterns of every outfit they would wear during the visit, so that they should be identical: cut, colours, fabrics, trimmings and accessories; ball gowns, riding habits, day dresses, coats, hats and shoes. Day and night the two sisters would be dressed alike, and thus, without the need to utter a word, the idea of an alliance between England and Russia, and by implication against Germany, would instil itself in the public's mind.

When the Russian Imperial Yacht berthed at Woolwich on 16 June there was a huge crowd at the quayside, the Prince and Princess of Wales among them. As the Tsarevich and his wife came down the gangplank, followed by Nicky aged five and his brother Georgei aged two, a great roar of approval went up. The Tsarevna was wearing a white day dress and straw bonnet decorated with cherries, the same in every detail as the dress and bonnet worn, they had already observed, by their own Princess of Wales. The carriage procession set out for London with an escort of the 3rd Dragoon Guards, the Queen having ruled out an escort of the Household Cavalry, since this visit was only semi-official. The crowd cheered the two sisters wildly. Later, at the ball given for the Russian guests at Lansdowne House, footmen struggled to prevent people standing on chairs, sofas, even tables, as they tried to catch a glimpse of the Princess of Wales and the Tsarevna in their identical ball gowns. 'The sisters set each other off,' wrote Lady Antrim, 'and became the centre of a glittering crowd wherever they went.'

Unfortunately, the Shah Nasr el Din of Persia was due on an official State Visit only two days after the arrival of the Tsarevich and his family. This was awkward in every respect. There was the problem of precedence: the Tsarevich and his family, being only semi-official, had to give way to the Shah, and the Russians were offended. Worse still, the Shah's European tour – announced with a suddenness which took everyone by surprise – had begun in St Petersburg, and it now appeared to the Russians that the British were trying to outdo them in the lavishness of their hospitality. 'Proud Albion is doing all she can by the pomp of her receptions to astonish the Shah, and to what end, only to outdo Russia and to efface the pleasing memory the Shah took with him from St Petersburg,' wrote the *Mir* of St Petersburg. *The Times* responded: 'Our Russian friends must not suppose we are always thinking about them. Our Queen, her Ministers, the Lord Mayor, the Lessees of the Opera, the Directors of the Albert Hall and the Crystal Palace, have not the slightest desire to make a demonstration against the Russian Government.'

Throughout the 1870s the problem of the Middle East was uppermost in politicians' minds. The Ottoman Empire was slowly crumbling, and the Great Powers were lining up to maintain the balance of power, as they put it, but in reality to ensure that they each got a piece of the cake. As for the great British public, most were completely uninterested in any political implications, only thrilled at the sight of a man literally dripping with jewels. Diamonds and emeralds adorned the Shah's chest, his epaulettes, and his astrakhan cap. The buttons on his tunics were rubies, and his belts were encrusted with gems of every shape and colour. The Shah upstaged the Russians with ease, and it was only those delightful matching outfits won by the Princess of Wales and the Tsarevna which saved the day.

The Tsarevich and the Tsarevna appeared unconcerned by all the fuss. Sasha spent most of his free time in the nursery at Marlborough House playing with Nicky and Georgei and the five Wales children, Eddy, Georgie, Louise, Victoria and Maud, who ranged from nine to four years old. Nicky was the same age as Victoria, or Toria as she was known in the family, and he remained closer to her than the others. He also formed a lasting affection for his uncle Bertie, who spoiled him. But it is unlikely that he played much with his cousins Eddy and Georgie, and not only because of the age difference. The Wales children, indulged by both parents, hardly knew the word 'discipline'. 'Wild as hawks' was how Queen Victoria described them. 'They are such ill-bred, ill-trained children I can't fancy them at all,' she had noted in her Journal the year before.

The Tsarevna meanwhile spent most of her time with her sister the Princess of Wales, causing a stir. Each morning they drove out in Hyde Park, seated side by side in an open carriage, wearing their identical outfits and waving gaily to the gaping crowds gathered at the railings. In the afternoons they might set off, now dressed more modestly, for the East End of London, an area of Dickensian poverty and squalor, to visit one of the many Houses of Refuge which Alexandra supported. In the evenings they attended dinners and banquets, or one of the balls given in their or the Shah's honour by all the great houses of London.

The whole of London was agape at the Shah's behaviour, which was spectacularly bad. He shouted at the servants, his table manners were disgusting, his time-keeping was rude, and his freedom with the ladies was shocking. He pulled food out of his mouth and either put it back if he deemed it good, or threw it over his shoulder if he did not. He soon abandoned knives and forks, wiping his greasy hands on the tablecloths and belching loudly. At the Gala Concert given in his honour at the Albert Hall he sat in the Royal Box between the Princess of Wales and the Tsarevna (in identical white evening gowns and matching tiaras), and put an arm round the chair of first one sister then the other, moving smoothly from the chair to their own royal persons, fondling them in full view of the thousands of guests. Unfortunately the two princesses did not maintain their dignity but broke out in hysterical giggles, scandalising the crowd. The Prince of Wales was more amused than his brother-in-law by the Shah. For years afterwards he liked to tell people about the night when they all went to Trentham to stay with the Duke of Sutherland, who was extremely rich. 'Too grand for a subject,' opined the Shah to the Prince. 'You'll have to have his head off when you come to the throne.'

In 1874 Bismarck, always convinced of the necessity for Germany to avoid war with her mighty neighbour Russia, formed the *Dreikaiserbund*, the Three Emperors' League. Its inauguration was glimpsed by a young French nobleman called François Ayme who was travelling back to Germany after the Franco-Prussian war to take up his post as Prince Wilhelm's French tutor. Ayme was studying at the University of Bonn in 1870, but when the war came he made a hasty retreat to France. Now he was back, recruited through a network of aristocratic contacts. He came with mixed feelings. The war had left France humiliated, and turned the young nobleman into a

Republican. Passing through Bonn, François Ayme joined the crowd to watch the three Emperors, Wilhelm I, Franz-Joseph of Austro-Hungary and Alexander II of Russia, parading up and down in public. They were apparently deep in serious conversation, but it was probably only an early example of a photo-opportunity.

There was little reason for Ayme to understand the full significance of this historic event. Bismarck was above all anxious to prevent further conflict with France, which might reverse the outcome of the Franco-Prussian war. Now that France was a Republic, he called the three Emperors together to join forces. For the time being the agreement between them remained no more than an 'understanding', in the subtle language of diplomacy; not until 1881 did it become the League proper. But a secret military agreement was also signed in St Petersburg by which Germany and Russia agreed to come to each other's aid in the event of an attack from a third European power.

However, Bismarck's memoirs make it clear that he feared the rise of socialism and revolution as much as he feared another war. Now that he had achieved a united Germany, he was concerned to maintain the status quo. The new constitution, drafted by himself, gave the Kaiser absolute and autocratic powers – but for now, only in name; in practice, Wilhelm I was entirely in Bismarck's hands, and happily so. It appears not to have crossed Bismarck's mind that another Kaiser might not be quite as malleable.

But there was no stopping progress. As François Ayme quickly noticed, the Franco-Prussian war had brought about a great change in newly-united Germany. The very atmosphere was different. Before the war everything had seemed charming and '*gemutlich*'. After it, Ayme sensed a new arrogance in the country, a driving energy and ambition which appeared to be shared by everyone, whatever their background. People everywhere were working feverishly. Industry was thriving. Bankrupts became commonplace. Germany was determined to become a world power, with Berlin a world capital. The Prussian military was unstoppable, and Bismarck was God. The earlier philosophical and sceptical outlook which had so appealed to François Ayme had disappeared, replaced by a fervent and simple belief in Germany's glorious future. But with this new-found confidence, prosperity and progress came the rise of Socialism.

In 1778 Bismarck began to introduce his draconian Anti-Socialist Laws, using two minor attempts on the Kaiser's life as his excuse.

Article 11 curtailed the freedom of the press; Article 17 made it a crime to join a banned organisation, with three months in prison for membership and up to a year in prison for those actively working for the organisation. But repression only caused the activists to go underground, where they flourished.

4

The Education of Three Royal Cousins

~

A T FIFTEEN, WILHELM was confirmed. It was another private
family event with public significance, the Protestant religion
being, for the future Kaiser of the German Reich, a matter of State.
Southern Germany remained Catholic, but it was Prussia and the
Protestant north which had emerged pre-eminent after Bismarck's
three wars of German unification, with the Protestant, autocratic
Kaiser standing somewhere between his people and his God. In future
years Wilhelm referred to himself in precisely these terms, insisting
that as Kaiser he was answerable to no one but God. His parents held
the more modest and liberal view that religion should embrace a
concern for humankind and inform one's behaviour in daily life: a
typically weak and sentimental English view.

The confirmation took place on 27 August 1874, in the
Friedenskirche where Sigi was buried. The church was filled with gar-
lands of greenery and Willy, in uniform, knelt at the altar, which was
draped in Sigi's white satin pall embroidered by his mother with a
golden 'S' and crown in each corner. His uncle Bertie had
travelled from England with the Princess of Wales to attend, representing Queen Victoria. Vicky looked tearful and edgy, having had a
row with the Kaiser that morning over Willy's education. After the
ceremony, Bertie read William a letter from his grandmother and
handed over her present of a bible, with an edifying letter enclosed.
'Willy was much pleased with your presents which were laid out in my
sitting-room,' he wrote dutifully. 'Your letter to him and the inscrip-
tion you wrote in the Bible I thought beautiful, and I read them to
him. All you said I thought so very true.' Then, as soon as possible,
both he and the Princess of Wales left, the Princess for Copenhagen,
the Prince for Baden and his usual amusements.

The British press, reporting the Baden visit, made reference to the
Prince of Wales's mounting debts. They were said to be in the region

of £600,000 – some four million in today's money. Moneylenders always hung about the hotels where he stayed when he was abroad, and rich friends such as Baron Maurice de Hirsch, Sir Ernest Cassel and the Rothschilds were often called upon to bail him out, being received at Court and entertained at Marlborough House in return. Sir William Knollys wrote to Queen Victoria that he had objected to the Prince of Wales's visit to Baden, and 'should equally do so if another visit to Paris in returning be in contemplation.' Knollys saw Paris as the den of iniquity.

In Berlin the row over Wilhelm's education ran along familiar lines. The Kaiser wanted his grandson to attend a military academy. Vicky and Fritz intended to send him away to an ordinary grammar school in Cassel on the Rhine, not far from his grandmother's castle at Coblenz. Like Queen Victoria, they believed that princes should know about the real world and be educated among ordinary boys. The Kaiser was appalled and went into a rage. But Vicky and Fritz got their way, and by the start of the autumn semester Willy was on his way to Cassel for the next three years of his education, accompanied by Dr Hinzpeter and his brother Heinrich who, being entirely unacademic, was to attend the nearby naval academy.

Dr Hinzpeter, determined that his royal pupils should arrive like ordinary schoolboys, decided they should walk, rucksacks on backs, for a large part of the way, and travel the rest by public transport. The net result was that when they finally arrived at the palace in Cassel, exhausted, hungry after a meagre breakfast of bread and beer, and wet in spite of Hinzpeter's umbrella, the porter would not let them in. 'Only after a long dispute between an extremely annoyed Hinzpeter and the porter, who was expecting two Prussian princes which we clearly were not, were we finally allowed to enter,' wrote Willy years later, with some humour. 'In fact our arrival in Cassel was altogether eccentric.' The eccentricity extended to the fact that the two princes lived not in a house, like any other student, but in a palace – two palaces, in fact: the town palace during the winter months and the beautiful palace of Wilhelmshohe in the hills above Cassel during the summer.

Willy had been extremely anxious at the thought of leaving home, his only consolation being that Heinrich was going too. But everything went much better than he'd expected. Within a week he felt so completely at home among his classmates at the grammar school that he could hardly imagine studying any other way. As for the teachers and the other students in his class, all local boys, Hinzpeter later recalled that after some initial hesitation they were soon reassured, for Wilhelm behaved with tact, keen to show he could be a good *Kamarad*. Willy remembered it in slightly less rosy terms. In his memoirs he made it clear that although he had a good relationship with all his classmates, he never developed a really close friendship with anyone. However much Hinzpeter wished it otherwise, the reality was that Wilhelm was different, and no amount of pretence could alter the fact.

The routine at Cassel was strenuous, strictly imposed by Hinzpeter, though his role was now less that of tutor, more that of general over-seer. The two boys were up at five in summer and six in winter, in order to finish their homework before breakfast. Classes at the grammar school ran from eight until twelve, when there was a two-hour break for lunch. Since mealtimes never lasted more than half an hour in the royal household, there remained a good hour and a half to fill with extracurricular activities: fencing lessons, swimming or going for walks, always with Hinzpeter. Then it was back to class from two until four, followed for Willy by an extra hour with Hinzpeter going over everything he had learnt that day. From five to six was supper, followed by at least two hours of homework, and bed at nine, or nine-thirty at the latest. The hour before bedtime was usually taken up, for Willy at least, by more schoolwork, either with Hinzpeter or with one of the special tutors engaged for lessons in English or French. Sunday afternoons the boys had to themselves, when they might go to the theatre, always a favourite pastime, but even these afternoons were often annexed by Hinzpeter for some elevating activity: a visit to a museum, or a debate with classmates on some serious issue. 'I like my life at Cassel very much,' Willy wrote dutifully to his grandmother in England, 'and going to school gives me great pleasure, as I like my masters, my studies and my schoolmates.'

Years later Wilhelm complained that it had not been a rounded education in any sense of the word. His studies were typical of a German grammar school, dominated by the Classics, which he found excessively dry though not necessarily difficult, thanks to his excellent memory. He liked the heroics of the *Iliad*, but thought Cicero a bore. On the other hand Classical art, especially sculpture, became something of a passion, defining for ever more Wilhelm's idea of what 'good' art was. His favourite subject remained German history, so much so that he read it in his spare time as well. But he also loved literature, German and English, including Charles Dickens. His grandmother sent him books from England, including one on the life of his grandfather, Prince Albert.

How did François Ayme, now joining the royal household at Cassel, find his new pupil, Prince Wilhelm of Hohenzollern? Of all those who knew Willy at this time, he – French and Republican, albeit with an aristocratic background, and with nothing to gain – is the least biased and the most reliable witness. From his book *Kaiser Wilhelm II and his Education*, published in French and German 1898, it is clear that Ayme liked Wilhelm. Although he was nervous on that first day, he felt at ease with his new pupil within minutes, describing him as polite, friendly, energetic and full of life. He judged him clever, quite original in his thinking, ambitious, and a hard worker, noting that he hated to fail. He was pleased to find that Wilhelm already spoke good French and liked to read the French poets, especially Victor Hugo. His manners were perfect. He did notice a tendency in Wilhelm to show off at times, but mostly he was restrained, with views which were upright and idealistic, still influenced by his parents and Dr Hinzpeter. Wilhelm was one of those pupils a teacher remembers with happiness, Ayme wrote. He thought the Prince could have made a good journalist, had he not been the heir to the Hohenzollern throne.

Most revealing of all is Ayme's account of how Wilhelm, living among ordinary boys of his own age, coped with his crippled arm. He noted that the arm was so useless that Wilhelm had trouble gathering his books and lifting them off the table. The only help his left arm offered was for leaning on the table to steady himself. But he always made light of it, wrote Ayme, impressed. As for Heinrich, he was neither bright nor hard-working, but he was likeable. Willy got twenty Marks pocket money a month, Heinrich ten.

During French lessons Ayme and Willy covered many topics. Ayme explained what it was to be a Republican. He noted that Wilhelm had no idea that Socialism in Germany was no longer in its infancy, but a well-developed and mature movement. Finally they got round to talking about a subject they had been avoiding for months: the Franco-Prussian war. Willy described the reaction at home on the day war broke out. 'We were just sitting down for dinner when my father rushed into the room looking pale and upset. His voice breaking and taking us into his arms he said, "It's decided. France wants war. Oh my children, what a disaster." ' Apart from the fact that Wilhelm put the blame on France, Ayme was touched. He was therefore extremely surprised when, coming back to the subject a few days later, Willy announced, 'Next time we'll do it better.' It was quite a while before they were back on speaking terms. Ignorant of how Wilhelm's loyalties were divided between liberal English and belligerent Prussian, Ayme was baffled by the contradictions. 'Together we could conquer the world,' Wilhelm told Ayme, meaning Germany and France, and restoring the peace between them.

Ayme is particularly good on the problems of being a prince. When a prince enters a room, he noted, everyone stops speaking. People stand still as statues, not even daring to move over to the window for a breath of air, then following at a respectful distance when the prince proceeds into the next room. Ayme had seen normally intelligent people, even of high rank, behave like fools when confronted with a prince. 'In a land where the monarchical principle rules, it is the flattering, manipulative people who rise to the top. The servile courtiers. It's actually a miracle that crowned heads don't make more mistakes than they do, or misuse their power more. How can they distinguish between true and false courtiers?' Thus did Ayme accurately predict Wilhelm's future life, and the people who would surround him.

As soon as the two boys had settled down at Cassel the Crown Prince and Princess paid them a visit. Ayme was keen to meet them and see what they were like. He was agreeably surprised. They were extremely informal. The Prince was tall and handsome in his uniform, and very relaxed. He told a good joke. The Princess was clever, rather serious, and clearly the one who had organised Wilhelm's schooling. She seemed genuinely proud of her son's progress. She spoke good French, and knew how to charm people. She was very little concerned about smart looks. However, Ayme also noted that she was very outspoken, not bothering to disguise her dislike of the Prussian aristocracy, nor her anti-clericalism. Writing years later, he thought that 'If the Crown Prince had lived, she would have been the ruler.' That evening Willy asked Ayme to join them for dinner. When the tutor entered the room, he found the four of them all talking happily together. As he sat round the table with them, relaxed and laughing, he thought that, at that moment, the Crown Prince and Princess had everything: a happy marriage, and the 'nimbus of majesty'. By 1898, when his book was published, it was a different story.

When his parents returned to Potsdam Willy began to write home regularly. They are strange letters, revealing a son fixated on his mother. 'I have again dreamt about you,' he wrote. 'This time I was alone with you in your library, when you stretched forth your arms & pulled me lower to your chair . . . I instantly seized your hand & kissed it . . . Then you gave me a warm embrace & put your right arm around my neck & got up and walked about the room with me . . . I dreamt about what we will do in reality when we are alone in your rooms without any witnesses . . . This dream is ALONE for YOU to know.' It was written, as usual, in English, and it was signed 'William'.

By now the German Court official who wrote *Recollections of Three Kaisers* had left Kaiser Wilhelm's service and joined the Crown Prince and Princess at the Neues Palais at Potsdam as a general factotum. The Neues Palais was a happy home in those days, he recorded. Holidays were spent *en famille*, often on the North Sea coast. Every day the Crown Prince took his children swimming or rowing or walking. In the evenings they might go to the theatre. Or he might read aloud to them. At this stage in his life, Willy loved his father. Later it became more complicated. 'The Christmas fair was the children's paradise,' recalled the Court official, 'and all Berlin thronged to it, young and old, rich and poor. The Crown Prince and his wife, arm in arm, with their children and all unattended, used to wend their way between the booths, regardless of the crush, just like any ordinary citizens, and the children loved spending their pennies just like ordinary little Berliners.' Family life was kept as natural and simple as possible.

Vicky had completely redecorated the Neues Palais, untouched since it was built by Frederick the Great in the mid eighteenth century. She also redesigned the gardens along English lines, with plenty of roses. Since Fritz was often away, frequently at war, Vicky devoted her excessive energy to every detail of the planning, as well spending a great deal more time with her children than was considered normal among the Prussian aristocracy, and doing her charity work. Visitors to the Neues Palais included writers, artists and musicians, German and foreign, who shared the Crown Prince and Princess's own liberal views. 'Whether commoner or nobleman, anyone with a name in the world of art or literature was a welcome guest, and well-known industrial and financial geniuses, whether Jew or Christian, were often invited to the Palace,' wrote the admiring Court official. Things were very different at the Kaiser's Palace in Berlin. The big

Court functions were dreary affairs, the old Kaiser insisting on the rigid Prussian etiquette dominated by the military nobility, and excluding commoners and Jews.

In January 1874 the Crown Prince and Princess left Berlin for St Petersburg for the marriage of Prince Alfred, Duke of Edinburgh and Saxe-Coburg-Gotha to Grand Duchess Marie, the Tsar's daughter. Alexandra and Minny had introduced Affie to Marie three years earlier during a Danish family holiday, always hoping to further their aim of an Anglo-Russian alliance. Everyone, including Bertie and Alexandra and Duke Ernest of Saxe-Coburg-Gotha, from whom Affie would one day inherit the 'dear small country', stayed at the Anitchkoff Palace with Sasha and Minny while Affie, as the bridegroom, stayed at the Winter Palace. 'I hope the cold at St Petersburg will not be too much for you,' Queen Victoria wrote to Vicky. 'I shall feel not being present for the first time at the marriage of one of our children, but at the same time I dislike now witnessing marriages very much, and think them sad and painful.' On the way home Bertie and Alexandra stopped off in 'the disgusting Berlin', as Alexandra described it to Minny. The bride and bridegroom meanwhile made their way to England and thence to Balmoral where the bride, accustomed to the heated hothouse of the Winter Palace in spite of deep snow outside, was astonished at the icy temperature in all the bedrooms.

Bismarck insisted that Vicky and Fritz leave Berlin for the duration of the Three Emperors' Conference due to take place in Berlin that autumn, for fear, as he said, of 'interference'. By now the Kaiser had been so turned against his son that he agreed, and ordered them to leave. Only too pleased, Vicky and Fritz set off happily with their children for England. 'No one wishes more, as you know, than I do for England and Germany to go well together,' Queen Victoria had written to Vicky earlier that year, 'but Bismarck is so overbearing, violent, grasping and unprincipled that NO ONE can stand it, and ALL agreed that he was becoming like the first Napoleon whom Europe had to join in PUTTING down.' However, she adds, 'I wrote a private letter to the Emperor Alexander, urging him to DO all he could in a pacific sense in Berlin, knowing the anxiety he had to prevent war.' The letter was, as she said, a private one, but it suggests that Bismarck's suspicions were not entirely unfounded.

By 1875 Georgie and Eddy, now ten and almost twelve, were still spending most of their time at Sandringham receiving what turned out to be a rather basic education from the Reverend Mr Dalton. In November their father the Prince of Wales embarked on a State Visit to India to represent his mother the Queen and Empress, and leaving his wife behind. He travelled with twenty-two ordinary servants as well as his valet, his stud groom, his page, three chefs, and a suite of eighteen gentlemen. His letters home to the two boys were full of exciting anecdotes about life in foreign parts, interspersed with vain hopes that the next letters he received from them would be better written than the last. 'My Dearest Eddy and Georgy,' he wrote from Goa, 'As I have not time to write to you each a letter, I write to you both together to thank you very much for your letters of the 3rd from Sandringham. They are not quite so well written as the last ones and Eddy made several mistakes in the spelling, so I hope you will be more careful next time. I had some wild boar-hunting last Tuesday, which is called in India "pig-sticking". We all rode with heavy spears and when a boar is seen, everybody rides up to him to try and spear him.' From Kandy in December he wrote to tell them about an elephant hunt and the jungle leeches 'which are very bad, and climb up your legs and bight you', proving that his own spelling was not always up to the mark.

Domestic life at the Anitchkoff Palace in St Petersburg was meanwhile proceeding smoothly, tightly supervised by the Tsarevna. In April 1875 she had given birth to their third child and first daughter, Xenia. Nicholai was now seven years old, and the time had come for him, like his royal cousins in Germany and England, to begin his formal education. A governess, Alexandra Ollongren, was employed for the first three years to teach him all the normal subjects studied by any other Russian child in middle school, at the end of which Nicky took the usual examination, which he passed with ease.

Nicky had two companions in the schoolroom at the Anitchkoff Palace, his brother Georgei and Vladimir Ollongren, son of the governess. Vladimir Ollongren provides the first real detail about the boy Nicky, describing him as a happy child with a 'charming, playful almost girlish laugh'. It soon became apparent that although Nicky was quite bright, with an excellent memory, he was immature for his age. The Tsarevna, much like her sister the Princess of Wales, was over-protective of her children, especially of Nicky, the son and heir. Added to which, Nicky was physically small and slightly built, taking after his mother rather than the father and uncles who towered over him.

Although Vladimir Ollongren describes Nicky's father as a cheerful man who liked to take the children outside and play with them, sawing wood or making snowmen, Nicky was always in awe of him, even frightened of him. Sasha appears to have been one of those men who got on better with other people's children. Certainly other children never saw him in one of his rages, which, though they passed quickly, were terrifying while they lasted. To his own children he could seem domineering. 'Neither I, nor the Grand Duchess, are going to make green-house flowers out of them,' he informed Alexandra Ollongren before she began her task. 'They must pray well to the Lord, learn, play and prank within reason. Teach them well, don't let them get out of hand, take special care to discourage idleness . . . I repeat, I do not need porcelain, I want normal, healthy Russian children. If they fight – let them. But the sneak will get the first whip.'

For Nicky, like his cousin Georgie in England and indeed Willy in Germany, it was his mother who was the centre of his life. She watched over him obsessively, to mould him for his future role as Tsar but also to protect him from danger, always present for the Russian Imperial family. 'Arm Yourselves with Knives and Pistols, for the Day of Your Deliverance Approaches' ordered the pamphlets produced on the secret printing presses of the Socialist revolutionaries in St Petersburg. Minny and Sasha only properly relaxed during those happy times when they were on holiday *en famille*, especially in small, safe Denmark.

But Minny was also the Tsarevna, the fashionable leader of St Petersburg society. Nicky saw her twice a day, once at 11 a.m. and once before bedtime. She was also often away on duties of State with his father. Much of his time was therefore spent with the servants, who, as Ollongren recalled, loved the Imperial family. Olga, Nicky's youngest sister, remembered how 'old Jim Hercules, a Negro, spent his annual holiday in the States and brought back jars of guava jelly as presents for us children.' Family life was conducted along self-consciously simple lines despite servants, footmen, pages, nannies and cooks. As one visitor to Anitchkoff Palace, used to the more splendid customs of Alexander II's home, noted: 'I don't like watching while people throw bread pellets across the table.' Obviously the idea of fun and games, learnt during holidays at the provincial Danish Court, had travelled to St Petersburg. Both parents were determined to keep their children simple and safe, largely cut off from the dramas unfolding in the world outside.

Those unfolding for Russia continued to centre on the disintegrating Ottoman Empire. In 1877 Russia declared war on Turkey, ostensibly to defend the Bulgarians against Turkish aggression, which was certainly brutal, but in fact because she wanted to expand her territory and gain access to the Dardanelles. When the Russians won the war, Turkish rule in Europe was effectively at an end. At the Congress of Berlin in July 1878 all the Great Powers vied for position and territorial gain. Half Turkey's European territory was confiscated and redistributed. Britain, assuming the high ground with practised hypocrisy, undertook to defend Turkey against any Russian encroachments on her remaining territory, Turkey ceding Cyprus to Britain in return. 'Turkey is in my pocket,' Disraeli wrote with his usual flourish to the Prince of Wales.

It did not make for good relations with Russia. 'We don't want to fight, but by jingo if we do, we've got the men, we've got the ships, we've got the money too' went the ditty as England stood ready and prepared to go to war. Even worse was Article 25 of the Treaty of Berlin, which gave Austria the right to administer, and keep within her sphere of influence, Bosnia and Herzegovina. The Treaty of Berlin was one of the most short-sighted settlements ever made.

In January 1877 Wilhelm and his seventeen classmates sat their final grammar school examinations, which they had to pass in order to go to university. Willy had been in the top four of his class all through his time at Cassel, and he passed easily. On 25 January the class celebrated the end of their schooldays in the school auditorium. For Wilhelm it marked the end of Dr Hinzpeter's eleven-year rule. Overnight the punishing regime was over. No more fourteen-hour days, no more harsh discipline, no more doing one's duty at all times, no more quiet and modest behaviour.

Wilhelm was free. In the same month he celebrated his eighteenth birthday and came of age. 'I received two high orders on that day,' he remembered with evident satisfaction. First the English Ambassador Lord Odo Russell came to the Neues Palais bearing the Insignia of the Garter, which as Willy proudly pointed out was usually only bestowed on Sovereigns and immediate heirs. In fact his mother had had to beg Queen Victoria for the Garter; the Queen thought the Order of the Bath quite sufficient. 'Willy would be satisfied with the

Bath but the Nation would not,' wrote Vicky, scratching around for a convincing excuse. After that ceremony the family proceeded to the Kaiser's palace in Berlin where Willy was solemnly invested by his grandfather with the Prussian Order of the Black Eagle in the Knights' Hall in the presence of the entire German royal family and assorted privileged military. Two grand orders in one day, the first English, the second Prussian. For Willy it was the perfect start to his new, adult life.

For his grandfather and Bismarck it marked the moment in which Prussian dominance over Wilhelm's life was to be asserted. The Kaiser now insisted that Prince Wilhelm take the normal route for a future heir to the throne and start his military career in the First Foot Guards, quartered at Potsdam. Willy could hardly have been more pleased. A week later he joined his regiment, and felt instantly at home. The life of a Prussian officer was essentially one of elegant idleness. There were parades and manoeuvres, but most of the time was spent in the officers' mess in the agreeable company of sons of the Prussian nobility, taking nothing too seriously except the punctilious rules of the officers' Code of Honour, which were taken very seriously indeed. The contrast with life at Cassel was complete.

Prince Wilhelm's parents watched his enthusiastic progress with mounting alarm. On 25 July 1877 Vicky wrote to Queen Victoria that she could not get Willy to read a book or write a line 'or do anything except ENJOYING having NOTHING TO DO'. The Court official summed it up nicely in his *Recollections*: 'It was after Prince Wilhelm became of age, like all German princes when only eighteen, that he began to feel himself a man and a Prussian – the synonym for all that was grand and great, and after he had served as a lieutenant in the First Foot Guards in Potsdam he was the typical narrow-minded and arrogant Prussian officer. He was the acknowledged idol of the younger military set, and the easy tool of Bismarck from the very beginning, and surrounded by flatterers.'

At Cassel Wilhelm had been so hard-working that after visiting his grandfather on his birthday he returned early, missing the evening party, to finish some homework. Now he seemed to have lost all interest in work. In fact he never regained that interest, and his restless lack of application and concentration soon became a daily problem for his advisers. He was quickly bored and easily distracted, apt to take up a subject – any subject, it sometimes seemed – with enthusiasm, only to drop it a few days later. He never lost his excellent memory, or his ability to spout verse after verse of his favourite poems. But, surrounded by flatterers, he came to believe he was cleverer than he was.

Even with the benefit of hindsight it is hard to pinpoint what caused the change. Possibly his mother had been too critical, and Hinzpeter too severe. The crippled arm must have had some psychological effect. But Willy was also born with a certain character. As a child he had earned the nickname 'Wilhelm the Sudden' for his extreme restlessness and quick changes of mood. In his teens his mother complained to Queen Victoria about his growing pride and arrogance, describing him as 'a regular Hohenzollern'. Now even his father, who had always seen the best in his son and been proud of his achievements, had his doubts. Perhaps Willy, free for the first time and keenly encouraged by his grandfather and Bismarck, was finally showing his true colours.

That same year, 1877, Georgie turned twelve and Eddy fourteen. The time had come for the next stage in their education. As the second son Georgie was always bound for a career in the Royal Navy. But what were they to do with Eddy, who was quite amiable and good-looking but had in no way improved with age and was still dependent on Georgie to steady him and galvanise him into any kind of positive action, though Georgie was a good deal smaller in size as well as younger in age. Queen Victoria thought Wellington College a good idea, but now Dalton, who was always firm in his views on the boys' education, stepped forward, arguing that, given Eddy's problems and the boys' affection for one another, they should not be separated. 'Prince Albert Victor requires the stimulus of Prince George's company to induce him to work at all,' he wrote, not mincing his words. 'Prince George's lively presence is his mainstay and chief incentive to exertion.'

Queen Victoria was not convinced. 'Their position (if they live) will be totally DIFFERENT and it is not intended that they should BOTH enter the Navy,' she wrote. 'The very rough sort of life to which boys are exposed on board ship is the very thing not calculated to make a refined and amiable Prince, who in after years (if God spares him) is to ascend the throne.' It was all right for Georgie, the second son, but not for Eddy, the future heir. The Prince of Wales agreed with Dalton and applied his well-practised tactic in dealing with his mother, suggesting they might try it 'as an experiment' and see how they got on. On this basis Queen Victoria was prepared to agree, and in September 1877 both boys joined the training ship *Britannia*, Georgie as a bona fide naval cadet, Eddy as an also-ran.

The *Britannia*, anchored on the river Dart in Devon, was an old ship with few comforts. The two princes arrived on board accompanied by Dalton. They were given no privileges apart from a cabin of their own in which to sling their hammocks. Georgie was soon known as 'Sprat' by his shipmates, being a very small 'whale'. Years later he told his librarian, Sir Owen Morshead: 'It never did me any good to be a Prince, I can tell you, and many was the time I wished I hadn't been. It was a pretty tough place, and, so far from making any allowances for our disadvantages, the other boys made a point of taking it out of us on the grounds that they'd never be able to do it later on. There was a lot of fighting among the cadets and the rule was that if challenged you had to accept. So they used to make me go up and challenge the bigger boys – I was awfully small then – and I'd get a hiding time and again. But one day I had a blow on the nose which made my nose bleed badly. It was the best blow I ever took for the doctor forbade my fighting any more.'

Not only that. There was a tuck shop on land, up the hill, but eatables were not allowed on the ship. The 'big boys' kept sending Sprat out to buy things for them and smuggle them back on board. Sprat was constantly getting caught, and the big boys never paid him back. They could hardly be expected to know that one of Queen Victoria's firmly held convictions was that princes must not be spoiled. The money came out of Sprat's own pocket, and it would have surprised his shipmates to know that he was allowed only one shilling a week. This kind of bullying would make anyone's life a misery, but for a young boy who had led a sheltered life, doted on by his parents, it must have been a horror. Homesickness was the worst. 'Please give Victoria my very best love and many kisses,' Georgie wrote to his mother from *Britannia*, 'and mind you kiss her properly, like I would if I was there because I am sure that when I send kisses to people in your letter you never kiss them.' Victoria was Georgie's favourite sister and later, during a summer holiday in Denmark, his Russian cousin Nicky's first love.

'It is impossible that two lads could be in more robust health or happier than the two Princes are,' Dalton wrote happily to Queen Victoria, showing that however clear-sighted he might be at home, on board ship he was blind as a bat. He added, somewhat wryly, and presumably in response to some query from the Queen: 'Their studies also progress favourably. Mr Dalton thinks there is no fear of the elder Prince working too hard, or overtaxing his powers, as Your Majesty seems to fear: in fact he might work harder than he does without any risk of detriment.' Still, Eddy and Georgie completed their two years in *Britannia*. Georgie managed the passing-out exams well enough, showing an unexpected aptitude for mathematics, as well as a less surprising aptitude for seamanship. Eddy showed no aptitude for anything at all. Their best times remained the holidays spent in the summer of 1876 and 1878 in Denmark, in the company of their Russian, Greek and Danish cousins.

'My own darling little Georgie,' their mother wrote, just as they were doing their exams and for Georgie's fourteenth birthday, 'Fancy my writing from Paris to wish you joy on your birthday, your 14th too. Victoria says "so old and so small"!!! Oh my! You will have to make haste to grow, or I shall have that sad disgrace of being the mother of a dwarf!!!' Tactful the Princess of Wales was not, but perhaps high spirits had overtaken her. It was extremely rare for Bertie to take his wife to Paris with him. Cynics noted that he was very likely prompted by a sense of guilt because he had lately become rather too attached to the actress Lillie Langtry, the unknown beauty from Jersey who had taken London by storm.

In Russia Nicky's serious education began when he was ten, in 1879. He was put in the hands of a not very inspiring military governor, General Danilovich. As a military man the General's strength was discipline, and he must have had something of a temper, because Nicky referred to him as 'Cholera'. Danilovich brought in specialists to teach the Imperial pupil history (his favourite subject), geography, chemistry and the four languages which were necessary to navigate European Court and family life: Russian, English, French and, as a poor last, German. Mr Heath, arriving some time in 1882 to teach the Imperial children English, seems to have been the favourite tutor.

Heath was a typical English schoolmaster, not a university man but an intelligent and nice man, who believed in the Victorian virtues of fair play and behaving like a gentleman, being polite at all times, especially to inferiors, and controlling the emotions. He did not find the Imperial children well-trained or well-disciplined, and he was not too fond of Georgei's green parrot, Popka, which soon learned to imitate his accent. But General Voeykov, last Commandant of the Imperial Palaces before the Revolution, later noted that Tsar Nicholai had learnt to curb his temper with a self-control first acquired from 'the English Mister Heath'.

At this time Nicky began an extensive correspondence with his mother, written mostly in Russian, though many phrases are in French or English, with all the names in their original language. Georgie is 'Georgie', Wilhelm is 'Wilhelm', Queen Victoria is 'Granny'. His mother wrote mostly in French, since Nicky's knowledge of languages never extended to Danish and her knowledge of Russian was always more of the spoken than the written language. It is an extraordinary correspondence, revealing on almost every page the extreme closeness of the relationship. There are more than five hundred letters in all, covering a period of almost forty years, the last one written by Minny, by then Dowager Tsarina, to Nicky in November 1917, only months before he and his family were assassinated by the Bolsheviks. The letters were later found in various Imperial palaces, and kept by the Bolsheviks in the State Archives in Moscow.

These letters offer fascinating insights into Nicky, the boy and the man. They are well-written, with a certain humour, and filled with affection. 'My Darling, Darling Mama', a letter might open, even when Nicky was a grown man, ending 'Goodbye, my dear sweet Mama. Yours with all my heart, Nicky'. The letters are often long, but the detail is mostly simple, that of everyday family life: who came for lunch or supper, what food they ate, where they went for a drive or a swim, the state of an aunt's health, the description of a birthday celebration, a military review, or a trip on one of the Imperial yachts, and rather a lot about favourite pets. Only in between, and almost by the way, come the comments on political events: the meetings, the wars and the revolutions.

The letters are strikingly reminiscent of those between Nicky's cousin Georgie and his mother, especially once Georgie and Eddy had embarked on the next stage of their education, a subject which caused hot debate between Queen Victoria, the Prince and Princess of Wales, their respective private secretaries, Dalton, the First Lord of the Admiralty and, finally, the Government.

It had already been decided that, because of Eddy's lamentable performance, the two boys should be kept together for a further three years. They would continue their naval training and general education by cruising round the world in HMS *Bacchante*, a corvette of 4,000 tons. The debate rested on the risk involved if both princes sailed in the same ship, and whether HMS *Bacchante* was safe and stable enough. Should the princes not have a warship each, with the added advantage that Prince Eddy could then have additional tuition on board from tutors specialising in the education of backward pupils? The Cabinet debated the issue on 19 May 1879 with W.H. Smith, First Lord of the Admiralty, supporting the 'two warships' argument. But the Prince of Wales, annoyed by what he saw as Government interference, insisted that his two boys be kept together. The Admiralty was despatched to carry out tests on *Bacchante*'s seaworthiness, and the naval officers to man her, under the command of Lord Charles Scott, were carefully selected.

On 17 September 1879 HMS *Bacchante* set sail from Spithead with both Eddy and Georgie on board. With them sailed Dalton, in the role of honorary Ship's Chaplain, and Charles Fuller, who had been the princes' devoted nursery footman since their birth. Their only privilege apart from the services of Charles Fuller was a cabin of their own. To cheer them up, the Princess of Wales presented the ship with a harmonium. Over the next three years they made three voyages, to the West Indies, to Spain and Ireland, and to Australia and New Zealand by way of South America, the Falkland Islands and, on the return journey in 1882, Japan, China, Singapore, Egypt, Palestine, Greece, Gibraltar and thence back to England. By the time they came home Eddy and Georgie had both been promoted to midshipmen.

The Princess of Wales was distraught at losing her boys. 'I hate letting any of you out of my sight even for a week,' she admitted. The boys felt no better. Prince George was crying as they left. 'Every evening I expect to see you coming in after tea,' she wrote to him, 'and every morning on awaking I can ALMOST fancy your two little voices squeaking into my ear but instead it is only the two white kittens which the sisters are putting on my pillow.' They came home during the summer of 1880, but were soon off again. 'My darling Motherdear,' wrote Georgie, now aged fifteen, as the *Bacchante* set sail, 'I miss you so very much & felt so sorry when I had to say goodbye to you and sisters & it was dreadfully hard saying goodbye to dear Papa & Uncle Hans [his mother's uncle] I felt so miserable yesterday saying goodbye. I shall think of you all going to Scotland tonight and I only wish we were going too . . . So goodbye once more my darling

Motherdear, please give darling Papa and sisters my very best love and kisses and much love to dear Uncle Hans. I remain your very loving son Georgy.'

Georgie read aloud to his mother every morning when he was at home, as her hair was being brushed, and every evening he said his prayers with her. Evening prayers and reading a passage from the Bible before starting each day were habits he kept all his life. He'd been homesick during the two years in *Britannia*, but that was in Devon, and there were plenty of visits to 'dear Sandringham' and Marlborough House. Now they would be gone for months at a time. 'How I miss you and long to see your dear little turn-up snout again,' his mother wrote, apologising at the same time for the silly tone of her letters. 'You say your letter is stupid,' Georgie replied, 'it is not, darling Motherdear, it is dear and charming and you write just as if you were talking.'

To cheer up his wife the Prince of Wales sacrificed his usual stay in Homburg that autumn to spend a month with Princess Alexandra in Denmark. His open relationship with Lillie Langtry may again have contributed to his decision, though the Princess of Wales appeared to take the liaison in her stride, even inviting Lillie to Marlborough House. The Tsarevich arrived in Denmark with less enthusiasm than usual, the terms of the Treaty of Berlin having once again played in Britain's favour. But for the two sisters Alexandra and Minny it was their happiest time, in each other's company, together with their children. And, once in the relaxed atmosphere of Denmark, the two brothers-in-law soon left the irritations of international politics behind them.

To Eddy and Georgie embarked on the high seas the Prince of Wales wrote about the grand parties he and the Tsarevich gave on board their respective royal yachts. 'Last Saturday we had a very pleasant cruise in the *Osborne* to Helsingborg. All the Relations and Cousins came, also the Crown Prince of Sweden . . . Uncle Sasha gave a luncheon last week to the officers of the Danish Guards on board the large Imperial yacht *Dirjava*, and I gave one on Monday last on *Osborne* to the officers of the Danish Hussars.' To homesick boys these letters filled with news of happy family gatherings possibly gave less pleasure than the sender fondly imagined. On their way home from Denmark the two royal couples spent a jolly week in Paris, where the Prince of Wales and the Tsarevich, giving their respective suites the slip, wandered incognito and arm-in-arm along the boulevards of Paris. Disraeli complained that the Prince of Wales had returned home very pro-Russian.

Dalton sent the Prince and Princess of Wales detailed reports on both boys. The settings changed, but the news was much the same: Georgie was doing well, Eddy was as bad as ever. All the tutors agreed that any attempt to educate Eddy was doomed to failure. 'This weakness of brain, this feebleness and lack of power to grasp almost anything put before him' was, wrote Dalton, 'a fault of nature.' Whether it came from his premature birth or an inherited weakness, either way Prince Eddy was not 'right'. Fortunately it made not a scrap of difference to his parents who, though worried, loved him none the less.

By contrast, Prince George's only real problem was a nerviness and lack of confidence, compounded by his modest intelligence and aggravated by his constant, nagging homesickness. 'Prince George's old enemy', Dalton reported, 'is that nervous excitable temperament which still sometimes leads him to fret at difficulties instead of facing them, and thus make mountains out of molehills.' But mostly Georgie was cheerful, straightforward and conscientious. Many years later, giving a talk to some cadets on a training ship, he listed the three qualities he considered indispensable – 'Truthfulness, Obedience and Zest' – without which 'no seaman is worth his salt'. For the rest of his life he held to them faithfully, though Zest sometimes eluded him.

5

Family Dramas

~

IN JUNE 1877 Willy went to Bonn, his parents having insisted that he leave his regiment and the militaristic atmosphere of Potsdam after six months to attend his father's old university. The Kaiser could not see the point, having had no academic education himself yet having managed, he felt, rather well. But since Wilhelm was still nominally in the care of his parents the Kaiser was forced to give in, and the Prince began the first of four terms studying a wide curriculum that included history, German literature, philosophy, political and social theory, history of art, and law. 'But I didn't only devote my time to hard academic studies, and didn't spend all my time with my professors during my time at Bonn!' he later recalled. That put it mildly. His uncle the Grand Duke of Baden, whose son Prince Friedrich was attending Bonn at the same time, was shocked by Wilhelm's extreme indolence, worried that he would be a bad influence on his son. The only actual work Willy seemed to enjoy was regular visits to the local museum with a young tutor in art history, Reinhard Kekule, who was an authority on Ancient Greek sculpture, those naked, idealised young athletes which Wilhelm already considered the only true form of art.

Willy's parents grew more and more worried. He was becoming increasingly arrogant, and the Crown Princess wrote in despair to her mother that he was behaving towards her with a new coldness and distance. Karl Justi, one of Wilhelm's professors at Bonn, summed him up as 'a very lively person, also in the way he grasps things, but by no means possessed of exceptional gifts. Moreover in his likes and dislikes he seems to be just as opinionated as he is hasty, and he refuses to have anything to do with contrary opinions.' One short year had apparently been enough to change the Wilhelm François Ayme had known into someone rather different.

Perhaps Bonn had not been the best choice. It was the most exclusive university in Germany, filled with the sons of the Prussian nobility, soon to become Prussian officers like Prince Wilhelm himself. Not surprisingly, Willy quickly felt completely at home. As soon as he could he joined the Borussa Fraternity, the elite of them all. From then on he spent most of his time carousing with his fellow aristocratic corps members, who practised a studied condescension towards anyone less noble than themselves. But while Prince Wilhelm would sing lusty songs with the best of them, it was soon noticed that he drank little and was prone to a pious religiosity. Wilhelm, they discovered, was a bit of a prude.

Nor did he appear to be very interested in women; if at all, he seemed happier with older women. He wrote frequently to Countess Marie von Dönhoff, an Italian aristocrat married to a German diplomat who was one of his mother's best friends. 'I have very few real friends,' he confided to her in English from Bonn. Later he shared with her his views on women, at least those he knew in Berlin society. They talked about nothing but clothes, he complained, adding rather piously that their constant flirting was 'something beneath a real man and a gentleman, especially I think it beneath myself, don't you think so too?'

In September 1878 Willy went to England and Scotland for his holidays. At Balmoral he was thrilled by a surprise his grandmother had waiting for him in his room: a full Highland costume in the Clan Stewart tartan of the Royal House. In his memoirs, thinking it likely that his readers might not know about the Stewart tartan, he explained it in detail. 'One can only imagine how great was my young joy as I came into my room and found this whole wonderful outfit which my grandmother had ordered to be laid out to surprise me.' John Brown was on hand to help him put it on correctly. Queen Victoria, as wily as Bismarck in her way, knew just how to bring her capricious grandson back on side. Before he left Balmoral she spoke a few wise words. Willy, all those years later, reproduced exactly what she said, in English, and it stood out oddly from the German text of his memoirs, printed in the old German typeface: 'My dear boy,' she said, 'never forget him! Your grandfather was the best man in the world. Try, as much as you can, to become like him. God bless you!'

The following year Prince William was back in England, this time with his parents for the wedding of Princess Louise of Prussia to his uncle the Duke of Connaught. The happy event was swiftly followed by a family tragedy. Eight days after their return to Potsdam, Willy's ten-year-old brother Waldemar died of diphtheria. The blow was the more keenly felt because only the previous November Alice in Darmstadt and one of her young children had died in the same epidemic. Vicky was grief-stricken. The loss of her sister, followed so quickly by that of Waldie, her favourite child after Sigi, caused what appeared to be a nervous breakdown. 'So many pretty and charming traits of Waldie's character come back to me!' she wrote to her mother. 'Oh that Willy had his warm and affectionate, spontaneous nature, his industry and activity and interest in everything . . . to everything that one used to have to URGE the elder brother one had almost to restrain Waldie from . . . His being strong and handsome made me so proud!' Pride was not something Vicky ever felt in poor Willy, with his difficult character and his crippled arm.

Meanwhile Bismarck's 'iron and blood' policy, applied to domestic as well as foreign affairs, had led to increasing unrest in Germany. The Socialist movement was gaining ground on the left, while the Liberals and the Catholics, holding the centre, publicly put their faith in the Crown Prince and Princess, since the old Kaiser could not live for ever. Bismarck set about infiltrating the Neues Palais with spies. Agents were carefully vetted, then persuaded to take menial jobs in the royal household as a cover. Particularly useful were the two spies in the accounts department, giving Bismarck access to details of the Crown Prince's expenditure – though not to the Crown Princess's, who kept separate accounts.

Whenever Vicky and Fritz returned to the Neues Palais from a trip they found evidence that locks had been forced and desks searched. Sir Robert Morier, the British Ambassador in Berlin, warned Vicky to write nothing incriminating either in her diary or in letters except in cipher, and to take care what she said in front of the servants. When Lady Ponsonby, one of Vicky's closest friends, came to visit from England she was alarmed by what she found, and wrote to her husband, Queen Victoria's Private Secretary: 'I don't think the Queen realizes what an extraordinary state of things exists in Germany in the way of espionage and intrigue. They, the Foreign Office, which means Bismarck, wanted to put a man of their own about the Crown Princess so as more effectually to control the Crown Prince when he became Emperor.' The last thing Bismarck wanted was a weak, liberal Kaiser, but there had already been three assassination attempts on Kaiser Wilhelm. 'My shame that a German was capable of committing such an act against our most venerated Ruler knew no bounds and I was utterly appalled,' wrote Willy from exile years later.

By the autumn of 1879 Willy was back in Potsdam, back with his regiment. He spent almost all his time with them: he drilled and paraded with them, he ate his meals with them, he spent his evenings with them in the officers' mess, singing rowdy songs, telling crude jokes (which for all his prudishness Wilhelm loved all his life), and playing cards or billiards. Years later he told his friend Philipp zu Eulenburg that it was with his regiment that he found his real family, his friends and his interests. To his confidante Countess Dönhoff he wrote in his stilted English: 'I never feel happy, realy [sic] happy at Berlin. Only in Potsdam that is my "el dorado" and that is also where Mama mostly likes to live, where one feels free with the beautiful nature around you and soldiers as much as you like, for I love my dear Regiment very much, those such kind nice young men in it.'

Prince Wilhelm now had his own apartments in the Neues Palais, with his own Household, headed by Major Wilhelm von Liebenau. But the man to watch was Willy's adjutant, Captain Adolf von Bülow. Bülow was a rough and rude Prussian officer with profoundly reactionary views which included a virulent hatred of England and everything she stood for. He was Bismarck's man. He had been to school with Bismarck's son Herbert, whom Bismarck was grooming, like a proper heir, to be his successor. The Bismarcks and Captain von Bülow agreed on the necessity of prising Prince Wilhelm away from the influence of his liberal parents and used his grandfather to further their aims. The Kaiser frequently invited Wilhelm to dine at his Berlin palace, engaging him in long and mutually satisfactory conversations on military matters and often favouring him with information which was being withheld from his son the Crown Prince. By the early 1880s Fritz was feeling not only frustrated and persecuted, but jealous of Wilhelm. Vicky was becoming disillusioned and bitter.

In May 1880 Willy's English cousin Georgie began a diary which he kept dutifully for the rest of his life, until only three days before he died. The entries were short, simple and schoolboy-neat, beginning almost always with the weather, regardless of the importance of the occasion – even on his Coronation Day. The diary is a record of facts, hardly ever of emotions, which perhaps accounts at least in part for the impression history has of George V as an unemotional man, a man without much feeling. The opposite was nearer the truth: Georgie wept easily and often, mainly at partings from people he loved, but also when reading the novels which he took with him on his voyages. He was particularly keen on romances. 'Such a lovely book,' he noted in his diary about one appealingly titled *Wrong on Both Sides*. 'I always cry over it.' He liked to read favourites like *Les Misérables* more than once. But his main sobs were kept for partings from his beloved Motherdear and Papa and his sisters, especially Toria, to whom he wrote regularly and, later in life, telephoned every day if he did not see her.

The year 1880 was a worrying one for Queen Victoria. In April Disraeli and the Conservatives who had been in power since 1874 were again displaced by Gladstone and the Liberals. The Queen wrote to her Private Secretary, Sir Henry Ponsonby, her grammar quite shot to pieces: 'The great alarm in the country is Mr Gladstone, the Queen perceives and she will sooner abdicate than send for or have any communication with the half-mad fire-brand who would soon ruin everything and be a Dictator. Others but herself may submit to his democratic rule, but not the Queen.' It is clear that at times Queen Victoria's views were not so different from those of the Kaiser in Germany or the Tsar in Russia. The real difference lay in the fact that Britain, alone of the three countries, already had a well-tried system of parliamentary democracy and a constitutional monarchy, so that the Queen was obliged to listen to her advisers and obey her Government. Ponsonby advised that 'Mr Gladstone is loyal and devoted to the Queen.' She did not believe him, but in time she adjusted, because she had no choice.

Fortunately there was also some good news. Willy, the difficult grandson, had decided to marry. He rather sprung it on his parents, and left his mother to persuade the Kaiser that it was a good match. He was just twenty when he proposed to Princess Augusta Victoria of Schleswig-Holstein-Sonderburg-Augustenburg, known as plain 'Dona'. The problem, as far as the Kaiser and the mighty Hohenzollerns were concerned, was that Dona was from a minor, impoverished branch of the extended royal family, not sufficiently *ebenbürtig*. Being *ebenbürtig* – understood by them as meaning 'of pure royal blood' – was a perfect obsession with the Hohenzollerns, even the usually liberal Crown Prince Frederick. Dona's mother was only just *ebenbürtig* while her father had many years since renounced his claim to his small principality, and the question arose: was Dona herself sufficiently *ebenbürtig* to marry HRH Prince Wilhelm? Fortunately Vicky and her mother were grand enough not to care. They were much more concerned to get Willy safely married, knowing that his 'bad tendencies' were not improving with time. Every man was in need of a good wife, they were the first to agree, and if Dona was one thing, she was certainly good. Neither beautiful, nor very intelligent, and perhaps rather narrow in her views and her blind adherence to the Protestant religion, but kind and dignified, and devoted to Willy.

The Augustenburgs were family friends, so the couple had known each other, though not well, since childhood. Early in March 1880 Dona was dispatched to England to be inspected by Queen Victoria. 'I am so delighted you think Victoria so gentle and amiable and sweet,' Vicky wrote to her mother on 26 March, once Dona was safely back home. 'She always struck me as such. I am sure she must win all hearts. Her smile and her manners and expression must disarm even the bristly, thorny people of Berlin with their sharp tongues.' The only worry was that Dona seemed too much in awe of Willy, agreeing with everything he said.

They were married on 27 February 1881. In his memoirs Wilhelm described the event, with evident relish, from the military point of view. 'By then I was Hauptmann in the Body Guard Company of my regiment . . . On the day before the wedding I was allowed to parade my Company through the Brandenburg Gates, down Unter den Linden to the Royal Palace below, enthusiastically cheered on all sides by the crowds who were awaiting the arrival of Princess Auguste Viktoria.' Dona never forgot it. On a freezing day, wearing a bare-shouldered Court gown, there she sat being rocked heavily from side to side in the cold royal carriage drawn by eight fine horses. The next day, their wedding day, the Kaiser promoted Prince Wilhelm to command the First Foot Guards.

Most of royal Europe was foregathered, including Willy's uncle, the Prince of Wales, who came to represent Queen Victoria but, noticeably, without his wife, Alexandra's hatred of the Prussians having altered not at all over the years. The bride wore light blue and gold brocade with pink and white China asters, with pearls and a pendant from Queen Victoria round her neck. The groom wore uniform. The ceremony lasted six hours, and Vicky found the weight of her tiara almost unbearable. The following evening the Prince of

Wales noted that fifty-four royal relations sat down to a family dinner given by Vicky at the Neues Palais. The next day, before leaving, he had a long and interesting discussion with Bismarck, during which Bismarck did most of the talking.

The royal couple did not go away on honeymoon but settled almost instantly into a pattern of married life which hardly altered over the years. The groom took up his command of the First Foot Guards with a speed and enthusiasm which might have disheartened a wife less devoted than Dona. They moved in to the Marble Palace on the outskirts of Potsdam, but Willy was rarely at home. He spent most of his time in the officers' mess, just as he had before his marriage. When he was not there, he was away on one of his hunting trips, leaving Dona in Potsdam in the company of her three ladies-in-waiting, known at Court, behind their backs, as the 'Hallelujah Aunts' because of their pious Protestantism.

Willy's restlessness did not improve with marriage; if anything, it grew worse. Even when he was home he was never without his entourage, all military men, permanently in uniform, as was Willy himself. Nevertheless, when he was with Dona people noticed that he was considerate and attentive, both to her personally and in all matters of Court etiquette. In May 1882 Dona produced a son and heir, followed in quick succession by five more sons and finally one daughter. As Wilhelm frequently pointed out, women were for *Kinder, Küche, Kirche*, children, kitchen and church. Perhaps, as Vicky's son, he had absolutely no wish for an ambitious wife, and it is possible that Dona was the perfect match for a man of his neurotic complexity. But she was none at all for the political rivalries and intrigues which lay ahead, and in the fight for his adherence between the English liberal and the Prussian military tradition, Dona was firmly and unthinkingly on the Prussian side.

The Prince of Wales had hardly reached home after Willy's wedding before news arrived from St Petersburg that Tsar Alexander II had been assassinated. 'I share your horror, condemnation and sorrow at the death (unparalleled) of the poor, kind Emperor Alexander. A sense of horror thrills me through and through! Where such a criminal succeeds the effect is dreadful. The details are too terrible,' Queen Victoria, thoroughly rattled, wrote to Vicky in Berlin. 'No punishment is bad enough for the murderers who planned it; hanging is too good. That he, the mildest and best sovereign Russia had, should be the victim of such fiends is too grievous.' When it came to assassination, sovereigns stood shoulder to shoulder. Gladstone, 'that half-mad fire-brand', was back in power, and Queen Victoria was not at all convinced that he had the political will to contain the Republican sentiments of some of her own subjects. 'This dreadful Radical Government which contains many thinly-veiled Republicans,' she wrote to Bertie a year later, 'as well as the utter disregard of all my opinions which after 45 years of experience ought to be considered, all make me very miserable, and disgust me with the hard, ungrateful task I have to go through.' In the teeth of public opinion, which considered the situation in St Petersburg too dangerous for their own heir to the throne, Queen Victoria gave her permission for Bertie and Alexandra to attend the funeral, mainly because 'dear Alix' was so attached to her sister Minny, who would now become the Tsarina.

Nicky was twelve when his grandfather was assassinated. He was having lunch with his brother Georgei in the Anitchkoff Palace when they heard the explosion. It was about two o'clock in the afternoon of 1 March, and a young revolutionary had thrown a bomb at the Tsar's carriage as it turned a corner by a canal in central St Petersburg. The bomb missed its target and the assailant, a nineteen-year-old anarchist called Rysakov, was held. But when the Tsar, unhurt, thoughtlessly got out to inspect the damage to his carriage, some fellow conspirators lurking nearby seized their chance and threw a second bomb. This time it was a direct hit. Tsar Alexander II fell to the snow-covered ground, gushing blood. He was rushed by sleigh to the Winter Palace. 'A frightened servant ran in telling us a misfortune had befallen the Tsar and that our father had given orders for us to go immediately to the Winter Palace by the first conveyance at hand,' Nicky later recalled. 'We hurried downstairs and drove down the Nevsky at top speed to the Winter Palace. As we went up the stairs we saw pale faces everywhere. On the carpet there were deep red stains. My grandfather was bleeding to death in his study.'

Nicky's parents – his mother still holding a pair of ice-skates – and his uncles and aunts all stood there. 'No one spoke. My grandfather was lying on the narrow camp bed he always slept in, covered by the military cloak he used as a dressing gown. His face was deadly pale and his eyes were closed.' Nicholai, his grandfather's favourite, was led up to the bed by his father, who said: 'Papa, your sunshine is here.' But it was too late. 'Silence please, the end is near,' announced a Court official. And then, moments later, the Court surgeon, having checked the pulse, pronounced the awful words: 'The Tsar is dead.'

Bertie and Alexandra rushed to be at Minny's side at this most daunting moment in her life. The Princess of Wales's favourite dog Joss accompanied them in the carriage which conveyed them to the royal train waiting at Victoria station. As the train left the station with Alexandra leaning out of the window, waving goodbye, Joss slipped his lead and ran down the platform in hot pursuit. A telegram in the Royal Archives, sent from London by Princess Louise to her anxious grandmother Queen Victoria at Windsor, records that Joss was later retrieved safe and sound.

Bertie and Alexandra found Minny pale and thin, but calm. Everything was draped in black, including the sleighs travelling up and down on the frozen Neva river. The two sisters spent all their spare time together, not in the Winter Palace, which was considered too dangerous, but at the Anitchkoff Palace, thought to be safer. Even so, from the windows, the sisters could see hundreds of men and women labouring to dig a deep trench all round the palace, as protection from bombs or mines. Sasha, the new Tsar, who so loved the outdoors, was confined to walking round and round a small, secure, snow-covered palace garden. Once a day he went under heavy guard to the church of St Peter and St Paul where his dead father lay in state. By the time Bertie and Alix arrived the body had started to decay, and the smell was awful. In accordance with Russian ritual the face of the Tsar was left uncovered, and royal mourners were required to kiss it.

A mass of European royals turned out for the funeral, but none so beautiful as the Princess of Wales in her Mary Stuart mourning cap and long black veil. The Prince of Wales was keen to leave as soon as possible afterwards: St Petersburg seemed not only a dangerous place for royals but also gloomy and boring, with everyone in mourning. He had been commanded by Queen Victoria to invest the new Tsar with the Order of the Garter before he left. The ceremony, which took place in the Throne Room at the Anitchkoff Palace, was redolent of good old English pomp, with the Insignia, star, ribbon, collar, sword and the garter itself all carried in on separate cushions of red velvet generously trimmed with gold.

After the funeral Alexandra begged to be allowed to stay at least another week with Minny, who now as Tsarina faced the daunting task of supporting her husband, who himself felt utterly unprepared for what lay ahead. 'Never mind, dearest Mama,' Alexandra wrote with commendable courage to Queen Victoria, who disapproved. 'I have nearly come to the end now and through this my poor sister has had a few moments more happiness. It really was very kind in [*sic*] my Bertie to let me stop but he knew how much our hearts were set on it – and after all it would have mattered much less if anything had happened to me than to him.'

Alexandra left at the end of March. In April Minny wrote to their mother in Copenhagen: 'We're never letting the boys out alone and always keeping them with us. And we keep everything sad and unpleasant far from them so that they will not feel the stressful times we are living through which of course would ruin their first childish impressions for the rest of their lives.' Nicky was almost thirteen by then, hardly a child. But she goes on: 'Nicky's often asking with interest how the case is going in the courts. And regarding all this he knows that the seven ruffians are going to be hanged – only we didn't tell him the date so he didn't think too much about it. The hanging took place on the 3rd at Smirow Place. Great security was taken to prevent people attacking the criminals who they would probably have torn to death, as they quite rightly are so angry with these criminals and everything seems to have taken place in an orderly manner.' Although Nicky was now heir to the throne, he was told almost nothing.

Not long after the funeral General Tcherevin, the new Chief of the Secret Police, advised that the Imperial family should move out of St Petersburg to the safety of Gatchina, a palace some thirty miles south of the capital. He himself would move there as commander of the Ochrana, the Tsar's personal guard. Here the Imperial family began a life Alexander III soon began to refer to as being 'in prison'. They were literally surrounded by the secret police, who kept a twenty-four-hour watch outside and inside the palace, each policeman within sight of the next, along the high palace wall, in the gardens, and in every room. In addition to the police guards, an Infantry brigade and a Guard Cavalry brigade formed a chain of horsemen riding round the palace walls day and night. This life of constant surveillance had the inevitable effect of cutting the Imperial family off from the outside world. Although he hated it, Alexander III accepted it as the inevitable outcome of the decision, taken on the morning of his accession, to make no concessions to the revolutionaries.

Gatchina was an enormous 600-roomed palace, serviced by a staff of 3,000, where the Imperial family nevertheless contrived to live simply in a series of low, vaulted rooms crammed with furniture, knick-knacks, photographs and china, rarely using the main State rooms. The Tsar's study was modest, adorned with a life-sized figure of a man blowing a hunting horn; he himself preferred to play the trombone. The main hall where they ate and played games was filled with stuffed bears. There was a full-scale miniature railway which ran round the palace grounds, and a lake with an Echo Grotto which could be reached by an underground passage.

The Tsar generally rose at seven every morning, had a cold bath, went for a heavily guarded walk in the park, had breakfast, then set to work in his study, reading reports, signing documents, and receiving ministers. His secretary Lanin reported that the Tsar's marginal comments on reports were of a basic and robust nature: 'They are a set of hogs!' or 'What a beast he is!' The single word 'Discouraging' was often used for reports on calamities such as famine and crop failure. After lunch there was another, long, walk in the enclosed grounds of the palace, this time with his wife Minny, often accompanied by the Chief of Police. The afternoons were filled with audiences. Dinner was at eight, usually just the family and a few members of the Imperial Household. Evenings were spent *en famille*, unless it was one of the Tsar's famous beer evenings, when his own band played the music. Invitations were much sought-after, and people would go so far as to learn an unusual instrument for a military band, just to ensure one.

The move to Gatchina meant that the lives of the five children – Nicky, Georgei, Xenia, Mikhail, known as Misha, and Olga – became even more protected and isolated than before. There is an unreal quality to descriptions of their upbringing behind the massive palace walls. They slept on army cots with hard mattresses and, like their father, rose at seven, followed by a cold bath unless their mother allowed them a warm one in her own bedroom. Then came a simple breakfast of porridge and black bread, much like that eaten by their peasant subjects, apart from the footmen. All three royal cousins appear to have been victims of the same parental illusion – that the only way to protect their sons from the corroding influence of flattery and Court life was to bring them up in conditions that were Spartan by the standards of many ordinary people.

The mornings of the five Russian siblings were spent with governesses and tutors, the afternoons outside in the grounds, riding, looking after their pets, chopping wood with their father or, in winter, sledging, or skating on the lake. It was always a good moment when their father tested the newly frozen ice, treading softly on it until it gave way under his enormous weight, leaving him up to his knees in water. In the evenings, once they were old enough, they had dinner with their parents in the great hall. If no one else was present, and sometimes if they were, they had the usual fun of throwing pellets of bread at one another. After dinner their father might read them a short story by Gogol or, once Mr Heath arrived from England, there might be some Shakespeare.

On the great feast days of the Russian Orthodox Church the Imperial family went to St Petersburg, always under heavy guard. 'Pray well to the Lord' was instilled into the children from an early age, and Nicky at least held to the precept all his life. Religious rituals constituted a fundamental part of Russian life, and the children could never quite forget that their father was the autocratic, semi-divine Tsar. 'After dinner we worked colouring eggs with Mr Heath,' Nicky wrote to Xenia at Gatchina from St Petersburg, where he had gone with his parents for the Easter celebrations. 'Yesterday we were at the Winter Palace for matins which lasted two hours. A lot of people exchanged triple kisses with Papa and Mama in the church.'

Nicky was thirteen when they moved to Gatchina, and it was there he began the diary he kept for the rest of his life. It is more detailed and informative than his cousin Georgie's diary, but not by much. It too concerns itself mostly with the comings and goings of family life, only occasionally touching on the larger political events as he gets older. But where Nicky's diary gains over Georgie's is in the feelings it reveals – his excitements, his sorrows, his frustrations and his anxieties, as he falls in love, faces a family death, resents the constraints of public life, or fears the burdens of office.

His first entry was for New Year's Day, 1882: 'In the morning drank chocolate; tried on the Life Guard Reserve full-dress uniform . . . went to the garden with Papa and made a great fire. Went to sleep about half past nine.' On other occasions: 'had classes' or 'my bullfinch came out of its cage and ate from my hands' or again, 'worked in the greenhouse'. War games, in preparation for their future military careers, were the greatest fun. 'Today was a march to the fortress,' he wrote on 24 June 1883. 'Sergei, Georgiy and I were with guns, the rest without. Both watch-teams behaved perfectly, disorder happened in the non-combatant team, but given time it will improve.'

Sometimes the family went to St Petersburg to the theatre or the circus, always shadowed by dozens of plain-clothes policemen pretending to be theatre-goers. 'After breakfast went to Ciniselli's [circus] and watched the clowns' various performances,' Nicky wrote on 31 March 1884. 'Everything was excellent; the clowns made us laugh terrifically.' When he was older they went to the Bolshoi Theatre to see ballets and operas. Mr Heath makes fairly frequent appearances in the diary, mainly because he was soon a favourite, prepared to join in their fun and games. Nicky describes shooting peas out of a peashooter at him 'between lessons', to which Mr Heath responds by chasing them and jovially beating them with his walking-stick. On one of their journeys in the Imperial train to holiday at the palace of Livadia in the Crimea Nicky writes: 'We had awful fun with Mr Heath. When passing a tunnel we started throwing pillows at him and he seemed very surprised at the ensuing darkness.' He might also have been surprised because Nicky was sixteen at the time.

M. Lanson, later famed for his textbook 'History of French Literature' and most insistent on a 'correct' French accent, soon arrived from France to join the Imperial family at Gatchina. He was surprised to find that the Imperial children helped with the housework, laying the table, packing and unpacking their own baggage, and putting everything away tidily where it belonged. Their mother read all the newspapers, including *The Times* from England and the *Figaro* from France as well as all the Danish papers. Knowing the children would not read the papers themselves, she had clippings cut out and pasted up on the dining room and corridor walls. Thursday afternoons were set aside for her letter-writing, but on other days she accompanied her husband on his long walks in the palace grounds.

For those who like to interpret history as a series of turning-points, the timing of the assassination of Alexander II offers a good example. On the liberal Tsar's desk on the morning of his assassination lay a document, already signed, offering a wider franchise to the people and a Consultative Assembly – a first, if small, step towards representative government. After the funeral, his son and heir Alexander tore it up. Perhaps it would be more accurate to say that his former tutor, Konstantin Pobedonostsev, tore it up, replacing it with a new one.

Pobedonostsev did not believe in Democracy, certainly not for Russia's inexperienced electorate. In his view Russia could only be ruled by an autocratic monarchy, advised in its turn by a carefully selected elite. Democracy was dangerous, and Pobedonostsev had no time for those educated middle-class liberals who promoted it. He held the view that education itself was dangerous, giving birth to radical students calling for revolution. The young Lenin and his elder brother Alexander were typical of the type. Alexander was executed; Lenin was exiled to Siberia. The assassination of Alexander II in 1881 proved to the Tsarevich, if proof were needed, that Pobedonostsev was right. In Russia, repression was the only solution.

Once the Manifesto of Tsar Alexander III was published, everyone knew how things stood: 'The voice of God commands Us to place Ourself with assurance at the head of the absolute power. Confident in the Divine Providence and in His supreme wisdom, full of faith in the justice and strength of his autocracy which We are called to maintain, We shall preside serenely over the destinies of Our empire, which henceforward will be discussed between God and Ourself alone.'

Ministers, grand dukes, provincial governors, officials and administrators, all were answerable to the Tsar alone. The police were given wide-ranging powers, exile to Siberia for political dissent became common, and the freedom of the press was severely curbed. One of Alexander III's first acts as Tsar was to appoint Pobedonostsev as Chief Procurator of the Holy Synod, a post which carried great power and which he held until 1905. Some observers felt that power in Russia effectively rested with a small clique, and that home-loving Alexander, the Autocrat of All the Russias, was largely in their hands. 'The new Emperor is a very stay-at-home kind of person, devoted to his wife and children, fond of music, and has hitherto surrounded himself with a small circle of very insignificant persons,' reported the British Ambassador Lord Dufferin to Queen Victoria in March 1881. 'There is still very little known about him, probably because there is very little to know.'

'Those who did not know the Tsar unjustly pictured him as limited, slow of mind,' wrote Count Witte of the new Tsar in his memoirs, putting Lord Dufferin in his proper place. Count Sergei Iulevich Witte should have known, for he was one of the ablest politicians of his age. He was born in the Caucasus, his father a top bureaucrat of Baltic German origin, his mother a member of the Russian nobility. After university at Odessa he quickly made a name for himself in the railroad business, marked out by his brilliant mind and his daring decisions. Soon he was made director of the Department of Railroad Affairs in the Ministry of Finance, and later Tsar Alexander III, spotting his potential, appointed him Minister of Finance, where he still was when Nicky in turn became Tsar. 'It is true that he was below average in intelligence and education,' Witte continued about Alexander III. 'I will not dispute the assertion that the Tsar was not well educated, but I do deny what is often said, that he did not have a good mind. Of course, one has to define what is meant by a good mind. Perhaps he did not have a good mind if the word is taken to mean mind-intellect. But he had an outstanding mind in the sense of mind-heart, the kind of mind that enables one to look ahead, to sense what is coming. Such a mind is more important than mind-intellect.'

In April of that same year, 1881, Queen Victoria had a personal sorrow to endure. Her 'best, most devoted, and kindest of friends', Disraeli, the politician who had known how to speak to her with subtle flattery, always keeping her well-informed in long, entertaining letters, and always remembering to ask her advice, had died, leaving her with hell-raiser Gladstone. But Queen Victoria was above all a pragmatist. By August she was writing to Gladstone in a slightly more conciliatory tone, thanking him for his regular and interesting reports of the proceedings of the House of Commons, though she could not resist a comment on the disgraceful character of many of the members, asking, 'But how can you expect better from so many Members of such low and revolutionary views?'

As the Prince of Wales was returning to London after Alexander II's funeral in St Petersburg, Prince Eddy and Prince George were arriving in South Africa, bound for Australia on their third and last tour. Wherever they anchored, Dalton was on hand to show them the sights and inculcate a little more education. 'We then passed an ostrich farm,' Georgie noted with a distinct lack of enthusiasm in his diary for 2 March 1881 from South Africa, 'and saw a good many ostriches.' On another occasion, in Barbados, there had been a mis-understanding. Newspapers reported that the two princes had been tattooed on the nose, and the news quickly spread to England. Although Prince George acquired many tattoos later in his naval career, and it is amusing when looking at photographs of him resplendent in his Coronation robes to think of all those dragons lurking beneath the ermine, in 1881 he as yet had none, neither on his nose nor anywhere else. 'How could you have your impudent snout tattooed?' wrote the Princess of Wales, appalled. 'What an OBJECT you must look, and won't everybody stare at the ridiculous boy with an anchor on his nose! Why on earth not have it put somewhere else?'

Between South Africa and Australia the HMS *Bacchante* hit a gale-force storm which lasted for three days and tore her sails to shreds. They were four hundred miles from the nearest port, drifting aimlessly, having lost contact with the rest of the squadron. Still, fear and drama were preferable to boredom. 'Weeks and weeks at sea, sometimes very monotonous weeks, living on food that was more than monotonous, and also exceedingly nasty. Mostly salt pork and ship's biscuit,' wrote a shipmate many years later. 'Remember there were no comforts in those days. No such thing as electrical freezing plant. So fresh vegetables, fruit and fresh provisions lasted a very, very short time after leaving harbour. Also, one got rather bored at seeing the same old faces round the same old table, and tempers at times were apt to get a little frayed and irritable. Yet in all those years I never remember Prince George losing his temper. I certainly never had even a cross word with him. Unselfish, kindly, good tempered, he was an ideal shipmate.'

Finally, in August 1882 they came home, Eddy by now nineteen, Georgie seventeen. They hardly had time to see everyone before they were off again, this time for six months to Lausanne, in the vain hope of making them fluent, or at least passably so, in French. Queen Victoria had complained that her grandsons could not speak anything but English. In such an international family, where everyone spoke a bit of everything, and certainly German and French, it was a surprising turn of events, though one which George, once he was King, seemed perfectly happy about. Why speak another language if you have English? remained his firm and patriotic conviction.

However, the Prince of Wales, a good linguist himself, agreed with his mother, and off the two princes went. On their return it was discovered that neither had learnt much French, but it was Eddy who again caused the greatest concern. 'It is indeed a bitter disappointment,' wrote the Princess of Wales to Dalton, who had again accompanied the princes, 'that instead of steadily improving as we hoped he had begun to do during the first half of his stay at Lausanne he should have relapsed into his old habits of indolence and inatten-tion.' Prince George was not home for long. By June 1883 he was pursuing his naval career, appointed to HMS *Canada* bound for the West Indies, while Prince Eddy, separated from his brother for the first time in his life, was off to Cambridge, though his tutors saw little point, claiming he hardly even knew the meaning of the words 'to read'.

At midnight on 10 June Princess Alexandra sat at her desk writing Georgie a letter of farewell for the following day. 'My own darling little Georgie,' she wrote, 'I have only just left you going to bed, after having given you my last kiss and having heard you say your prayers. I need hardly say what I feel – and what we both feel at this sad hour of parting – It will be harder for you this time to have to go quite by yourself – without Eddy, Mr Dalton, or Fuller – but remember darling that when all others are far away God is always there – and He will never forsake you – but bring you safe back to all of us who love you so.' Thinking perhaps of her husband, she urged Georgie not to let anyone lead him astray. 'Remain just as you are – but strive to get on in all that is good – and keep out of temptation as much as you can,' she wrote, adding, 'and also never forget either your morning and evening prayer.' It is hard to remember that Prince George was eighteen by then. Almost as distressed as the Princess of Wales was Charles Fuller, 'my dear excellent Fuller' as Prince George always addressed him, who had been Georgie's constant companion during the past three years and was now left behind at Sandringham. 'It is just a week since you left us,' Fuller wrote on 20 June 1883, 'and you cannot think how much I miss your dear face, the place don't look the same!'

6

Family Strife

~

IN MAY 1883, a good two years after his accession, Alexander III was crowned Tsar of All the Russias in the Church of the Assumption in Moscow, within the walls of the Kremlin. The long interval between the two events was a consequence of the ever-present fear of assassination. Charles Lowe of *The Times* had the honour of being the sole representative of the English Press at the Coronation, an occasion of, as he put it, 'unparalleled pomp'. Lowe described Alexander III's triumphal entry into the city a few days before the Coronation, preceded by the deputies 'from all the Asiatic tribes and peoples subject to his sway – Kalmucks, Khirghiz, Khivans, and the denizens of the Kizil Kum and the Kara Kum, dwellers on the banks of the Jaxartes, and the Oxus, roaming warriors from the far Siberian steppes and the great Mongolian rivers – on they rode, in all the gorgeous variety of their picturesque costumes, before the mighty monarch whose sway extended from the amber-yielding shores of the Baltic to the ice-bound Straits of Behring. On passed the procession amid a never-ceasing roar of cheers from the immense multitudes which lined the route, the booming of guns, and the deafening clangour of all the city bells – a most dazzling and kaleidoscopic cavalcade, relieved at intervals by the gorgeous state coaches of the Empress and the other ladies of the imperial family and Court, each drawn by beautiful and richly caparisoned cream-coloured steeds; and in the centre of all the mighty Tsar himself, in his simple dark green uniform and sheepskin cap, on a snow-white palfrey – the picture of Spenser's "very perfect, gentle knight".' No wonder Lowe had been given his privileged position. As for the English royal family, they were represented by good old Affie with his Russian wife Marie, sister of the Tsar.

After Tsar Alexander II's funeral Minny and Alexandra did not see each other again for two years, but then came the happy summer of 1883 following the Coronation, when the Tsar and Tsarina, with

94

Nicky, now aged fifteen, and their four other children, were able to get away from their 'prison' at Gatchina to the safety and peace of Copenhagen. They arrived on 30 August in the Imperial Yacht and were received by the King and Queen of Denmark, Crown Prince Frederick and Prince Waldemar. The charmingly obsequious Court official was still in service at the Danish Court. He found Tsarina Dagmar as young and lovely as ever, and the Tsar also unchanged, 'his tall, stately, knightly figure with the full beard waving over his chest, and his honest blue trusting eyes. No dark storm cloud casts a shadow over his manly features.'

Then the Court official turned his attention to other members of the Russian Imperial family. 'I must say there is life and merriment at the palace now. All the princely youth who have gathered here are letting their hair down. There is sunshine and laughter in all the corners of the palace, in all the corners of the park, as if a swarm of twittering birds had arrived. And the very youngest of the royal and princely children have found their leader in none other than the Tsar of Russia. Tsar Alexander is a lover of children like few. When he is present one can be sure that the children will flock around him like new shoots round a strong and broad oak tree. The little fellows show no respect for his Russian Majesty. They fearlessly ride on his knee, pull his beard and do a hundred pranks with their Imperial playmate.'

All six of the King and Queen of Denmark's children were together for the first time in twenty years during that summer holiday of 1883, arriving with their many children, the 'twittering birds'. Willi came from Greece, Alexandra from England, bringing Eddy and Toria as well as Louise and Maud. Only poor Georgie was missing, doggedly pursuing his career in the Royal Navy.

Perhaps inevitably, that summer Nicky fell in love with Toria, who was the same age as himself. 'I am in love with Victoria, and she seems to be with me, but I don't care. Yes, it is still more pleasant if she loves me,' he confided to his diary. 'Awfully enjoy being with her, and I feel dull without her.' The two cousins did everything together. They sketched together, went for walks together, talked endlessly together, had Danish lessons together, and ate together, always sitting side by side. In the true spirit of Danish family life, the thing they liked best was playing games together. 'My evening game with Victoria is that she hides and I seek. When I find her too soon, she gets cross and starts chasing me. If she catches me, she tries to knock me down, but she fails. Then she beats me with her fists, and I bear it like the Lamb of God,' he wrote on 6 September. Then, two days later, 'It seemed to me that Victoria despised me, but luckily I was very much mistaken. The less I cared for her, the more she followed me, and I secretly rejoiced. In the evening I tried to be alone with her and kiss her. She is so lovely.' The next day the tables were turned: 'The more Victoria torments and teases her prey, the more the prey loves her. This prey is ME.'

The September days were filled with trips to Copenhagen, parties on the royal yachts, and visits from relations and friends. But by 9 October Nicky was writing: 'Still more and more I love Victoria, awfully sorry we'll have to leave soon. There'll be no playing and romping with her in the small corner room.' They promised faithfully to write, and to meet again in two years' time. Two years later much had changed, and the intensity of that first love was never recaptured, but the deep friendship lasted for the rest of their lives. Toria wrote and sent Christmas cards to 'My darling old Nick' long after he was married. She herself never married. Nicky never lost his affection for her and extended it to her brother Georgie, his English cousin, whom he always much preferred to bombastic Willy in Germany.

When the summer came to an end the two sisters, Minny and Alexandra, had once again to part. Alexandra wrote to Georgie, on the high seas, about 'the AWFUL moment of tearing ourselves away from one another, not knowing WHERE and HOW our next meeting may be. Poor little Minny, I can see her now, standing on the top of the steps in utter despair, her eyes streaming over with tears, and trying to hold me as long as she could. Poor Sasha too felt the parting very much and cried dreadfully.' Partings were always difficult for the Danish royal family, who were in the unhappy position of being very close, while living very far apart. But for Minny and Sasha, returning to 'the prison' of Gatchina, they were awful on a scale which no one else could really understand.

The following year the Danish Court painter Laurits Tuzen was at Gatchina, finishing a painting of the Danish royal family which he had started in the garden room at Fredensborg the previous summer. He provides a vivid description of life at Gatchina for those unhappy guests uninitiated in the odd ways of Court life: Tuzen spent two months there, and hated every minute. 'Grandeur and loneliness go together,' he concluded. He had a large bedroom, a fine drawing room, and his own personal servant, which sounds splendid but meant that he saw no one. He ate alone and he spent his interminable hours of leisure alone, walking down the long, empty, completely straight roads outside the high palace walls. His only human contact was when the Tsarina or the children posed for him. 'In order to go from my room to the big room where I was painting, I had to go very fast through room after room and door after door for five minutes.'

One day the Tsarina asked why they never saw him on their after-noon walks in the palace park. No one had given him permission, he replied. The Tsarina quickly put that right, but it was not much of an improvement. Every hundred steps he was stopped by a soldier demanding 'Your name?' Plain-clothes policemen lurked in every bush. One day Tuzen met the Tsar on a small bridge over a canal. He took off his hat and asked the Tsar for one more sitting for the paint-ing, then put his hat back on. 'We'll see,' answered the Tsar abruptly and strode off. As Mr Lowe of *The Times* later put it: 'Outside the narrow circle of his family the Tsar was never very communicative or cordial. He was taciturn, and as he always felt uncomfortable, was rather awkward.' Tuzen realised it had been a *faux pas to* put his hat back on again in the Tsar's presence. He never got his sitting, and he learnt a fundamental fact: that the Tsar in Denmark was one thing, the Tsar in Russia quite another.

On 15 May 1884 Nicky wrote to his mother from Gatchina: 'My Darling Darling Mama, Today we are impatiently expecting the courier with letters from you. It will be a real pleasure for me if he brings me a letter. It's a beautiful day, the weather has never been so warm yet. There are plenty of flowers everywhere and cowslips, just when you are not here. I am sending you a cowslip which I plucked last night on my way home.' He ended: 'Good-bye, darling Mama, I kiss you tenderly, and also everybody who is here and, of course, Xenia. Once more, I am glad that the courier is coming today – I remain, Your loving, Nicky.' At sixteen Nicky's emotional life was still tied up with his mother and the family, perhaps the inevitable result of an over-protected childhood.

In 1884 one of those family rows blew up which acquire an ominous significance in hindsight. Once again it centred on a spot of match-making, Vicky and Queen Victoria ranged on one side, the Prussians on the other. The subjects were the Battenberg brothers

Louis, Heinrich and Alexander, handsome and charming German princes all three, but minor royals and impoverished and out to make good matches, which two of them managed with some brilliance. Louis married Princess Victoria of Hesse-Darmstadt, Queen Victoria's granddaughter. The Queen had effectively adopted the Hesse children when their mother Princess Alice died of diphtheria in 1878, and Louis now agreed to live in England, where he joined the Royal Navy and later became First Sea Lord, later still Marquess of Milford Haven. Heinrich went one better: he married Beatrice, Queen Victoria's own daughter, also agreed to live in England, and became Henry in the process.

But Alexander, known as Sandro to distinguish him from other royal Alexanders, was another matter. In 1879 Sandro had been nominated to the Bulgarian throne, in much the same way as Willi of Denmark had been nominated to the Greek one, Bulgaria being in need of a monarch because of the continuing collapse of the Ottoman Empire. Sandro was Tsar Alexander II of Russia's nephew. He was personable and, it was supposed, duly grateful. The Great Powers agreed that Bulgaria should be placed within Russia's sphere of influence, and the deal was sanctified with a grand coronation. But Alexander of Bulgaria, as he now was, did not play by the rules of the game. He was soon siding with the Bulgarians, 'his people' as he now called them, who wanted independence from Russia. Tsar Alexander was outraged.

Sandro offended further in April 1884, when he set about courting Princess Victoria, the nineteen-year-old daughter of the Crown Prince and Princess of Prussia, and Willy's sister. Now it was Willy's turn to be outraged, along with Bismarck and the Kaiser. They could not afford to offend the Tsar, or to risk any misunderstandings about their intentions. Willy was additionally enraged because in his view Sandro was not even *ebenbürtig*. Queen Victoria and Vicky begged to differ. The Queen called it 'extraordinary impertinence and inso-lence' when Willie, as she persisted in spelling him, raised the same matter a year later over the marriage of Heinrich to Princess Beatrice. 'As for Dona,' she added, not yet done, 'a poor, little, insignificant Princess raised entirely by your [Vicky's] kindness to the position she is in, I have no words.'

Beatrice married Heinrich or Henry, and the Darmstadt wedding was one of the grand royal gatherings sanctified by the presence of

Queen Victoria herself. Breezily oblivious of any political considerations which might be troubling Bismarck and the Kaiser, she and the Crown Princess, who should perhaps have known better, expressed themselves delighted with the romance between Sandro of Bulgaria and Princess Victoria of Prussia, which blossomed at the wedding. 'I think him very fascinating,' Queen Victoria later confided to Vicky, 'and (as in beloved Papa's case) so wonderfully handsome.'

Bismarck warned the Prince of Wales, also at the wedding and naturally on the English side in the argument, that romance counted for nothing when weighed against German political interests. Bertie thought that 'a bit hard', and promptly cancelled an admittedly boring engagement in London in order to escort the Prince of Bulgaria to Berlin and help him persuade the Crown Prince, who was less convinced than his wife, of the suitability of the match. At a banquet at the Neues Palais in Potsdam Vicky pursued her goal with her usual lack of diplomatic finesse: it was noted that not only was Alexander of Bulgaria seated next to the Crown Prince, with the Prince of Wales on his other side, but the Crown Prince was treating him 'with quite unusual cordiality . . . So the Crown Princess has got him round once again.'

The English faction appeared to have won. But Bismarck was not done. There was another ostensibly private royal event in prospect: Nicky's coming-of-age. In a fury the Kaiser bypassed his son the Crown Prince and sent Prince Wilhelm to represent him instead. It was Willy's first important diplomatic mission, and he accepted with ill-disguised glee. By sending Prince Wilhelm and not the 'English influenced' Crown Prince, Bismarck signalled to the Tsar that the Prussians sided with him in the Sandro affair.

Willy set off in high spirits on his twelve-day visit to Russia, accompanied by his Marshal of the Court, von Liebenau, his two adjutants, von Krosigk and von Bülow, and General Count von Waldersee, all keen supporters of Bismarck and enemies of the Crown Prince and Princess. Willy was to present Nicky, the Tsarevich, with the Order of the Black Eagle, the most prestigious order of Imperial Germany, and he himself would be appointed à la suite to Tsar Alexander's Grenadier Guards Regiment No. 1, which happily possessed a fine uniform.

In St Petersburg Willy, aged twenty-five and still impressionable, was for the first time confronted with a fully autocratic monarch, and he never forgot the experience. He also became acquainted with Herbert, Bismarck's favoured son, who happened, most conveniently, to be in St Petersburg as part of the German Legation. Neatly bypassing the German Ambassador, Willy asked Herbert for advice as to how to make the best impression on the Tsar. 'Show joy and interest in everything Russian,' Herbert Bismarck replied.

Willy was given splendid rooms in the Winter Palace and treated with flattering respect. On 18 May he presented Nicky with the Order of the Black Eagle, quickly racing back to his rooms to change into his splendid Russian uniform for Nicky's coming-of-age ceremony. Count von Waldersee, looking to the future, noted in his diary that evening that the Tsarevich looked 'quite conspicuously small and delicate', then went on to record the fabulous details of the ceremony. 'Hordes of generals, high ranking officers, court officials, senators, clergy, and naturally the entire diplomatic corps and a great many ladies in Russian costume completely filled the colossal halls. The procession with the Tsar and Tsarina in front, then Prince Wilhelm with the Queen of Greece etc. paraded through all the rooms until the church was reached. The heir to the throne took his oath in a firm voice. From there, the procession once again passed through the many rooms until it reached the throne, where all the banners were assembled, and the soldiers' oath was taken, then back through the lines of troops presenting, to the Emperor's chambers.'

At a banquet in honour of the heir to the throne, Alexander III ordered all the grand dukes who possessed one to wear the Order of the Black Eagle. His Foreign Secretary von Griers noted that the Tsar had never seemed more relaxed, and had spoken for the first time of a friendship and alliance between 'the three Empires'. Willy, blissfully unaware of the Tsar and Tsarina's intense dislike of Prussia, took it all as a tribute to his own diplomatic skills. He and the Tsar had a most gratifying conversation, in confidence and lasting over an hour, about the international situation. Willy donned his Russian uniform for the occasion, and rushed to tell Waldersee all about it the moment it was over.

During the conversation the Tsar broached the tricky question of Alexander of Battenberg and the problem of Bulgaria. Wilhelm was able to reassure the Tsar on both counts: 'The Reich has no interests in the Prince,' he said, nor would the Kaiser give his permission for Alexander's marriage to Princess Victoria. When the Tsar hinted that

Alexander might not be in his regal position much longer, Willy airily declared that this 'would not be such a terrible tragedy.' With that, the Tsar sent Willy's disenchanted parents a telegram redolent of hypocrisy. 'It is a true joy to see your dear son among us on such a festive occasion,' he wrote, 'and we will cherish the fondest memories of him.' Willy returned to Berlin with a new swagger and arrogance about him. His parents could only watch the unfolding events in despair.

In his memoirs written so many years after the event, Wilhelm added a postscript. 'That my relationship with my mother was very badly affected by this hurt me very much, and I was also deeply affected by my sister's personal destiny. But since it concerned the well-being of the Vaterland, all personal concerns had to be put aside.' Willy returned to Germany convinced that he had charmed the Tsar. As to his opinion of his cousin Nicky, to judge from later comments Willy had early made up his mind that Nicky, unlike his father, was small and weak, something of a push-over. For his part, Nicky took very little notice of Willy, and was soon involved in more exciting events.

On 27 May 1884, a few days after Nicky's coming-of-age ceremony, the European royals met again, this time for a royal wedding at the Imperial palace of Peterhof, some fifteen miles from St Petersburg. Grand Duke Sergei Alexandrovitch, the Tsar's younger brother, was marrying Princess Elizabeth of Hesse-Darmstadt, another of Princess Alice's daughters, known in the family as Ella. Uncle Willi and Aunt Olga, the King and Queen of Greece, had stayed on and Nicky's sister Xenia, recently married to another Sandro, this a Russian one, was there too. Russian Sandro hated Grand Duke Sergei, his uncle by marriage. 'I would have given ten years of my life to stop her [Ella] from entering the church on the arm of haughty Sergei,' he wrote in his memoirs. 'Obstinate, arrogant, disagreeable, he flaunted his many peculiarities in the face of the entire nation, providing the enemies to the regime with inexhaustible material for calumnies and libel.' Among his peculiarities was an extravagant homosexuality. He and Ella never had children. Of the bride Sandro wrote: 'Ravishing beauty, rare intelligence, delightful sense of humour, infinite patience, hospitality of thought, generous heart, all gifts were hers. It was cruel and unjust that a woman of her calibre should have tied up her existence to a man like Uncle Sergei.' Royal marriages were royal marriages, however, and the choice for the Hesse sisters, as grand-children of Queen Victoria, was limited.

Ella's sister Alexandra, known as Alix or Alicky, also came to the wedding. She was only twelve at the time, but already showing signs of her later beauty, a beauty not lost on Nicky. 'The weather today was wonderful. We lunched as always with the Darmstadts,' he wrote in his diary on 12 June. 'We jumped about with them on the net [trampoline]. At 3 o'clock I went out with them in the four-horse break [*sic*]. Papa drove in front in the family char-à-banc with Aunt Marie and Victoria. We looked at Oserki and everyone signed their name in the book at the mill. We drank fresh milk and ate black bread. We dined with Ernest, pretty little Alix and Sergei. Alix and I wrote our names on the rear window of the Italian house.' In brackets he added, 'We love each other'.

The following day, after church, Nicky put on his uniform of the Preobrajenski Regiment and went to the parade of the Horse Grenadiers and Uhlans. After lunch Alix and her brother Ernie came to visit. 'We jumped about together on the net. Ernie, Alix and I told each other secrets. We had a terrific romp around the rooms of the Italian House. We had dinner all together. I sat and chatted to darling little Alix. Wrestled with Ernie.' The chatting was in English, the only language they had in common. Nicky was sixteen but he loved horsing about – more like a twelve-year-old, as Count von Waldersee had noticed. A week later Nicky was writing: 'We fooled around a lot on the swings. Papa turned on the hose then we ran through the jet and got terribly wet.' And the following day, 20 June: 'We had dinner together in my rooms. We jumped on the net and told each other secrets in the Italian Pavilion. We romped around in the wigwam on Xenia's balcony.' And then, at last: 'I am very sad the Darmstadts are going tomorrow and even more so that dearest Alix is leaving me.'

Although they did not see each other again for five years, and Nicky fell in and out of love a few times in between, his love for twelve-year-old Alix of Hesse turned out to be the passion of his life. Their relationship was an intensely private affair, almost symbiotic, which under normal circumstances would have had no repercussions. As it was, the private love story was played out on the very public stage of European politics, with awful consequences.

Nicky's cousin Georgie was meanwhile pursuing his naval career with Truthfulness, Obedience and Zest, but also with Homesickness, a pain which never quite left him. Letters from his parents may or may not have helped. In March 1886 the Prince of Wales saw his son off from Genoa, following another home leave in England, before moving swiftly on to Monte Carlo. From Monte Carlo he wrote to Georgie: 'On seeing you go off by train yesterday, I felt very sad, and you could, I am sure, see that I had a lump in my throat when I wished you good-bye. We have been so much together, and especially lately, that I felt the parting doubly . . . On returning to Cannes today I shall miss you more than ever, my dear Georgy, and at the ball at Baroness Hoffmann's – How I wish you could be at it! Now God bless you, my dear boy, and may He guard you against all harm and evil, and bless and protect you. Don't forget your devoted Papa. A.E.'

When they were young the Prince of Wales could never bear to be parted from his boys for more than a few weeks at a time, though a good shoot in Hungary or a lucky streak of gambling at Baden might occasionally ease the sorrow. Now, as Georgie set off on yet another voyage, the feelings of sadness were real enough, but the charms of Cannes soon put him right. 'You are, I think, rather hard upon me when you talk of the round of gaieties I indulge in at Cannes, London, Homburg and Cowes,' Bertie wrote to his mother the following year. 'I like Cannes excessively, especially for its climate and scenery, just the same as you do Aix, which you tell me you are going to this year . . . Nobody knows better than I do that I am not perfect – still I try to perform the many and ever-increasing duties which lie before me to the best of my ability . . . There is an old English saying that "all work and no play makes Jack a dull boy" – and there is a great deal of truth in it.'

Dull the Prince of Wales was not. Off he went to Cannes, taking boisterous part in the famous Battle of the Flowers. He also managed to see 'dear Georgy' again, when he came over from Malta to join his father. Then Bertie moved on to Berlin for the Kaiser's ninetieth birthday celebrations. By August, after a spot of racing and shooting in England as well as a good run of balls, dinner parties and theatres, he was back on the Continent, at Homburg, and back to the gaming tables, where he managed to add another large sum to his mounting debts.

Georgie had meanwhile returned to sea, still feeling homesick. 'I wonder who will have that sweet little room of mine, you must go and see it sometimes and imagine that your Georgie dear is living in it,' he wrote to his mother, reliably at home at Sandringham. 'Think sometimes of your poor boy so far away but always your most devoted and loving little Georgie.' The Prince of Wales, not at home, nevertheless found time to write to his old friend Captain Henry Stephenson, commander of the battleship *Thunderer* which formed part of the Mediterranean Fleet in which Georgie was currently serving. 'I feel that in entrusting my son to your care I cannot place him in safer hands only don't SPOIL him PLEASE!'

Georgie was in fact becoming less and less keen on naval life. But when he broached the subject tentatively with his father he met with a less than indulgent response. Although Bertie had seen his son off that August with the usual lump in his throat, lamenting that it was the bane of his life, having to say good-bye to his children and family, he then wrote to his son making it quite clear where he stood on the matter of Georgie's naval career. 'I was sorry to learn from hints that you dropped that you were not as keen about the Navy as formerly. This I should greatly deplore — as no finer profession for an Englishman exists in the world and our great wish is that you should be fond of it. Every year as a profession it becomes more interesting, and some members of our family ought always to be actively employed in it. If you left the Navy, what would you do? Would you like to lead an idle life? I feel sure not.'

What Georgie's feelings were as he contemplated years and years of life at sea is not too difficult to imagine. But he knew that in his case, as the second son, there was no alternative. He seems never to have mentioned the matter again. As for Bertie, he was off again to Homburg before joining his wife and the rest of the family in Denmark. From Copenhagen, where the Tsar and Tsarina and Nicky, now heir to the Russian throne, were also present, he wrote to Georgie again. 'You can picture our life here and all the noise and racket . . . We are a very happy family. WE ARE! You are the only one wanting to make it complete.' Little comfort for Georgie, marooned on the high seas.

By this time the row between the Prince of Wales and his nephew Wilhelm/William had escalated through several stages. Queen Victoria, outraged by Willy's support of Bismarck and the Kaiser against his own mother, which she called 'extraordinary impertinence and insolence', and still irked by Willy's attitude to the Battenberg marriage plans, had been minded to teach her arrogant grandson a lesson. 'As for Willie,' she wrote to Vicky, 'that very foolish, undutiful and I must add unfeeling boy, I have no patience with, and I wish he could get a good "skelp'g" as the Scotch say and seriously a good setting down.' Perhaps unwisely, she enlisted the Prince of Wales as her messenger.

In October 1885, after his usual stay in Denmark with the Princess of Wales and the Tsar and Tsarina, Bertie had moved on to Hungary for a spot of rather more lively social life. From Budapest he telegraphed to Willy to join him there as soon as possible to hear something urgent and private. Willy took his time, only arriving the day before his uncle was due to leave. Waiting for his nephew, the Prince of Wales sat down to write to Georgie, who was by that time a sub-lieutenant, completing a training course at the Royal Naval College at Greenwich and another on HMS *Excellent* at Portsmouth. Georgie had done extremely well at Greenwich in Practical Navigation and reasonably well in most other subjects, but shockingly badly in Mechanics, gaining only 9 marks out of 125. At Portsmouth he did well at Gunnery and Torpedo Work and Seamanship, but just missed getting a First in Pilotage. 'You have, I hope, got over your disappointment about a First,' wrote his sympathetic father. 'It would, of course, have been BETTER if you HAD obtained it; but being only within 20 marks is VERY satisfactory, and shows that there is no favouritism in your case.'

When Willy finally arrived in Budapest his uncle informed him with ill-disguised satisfaction that Queen Victoria was displeased with him, and had no wish to receive him in England that autumn. Willy would understand that under the circumstances he and the Princess of Wales could not entertain him at Sandringham either. This was a snub of the highest order, and rather short-sighted. The following morning the Prince of Wales left for Vienna and Paris, apparently unaware of or unconcerned by the rage and resentment he left behind. When Wilhelm next saw Herbert Bismarck, now back in Berlin as his father's Secretary of State at the Foreign Office, he referred to his grandmother as 'the old hag', adding that 'he was very glad he now had a weapon he could use against his mother if she should reproach him with not being sufficiently well disposed towards the Queen of England.' The Bismarcks could not have been more pleased. Herbert reported the whole story, including Wilhelm's angry remarks, to his Foreign Office colleague Friedrich von Holstein, in whose diary it is to be found.

In June 1887 came Queen Victoria's Jubilee. The greatest nation on earth went wild with excitement and patriotism. The stalls in the

Strand sold everything from commemorative books, portraits, busts and coins to teapots representing the Queen's head and musical bustles which played 'God save the Queen' each time the lady wearing it sat down. Thousands of letters and telegrams of congratulation poured in to Buckingham Palace. Countless gifts of precious jewels and ornaments in gold and silver arrived from across the world. The Poet Laureate, Tennyson, wrote his 65 lines.

The crowds gathered for days outside Windsor Castle and Buckingham Palace were thrilled by guests from eighty countries and the Colonies clad in fabulous national costumes and headdresses. Passing quickly over the deputations of grey London councillors, mayors and freemasons, they craned their necks to spot the next Maharajah decked in diamonds. There were receptions, dinners, balls, ceremonies, naval reviews, exhibitions and dedications of buildings. And everywhere the Prince of Wales moved about, organising, greeting guests, and enjoying himself. Only the Queen remained unenthusiastic. 'The day has come, and I am alone,' she wrote dolefully in her Journal on 20 June 1887, 'though surrounded by many dear children. I am writing, after a very fatiguing day, in the garden at Buckingham Palace, where I used to sit so often in former happy days. Fifty years today since I came to the Throne! God has mercifully sustained me through many great trials and sorrows.'

Her greatest trial among many at the time of her Jubilee remained her grandson. Willy had bombarded the Queen with requests to attend the celebrations in place of his father, who was by now ill with throat cancer, though no one yet knew quite how serious it was. Receiving no encouragement from his grandmother, who was still angry with him, Willy went to ask his grandfather, the aging Kaiser, for permission to attend as the official representative of the Hohenzollerns. His grandfather agreed, and Willy promptly presented Queen Victoria with the *fait accompli*, claiming it was on the Kaiser's orders. This 'impertinence' enraged Queen Victoria, who was now minded to cancel Willy's invitation altogether.

Instead, she and Vicky made sure not only that Fritz attended as the official representative of the Hohenzollerns but that he took pride of place in the procession, riding in front of the Queen's carriage through the garlanded streets to Westminster Abbey looking like Siegfried himself, seated on a fine white charger and resplendent in the white uniform of the Pomeranian Cuirassiers, the diamonds of his

Garter Star gleaming, easily capturing the greatest applause from the gaping crowds. Vicky, the favourite daughter, was given the place of honour in the carriage beside her mother the Queen, together with her sister-in-law, the Princess of Wales. Willy meanwhile was literally put in his place, riding well back in the procession, lost in the crowd of other princes and Royal Highnesses. He complained that his uncle Bertie was deliberately ignoring him, and he was outraged when the black Queen of Hawaii was given precedence over Dona at a Court function, an insult which was never forgotten.

As far as Georgie was concerned, the Jubilee celebrations gave him an opportunity to be at home with his beloved family. He had badly missed Christmas at Sandringham that year. 'How delightful to be in dear old England again,' he wrote in his diary on 16 June. 'Got to Kings Cross at 8 [p.m.]. Dearest Papa, darling Motherdear, Eddy and sisters and George of Greece came to meet me. So happy to be home again. Dined at 9. At 11.30 we all went to a dance at the Wombwells. Home at 4.30. Talked with Motherdear. Bed at 5.30.'

The days which followed were filled with trips to various stations to greet a stream of royal guests: the Denmarks, the Germans, the Austrians, the Greeks, the Swedens, the Spanish, the Portuguese, as well as the Battenburgs, the Hesses and the dear Coburgs. Favourites among them all for Georgie were his Danish relations and his Russian Aunt Olga who was married to his uncle King George of Greece, one-time Willi of Denmark. Queen Victoria was not keen on her grandson's affection for this Danish/Greek side of the family, and frowned on his frequent visits to the palace at Athens when he was based in the Mediterranean. 'Why on earth should I not?' he wrote to Motherdear in one of his occasional outbreaks of fret. 'Why may I not go and see Uncle Willy if you and Papa wish me to? It is the greatest BOSH I ever heard.' But he had the sense to add, 'Please don't leave this letter lying about, Motherdear, as there are some things perhaps that I ought not to have said, but I always tell you everything you see Motherdear. Better burn it.' His grandmother had created her favoured grandsons Prince Eddy and Prince George her personal ADCs for the duration of the Jubilee celebrations, and they rode beside her coach to the Abbey to 'deafening applause'. The other, unfavoured grandson, Willy, was left out in the cold.

Georgie's life appeared to be mapped out for many years to come, his naval career progressing smoothly in spite of persistent sea-sickness and a lingering longing for home. In 1888 he managed to get home for a long Christmas leave, and 1889 therefore opened at Sandringham, duck-shooting with Papa and Eddy in Woodcock Wood. There was tea in the hall at 5 and a spot of dutiful letter-writing before dinner at 8.45, followed by a game of billiards and another of bowls in his father's bowling alley. Later he sat and talked to Motherdear, and 'Bed at 1.' It was, in Georgie's terms, the perfect day.

There was only one problem to spoil the perfection. About this time the name Julie Stonor crops up frequently in Prince George's diaries. She was the daughter of Mrs Francis Stonor, onetime lady-in-waiting to the Princess of Wales. But Mrs Stonor had died in 1883, leaving her teenage children Harry and Julie motherless. Since they lived locally the Princess of Wales took them under her wing and they were frequent visitors at Sandringham. Prince George, home on leave, fell in love with Julie, who was pretty, sweet-natured and in need of love and protection. When he was away at sea they wrote each other long letters filled with affection. But Julie Stonor was a commoner and a Roman Catholic. Georgie's mother, indulgent in everything concerning her sons except the matter of royal marriage, wrote to Georgie saying how much she liked Julie, 'such a pretty simple unaffected dear,' but firmly adding, 'There it is and, alas, rather a sad case I think for you both, my two poor children! I only wish you could marry and be happy, but, alas, I fear that cannot be.'

7

I Bide My Time

~

By 1884, WHEN Willy went to Russia, he was already firmly aligned with the conservative forces in German politics, led by Bismarck. In spite of all his mother's efforts to influence him in the English way, he had turned out to be what she called 'a regular Hohenzollern'. But, as Willy's grandmother Queen Victoria had written to her daughter when Willy was twelve, 'It is a terrible difficulty and a terrible trial to be a Prince. NO ONE having the courage to tell them the truth or accustom them to those rubs and knocks which are so necessary to boys and young men.' This could hardly be said to apply to Georgie, in view of all the rubs and knocks he endured in the Royal Navy. But she was right about Willy.

Flattery was certainly a problem for all three royal cousins, but especially for a young man like Willy who appeared to combine a natural pride with a troubling lack of confidence exacerbated by his crippled arm. But the greater problem was that from the time he stepped into public life he was surrounded by political intrigue. By 1884 it was clear which faction had won. 'I Bide My Time' Willy wrote with a flourish at the bottom of a photograph of himself in full Highland dress that year, signing it William Prince of Prussia. It was a joke, what with the costume, a gift from his grandmother Queen Victoria, and the use of the English version of his name. But, as so often with Willy's jokes, not everyone was likely to appreciate it. Watch out, he was saying.

The 1884 trip to Russia was something of a turning-point for Willy. 'The Prince has made a brilliant impression here,' Herbert Bismarck reported to Berlin. 'Both sexes are enthusiastic about him.' Willy, flattered by all the praise, sent his parents a smug telegram: 'Truly moved by the lovely ceremony. Report my appointment to commander of the Vyborg regiment.' He knew very well that his father had been 'thunderstruck' by the original decision, had even on one occasion broken down in tears of bitterness and frustration at the way the Kaiser and Bismarck were bypassing him. What Willy did not realise, however, was that the rival camps were lining up to flatter him for their own gain.

The man Herbert Bismarck was reporting to in Berlin was Friedrich von Holstein, the very person who had noted that Alexander Battenberg was placed between the Crown Prince and the Prince of Wales at the banquet following the Darmstadt wedding and that the Crown Prince was chatting 'most cordially' to him 'so the Crown Princess has got round him once again.' Holstein was the powerful Geheimrat at the Foreign Office in the Wilhelmstrasse, best described as Senior Counsellor. His network of informers was so efficient that it was rarely more than a day before the Geheimrat knew of anything important that happened, either at home or abroad.

Adolf von Bülow, who accompanied Prince Wilhelm to Russia, was the son of Bismarck's former Secretary of State at the Foreign Office and brother of Bernhard von Bülow, one day to be Willy's Chancellor. He and Herbert had been school friends. Now, in Russia, Bülow presciently warned Herbert Bismarck: 'You are seeing the Prince at his very best at this time; he still feels unsure of himself, & this feeling induces him to heed good advice, for he wishes to succeed. The way he is treated here pleases him greatly. His parents constantly put him down & treat him like a green little boy, while here all the honours of a direct heir to the throne are bestowed upon him in pro-fusion.'

One of the interesting side issues of Willy's visit to Russia in 1884 was that he did *not* stay for his cousin Ella's wedding, which took place in St Petersburg only days after he left. This might have had little significance but for the fact that Willy had once planned to marry Ella himself. When he was a student at the grammar school in Cassel, visiting his cousins and his aunt Alice in Darmstadt, it was Ella, the second daughter, who took his fancy. 'I cannot describe to you how nice our stay in Darmstadt was,' Willy had written to his mother in April 1875, in English as usual. 'Ella – who is my SPECIAL pet – is very much grown & exeedingly [*sic*] beautiful; in fact she is the most beautiful girl I ever saw. She & I, we both love each other warmly; she showed me the hot house & garden at Darmstad [*sic*] & we were together the whole day. I think that, if God grants that I may live till then I shall make her my bride if you allow it.' The letter is typical of those he sent his mother at that time, revealing both his dependence on her opinion and his oddly personal relationship with God, which later developed into a relationship so exclusive that no one else could tell him what to do. Strangest of all is the fact that Ella was just eleven at the time.

Surprisingly, Vicky was not keen on her son's marriage plans even though his intended, as Ella remained, was her own sister Alice's daughter. Her stated reason was that they were too closely related, but that was unconvincing: in royal circles, cousins constantly married other cousins. The truth lay elsewhere.

In 1873 a sad accident had occurred in the Darmstadt household when three-year-old Frittie fell out of a palace window onto the terrace below while playing with his brother Ernie. Frittie had only recently been diagnosed as being a haemophiliac, and he bled to death. His uncle Leopold, Queen Victoria's son, also a haemophiliac, wrote with his condolences and in a touching effort to console: 'I know too well what it is to suffer as he would have suffered, and the great trials of not being able to enjoy life or to know what happiness is . . . I cannot help saying to myself that it is perhaps well that the dear child has been spared all the trials and possible miseries of a life of ill health like mine.' Ten years later Leopold himself died after falling down a staircase. It was known that haemophilia was passed down to sons through the female line, and Vicky and Fritz were determined to avoid any chance of a future grandson and Kaiser of the German Reich being so afflicted.

The effect on Willy of his mother's disapproval of his plan to marry Ella was dramatic, and distinctly odd. Vicky preferred one of the two princesses of Schleswig-Holstein-Sonderburg-Augustenburg: their grandmother had the advantage of being a cousin of Prince Albert, and Vicky's own sister Helena had married their uncle. Now, quite suddenly, and overnight it seemed, Willy changed his mind. On 30 August the two Holstein princesses were invited to Potsdam with their parents. When they left the following day, and before setting off to visit his grandmother at Balmoral, Willy asked their father the Duke if he might write to him on a certain subject when he returned from Scotland. He followed this by writing to his Aunt Helena, who was in England at the time, that Victoria, Dona, was 'the only one I have ever loved'. Helena promptly sent a copy of the letter to Vicky, who forwarded it to Fritz with the comment that Willy's letter was 'so curiously pompous & ornate.' Fritz was perplexed at what he called Willy's 'sudden changing of saddle'. The Kaiser saw it as another example of Vicky's plotting, unaware that Dona would turn out to be one of his best allies, and that Vicky would soon enough have cause to regret her choice.

As a disillusioned old man exiled at Doorn in Holland after the First World War, Wilhelm admitted to his grandson that his marriage had been nothing more than 'duty'. It is a word that surfaces again and again in the lives of all three royal cousins, Willy, Georgie and Nicky, but not necessarily with the same meaning. For Willy, in this case, 'duty' meant getting on with it, marriage and procreation being something which simply had to be done, since providing an heir was the first duty of a hereditary monarch. He already knew what he felt about women. In his memoirs Willy describes his wedding day in one page; ten pages on either side describe his life in the military with his officer friends in his regiment at Potsdam.

Willy's real emotional interests, as future events revealed, lay elsewhere. His regiment at Potsdam was his 'el dorado', as he described it to Countess Dönhoff, 'with soldiers as much as you like'. Countess Dönhoff was by now divorced from her German diplomat husband and married to Bernhard von Bülow, ambitious brother of Willy's ADC Adolf von Bülow and himself a rising diplomat, who ended as Willy's Chancellor. The charming and clever Countess was one of Willy's few confidantes, and she surely knew where his interests lay. The 'nice kind young men' in his regiment were essentially the same aristocratic friends from his university days. Bismarck, in his memoirs, noted Wilhelm's liking for *lange Kerls*, long-limbed young men. His son Herbert made a point of reporting from Russia that Prince Wilhelm was a success with 'both sexes'. By 1886, Wilhelm had met the man who was to become his best friend, Count Philipp zu Eulenburg und Hertefeld, known as 'Phili' or even the feminine 'Philine' to his intimate friends. The Berlin police had a file on Phili, who was suspected of being a homosexual.

When the industrialist Walter Rathenau first met Wilhelm, he was quite taken aback. Believing the image and the propaganda, he was expecting a powerful and energetic man. 'There sat a youthful man in a colourful uniform, with odd medals, the white hands full of coloured rings, bracelets on his wrists; tender skin, soft hair, small white teeth,' he wrote in his memoirs in 1923, adding with unusual insight: 'A true

Prince, intent on the impression [he made], continuously fighting with himself, overcoming his nature in order to wrest from it bearing, energy, mastery. Hardly an un[self]conscious moment; unconscious only – and here begins the part which is humanly touching – of the struggle with himself; a nature directed against himself, unsuspecting. Men have seen this besides me: neediness, softness, a longing for people, a childlike nature ravished, these were palpable behind athletic feats, high tension and resounding activity.'

Willy himself may not have been actively homosexual, and in many senses he was devoted to and certainly dependent on his wife, and had even had some experience with prostitutes as a young lieutenant, but his sexual interests were clear. This would have been of minor significance had he not been the heir to the throne. As things were, it opened up a rich avenue of political influence which the Bismarck clique was not slow to exploit.

It is hard not to feel sorry for Willy. Different by birth, handicapped, misunderstood by his parents, split by his dual Prussian/English identity, and confused by all the flattery and political intrigue which surrounded him, he hardly knew which way to turn. 'Cold as a block of ice' noted Herbert Bismarck just as coldly, but not the only one to pinpoint a fateful void at the heart of all the posturing.

In 1886 Willy had been married to Dona for five years and three of their seven children had been born: Princes Wilhelm, Eitel Friedrich and Adalbert. By 1890 they had been joined by August Wilhelm, Oskar and Joachim; and, finally, in 1892, came Victoria Louise, the only daughter and her father's favourite. Dona continued to devote herself exclusively to children and church, if not the kitchen. 'The new Hohenzollern Princess was amiable and virtuous,' wrote the anonymous Court official. 'She had been very simply brought up and under the tuition of the ducal chaplain had become very pious and strictly orthodox. With other creeds and with those who professed them the Princess never sympathised, but held as much aloof from them as possible.' One can imagine how well that went down with her liberal mother-in-law.

As before, Dona often saw her husband only at breakfast, and that only when he was not away on his increasingly numerous travels. Immediately after breakfast he left to attend to his regiment, sometimes returning for lunch, after which husband and wife would go for a ride in the countryside around Potsdam, always accompanied by Prince

Wilhelm's ADCs. But often Wilhelm remained with his regiment all day, and much of the evening. If he was not with his regiment he might visit his grandfather the Kaiser, drinking tea with him, helping him with his correspondence, or dining with him at his palace in Berlin. Sometimes Bismarck joined them, and then, at this early stage at least, a happier threesome could hardly be found.

The Kaiser had promoted Wilhelm to command of the elite and socially exclusive Guards Hussars without so much as a nod in the direction of his son and heir, the Crown Prince, causing another bitter outburst of frustration and hurt pride. Wilhelm, swaggering around in his newest and most splendid uniform, making loud pronouncements on military matters and his own brilliant successes at home and abroad, began increasingly to believe in his own fictions. To his father, who had been a real soldier fighting real wars, this 'tinsel soldiering' was an unbearable affront. Prince Wilhelm seemed not to know the difference, and his tendency to fantasy was only made worse by the flattering courtiers and military men who surrounded him.

Most of all Wilhelm liked the company of his fellow officers. If he rode and paraded with them during the day, in the evenings he liked to carouse with them in the officers' mess, or in a more serious mood lecture them at length on some aspect of military history. The officers' mess was an exclusively male society. The officers' honour code was sacred. He who offended against it was challenged to a duel. As his friend Eulenburg later found out, for Wilhelm the Prussian officer could do no wrong. 'Here I found my family, my friends, my interests,' Wilhelm told him, 'everything which I had up to that time had to miss.'

'Britain must be destroyed,' Wilhelm had announced on his return from Russia in 1884. Or so Herbert Bismarck claimed. 'After the experience of Petersburg, the Prince considered himself to be a Russian specialist,' he wrote, unwittingly revealing his contempt. 'He sent me billets on how we should strive to destroy Battenberg, & sent letters direct to the Tsar, which I never saw.' Herbert may have exaggerated, but he was right about Wilhelm's letters to the Tsar. Buoyed up by his new role of diplomat, Wilhelm sent the Tsar confidential letters which were far from diplomatic. 'He loves being contrary,' he naively confided to the Tsar about his father, the Crown Prince, 'and is in the hands of my mother, who is directed in turn by the Queen of

England and makes him see everything through "English spectacles". I assure you that the Emperor, Prince Bismarck and I are in agreement, and I will never cease to regard as my very highest duty the consolidation and maintenance of the Three Emperors' League. The triangular bastion must defend monarchies and Europe against the waves of anarchy, and it is precisely that which England fears more than anything else in the world.' With its florid language and bragging opinions, this has all the hallmarks of the later Wilhelm.

Interestingly, in his account Herbert Bismarck adds that Gladstone in England did not rise to any of this. What Herbert calls the 'Wales–Copenhagen' link kept Gladstone well informed, he wrote, revealing to him that the Germans might want to instigate war, but in Gladstone's phrase 'one should not do them the favour'. The two sisters, Alexandra and Minny, wrote weekly letters to one another, filled with news of every sort.

Oblivious of these undercurrents, the impressionable Prince played neatly into the hands of the Anglophobes who surrounded him. These included most of his fellow officers, General von Waldersee with his stiff military bearing, his ambitions and his profoundly reactionary views, who already had his eye on the aging Chancellor's job, and Captain von Kessel, a coarse-mannered soldier and a cousin of the Bismarcks, who came to replace Adolf von Bülow as Wilhelm's ADC.

In September 1886 Wilhelm was again sent by Bismarck to see the Tsar. Since he considered his first effort to have been such a spectacular success, he was perhaps surprised to be invited for only two days. Tsar Alexander, keen to keep the visit as short as possible, suggested that Willy attend the Russian manoeuvres at Brest Litowsk, rather than travelling all the way to St Petersburg. The Tsar had little need of Wilhelm now: Alexander Battenberg, Prince of Bulgaria was about to be kidnapped, summarily deposed, and sent packing.

The irritation Wilhelm felt at having his visit thus curtailed comes across in his account of the meeting as recalled years later in his memoirs. In spite of the Tsar's outward cordiality, the message was clear: Prince Wilhelm had to fit his diplomacy into the brief pauses between lengthy displays of military exercises. 'His [the Tsar's] response ran thus,' wrote Wilhelm. 'If he wanted Istanbul, he would have it. He had no need of Prince Bismarck's permission for it. Though at the same time he said he would hold to the Three Kaisers'

Alliance to maintain the peace in Europe, and also sent my grandfather heartfelt greetings, and was, in a personal sense, altogether very friendly.' The impressive military exercises, noted Willy, were saying 'We are ready.' Behind his comments one can detect General von Waldersee's conviction that Russia was belligerent, and that in view of this, 'the best defence lies in attack.' Waldersee wanted a pre-emptive war against Russia – for Russia, as everyone knew, was not in fact ready at all. Willy raced to report everything to his grandfather the Kaiser as soon as he got back to Berlin.

'How badly behaved he is FIRST visiting his grandparents & then you! How can this be possible!' wrote Vicky in capital commiseration to her husband Fritz from the South Tyrol where she was holidaying. 'The nonsense provoked by entrusting delicate & important matters to such INEXPERIENCED hands – and those of such a GREEN & IMPETUOUS young man. It DAMAGES THE CAUSE, sets HIS head spinning, and is an outrage against you.' Vicky knew exactly where the problem lay. 'The intriguers will leave no stone unturned.'

Willy's head was already spinning. In May he had met Count Philipp zu Eulenburg, the man who was to gain his deepest love and have the profoundest influence over him, with the most disastrous results. As Eulenburg's biographer and apologist Haller wrote in 1924, 'In general one can say that until the end of the 1890s there was scarcely a single important domestic or international affair of concern to the government agencies in which he [Eulenburg] did not in some way participate.' Haller wrote this with pride; others took a very different view as Eulenburg's power grew and grew.

The circumstances leading up to and surrounding that May meeting are worth examining in some detail. On 19 April Count Eberhard von Dohna-Schlobitten wrote inviting Eulenburg to stay for a few days at Prokelwitz, his brother Richard's vast estate in Silesia. The reason? Prince Wilhelm was to visit Prokelwitz, and someone somewhere had decided that Eulenburg might be the man to influence the Prince in favour of the Bismarck faction. Since all Eulenburg's close friends, including Herbert von Bismarck, knew of his sexual orientation, it must be assumed that they were also aware of Prince Wilhelm's own ambivalence. Eberhard and Eulenburg had been intimate friends since boyhood, and during the first war of

German unification had enlisted together along with their friend Edgard von Wedel, who later became Wilhelm's *Kamerherr* or Gentlemen of the Chamber and was eventually discovered to be homosexual. Eberhard and Eulenburg joined the War Academy at Cassel together, where Eulenburg met Kuno, Count von Moltke, the man who became Eulenburg's closest friend, and played a key role in the dramatic homosexual trials which broke on a shocked public in 1907/8.

After the Franco-Prussian war Eulenburg left the army, which had never really suited his artistic temperament, to study law at the University of Leipzig. Here he made a new friend, Axel von Varnbüler, and together they moved to Strasburg to finish their law studies. There they formed a close circle with Karl von Dornberg and Alfred von Bülow, later also accused of homosexuality. Karl von Dornberg, referred to as 'the little one' by the friends, committed suicide in 1897, just as the homosexual scandals were beginning to surface.

Eulenburg was the undisputed leader of the group, the man everyone turned towards as he entered the room, the man they all loved. He was something of a dilettante, a gifted writer and musician and an amusing raconteur. He composed ballads, often on ancient Nordic themes, and performed them charmingly, accompanying himself on the piano. His plays enjoyed a certain success in Munich and Berlin. But he only passed his law exams in Strasburg at the second attempt, suggesting that in purely intellectual terms Eulenburg was perhaps not quite as clever as some thought he was.

Most of Eulenburg's intimate circle married at some stage, but when Kuno von Moltke did so, Eulenburg was horrified. 'This marriage was extremely GRUESOME to me,' he later wrote, 'and I'm afraid that the "young bride" noticed it.' Eulenburg, Varnbüler and Kuno von Moltke formed an inseparable trio. Varnbüler was already married. So was Eulenburg, who had married Augusta Sandels, a Swedish countess he had known for many years. 'Dearest Axel, I am at the goal!' he wrote to Varnbüler, adding, 'but do not expect any "Brideletter" – I am just as I was, completely calm and not at all silly.' The couple moved to a small house near Liebenberg, his parents' estate in East Prussia. Eulenburg adored his mother, writing to her most days when he was away from home, and confiding in her about his 'real self'. She shared his artistic temperament and understood him, unlike his stiff Prussian officer father, who understood him not at all. 'My beloved Mama,' he wrote to her after one of her visits, 'I have the feeling, since you left, that I've lost all power of speech.'

With Karl von Dornberg and Alfred von Bülow, Eulenburg did his law tutelage under a district judge named Laemmel. The agreement with his stern father was that he would enter the diplomatic service once his law studies were completed, and April 1886 found him at the Prussian Embassy in Munich, having already served in Stockholm, Dresden and Paris, where he first became friends with Bernhard von Bülow, who was Second Secretary. Bernhard was clever, charming, highly ambitious, and by 1886 married to the Countess von Dönhoff, Prince Wilhelm's confidante.

Prince Wilhelm's Prokelwitz visit at the beginning of May 1886 could hardly have met with greater success. It was a small intimate group of friends: Richard and Eberhard von Dohna, Philipp zu Eulenburg, Prince Wilhelm and just one favoured ADC. Eulenburg found time, on 11 May, to report to Bismarck's son. 'My dearest Herbert,' he wrote, happily describing how he had spent hours in Wilhelm's company, going out hunting every day, till he felt he had come to know the Prince 'right to the depth of his private and political heart.' In another letter to his wife he wrote: 'Prince Wilhelm is full of friendship for me and so enchanted with my Nordic Ballads that he wants to hear them again and again. He stands beside me at the piano, and turns the pages of the sheet music. We are on the very best of terms.' He added that he should have left Prokelwitz on 9 May, but Wilhelm would not let him go. Eulenburg felt that the future of the Reich was in safe hands, 'in the best and truest Hohenzollern fashion.' As far as the Bismarcks were concerned, things were developing very nicely.

On 11 June Wilhelm sent Eulenburg, still based at the Prussian Embassy in Munich, a telegram in preparation for their next meeting. 'Request exact information private on arrangements. Still swoon about "Atlantis" and know "Hokum and Harald" by heart. Will probably leave for Reichenhall on Thursday. Wilhelm Pr v Pr [Prince of Prussia].' 'Hokum and Harald' was one of Eulenburg's ballads, about a deep friendship between two young men. From 1886 onwards the other two young men, Prince Wilhelm and Count Philipp zu Eulenburg, met at Prokelwitz every May to celebrate, like lovers, their first meeting. Soon Wilhelm, like his other close friends, was calling

Eulenburg 'Phili.' And the friends, all passionate monarchists like Eulenburg himself, were soon referring to Prince Wilhelm as 'Der Liebling', 'the darling one'.

That first year Herbert wrote back to Eulenburg: 'My dear Phili, many thanks for your most interesting letters, the last of which I received early today. I have sent them direct to my father, and your reflections have been noted.' In another letter he told Eulenburg that Prince Wilhelm had been praising him loudly, adding 'you must make good use of this, and talk to him again when you see him in Reichenhall and train him up . . . so that his Potsdam Lieutenant's opinions can gradually give way to reflections worthy of a statesman.' Herbert and his father clearly had a lower opinion of Prince Wilhelm's capabilities than did starry-eyed Eulenburg. They were also worried about the Prince's health. Wilhelm was highly strung, and given to unaccountable rages and nervous fits from time to time. Eulenburg planned to take him to hear Wagner at Bayreuth, a passion Wilhelm was learning to share with his new friend, and Herbert warned, only half jokingly: 'I hope you look after the dear man carefully, so that the Wagner tones don't damage his bad ear . . . because his health is quite simply priceless to the German Fatherland.'

Ever since his dangerously mismanaged birth Wilhelm had had serious trouble with his inner ear, and despite constant medical attention it seemed to be getting worse and worse. His health was 'priceless' because his grandfather was almost ninety, and his father the Crown Prince was being openly championed by the Social Democrats.

Before Prince Wilhelm set off to join his new friend in Munich, Eulenburg sent him a 'private and confidential' report on the political situation in Bavaria. Within two days Friedrich von Holstein knew about it, and contacted Eulenburg in a most friendly fashion, saying that Herbert von Bismarck had written to him, and offering a few words of advice of his own. Eulenburg wrote back with gratified thanks. At this early stage at least it would seem that Eulenburg, though he was already a deft courtier who knew how to advance himself, was as much manipulated as manipulating. Willy, the darling one, spent many happy hours with Eulenburg that fateful summer of 1886, never suspecting the intrigue which was fermenting all around him.

On 22 March 1887, just before Queen Victoria's Golden Jubilee in

June, it was the Kaiser's ninetieth birthday, an event enthusiastically celebrated by the German nation. As François Ayme noted, a great change had come over Germany after Bismarck's final war of unification. There was now a seemingly unstoppable swell of national pride and ambition, with the economy growing so fast that it had already overtaken those of Russia and France and was well on the way to overtaking Great Britain's. The new German Empire, personified in Kaiser Wilhelm I, meant to claim her rightful place in the world.

But what would happen when the old Kaiser died? It was decided that Prince Wilhelm should be given some training in affairs of state. As usual the Crown Prince – the Kaiser's son and heir – was not asked for his opinion, leaving him once again outraged and humiliated. Herbert von Bismarck suggested a short stint at the Foreign Office for Wilhelm. Far-sighted Friedrich von Holstein was not in favour, feeling that the Bismarcks were gaining altogether too much influence over the heir apparent, but the plan went ahead regardless. It did little good. Although Willy was clever enough, he lacked concentration, and his interest in diplomatic papers was at best superficial. It was the same when he was given a brief introduction to economic affairs at the Prussian Finance Ministry. The main effect was to increase his already overdeveloped sense of his own importance. As Vicky wrote to Queen Victoria in a fury, 'He is so headstrong, so impatient of any control, except the Emperor's, and SO SUSPICIOUS of everyone who MIGHT be only a half-hearted admirer of Bismarck's that it is quite USELESS to attempt to enlighten him, discuss with him, or persuade him to listen to other people, or other opinions! Fritz takes it profoundly AU TRAGIQUE, whilst I try to be patient and do not lose courage.'

Vicky wrote this letter in April 1886. By the autumn Fritz was ill. The first signs were a hoarse throat; by Christmas it was so bad he could hardly speak, and the following March a growth was discovered on the Crown Prince's left vocal chord. By May six separate specialists had offered their opinion that the growth was cancerous, and that it must be removed immediately if the patient's life were to be saved; his power of speech, however, must be sacrificed. The political implications of this did not have to be spelt out. A further specialist, this time English, arrived to offer a final opinion 'Got a cipher telegram from Vicky begging me to send Dr Morell Mackenzie at once for consultation,' wrote Queen Victoria in her Journal on 19 May.

To the Germans' surprise Dr Morell Mackenzie of Harley Street found no trace of a malignancy. He suggested some months' recuperation in a sunny climate, after which all should be well. Vicky and Fritz seized on the good news with a determination born of despair. Both personally and politically, the prospect of Fritz being mortally ill was impossible to contemplate. Few others in Germany believed the English diagnosis. The Social Democrats were terrified of losing their liberal Crown Prince. The Bismarcks too were worried, but for quite other reasons: immature and unpredictable, Prince Wilhelm was not yet ready to rule. Only Eulenburg and his rabid monarchist friends were thrilled by this fateful turn of events. General von Waldersee contemplated the situation and, like many others, now shifted his attention to Prince Wilhelm, redoubling his already immoderate flattery. As the news of the Crown Prince's illness became public that May, most people in Germany felt that the dubious diagnosis was yet another example of the Crown Princess's obstinately wrong-headed Englishness.

Meanwhile, plans for Queen Victoria's Golden Jubilee went ahead. Vicky and Fritz, quoting Dr Morell Mackenzie, insisted that Fritz was well enough to attend. The Kaiser reluctantly agreed, but Willy insisted that he also be allowed to attend. Queen Victoria reluctantly agreed, only to be enraged by the size of Wilhelm's suite. Willy, displeased in his turn, told his new friend Eulenburg, a man with no affection for Willy's maternal nation, that 'one cannot have enough hatred for England.' The Crown Prince may have looked like a knight in shining armour as he rode in pride of place in the Jubilee procession, but the knight could hardly speak, and before the year was out Mackenzie of Harley Street had changed his mind. The growth was indeed cancerous. Fritz and Vicky and their three younger daughters, whom Willy liked to refer to as 'the English colony', moved to San Remo, hoping the Italian sun might effect a miraculous cure.

On 10 March 1888 the Prince and the Princess of Wales celebrated their silver wedding anniversary at Marlborough House. Bertie gave his long-suffering wife a diamond and ruby cross. From Russia, Minny and Sasha sent her a beautiful ruby and diamond necklace. Queen Victoria arrived bearing a very large silver loving-cup. Three hundred and sixty-five society ladies gave a diamond tiara, the United Grand Lodge of Freemasons a diamond butterfly; and Lord and Lady Rothschild outdid everyone by sending a gold bouquet holder encrusted with precious stones and a huge pair of diamond and pearl earrings. The Kaiser and Kaiserin sent a couple of dreary Dresden vases.

Willy arrived in San Remo in time to hear the doctors pronounce the cancer incurable. He wrote to Queen Victoria that his father had received the news 'like a Hohenzollern and a soldier.' By now Willy's head was so turned by flattery that his language had apparently lost touch with reality altogether, to be replaced by that of Prussian myth and romance. 'Gentlemen, I am a soldier,' he ended one of his first public speeches, given earlier that year. 'Hence, let me quote, in con-clusion, the words which were pronounced by our great Chancellor in the Reichstag on the 6 February, the day on which the House gave the splendid spectacle of the representatives of the people walking hand in hand with the government: "We Brandenburgers fear God, but nothing else in the world." '

Within months both Willy's father and his grandfather were dead, and Willy was Kaiser. After all the years of waiting, Fritz reigned for only ninety-nine days. Not much could be achieved in such a short time, but Kaiser Friedrich III, as he so briefly became, immediately awarded his wife the Empire's highest honour, the Order of the Black Eagle. For her part, Vicky at once took up the battle of the Battenberg wedding, apparently unaware that since his abrupt removal from Bulgaria by the Russians Sandro had lost either his nerve or his inter-est, for he no longer wished to marry her daughter Princess Victoria. Willy, high on his horse now that he knew he would soon be Kaiser, was outraged by his mother's behaviour, writing to Eulenburg on 12 April 1888: 'What I have endured here in the last 8 days simply defies description and even mocks the imagination! The sense of deep shame for the sunken prestige of my once so high and inviolable House – that is the strongest feeling! I see it as something sent to try me and all of us, and am attempting to bear it with patience. But that our family shield should be besmirched and the Reich brought to the brink of ruin by an English princess who is my mother – that is the most terrible thing of all!'

In late April Queen Victoria travelled to Potsdam to visit her dying son-in-law, the man in whom she and Prince Albert had invested so many of their hopes for a united and liberal Germany. Lord Salisbury, returned to power as Prime Minister in the wake of Gladstone's defeat over the Irish Home Rule Bill, was anxious about the visit, well aware of how critical the Queen was of Prince Wilhelm, soon to be Kaiser. 'She thinks very badly of him,' he confided to a friend, 'resents his conduct to his mother, and has more than once shown her resentment very plainly. He is intensely irritated at this treatment, being quite conscious of his position . . . She is very unmanageable about her conduct to her own relations; she will persist in considering William only as her grandson. But the matter has become political and very grave, and she must listen to advice.' Luckily Queen Victoria, the constitutional monarch, was bound to listen; Wilhelm, about to become the All-Highest Kaiser, was not.

On 24 April Queen Victoria confided to her Journal: 'After I had tidied myself up a bit, dear Vicky came and asked me to go and see dear Fritz. He was lying in bed, his dear face unaltered, and he raised up both his hands with pleasure at seeing me and gave me a nosegay. It was very touching and sad.' The following day Bismarck came to the palace to pay Queen Victoria a visit, and they had a private conversation in her room, mostly about Prince Wilhelm – or William, as she persisted in calling him. The Queen expressed her anxiety at his 'inexperience and his not having travelled at all.' Bismarck agreed, but thought that if and when he was 'thrown into the water' he would be able to swim. The Queen expressed surprise at finding Bismarck 'so amiable and gentle'. She soon had occasion to find out how misleading first impressions can be.

Kaiser Friedrich III died on 15 June at his beloved Neues Palais at Potsdam. 'I am broken-hearted,' Queen Victoria telegraphed her grandson, the new Kaiser. 'Help and do all you can for your poor dear Mother and try to follow in your best, noblest and kindest of father's footsteps.'

Kindness was not uppermost in Willy's mind. The moment his father died he put a long-laid plan into action. Major von Nutzmer, the officer in charge of the Guards Hussars, galloped round the perimeter of the palace shouting the order to lock all the gates. No one could enter or leave without a signed permit, not even the doctors. Every letter and parcel was opened and examined. Once everything was sealed off, guards officers waiting at strategic points inside the palace began systematically to ransack the rooms, searching for incriminating evidence of a liberal plot supposedly hatched by Kaiser Friedrich and his wife, the English Princess. They forced open every desk and searched every drawer for private papers. When the Minister of Justice, Heinrich Friedberg, arrived unexpectedly, he told Wilhelm that although it was true he had the power to do this, 'if you exercise the power, you will begin your reign badly.' This did nothing to deter Wilhelm, but his officers found nothing. Fritz and Vicky's private papers were already safe in England, stored at Buckingham Palace. They themselves had taken the first batch when they went to London for Queen Victoria's Jubilee. Most of the rest had been put in a chest and spirited out of the Potsdam palace by one of Dr Morell Mackenzie's junior doctors who handed them to Malet, the British Ambassador, on 13 June, just two days before Fritz died. A further batch had already been burnt by Vicky at San Remo.

The Prince of Wales attended the funeral, accompanied by the Princess of Wales and Prince Eddy. It was Alexandra's first visit to Berlin in eleven years. Queen Victoria confided to her Journal that she was 'greatly relieved to hear that dear Alix would go with Bertie to Berlin, as I begged her to.' The Princess did not go with good grace. She believed that Fritz, as Kaiser, had intended finally to make some reparation to Denmark, and now that chance was irretrievably lost. She quickly extended her hatred of Bismarck and Prussia to Willy, calling him 'that young fool William', and writing to Georgie, 'Instead of William being a comfort and support to her [his mother] he has quite gone over to Bismarck and Co. who entirely overlook and crush her. Which is too infamous.' Emotional Bertie, genuinely affected by the loss of his brother-in-law, also wrote to his sailor son: 'Try, my dear Georgy, never to forget Uncle Fritz. He was one of the finest and noblest characters ever known. If he had a fault, he was TOO good for this world.'

The Prince of Wales had every reason to feel distressed. Had the Crown Prince lived they would have made a perfect team in further-ing a liberal and democratic Europe. Bertie's would have been the ideal position, as brother-in-law of the Kaiser on one side and the Tsar on the other, enjoying happy and fruitful relationships with both. Both the Kaiser and the Tsar had real power. Bertie himself, once King, had little real power, but plenty of influence. Had Fritz lived there would certainly have been a battle with Bismarck, but the German Constitution, drawn up by Bismarck himself, invested the Kaiser with the ultimate power, and the Liberals and Social Democrats were already gaining ground in the Reichstag. Between 1870 and 1910 the urban population in Berlin alone increased from near 800,000 to more than two million. In 1891 there were 344,000 Trade Union members in the Reich; by 1913, just before the outbreak of the First World War, there were 3,024,000. Had Fritz lived, the English influence might well have prevailed over the Prussian.

After Friedrich III's funeral the Prince of Wales made a careless mistake: he raised the issue of Denmark with Herbert von Bismarck, disingenuously wondering aloud whether Kaiser Friedrich had intended to make some reparation for the loss of Schleswig-Holstein. It went down very badly indeed. Wilhelm was infuriated by what he saw as his uncle's interference and took the opportunity of scotching any rumours in a rousing speech he made at Frankfurt an der Oder that August, calling Bertie's remarks 'intolerable insults' and insisting that his father would never have yielded a single gain won by 'the Prussian sword'. The fact was, the tables had been turned. Willy was top dog now, his uncle still no more than an heir, waiting idly in the wings. Bertie took to calling his nephew 'William the Great'. Willy, for his part, called his uncle 'the Old Peacock'.

Queen Victoria waited in vain for a letter from her grandson the Kaiser following the death of his father. 'But as you have not written I will just send you a few lines by the messenger,' she wrote on 3 July 1888. After broaching the delicate subject of where his 'poor dear Mama' would now live, she came to the main purpose of her letter: 'There are many rumours of your going and paying visits to Sovereigns. I hope that at least you will let some months pass before anything of this kind takes place, as it is not three weeks yet since dear beloved Papa was taken, and we are all still in such deep mourning for him.' There was no good news on either score. Willy quickly forced 'poor dear Mama' to move out of the Neues Palais so that he might move in himself, and within a few weeks he had embarked on his first State Visit, to Russia, quickly followed by Vienna and Rome, heedless of the advice of his wise old grandmother, to whom he began to refer as 'the Empress of Hindoustan' to amuse his England-hating friends.

'How sickening it is to see Willy, not two months after his beloved and noble father's death, going to banquets and reviews!' wrote Queen Victoria to Bertie. 'It is very indecent and unfeeling!' Very true, thought the disconsolate Prince, who had retreated to Sandringham for the duration of the long period of Court mourning. The Princess of Wales contemplated Vicky's 'lonely life and terribly sad' and counted herself lucky. In contrast to the bitterness and intrigue in Berlin, life in England was pleasant indeed. 'We are a most happy family and I thank God for having given me such good and affectionate children who are my real comfort in this world,' she wrote to Georgie. Georgie, home at Sandringham on Christmas leave, wrote simply in his diary on the last day of 1888: 'Goodbye dear old diary & don't let anyone read you. You are full now, so I shall not write in you any more.'

In Berlin the much more complicated royal cousin Willy had started as he meant to go on: as the Autocrat, answerable to no one but God. Sergei Witte, now one of the most powerful statesmen in Tsarist Russia, had already noted Wilhelm's attitude to emperors when he met him during his second visit to the Tsar at the military manoeuvres at Brest in 1886. 'The scene at Brest, minor but revealing, is etched in my memory,' he wrote in his memoirs, and went on to describe it. Alexander III, wearing his Prussian uniform beneath a Russian military greatcoat, alighted from the Imperial train, handing the greatcoat to an attendant Cossack: 'Upon completion of the greetings by the ceremonial honour guard, the Emperor shouted for his greatcoat. At that, Wilhelm, who understood a few words of Russian, dashed over to the Cossack, snatched the greatcoat out of his hands, carried it back, and placed it around the Emperor's shoulders.' Witte had already seen Wilhelm behaving in much the same way with his grandfather the Kaiser, obsequiously helping him with his correspondence 'like an office boy', and he deduced from these incidents that Wilhelm had an almost holy reverence for Emperors. 'He holds the opinion that an Emperor is a superman,' he concluded.

At dinner that evening in Brest Witte had observed another side to Prince Wilhelm. He was 'foppish', he noted, 'the typical Prussian guards officer, with his turned-up moustache, his mannerisms in walking, his affected elegance.' And now, quite unexpectedly, the foppish guards officer was himself the Kaiser, and all his defects seemed to multiply overnight. Wilhelm could not wait to exercise his autocratic powers, and the vulnerable young man Rathenau had spotted became increasingly lost in an elaborate masquerade of masculinity and Imperial might. The clique of flattering monarchists who surrounded him did nothing to prevent this – a highly dangerous tactic when dealing with a man of Wilhelm's neurotic personality, boastful and posturing on the outside, nervy and impressionable on the inside, as many of them would soon have cause to discover.

8

Willy, the Kaiser

~

WILHELM'S FIRST ACT as Kaiser was to issue three Proclamations, the first to the Prussian Army, of which he was now the Supreme Commander, the second to the Navy, and the last to the Prussian people. 'It is with deep emotion that I first address myself to my Army,' declared Wilhelm II. 'We belong to one another, I and the Army. We were indeed born for one another, and therefore let us always hold firmly together, whether God ordains peace or storm.' In case someone missed the point, he changed the name of the Army headquarters from Maison Militaire to Hauptquartier Seiner Majestat. The Navy, which was almost non-existent, he addressed in similar style: 'It is with deep emotion that I have to inform the Navy that today, at five minutes past eleven o'clock in the forenoon, my dear father, His Majesty the German Emperor and King of Prussia, Frederick III, gently fell asleep in the Lord, and that, in assuming the position destined for me by the will of God, the government of my ancestral lands and with it the chief command of the Navy, has passed into My hands.' Everything, it seemed, was now His. So, lastly, he addressed 'My People', again invoking 'the Throne of my Ancestors' and bowing only to 'the King of Kings'. He waited another week before addressing the Reichstag. Wilhelm's autocratic streak was already in evidence, presenting the German Government with a problem they failed again and again to solve.

In England the liberal and socialist press saw the problem clearly. *Truth* on 21 June 1888 wrote that Germany's aim should now be to alter and amend her constitution, to be dictated thenceforward by the people, 'and not by a single individual who – the accident of an accident – happens to be on the throne. Here with us the Monarch reigns, but does not rule. This should be the case in Germany.' *Justice* on 30 June put it more vividly, describing the system in Germany as 'jackboot Junkerism of the most brutal type', and pointing out that

'William II is said to hate England and Englishmen. But what William hates in us is that modicum of real liberty which our fathers conquered for us.'

Lord Salisbury, now Prime Minister, was equally worried. In the summer of 1888 he received a visit from a doctor named Erichsen who brought with him a medical report written in the 1870s when Prince Wilhelm, still an adolescent, was once again suffering from the ear problem caused at his birth. The report concluded that the damage to his inner ear, so close to his brain, was a possible reason for Wilhelm's 'sudden accesses of anger' which prevented his 'forming a reasonable or temperate judgement'. From then on, whenever there was another outburst from the Kaiser, Salisbury would be seen to tap his head and mutter the word 'Erichsen'. He summarised the problem for Queen Victoria: 'It is nevertheless true, most unhappily, that all Prince Wilhelm's impulses, however blameable and unreasonable, will henceforth be political causes of enormous potency.'

Knowing his mother's hatred of all Prussians, Georgie, still on the high seas, commented with some amusement on Willy's antics, now that he was Kaiser: 'I see William is now going to Vienna & Rome. I suppose he considers that he has not shown himself sufficiently yet, he must have been to nearly every capital in Europe by this time except London, & I don't think he will come there, what do you think? Whatever he may think of himself, he is much too frightened to do that.'

This was a fundamental misunderstanding of cousin Willy on Georgie's part, and to that extent a presentiment of things to come. Georgie, the most simple and straightforward of the three cousins, could not 'read' Willy, who was certainly the most complicated and unpredictable. Georgie's letter referred to the Battenberg row which had broken out when Willy was still plain Prince Wilhelm of Prussia and ranged against his uncle Bertie, Georgie's father, who was Prince of Wales, heir to the greatest throne on earth. But now that Willy was Kaiser, neither his grandmother nor his uncle Bertie held any fears for him.

Wilhelm's first impulse was to replace Army personnel and Court officials he did not like or trust with people who were part of his own clique. Foremost among the favoured was General Count von Waldersee, one of the first to be admitted to the Imperial presence on the day Friedrich III died, who now became Chief of the General

Staff. Wilhelm von Hahnke, related to the Bülows, became Chief of the Military Cabinet, and Liebenau got the post of Grand Marshal of the Court, managing its entire expenditure, including ceremonies, travel, and 76 royal palaces and 500 servants. Beneath the Grand Marshal came the Marshal of the Household, in charge of personal family matters, then the Marshal of the Court who managed the royal kitchens, the forty cooks, the dinners and the banquets, and the House Marshal who concerned himself exclusively with the royal possessions. Each had an extensive subsidiary staff. The Grand Marshal presented himself to the Kaiser at nine o'clock every morning, whether at home or abroad, to plan the day. At least two of the Marshals accompanied the Kaiser everywhere on his travels, and these grew so numerous that people were soon dubbing him 'the travelling Kaiser'.

'Things began to hum at the palace,' recalled the anonymous Court official, now transferred from Empress Frederick's service to that of the Kaiser. 'The retinue and the household were increased by numbers innumerable. An idea of the food consumed daily there, exclusive of State dinners, may be gained from the following items. This was the amount of meat for one day's consumption when there were no visitors: 100 lbs of beef; 200 lbs of mutton and pork, each; 350 lbs of veal; 10 pickled ox-tongues; 4 calves' heads. Fish, poultry, game and vegetables were in the same proportion, and butter was often used at the same rate of 100 lbs a day.' The Kaiser's palace in Berlin had 650 rooms, and the kitchens were a mile away from the dining hall, so that a soufflé could never be served because, as he explained, it would have fallen flat long before it arrived. From his humble position in the Imperial household he could not fail to notice how Wilhelm now treated his mother, swiftly relegating her to the sidelines, often ignoring her completely. 'The widowed Empress suffered in silence, but she did suffer horribly from the treatment she received from her eldest son, from Bismarck and his party.'

As it turned out, Bismarck himself was heading for trouble. In 1871 he had fashioned a Constitution for the new German Empire which gave the Kaiser autocratic powers, secure in the knowledge that Wilhelm I would always heed his Chancellor's advice and act accordingly. But now Bismarck found that the omnipotent new Kaiser, keenly encouraged by his entourage, was taking those powers literally, and listening less and less to his Chancellor. Wilhelm's Chiefs of Cabinet, both military and civil, were soon ordered to report direct to him or General von Waldersee, bypassing Bismarck. Since the Cabinets also selected the personnel of the officer corps on the one hand and the bureaucracy on the other, their power was immense. As for the Government, Wilhelm the Autocrat rarely bothered to see any of his ministers, calling them 'a bunch of noodles'. Instead there was a proliferation of *Immediatstellen*, advisers who had the right to see the Kaiser without a minister being present. Wilhelm was always surrounded by a posse of uniformed ADCs, and it became almost impossible to penetrate the wall they created around him. He took to seconding spare ADCs on overseas postings as military attachés to Germany's embassies, from where they reported directly back to him, bypassing the ambassadors. It did nothing to endear the Kaiser to the diplomats at Wilhelmstrasse.

But Bismarck was still too powerful to beat. When Wilhelm tried to appoint his friend Eulenburg Prussian Ambassador in Munich, one of the top diplomatic posts, Bismarck held his ground, writing to his son Herbert that although he liked Eulenburg personally, 'in the political field he's got no eye for what's important or unimportant, and he listens to carping gossip, which he then passes on, which gets people needlessly annoyed.' Eulenburg was fit for the smaller diplomatic postings, Oldenburg or Braunschweig or Lippe, but for a major posting such as Munich was 'impossible'. As a shrewd assessment of the favourite's essential mediocrity, it did not augur well for the future.

Eulenburg himself had no real wish for promotion. He was not even sure he wanted to forsake an artistic life for a political one, but in effect the matter had already been decided for him by his political allies who, for the time being at least, needed him close to the Kaiser, as the Kaiser's best friend. 'I have known for a long time', wrote Herbert von Bismarck to his father on 5 October 1888, 'that HM loves Phil Eulenburg more than any other living person.' He thus had all the power and the influence they could wish, all the better for it not being exercised in the public eye. Essentially unconstitutional, bypassing all the usual constraints and scrutinies of Government, Eulenburg's power continued as it had begun, hidden in the shadows, where he could carry on his private life as he wished.

Willy's already strained relationships with his extended family were not improved by his England-hating entourage. Herbert von Bismarck was active in stirring up the German press against England in general and the Prince of Wales in particular. Wilhelm himself remained ambivalent, hating England one minute and loving her the next. The previous autumn he had refused to meet his uncle in Vienna, but now he wished to follow his state visits to St Petersburg, Vienna and Rome with one to England. Lord Salisbury, always concerned that family quarrels should not disrupt the delicate business of international politics, went to the Prince of Wales at Marlborough House. He told the Prince that the German Ambassador had offered the excuse that the Kaiser was not in Vienna to meet him because it might have aroused Russian suspicions 'at a moment when matters were very delicate, without offering to Germany any substantial compensation in the shape of a genuine English alliance.'

It was true that Salisbury was unwilling to enter into a formal alliance with Germany for fear of jeopardising England's relations with France. But privately Bertie knew quite well that Willy had simply wanted to show that he, as Kaiser, was the master now. The ambassador had added that the Prince had offended Wilhelm by treating him 'as an uncle treats a nephew, instead of recognising that he was an Emperor.' 'Oh he is mad and a conceited ass,' wrote the Princess of Wales to Georgie, 'who also says that Papa and Grandmama don't treat him with proper respect as the EMPEROR of old and mighty Germany. But my hope is that pride will have a fall some day and won't we rejoice then!' Salisbury added when talking to the Prince of Wales that the Kaiser seemed to be 'a little off his head' and 'not quite all there'.

The Prince of Wales took it well enough, happy to agree that William the Great was probably 'a little off his head'. Queen Victoria was quite another matter. She reverted to her capital letters, describing it to Salisbury as 'PERFECT MADNESS' that Willy wished to be treated as 'His Imperial Majesty' in private as well as in public. It was 'really TOO VULGAR and too absurd, as well as untrue, almost TO BE BELIEVED,' adding, 'IF he has SUCH notions, he had better NEVER come HERE. The Queen will not swallow this affront.'

Salisbury insisted that the Kaiser's State Visit to England would have to take place. The Prince of Wales insisted that unless Willy apologised, he would not be able to meet him. Finally the Queen, urged by Salisbury, sent her grandson a mildly conciliatory letter, to which William the Great airily replied, 'The whole thing is a fixed idea which originated either in Uncle Bertie's imagination, or in somebody else's. Who put it into his head? I am very glad to hear that this affair has come to an end.' Francis Knollys, Bertie's devoted

Private Secretary, was outraged, saying that the Prince of Wales had been sacrificed by Salisbury for 'political expediency'. Herbert von Bismarck noted that Wilhelm was 'almost in ecstasy, like a child on Christmas Eve', when the news came through that his visit to England was to go ahead after all.

The visit took place, and the Prince of Wales was persuaded to forgo his apology, agreeing that his absence would have caused unhelpful gossip and comment in the press of both countries. In this he was well advised, advice he accepted with his usual good grace, putting the matter behind him. In a small way, it was an illustration of the effective workings of constitutional government, the kind Willy needed more than most, but did not have. In a great show of neighbourly friendliness Bertie even went to greet the Kaiser at Spithead, accompanied by both Prince Eddy and Prince George, now a lieutenant in the Royal Navy. Willy arrived in his new Imperial Yacht *Hohenzollern*, escorted by twelve units of the emergent German Navy. Ever since his holidays in England as a child he had been fascinated by the splendour of the Royal Navy, reaching across the globe, bringing trade and prosperity and protecting Britain's interests throughout her Empire. Germany might have the most powerful Army in the world but her navy was small, a shortcoming Wilhelm meant to put right as soon as possible. Unaware of Willy's grand ambitions for a German navy powerful enough to rival Britain's, the Queen was induced to indulge the Kaiser by awarding him the honorary rank of Admiral of the Fleet. Willy was doubly thrilled: not only was he a British admiral, but he could add a fine uniform to his collection.

If the Kaiser and the Prince of Wales shared one thing, it was a liking for a good uniform, and at Spithead uncle and nephew, so recently at loggerheads, greeted one another warmly, each splendidly attired as an Admiral of the Royal Navy. The visit went off better than anyone might have expected. Willy could be most charming when he wished, and now that he was on English soil, he wished. The Prince of Wales, equally charming, agreed to visit Berlin the following January for the Kaiser's birthday. 'The visit here is going off quite well,' Queen Victoria wrote to her granddaughter Victoria, married to Louis of Battenberg, on 7 August 1889, 'though it is very hard to swallow the horrid Herbert Bismarck who everyone dislikes . . . Willy is quite amiable; he is grown very large and puffed in the face. He seems pleased with everything.'

The Queen was right. Suddenly Wilhelm *was* pleased with everything English again. The word 'gentleman' again peppered his sen-
tences, and the English country house again epitomised everything
desirable in attractive living. He decided his Berlin Court was stuffy
and provincial and should from now on be more like the English
Court, conducted with easy elegance and sophistication. He made a
start by ordering the same silk stockings for his footmen as those
worn by the footmen at Buckingham Palace. Herbert von Bismarck
noted sourly that the Kaiser had returned home a complete
Anglophile.

In June 1889 Georgie was briefly back in London for the HMS
Bacchante Old Ship Dinner, named among the list of officers present
as Lieut HRH Prince George of Wales. The menu for the dinner has
a time-honoured predictability to it: Consommé, Whitebait, Saddle
of Lamb, Asparagus, Gooseberry Tart and, to round things off,
Anchovy Canapés. In October he joined his parents, Eddy, his sisters
and his Danish grandparents at another grand family reunion, this
time a royal wedding in Athens. 'Friday Oct. 25th. The Palace.
Athens. Got up at 8.30. Breakfast at 9.30' his diary for that day begins.
Everyone set off to Piraeus to meet the next Royal Yacht, the
Amphitrite, bearing Aunt Vicky from Germany with her four daugh-
ters, including Sophia, the bride-to-be, who was marrying Prince
Constantine of Greece, known in the family as Tino. 'Sophie met
with a splendid reception everywhere, great crowds, town decorated,'
Georgie noted in commendable shorthand. The next day there was
another trip to Piraeus 'in full dress', this time to meet Willy and
Dona, and Willy's brother Prince Heinrich, for the time being known
as Henry. The reception committee boarded the Imperial Yacht
Hohenzollern before everyone returned to Athens and a royal procession through the streets to the Palace. 'William brought 67 gentlemen
with him, a pity he didn't bring a few more,' Georgie told his diary
with unusually sharp humour, revealing his true feelings, but only in
private.

Willy arrived wearing his British Admiral's uniform and, forgetting
that his rank was no more than honorary, proceeded to offer his
English relations some words of advice on Britain's naval strength in
the Mediterranean – he deemed it dangerously low. After dinner
en famille, everyone sat about listening to the band for a time before
retiring to their rooms. Upstairs Georgie talked till after midnight

with Eddy and their Danish, Greek and Russian cousins, including Nicky, the Tsarevich, who had arrived from Russia. There is no mention of the other cousin, Willy.

In Germany the new Kaiser had been hyperactive with plans since his accession, no detail too small for his attention. He tightened up Court and military etiquette, firing off memos to heads of departments. He redesigned uniforms. He spent millions of Marks on schemes to extend his palaces. He commissioned a new Imperial train, all pastels and creams, with eleven carriages, a fully-equipped kitchen, a dining carriage with a table long enough to seat twenty-four guests, two sleeping carriages for the gentlemen, two more for the ladies, another for servants, and two day saloons with armchairs, sofas and writing desks, with two more saloons for his own personal use, only occasionally to be shared by the Kaiserin. The people were soon joking that the national anthem 'Heil Dir im Siegerkranz' (Hail to Thee in Thy Laurel Crown of Victory) would be changed to 'Heil Dir im Sonderzug' (Hail to Thee in Thy Royal Train).

But Willy's grandest commission remained the Imperial Yacht *Hohenzollern*. Bearing the name of the Prussian Royal House, and splendid enough to compete with those belonging to his relations in England and Russia, it had been built in the Kiel shipyard. It was the largest private yacht afloat, with cabins for up to eighty guests and staff, serviced by a permanent body of 350 sailors who were each required to play at least one musical instrument as well as perform all their usual duties. The hull was cream decorated with gold, the two funnels belching out the smoke from the hundreds of tons of coal consumed by the two massive boilers down below. On the upper four decks there were kitchens, dining rooms and salons filled with heavily stuffed furniture, as well as the Kaiser's own splendid personal suite. The technology was ultra-modern, with electric lighting and German tiled ovens providing central heating. The upper deck was large enough for the Kaiser to lead his guests in morning gymnastics, an activity he particularly enjoyed on his annual, exclusively male North Sea cruises. He insisted on even the oldest generals turning out, slapping them heartily on the back for encouragement, and hooting with laughter as they struggled to keep up. In another role, as head of the German Protestant Church, he liked to take the morning service, giving the sermon himself. At other times of day it was pleasant to sit on deck, everyone in their uniforms, smoking cigars, listening to the band, and enjoying the camaraderie of close friendship, surrounded by his dogs, a pack of royal dachshunds.

In March 1890 Prince George accompanied his father and Eddy on a State Visit to Berlin. His mother stayed at home. They took with them a list of German princesses compiled by Queen Victoria, hoping to find a bride for Prince Eddy. Hopeless Eddy had been commissioned into the Tenth Hussars but was, in the words of the Duke of Cambridge, Commander-in-Chief of the Army, 'Never ready, never there'. It was clear to everyone that Eddy needed a wife. Princess Margaret, the Kaiser's youngest sister, was high on the list, but Mossy, as she was known in the family, was not pretty enough for dashing Eddy, and in any case seems to have declined the honour. The same applied to Princess Alexandra of Hesse, Queen Victoria's favourite granddaughter, who later married Nicky, the Tsarevich. Despite the prospect of the greatest throne on earth, no one seemed keen to marry 'Collar and Cuffs', as the Prince of Wales liked to call his vain son teasingly. Eddy was reputed to visit a homosexual brothel in Cleveland Street, but he also had a girl in St John's Wood. 'She's a ripper,' wrote his brother Georgie in his diary, which suggests that he too shared the lady's favours. That year, to prepare Eddy for his future role and provide him with a seat in the House of Lords, Queen Victoria had created him Duke of Clarence and Avondale.

The Kaiser awarded his cousin Prince George the Order of the Black Eagle, along with five others. The ceremony was at 11.45. 'We were brought in by a Knight and after making three bows to William, the statutes were read out,' Georgie noted with careful attention to detail. 'We then put our right hands on the book and said "*Ja, ich glaube es*" & then our robes were put on . . . [William] put the collar on & kissed us three times . . . Heralds played "fanfares" all the time.' That evening he wrote a long letter to his mother. The next day there was a church service for all those who had received the Order of the Black Eagle, and in the afternoon William made Georgie a Captain in Grandmama's Dragoon Regiment. 'I tried on the uniform,' Georgie noted with some satisfaction, and went off to have his photograph taken with Eddy, he in his uniform, Eddy in the uniform of the Blücher Hussars, of which he was Honorary Colonel.

None of this pleased Georgie's mother. 'And so my Georgie boy has become a real live filthy blue-coated *Pickelhaube* German soldier!!!' she wrote, high on exclamation marks. 'Well I never thought to have lived to see THAT! But never mind; as you say, it could not have been helped – it was your misfortune and not your fault – and anything was better – even my two boys being sacrificed!!! – than Papa being made a German Admiral – that I could not have survived – you would have had to look for your poor old Motherdear at the bottom of the sea, the first time he adorned himself with it!' The Prince of Wales took the opportunity to remind his mother the Queen that the visit had left him somewhat out of pocket. 'When you next write to him [William] please thank him, as he has treated me quite like a Sovereign and considered my visit as in your name – in fact as your representative, and I am very sorry to say that my expenses, in consequence, have been heavy.'

Gladstone, Leader of the Opposition, had helped to persuade the House of Commons to raise the Prince of Wales's annual income to £36,000 and to vote him a further sum of £60,000 to help with his expenses. The Radicals were in uproar. Five per cent of the labouring poor had been forced to leave England for the colonies and America, scraping together the fare of £6 for the ten-day voyage to Boston. Workers were forming themselves into trade unions, to force employers to improve their pay and working conditions; the well-organised dockers' strike of the previous year had resulted in a significant increase in Trade Union membership. And now, in the midst of this hardship and struggle, the Prince of Wales was voted an extra £60,000 as well as a thumping rise to his annual income, all supported by the Leader of the Opposition. It was a disgrace. The Prince of Wales agreed. It was nothing like enough to cover his debts.

On 18 March 1890 the Kaiser, headier and headier with power, astonished the world by dismissing his Chancellor, Otto von Bismarck. The Kaiser's subjects were stunned. Bismarck was their hero. No one could believe it. No one except Waldersee and Eulenburg, who had orchestrated the event with the help of wily Friedrich von Holstein at the Foreign Office. Each had his reasons for wanting to be rid of Bismarck. Waldersee wanted power, and saw Bismarck's fall as his chance. Eulenburg and his friends, known as the Liebenberg Circle after Eulenburg inherited the estate at Liebenberg in East Prussia from his father, were ideologues who believed in an absolute monarchy with power vested solely in the Kaiser, not in the Chancellor, and certainly not in Parliament. Only Holstein, who had carefully maintained a correspondence with Eulenburg since the early days of his role as the Kaiser's best friend, perhaps had mixed motives. As a senior Foreign Office man he knew that maintaining the balance of power in international affairs was critical – and the only way to ensure that was to attempt to control the increasingly uncontrollable Kaiser. Holstein's chosen route was through Eulenburg. Wilhelm, of course, thought he had done it all on his own. But as soon as news of Bismarck's dismissal reached St Petersburg, Alexander III began negotiations for a Franco-Russian alliance. As the Tsar had told Bismarck in 1889, 'I certainly have full trust in you, but unfortunately your Kaiser gives others his ear, especially General Waldersee, who wants war. That we are certain of.'

Bismarck's dismissal was preceded by many clashes with the Kaiser. In the first year of his reign Wilhelm had favoured a softening of social policy in Home Affairs, probably influenced by his old tutor Hinzpeter, who liked to send his former pupil long tracts on social issues and was always admitted at once to the royal presence if he went to Berlin. In May 1889 the Krupp works at Essen were forced to close down because of a strike by coal miners, and troops were called in to maintain order. The miners were demanding higher pay, an eight-hour day, no work on Sundays, and better conditions for women and children. To Bismarck's dismay Wilhelm invited the strike leaders to the palace to put their case. They must have been confused when he warned them not to have anything to do with the Social Democrats, and followed this with one of his flamboyant speeches. His mother the Dowager Empress watched her son's antics with horror. 'The strike of coal miners is a very serious thing!' she wrote to her mother at Windsor. 'I was more than horrified at William's speech. Wm told the men that if they had anything to do with the Social Democrats "Ich werde Euch allen uber den Haufen schiessen lassen (I'll have you all shot)". It's just like him! He uses *les gros mots* wherever he can and thinks himself very grand! I think such words in the mouth of a Sovereign, and so young and inexperienced a man, most brutal and unbecoming.' Wilhelm's language grew increasingly alarming. Soon he was calling the Reichstag 'that pigsty' and the Social Democrats 'that rabble who shit in their pants'.

More strikes threatened. Bismarck insisted that the current Anti-Socialist Law be extended to include an Exclusion Bill which could exile socialist agitators to the countryside. When the Kaiser resisted, Bismarck threatened to resign. The real issue was, who held the power in Germany, the Kaiser or the Chancellor? By February 1890 Bismarck was again offering his resignation, not realising that Wilhelm, with the help of Holstein and Eulenburg, had already chosen his successor – General Leo von Caprivi, whom the Kaiser had summoned to Berlin on 1 February. By mid February Bismarck was seriously considering a *coup d'état*, to force the Kaiser into line. He told Malet, the British Ambassador in Berlin, that although the Kaiser was still friendly towards him, 'he wishes himself to govern . . . He has no doubts. He thinks he can do all things and he wishes to have the entire credit all to himself.' Malet swiftly repeated this to Salisbury, adding that Wilhelm himself had complained to Malet that Bismarck treated him 'like a schoolboy'.

The final act came when Bismarck, calling on a Cabinet Order of 1852, reminded ministers that no one other than the War Minister could have an audience with the Kaiser or send him reports without the Chancellor's permission. After another great row Wilhelm ordered Bismarck to hand in his resignation; he did so on 19 March, and the Kaiser accepted it. Bismarck and his wife left Berlin for Friedrichsruh, their estate near Hamburg, on 29 March. The streets were lined with thousands of well-wishers who had come to show their respect and love for the Chancellor who had made Germany great. At the railway station the entire diplomatic corps was lined up, along with numerous officials and a guard of honour. Bismarck was presented with two flower arrangements personally designed by the Kaiser. But the Kaiser himself was absent.

'I am sorry to say poor Dona is not a help but an obstacle,' Vicky wrote to Queen Victoria. 'Her pride is so great that she thinks she knows better than everyone, because she is the Empress, and she is always on the defensive, and ridiculously *exigeante*. The flattery that is lavished on both of them is enough to turn any lady's head and it is no wonder hers is turned . . . They have not a single wise or steady head about them; some very respectable and well-meaning people, others who are dangerous and intriguing, but not a single superior man or woman.'

By May Prince George had assumed command of HMS *Thrush*, a first-class gunboat, bound for Jamaica. He was due to be absent from home for over a year. It was particularly galling to hear that the Kaiser had paid a visit to Copenhagen, his own favourite destination. 'I see William the Fidgety has just been to Copenhagen, what the devil does he want to go there for,' he wrote to his mother in July, 'he must always be racing about somewhere interfering in other people's business which does not concern him.' Queen Victoria meanwhile was extending her match-making efforts to Georgie. 'I quite agree with you, dearest Grandmama & understand your reasons for wishing Eddy & I to marry as soon as possible,' Georgie wrote diplomatically in February 1891 from Jamaica. 'But still I think marrying too young is a bad thing, but I don't call Eddy too young, he is 27 . . . One thing I never could do is to marry a person that didn't care for me. I should be miserable for the rest of my life.'

Eighteen ninety-one was a bad year for the Prince of Wales. First there was a gambling scandal involving a young man named Gordon-Cumming, who had been caught cheating at baccarat. The Prince of Wales had not been playing, but he was present. The British public felt he was setting a bad example to the young. Then came a scandal surrounding the beautiful and clever Lady Brooke, a leading member of the Marlborough House Set and one of the Prince's favourites, who had an affair with Lord Charles Beresford, another member of the Set. The Prince took Lady Brooke's part and thereby fell out with the Beresfords, who were now reconciled. 'People are beginning to ask themselves how much more evil the Prince of Wales will work in an endeavour to deteriorate Society, which is already at a low ebb,' commented Lady Charles. Rumours of the scandal quickly spread to Denmark where the Princess of Wales was staying as usual with her parents and Minny and Sasha and their children. On the spur of the moment she decided to teach her 'naughty little man' a lesson: she would not to return to England in October, but travel with the Tsar and Tsarina to their palace at Livadia in the Crimea to celebrate their silver wedding anniversary.

Prince George, on home leave, made his way to Denmark for the summer. From Copenhagen he wrote a dutiful letter to his grandmother, keeping her up to date with the news but certainly not the scandal. 'My dearest Grandmama,' he wrote, 'I received my Commander's Commission with which I am delighted; I have been a Lieutenant for nearly six years and I served nearly all that time abroad in eight different ships . . . I was delighted to see all the many relations again. Apapa and Amama [his Danish grandparents] are wonderful, they do not look a day older. Uncle Sacha and aunt Minny arrived on Monday, they are all very well. Nicky was quite delighted with his visit to India and has told me all about it.' Nicky was twenty-three, Georgie twenty-six. The future Tsar of Russia and the future King of England always had plenty to talk about.

It was a disconsolate Prince of Wales who celebrated his fiftieth birthday at Sandringham on 9 November, alone, attended only by his two sons Eddy and Georgie. Three days later Georgie suddenly developed a high temperature. The Prince of Wales quickly had him transferred to Marlborough House where he could receive the best medical attention. Typhoid was diagnosed. A telegram to Livadia brought the Princess of Wales racing across Europe with her three daughters to arrive in London on 22 November, all thoughts of the quarrel with her husband forgotten. By then the crisis was almost over and Georgie was soon on the mend. At the end of December he was able to return to 'dear old Sandringham' in the happy knowledge that his parents were reunited. 'Thank God English George is now better,' Minny the Tsarina wrote from Russia to her brother Willi, the King of Greece, who also had a son called George, not to be confused with her own Georgei.

In Berlin, Herbert von Bismarck saw no possibility of continuing as Secretary of State at the Foreign Office now that his father had gone. He was swiftly replaced by the Prussian envoy to Baden, Baron Adolf Marschall von Bieberstein, another of Holstein's men who had been waiting in the wings. What the Bismarcks did not know was that Friedrich von Holstein had written to Eulenburg on 11 March telling him to go to Berlin as soon as possible to advise the Kaiser correctly through the chaotic days leading up to the Chancellor's dismissal. Marschall von Bieberstein had also written to him. Eulenburg had already met Caprivi in Hanover, on 6 March. Everything was falling into place just as planned. Hermann von Lucanus, the Civil Cabinet Chief, was already in his post. But Eduard von Liebenau, Marshal of the Court, who had served Wilhelm for years, was now a problem. As Waldersee told Eulenburg, 'He serves at the same time and even more [than the Kaiser] the house of Bismarck and is therefore a traitor.' He was swiftly replaced by Count August zu Eulenburg, brother of Botho zu Eulenburg, the Minister of the Interior, and cousin of Philipp zu Eulenburg. In fact, August zu Eulenburg turned out to be brilliant at the job, cleverly keeping in the background, from which position he was quietly influential. Still in his job in 1918, he was the only person in Wilhelm's entourage consistently advising him not to abdicate.

As for Philipp zu Eulenburg, for a man not sure he wanted to be in politics, he was doing remarkably well. Only two years earlier, when Wilhelm came to power so unexpectedly, he had written disingenuously: 'I am tortured by the thought that the gulf which separates us socially but which our friendship has bridged, must, with the Imperial Crown, become ever wider and deeper.' He need not have worried. Quickly reassured by Willy, he wrote: 'How happy it makes me to be able to write so frankly to you. You understand everything that concerns me – serious matters, raillery, duty, learning, art, each neatly separated from the others yet each entirely comprehended. Thus you are and so I hope also to remain, and God will give us His blessing so to be if we in all our affairs are convinced that we can reach the highest only through Him.'

The effusive tone is typical of the letters Eulenburg wrote to Wilhelm. Isabel Hull, in her study of the Kaiser's entourage, argues convincingly that many of the letters between the intimate male friends of the Liebenberg Circle were written in a form of code, enabling them to talk 'frankly' to one another about things other people did not understand, and would perhaps not countenance. But that did not matter, because He the Liebling understands, and gives His blessing. They talk about their 'real' selves, their '*Eigenart*', their uniqueness or individuality, and describe their friendships as being on a higher, idealised plane, far above the crude judgements of the insensitive rabble. Wilhelm himself had described his youth to Eulenburg as 'such horrible years when no one understood my individuality'. 'Individuality' most often meant 'sexuality'.

Eulenburg's letters were his way of influencing Wilhelm, privately and secretly. In the spring of 1894 he explained his method of handling the Kaiser to Lucanus, likening it to a game of tennis. 'He lets me say anything to him about politics, precisely because I play tennis with him, and between flying balls and during short intervals in the play, I have the Kaiser's ear, and in a good mood, so he's predisposed to giving his consent to difficult matters, and with good humour. *Ludere pro patria et imperatore* (Play the game for your country and your Emperor)! Mad world!'

The place to play the game was not in Berlin, where his presence would be noted, but from a distance, and by letter. By 1894 Eulenburg had secured the post of Prussian Ambassador in Vienna, with some help from Friedrich von Holstein, who briefed him carefully for a meeting with the Austrian Foreign Minister in Vienna, and after the meeting helped him prepare a report for the Kaiser. Wilhelm noted that it was 'the first sensible and interesting report to come out of Vienna for a long time'. Eulenburg's letters were reinforced by private meetings and fleeting visits to Berlin whenever Holstein or Marschall von Bieberstein, and later Bülow, thought some matter particularly urgent. But most effective of all were the three occasions in the year when Wilhelm and Eulenburg spent time together away from Berlin in the intimate atmosphere of the Liebenberg Circle. In May there was the annual celebration of Wilhelm and Phili's first meeting at Prokelwitz. The *Nordlandreise*, or North Sea cruises, took place every June on the Imperial Yacht *Hohenzollern*. And in the autumn there was the annual visit to Eulenburg's estate at Liebenberg for the *Kaiserjagt*, the Kaiser Hunt, followed by another at Rominten, the royal hunting lodge. There were no women present on these occasions, only favoured male friends, mostly members of the Liebenberg Circle. These included the Eulenburg brothers, August and Botho, Alfred von Bülow, Bernhard's brother, and his long-standing friend Karl von Dornberg, Kuno von Moltke and Axel von Varnbüler, Eberhard von Dohna who had had an 'intimate relationship', as his brother described it, with Eulenburg since their schooldays, Emil Görtz zu Schlitz who had known Wilhelm since Hinzpeter introduced them as boys, and Georg von Hülsen-Haeseler, who became director of the royal theatre, first at Wiesbaden and later at Berlin.

Phili and Wilhelm had adjoining cabins on *Hohenzollern* and adjoining rooms at Rominten, where Willy kept a photograph of Phili on his desk. Other photographs show large groups of hearty men, all in uniform, even on *Hohenzollern*, or in green hunting dress with jaunty feathered hats at Rominten. The mood was one of jovial pranks and coarse jokes, with Wilhelm slapping people's backs, digging them in the ribs, chasing them about the corridors, drilling them in stiff morning exercises, and cutting their braces with scissors when they were not looking. Anyone not used to such antics would surely have agreed with Lord Salisbury's assessment that the Kaiser was 'a little off his head'. But instead of calming this misplaced exuberance, Eulenburg and the other members of the Liebenberg Circle played up to it, holding on to their power. They laughed heartily at all Wilhelm's pranks, agreed with everything he said, and listened to his endless talk, for by now he could hardly stop talking. Their only problem was to keep their restless and nervy Kaiser amused. Endless 'entertainments' were devised for the long evenings. These might involve music, storytelling, puppet shows or magic, but cabaret was the favourite, preferably risqué. In preparation for the Liebenberg Kaiser Hunt in 1892 Georg Hülsen wrote to Emil Görtz, 'I'll parade you like a clipped poodle! That'll be a hit like nothing else. Just think: behind SHAVED, in front long bangs [fringes] out of black and white wool, in the back, under a real poodle's tail, a noticeable rectal opening, and, as soon as you stand up on your hind feet, in FRONT a fig leaf. Just think how terrific when you bark, or howl to music; shoot off a pistol or do other foolish things. It'll be simply splendid! Nobody can make a costume as good as you can; you can model the head yourself – I already see it in my mind's eye, HM laughing like us – and I'm counting on a *succès fou*.'

Eulenburg always suffered from complete nervous exhaustion by the end of the Liebenberg Kaiser Hunt, where he was sole host. But it was all in a good cause. Throughout the 1890s most political decisions and policies were made during one of the three annual events, always followed by a letter filled with flattery to confirm what had already been informally agreed. It was a system far removed from responsible government.

Ministers of the Kaiser's Government hardly got a look-in. Whenever Wilhelm was away, he was out of reach. Couriers followed him about with Government papers, but they often took days to arrive and days to return. The Kaiser was in Berlin for the Season in January, but after that more often on his travels than at home. In February there were hunting trips as well as his annual visit to Wilhelmshaven to swear in naval recruits; in March and April he went to Italy or the Mediterranean to recuperate, as well as making his annual visit to the royal theatre at Wiesbaden, his state visit to Alsace-Lorraine, and his romantic visit to Prokelwitz. These were followed by a yachting week at Kiel, instituted by Wilhelm to compete with his uncle Bertie's Cowes Week. The North Sea Cruise was followed by a trip to England for Cowes, where he competed so furiously with his uncle that the Prince of Wales, somewhat short of money, eventually gave up yacht-racing altogether. August was spent at Wilhelmshohe, the Kaiser's favourite summer royal residence since his student days at Cassel, and usually with his family. In September he was briefly back in Berlin and Potsdam for the great military parade at Tempelhof, and military and naval manoeuvres. But by October he was off again hunting, at Rominten and the royal hunting lodge at Cadinen, followed after a short interval in Berlin by the annual Liebenberg visit in November and some more hunting in Silesia. All this with an entourage so numerous that Queen Victoria refused to entertain him and his suite at Osborne during Cowes Week, forcing him to stay on board *Hohenzollern*. Finally, December saw the Kaiser at Potsdam again, to celebrate a happy family Christmas.

Caprivi lasted only four years. He was no liberal, but he was soon too liberal for the Kaiser, strongly backed by his military entourage and Eulenburg. All went well enough until Caprivi, faced by outrage in the Reichstag, proposed lowering the military budget. The Kaiser replied that he had his own plan, which involved higher not lower expenditure, and troop increases not decreases, a plan he had made 'before God and my Ancestors'. In January 1892 Eulenburg wrote Wilhelm one of his letters, telling him, between 'tennis balls', that Caprivi's Education Bill was far too liberal. Wilhelm at once called in the ministers who supported it, to inform them that he rejected the Bill in its entirety. Eulenburg wrote again, telling His Majesty to tone down his language. In a Crown Council a week later the Kaiser duly announced that he would only accept the Bill if it were modified. 'There is only one ruler in this Empire and I am he. I will tolerate no one else,' declaimed Wilhelm in a typical speech in May 1891. In reality, it seemed Eulenburg only had to click his fingers for Wilhelm, the Liebling, to fall into line.

It was becoming increasingly clear to Caprivi that responsible government was anathema to the Kaiser, who saw everyone he wanted to see behind his Chancellor's back and made every appointment he wanted to make in the same fashion, including Eulenburg's as Ambassador in Vienna, Kuno von Moltke's as one of his own ADCs, and Axel von Varnbüler's as Württemberg envoy to Berlin. 'Kuno aide-de-camp! The Kaiser telegraphed it to me full of joy. It is good to have him in Berlin,' Eulenburg wrote to Varnbüler once Kuno was in daily contact with the Kaiser, neatly placed to keep Eulenburg well informed. In October 1893, after a series of moves as complicated as a game of chess, Eulenburg used the annual hunt at Rominten to brief the Kaiser about Varnbüler's imminent appointment to Berlin. 'The bomb is ready to explode!' Kuno wrote to Varnbüler, adding, 'Phili asks you to keep the matter strictly secret.' Caprivi was consulted on none of it.

By now the Kaiser, once seemingly in favour of social reform, had completely changed his views. In 1890 and again in 1893 the Socialists gained ground in the Reichstag and demanded reforms, both social and constitutional. The Kaiser's reaction was to present the Reichstag with a tough Anti-Revolution Bill. Keenly watching developments from his estate at Friedrichsruh, Bismarck must have had a sense of *Schadenfreude*. In the field of foreign affairs, too, Bismarck's fears were soon realised. The Kaiser, influenced by Waldersee, who still favoured a pre-emptive war against Russia, and by an entourage which was almost entirely pro-Austrian, did not renew the Russo-German Pact. Instead, and for good measure, he renewed the Triple Alliance with Austria and Italy. Convinced of his supreme powers of diplomacy, the Kaiser felt he could nevertheless make everything right with Tsar Alexander III by offering promises of friendship as between 'colleagues'. Alexander was not fooled, commenting 'Wilhelm is as good a liar as his manners are bad.' The truth was that the Tsar and Tsarina never had liked and never would like Willy and the strutting Prussians. The Tsar promptly invited a French naval squadron to call in at Kronstadt, the port which served St Petersburg, and from then on Russia was aligned, whether formally or informally, with France and against Germany.

In the event Waldersee did not fare well in the new regime, and he was soon sidelined. Holstein had never liked or trusted him, seeing him as a bad combination of the very ambitious and the not very bright. Eulenburg had never liked him either, seeing him as a competitor for Wilhelm's affections. Waldersee was no great loss. But in other matters the Kaiser's unpredictability and loosening grip on reality was becoming a serious problem. The tragedy for the Kaiser and the German Reich was that the more Wilhelm needed careful and objective advice, the less he got it. 'Every day I feel the blessing of a strong Government in such safe and strong hands as yours,' Queen Victoria in England was able to write to her Prime Minister Lord Salisbury in March 1896. In Germany the Chancellor and the Government had little say, power being entirely vested in the Kaiser, who was advised not by his ministers but by his best friend, Philipp zu Eulenburg.

In the matter of his relationship with Great Britain, Wilhelm/William got no help at all. 'In the early years of his reign the Kaiser repudiated on every possible occasion his kinship with England,' wrote the German Court official. 'Once on a shooting expedition he caught his hand in a bramble, scratching it rather badly. Shaking off the tiny drop of blood he muttered angrily "*Dies verdammte englisches Blut* [This damned English blood]!" Though but a small incident, it was very typical. Later on in life he has become outwardly, at least, more tolerant, but the efforts of certain sycophants to prove that he was not of English extraction and had no English blood in his veins met, nevertheless, with his entire approval. One such patriotic historian drew up [a family] tree as a proof of Kaiser Wilhelm's pure German blood.'

There followed a family tree which began with Georg I (not George) and came to Queen Victoria through her father, the son of Georg III and Charlotte von Mecklenburg-Strelitz. Among the Prussian nobility in the Germany of the 1890s the matter of 'pure blood' was as serious as it later became in the Nazi period. Eulenburg and the Liebenberg Circle were racists of a particularly pernicious type, introducing Wilhelm to Gobineau and Houston Stewart Chamberlain, both rabid racial theorists, one from Germany and the other from England. Wilhelm was soon blaming the Jews for everything – his father's death, at the hands of Jewish 'trash'; social unrest, fomented by the Jewish 'rabble'; and criticism in the press, orchestrated by Jewish 'scum'. Big business was run by Jews who were sucking the Reich dry. Only the Kaiser's Court was uncontaminated, happily free of all Jews. It was one of the mysteries of the English Court, opined Willy and Dona, that not only were Jews permitted to attend, but some were uncle Bertie's best friends. 'The Old Peacock' seemed not to realise that the Jews were part of an international conspiracy, lending him money to pay off his debts in order to further their own ambitions. As far as the German Anglophobes were concerned, it was all grist to the mill.

9

A Wedding and a Betrothal

~

IN ENGLAND PRINCE Eddy, as heir to the throne, still needed a wife. He had been keen to marry Princess Hélène d'Orléans, but she was a Catholic, and the match was impossible. Now Queen Victoria had someone more suitable in mind. She was not a major royal, she had no money, and though pleasant-looking, was no beauty. But she was nice, quite clever, and possessed that most valuable quality: she was sensible. She was also English, more or less. Most important of all, she was devoted to the monarchy. Her name was Princess May of Teck and she had grown up at Kensington Palace, within a stone's throw of Buckingham Palace.

May's father, the Duke of Teck, was half-German, half-Hungarian. Her mother was Princess Mary of Cambridge, a granddaughter of George III, unkindly known as 'Fat Mary' because she needed two of the small Court chairs to accommodate her generous frame. Queen Victoria had long taken an interest in the family and provided them with a grace and favour apartment. May had three brothers, and sometimes the Teck children were invited to play at Marlborough House, where they found the Wales boys very wild. The Princess of Wales, it turned out, was also keeping an eye on little May. By 1881 she was writing to Georgie, 'May has grown quite a tall lady since you were away, with her hair done up and long petticoats, nearly as tall as I am.'

'I think the preliminaries are now pretty well settled, but do you suppose Princess May will make any resistance?' wrote Francis Knollys to Sir Henry Ponsonby, Queen Victoria's Private Secretary, on 19 August 1891. 'I do not anticipate any real opposition on Prince Eddy's part if he is properly managed and is told he MUST do it – that it is for the good of the country, etc, etc.' In December Eddy and May were engaged. For the next few weeks the papers were filled with news of the royal couple, their dress, their dinners, their drives in Hyde Park, and the nation rejoiced. But at the beginning of January

Prince Eddy, at Sandringham for Christmas and New Year, was in bed with influenza, which quickly developed into pneumonia. By 14 January 1892 he was dead. 'Poor, poor parents; poor May to have her whole bright future to be merely a dream! Poor me, in my old age, to see this young promising life cut short!' wrote Queen Victoria in her Journal on that day, neatly summing up the situation while assessing Eddy's life with some lenience. To Vicky in Berlin she wrote that Bertie had cried throughout the funeral. 'He is broken down, and poor dear Alix, though bearing up wonderfully, does nothing but cry, Bertie says.'

Georgie was shocked by Eddy's death. 'I am sure no two brothers could have loved each other more than we did,' he wrote to his grandmother on 18 January. 'Alas! it is only now that I have found out how deeply I did love & I remember with pain nearly every hard word & little quarrel I ever had with him & I long to ask his forgiveness, but, alas, it is too late now!' Georgie was now the next heir to the throne, and began to suffer sleepless nights of anxiety at the prospect on top of the sorrow he felt at the loss of a brother with whom he had shared almost every day of his life until Eddy went into the Army. Secretly the politicians were highly relieved, and quick to transfer their attentions to the much more promising and biddable younger brother.

Prince George now needed a territorial title and a seat in the House of Lords: in the Birthday Honours list of 24 May 1892 he was duly created Duke of York, Earl of Inverness and Baron Killarney. 'I am glad that you like the title of Duke of York,' Queen Victoria wrote to him from Balmoral on 27 May. 'I am afraid I do not, and wish you had remained as you are. A Prince NO ONE else can be, whereas a Duke any nobleman can be, and many are!' The Princess of Wales was much more accommodating: 'Fancy my Georgie boy doing that [taking his seat in the Lords] and now being a grand old Duke of York!' she wrote to him in high amusement. The Prince was now provided with his own apartments in St James's Palace, suitably named York House, and a personal staff which included Major-General Sir Francis de Winton as his Comptroller of the Household and Lieutenant Charles Cust, an old Navy friend, as his equerry (Cust remained devotedly at his side for thirty-nine years). At Sandringham Georgie was allocated the Bachelors' Cottage for his own personal use. His financial position also improved, because he now inherited Eddy's allowance in addition to his own.

In July he was commanding HMS *Melampus* in summer manoeuvres, with a notable lack of enthusiasm. 'The Flagship made any number of mistakes,' he confided to his diary on the 27th, adding: 'I hope I shall never be in any other manoeuvres . . . Hate the whole thing.' He was soon able to give 'the whole thing' up to concentrate on his future role. Although he never lost his enthusiasm for the sea, Prince George was happy to be home. First, however, he was despatched to Heidelberg for a short course in what his mother dismissively described as that 'sauer-kraut' language. His father meanwhile instructed him to take 'yr whole German uniform with you . . . as William is going to Carlsruhe next month (no distance fr Heidelberg) to stay with Gd Duke & Gd Duchess of Baden so you could pay them a visit altogether. In case there should be a service or anything it is best to bring the whole kit.' Georgie should also take ALL his German orders, as well as the Garter, and fresh epaulettes were on order. Georgie duly attended the annual Lutheran celebrations at Wittenberg, fully attired, travelling there with cousin Willy in his cream and blue Imperial train. He was surprised to find William extremely attentive and civil, nicer than he had ever known him; apparently it did not occur to Georgie that his new position was responsible.

Once at home again, Georgie embarked on his new life as future heir to the throne. He received lessons in constitutional history from J.R. Tanner of Cambridge University, who introduced him to Walter Bagehot's *The English Constitution*, and it was suggested that he should learn something of politics, a subject completely absent from his previous naval career. The Conservatives had been defeated in the general election that August, and Gladstone had replaced Lord Salisbury as Prime Minister. Queen Victoria was not pleased, being especially put out by Gladstone's Home Rule Bill for Ireland. Georgie, more open-minded, went to the House of Commons on 13 February 1893 to hear Gladstone introduce the Bill and listen to the debate. 'He made a beautiful speech and spoke for 2 and a quarter hours, which is wonderful for a man of 83,' he noted, full of admiration. Georgie had started making speeches himself, one to the Society for the Prevention of Cruelty to Children, another when he received the Freedom of the Merchant Taylors' Company. It was a new duty, not greatly to his liking. 'I was horribly nervous,' he admitted to his diary.

Prince Eddy was scarcely buried before Queen Victoria turned her attention to Georgie and the necessity of finding him a suitable wife.

And who better than Princess May, charming, sensible and devoted? In April the Queen wrote to Georgie from the French Riviera, where she was enjoying a holiday: 'Have you seen May and have you thought more about the POSSIBILITY or FOUND OUT what her feelings might be?' she asked disingenuously. The letter did not have far to travel. By some happy chance both the Waleses and the Tecks were also holidaying in the South of France, the Waleses at Cap Martin and the Tecks at Cannes. 'Papa and I are coming to Cannes towards the end of the week for a few days (incog.) and so I shall hope to see you then,' Georgie had already dutifully written to May on 29 March, ending, 'Goodbye Miss May . . . ever your very loving old cousin Georgie.'

Thereafter matters moved fast. In late November 1892 Princess May and her parents went to stay at Sandringham for the Princess of Wales's birthday, the anniversary of May's first engagement to Prince Eddy in early December not however forgotten. 'Poured,' noted Princess May succinctly in her diary on Motherdear's birthday. 'At 11 she was given her presents, some of them quite lovely, she was terribly upset, poor thing. We went out to lunch in a tent with the shooters, dreadful weather . . . After tea I played bezique with George.' On 3 December, the day of the anniversary, May wrote: 'Dull wet day. This day last year was our engagement day, such a sad contrast.' By now the second engagement was pretty well a foregone conclusion. 'May is a smart *erscheinung*, still all in black of course, but she seemed to me a little stiff & cold! I hear her praised on all sides by those who know her well,' wrote Vicky, Dowager Empress of Germany, to her daughter from Windsor, where she was staying with the Queen. 'She is certainly very nice in manner &c but I do not think she has much charm or is very fascinating! She may have been shy with me seeing me again after all this sorrow! And it is a difficult position for her – as the newspapers are perpetually talking of her Betrothal to Georgie.' The Princess of Wales was not making things any easier. 'There is a bond of love between us, that of mother and child, which nobody can ever diminish or render less binding,' she wrote to Georgie, 'and nobody can, or ever shall, come between me and my darling Georgie boy.'

'Received a telegram from Georgie . . . to say he was engaged to May of Teck, and asked for my consent. I answered that I gladly did so,' wrote Queen Victoria in her Journal with formal surprise on

3 May 1893. The betrothal pleased British public opinion, which had been in favour of the union for a long time. People felt sorry for Princess May, and just like Queen Victoria saw it as romantic as well as convenient, and not at all odd. The royal couple themselves were not so confident. 'I am very sorry I am still so shy with you, I tried not to be the other day, but alas failed, I was angry with myself! It is so stupid to be so stiff together and really there is nothing I would not tell you, except that I LOVE you more than anybody in the world, and this I cannot tell you myself so I write it to relieve my feelings,' wrote May. Georgie replied at once, throwing punctuation to the winds. 'Thank God we both understand each other, and I think it really unnecessary for me to tell you how deep my love for you my darling is and I feel it growing stronger and stronger every time I see you; although I may appear shy and cold.'

The wedding was fixed with almost undue haste for 6 July 1893, in the Chapel Royal at St James's Palace. Knowing that May had no money of her own, her aunt and uncle the Grand Duke and Grand Duchess of Mecklenburg-Strelitz paid for her trousseau, described in the *Lady's Pictorial* as including forty outdoor suits, fifteen ball-dresses and five tea-gowns, as well as a number of matinée gowns, travelling wraps and walking costumes of Harris Tweed, with matching bonnets, shoes and gloves – all this 'but a portion of the trousseau'. It was however noted approvingly that 'Princess May cannot be called a dressy woman and has no extravagant taste in dress, preferring always to look neat, lady-like and elegant.' The national weeklies commented on every aspect of the Princess's life, including the somewhat surprising comment that 'no young lady of the present day – Princess or otherwise – is more thoroughly grounded in the English classics, or more happily at home in modern literature than our future Queen.' Presents, 15,000 of them, poured in from the four corners of the earth, reportedly valued at £300,000 (this at a time when a working man was lucky to bring in three pounds a week).

The foreign royal wedding guests began to arrive, headed by Georgie's Danish grandparents, Amama and Apapa; Prince Henry, or Heinrich, of Prussia, representing the Kaiser; and Nicky from Russia. 'My darling Mama,' Nicky wrote to his mother the Tsarina from Marlborough House, where he was staying, 'Arrived well. The crossing was very comfortable owing to the courtesy of the Queen who sent her yacht *Victoria and Albert* to Flushing.' He was met by 'the dear Wales family' at Charing Cross and escorted straight to Marlborough House. He was given a room next to his first love Toria, and her sister Maud. 'Victoria has got much thinner and unfortunately does not look well; Maud on the other hand has put on weight,' he noted succinctly in his diary. Uncle Waldemar, from Denmark, was just down the passage. His grandparents Amama and Apapa were on the floor below. He felt completely at home, and found Uncle Bertie in very good spirits and most friendly – almost too much so. 'Uncle Bertie has sent me a whole bevy of tailors, shoe makers and hatters! He is very funny in that respect, but he has always been extremely attentive and kind to me.' That afternoon Nicky went to Clarence House to have tea with Uncle Affie and Aunt Marie. During the following days he and Georgie had their photograph taken together, looking like twins – the same height, hair, eyes and lovingly tended moustaches. In the mornings the two cousins talked in Nicky's bedroom. One afternoon Georgie took Nicky to see his new home in St James's Palace.

Nicky was delighted with London. 'I never thought I would like it so much,' he told his mother, and he was delighted with May, whom he met at the family dinner and found much better-looking than in her photographs. As for all the presents, someone even managed to give the royal couple a cow, he told his mother. He did some sight-seeing and some shopping, always attended by a Colonel Clarke who was attached to him throughout his visit. He enjoyed the State Ball and danced a lot 'but didn't see many beautiful ladies', preferring the society women he saw out riding in Rotten Row in the mornings. One day he went to hear Gladstone speak in the House of Commons. On another he went to Windsor with Uncle Affie to see Queen Victoria and receive the Order of the Garter, nicely describing the august Queen as 'a round ball on unsteady legs'. Whenever the people crowding the royal routes caught sight of the Tsarevich, they cheered loudly. It was his uncanny resemblance to the Duke of York which caught their imagination. Queen Victoria was amused that it led to 'no end of funny mistakes, the one being taken for the other!'

'The great day, so anxiously looked forward to, was very bright and fine, but overpoweringly hot,' Queen Victoria wrote in her Journal on 6 July. Lying in bed at Buckingham Palace that morning she could already hear 'the distant hum of the people' and out of her window she could see troops – infantry, cavalry, volunteers – crowds and bands. At eleven-thirty precisely the first carriage procession of twelve scarlet and gold open State Landaus each drawn by four cream-coloured horses made its way to the Chapel Royal, bearing all the royal guests in reverse order of precedence. The second procession left at eleven-forty-five sharp: the bridegroom, his father and their suite. A great roar went up in the crowd. Then came the Queen in the 'Glass Coach', attended by a Sovereign's Escort of the Household Cavalry. Beside her sat the Duchess of Teck, beaming. Another, greater, roar went up. Finally, to the greatest cheer of them all, came the bride's procession, with Princess May of Teck in the last carriage beside her father the Duke. Her dress was exquisitely simple, white and silver, decorated with silver roses, shamrocks and thistles. On her head she had a small wreath of orange blossom, myrtle and white heather. The veil was fixed with a Rose of York diadem with a single diamond, given to her by the Queen. She waved to the crowd, smiling shyly. There were ten bridesmaids, and as the bride came up the aisle her waiting groom, Prince George, in naval uniform, made her a spontaneous bow. 'I am indeed lucky to have got such a darling and charming wife,' he confided to his diary that evening.

'The young couple go to Sandringham to the Cottage after the wedding, which I regret and think rather UNLUCKY and sad,' wrote Queen Victoria to Vicky, still thinking of Eddy. Not so Georgie, who loved Sandringham better than anywhere in the world, and his own part of it, the Bachelors' Cottage, now renamed York Cottage, so much that he went on living there for the next thirty-three years. York Cottage was memorably described by Harold Nicolson in his entertaining biography of King George V as 'a glum little villa, encompassed by thickets and rhododendron . . . the rooms inside, with their fumed oak surrounds, their white overmantels framing oval mirrors, their Doulton tiles and stained glass fanlights, are indistinguishable from those of any Surbiton or Upper Norwood home.' What better example of the fact that the British monarchy had more in common with the man in the street than with the snobbish upper classes, of whom Queen Victoria so often disapproved. The Duke of York was not at all put out by the fact that the rooms were small and dark, the bedrooms cold and (conveniently) so few that it was impossible for guests to stay. As the family grew, the children were squeezed in on the top floor, under the mock Tudor eaves. The private secretaries did their work in their bedrooms, there being no space for an office or study. There was only one telephone, and that was in the hall. The servants were billeted out to cottages on the estate. In a fit of enthusiasm the Duke of York, in preparation for his new wife, had furnished the cottage entirely in the modern style, from Maple's Emporium in the Tottenham Court Road.

Nicky had been hoping to meet Princess Alix of Hesse at Georgie's wedding, but she had refused the invitation, with the excuse that she could not afford to attend. They had only met twice since their original meeting, once in 1889 when Alix spent the winter in St Petersburg visiting her sister Ella, and then again, briefly, in early 1893 at the wedding of the Kaiser's sister Mossy in Berlin.

At the time of the 1889 visit, Nicky was twenty and following the traditional route for the heir to the Russian throne, serving as an officer in the Preobrazhensky Guards, the elite regiment of the Russian Army. Like Willy in Germany, but unlike Georgie in England who was not expected to succeed to the throne, Nicky had begun his training as future Tsar when he was seventeen. There were lessons in history, international law and the art of government from leading politicians, academics and military men. Nicholas Bunge, a former Minister of Finance, taught him the history of economics in general and of the Russian economy in particular. Bunge was a man of charm and humanity, a liberal by instinct and training, with first-hand experience of the workings of capitalism and the modern banking system in other parts of Europe. But the greatest influence on Nicky turned out to be Pobedonostsev, the forceful arch conservative who was Alexander III's former tutor, the man who had redrafted Tsar Alexander's Manifesto along much less democratic lines, holder of the powerful position of Chief Procurator of the Holy Synod during Alexander's reign and Nicholas's. His views remained the same throughout: democracy was dangerous, even disastrous for a vast and unruly Empire like Russia. The only possible system for Russia was an autocratic monarchy, heavily backed by the police and military, and advised by a carefully selected elite. Religion and Nation were the corner-stones of Russian life, and the Tsar, the Autocrat of All The Russias, was the absolute head of both.

Meanwhile the future Autocrat of All the Russias was having an extremely pleasant time in his exclusive Guards regiment, where life was spent in the company of like-minded aristocratic young men in the officers' mess, doing not very much apart from having a good time. Like Willy in Germany, Nicky had always loved the Army – the traditions, the uniforms, the codes of behaviour. For Nicky, brought up in the over-protective atmosphere of heavily fortified and policed Imperial palaces, regimental life was a heady liberation. 'I am now happier than I can say to have joined the army,' he wrote to his mother from camp at Krasnoe Selo in June 1887. They drilled in the mornings and did target practice in the evenings, or the other way round, and for the rest, it was business as usual. 'I like my bungalow awfully and were you to see it, darling Mama, you would most likely fall in love with it. My little bedroom and study are wonderfully comfortable and attractive. The dining-room is rather big in comparison with those rooms. It has a door leading to a balcony and a small garden which leads right into the centre drive. We have lunch at 12 o'clock and dine at 8, with siesta and tea in between. The dinners are very merry; they feed us well. After meals, the officers practise hard on the *pas de géant* or play billiards, skittles, cards or dominoes. I always play skittles in spite of the poor condition of the skittle-alley.'

'Never forget that everyone's eyes are turned on you now, waiting to see what your own first INDEPENDENT steps in life will be,' wrote his mother. 'Always be polite and courteous to everybody, see that you get along with all your comrades without discrimination, although without too much familiarity or intimacy, and NEVER listen to flattery.' Nicky no doubt heeded the advice, but army life was army life. 'Woke up and felt as if a squadron had spent the night in my mouth,' he confided to his diary, but not his mother.

On 30 January 1889 Nicky went 'in uniform' to meet Alix at St Petersburg station. The reception party included his father the Tsar, Ella and Sergei, and various Grand Dukes. Alix was seventeen. She arrived with her father Grand Duke Louis of Hesse, who had brought her up since her mother's death, and her brother Ernie. They drove to the Anitchkoff Palace where Aunt Minny, the Tsarina, awaited them. There they all took tea together. 'She has grown up a lot and become prettier,' noted Nicky in his diary that evening. Alix was staying with Ella and Sergei. It was a winter of skating, visits to the theatre, Court balls and the occasional reception. Alix, another diary-writer, recorded a typical day on 29 January: 'I skated and slid down the hills in the afternoon in the Anitchkoff garden. Supper at 7 thirty, then Ella and I went to the Winter Palace where we dressed for the ball (white diamonds, white flowers and sash).' She notes that she danced a quadrille with Paul and a cotillon with Nicky. The next day Nicky wrote: 'At the skating rink we again fooled around a lot with Aunt Ella and Alix. After the *Zakuska* [light snack] I went with Papa and Mama to the *Mikado*, where we had a lot of fun and laughed a great deal.'

Nicky spent a lot of time with Ella and Sergei and Alix. On 16 February they all went skating again, and in the evening they went to the French Theatre to see Zola's play *L'Assommoir*. 'A terrible drama,' noted Nicky, not keen on too much realism. A few days later there was a family dinner at Ella and Sergei's, followed by dancing. 'We danced till we dropped and had a wonderful time. I danced the mazurka with Alix,' Nicky told his diary. Two days later he confided, 'Was in a very animated mood, I don't know quite why?' The following day they played hide-and-seek, just like children. On 11 March, after an evening spent playing chess with Alix, he wrote: 'Was in a sad mood.' Alix was to leave the following day.

They began writing to one another, in English, the only language they had in common. 'It was so good of you to write and it gave me great pleasure,' wrote Alix from Darmstadt. 'Thank you so much for your dear little letter,' wrote Nicky from St Petersburg, adding that he had shot his first bear that day, and signing himself 'With much love, your ever loving Nicky.' Ella and Sergei were busy fanning the flames. Ella gave Nicky a photograph of Alix in a ball dress, 'a charming photograph, which is constantly before me,' he wrote. By June Nicky had taken Ella into his confidence. 'Darling Nicky,' she wrote in response, 'The whole day I have been thinking and thinking about our conversation and your little note I have received gave me such pleasure, most hearty thanks.' She had told Sergei, but would of course not tell anyone else. And she had written to Alix. Did Nicky know that if one prayed in a church which was about to be consecrated, God would hear one's prayers?

Queen Victoria was not pleased by the thought of Alix disappearing off to dangerous Russia, and she knew exactly who was behind it all. 'It is about Alicky and N [Nicky],' she announced in a letter to Victoria, Alix and Ella's sister, who had sensibly married Louis of Battenberg and come to live in England. 'I had your assurance that nothing was to be feared in that quarter, but I know for certain that . . . behind all your backs Ella and Sergei do all they can to bring it about, encouraging and even urging the Boy to do it! – I promised not to mention who told me – I must do to you, it is Aunt Alix who heard it from Aunt Minny herself who is very much annoyed about it. You must never mention Aunt Alix's name, but this must not be allowed to go on . . . The state of Russia is so bad, so rotten that at any moment something dreadful might happen and though it might not signify to Ella, the wife of the Thronfolger [heir to the throne] is in a most difficult and precarious position.' There was much truth in this, as future events would reveal, but the objections are mostly those of a grandmother who did not wish to lose her favourite grandchild, for when would she ever see Alicky again if she went to Russia? There was also the old problem of private relationships having public repercussions. 'It would have the very worst effect here and in Germany (where Russia is not liked) and would produce a great separation between our families.'

In Russia Nicky's father the Tsar was not keen either. But for the time being he had other things on his mind. In November 1890 four terrorists were condemned to death by hanging, one a woman, whose sentence was commuted. The group had connections with some revolutionary bomb manufacturers in Zurich, and with a Nihilist cell in Paris who were planning another attempt on the Tsar's life. Then came the terrible famine of 1891, which the Nihilists described in inflammatory pamphlets as the inevitable consequence of the system of government, which needed urgently to be replaced by a national assembly. Revolutionary activity increased again, and police found secret printing presses in seven separate towns, producing proclamations addressed to the 'persecuted and oppressed nation' and ending 'Long Live Liberty and Revolution'. Two hundred and forty people were arrested in Moscow alone, including fourteen officials, four schoolmasters, and six officers. Some of those arrested came from the educated and upper classes. After an earlier attempt on the Tsar's life, several students had been arrested and hanged. One of them was Lenin's brother. In the Customs department at the French Exhibition in Moscow four large boxes of dynamite were discovered, meant for use when the Tsar visited the exhibition.

The country was in crisis, and the harsh and repressive measures which followed only made matters worse. Mr Lowe of *The Times*, who had once been so impressed by Tsar Alexander III, now found him extremely reactionary, and much influenced by Pobednostsev. But his old source 'Mr Lanin' reminded him that the Tsar was cut off from everyday life, always under heavy guard in the Imperial palaces, and surrounded by spies. When he travelled in his Imperial train, troops stood guard the length of the railway line. 'Any man who saw, as he did, his own father mutilated and bleeding to death; who himself, more than once, narrowly escaped a similar fate . . . a man who has had such experiences as these entertains not the slightest doubt that the hairs on his head are numbered,' Mr Lanin told Mr Lowe.

By now Nicky was embarked on a nine-month grand tour to the Far East by way of Greece and Egypt, to broaden his mind and further educate him for his future role. He travelled with his younger brother Georgei and his cousin Prince George of Greece, two of his friends, Prince Bariatinsky and Prince Obolensky, and Dr Rombach, the Court physician. Various people joined the entourage at different points in the journey to offer specialist knowledge and insights. Prince Ukhtomsky was an expert on Asian religion and culture. M.K. Onu, who joined the party in Egypt, was an authority on Middle Eastern Affairs. In India they had the benefit of Sir Donald Mackenzie Wallace. It may be that the Tsar and Tsarina hoped the voyage would make Nicky forget the beautiful dancer Mademoiselle Kshessinskaya with whom he had had a brief liaison, but they were probably more concerned that he should forget Princess Alix of Hesse.

By the time the royal party reached India, where they were treated to the full pomp of the British Raj, Nicky's brother Georgei was unwell, and was soon obliged to return to Russia, where it was discovered that he was suffering from tuberculosis. The rest of the party travelled on through Siam to China and Japan, which they reached in May. Here their voyage came to an abrupt end. As they were sight-seeing in the Japanese town of Otsu, Nicky was attacked by a policeman wielding a sword. Only the quick reactions of Greek George, who leapt on the assailant, saved Nicky from death. He bore the scar on his head for the rest of his life. No one ever found out the reason for the attack, but it was enough to send the royal party back to their ship, bound for home. On hearing the news the Tsarina wrote to her son, distraught: 'My more than dearest Nicky – God be praised! No words can tell what dread and sorrowing tears we received that TERRIFYING news with! I could not believe my eyes and thought I must be going mad. How lucky your telegram telling us you were safe came first . . . What joy that you are leaving that horrible Japan today the 7 May for Wladivostok. The Empress Haruko sent me the most touching telegrams every day with news about you.'

They were to stop in Vladivostok in Siberia on the way home for a religious dedication ceremony marking the start of the construction of the Trans-Siberian Railway. Among Alexander III's finer legacies to Russia, along with the maintainance of peace abroad if not at home, were the many great engineering projects – roads, bridges, railways – which helped to bring his huge and backward Empire into the modern age. Sergei Witte, now the Finance Minister, had suggested to the Tsar that Nicky serve as Chairman of the committee for the construction of the railway, thinking it would be good preparation for Nicky's future role. The Tsar disagreed. 'But he is absolutely a child,' he said. 'He has the judgement of a child – how would he be able to be chairman of a committee?' Nicky was twenty-four. Witte got his way, and Nicky attended the ceremony. He was also appointed to chair the Special Committee on Famine Relief, with the useful result that he came to know some of Russia's leading officials, as well as finding out something about the harsh realities of everyday life in the Empire.

By August 1891 Nicky was back with his grandparents in Denmark, having good long talks with English Georgie. In December, at Gatchina, he approached his parents about Alix. 'Inevitably this conversation touched the most sensitive string of my heart, and touched that DREAM and that HOPE I live with from day to day. It is already a year and a half since I talked about it to Papa at Peterhof, and since then nothing has changed either for better or worse!' he confided to his diary on 2 January 1892. 'My dream – one day to marry Alix H., I have loved her for a long time, but more deeply and strongly since 1889 when she spent six weeks in Petersburg during the winter! For a long time I resisted my feelings, and tried to deceive myself about the impossibility of achieving my most cherished wish! But now that Eddy has withdrawn or been rejected, the only obstacle or gulf between us – is the question of religion.'

That, and his parents; even, on certain days, himself. He noted that he was still a little in love with the dancer Kshessinskaya. 'What a surprising thing our heart is! At the same time I never stop thinking of Alix! Would it be right to conclude from all this that I am very amorous?' Whether he was amorous or not, the matter was effectively taken out of his hands by Alix, who wrote to him in Denmark the summer following Georgie and May's wedding in London to say she could not marry him because she could not change her religion. They had met briefly earlier in the year, at Mossy's wedding in Berlin. But he had hardly seen her, let alone talked to her. Instead he was beset by Willy, who insisted on bestowing the highest Order of the Black Eagle on him. 'I had to put on a particularly uncomfortable red cloak – I nearly died of heat in it!' he told his diary. Nor did the wedding ceremony please. 'I did not like the service. There was some singing, a little music from a string choir, the pastor gave a sermon – and that was it – there was nothing to convey that marriage is a sacrament! In the great hall, the newlyweds received congratulations in the most tiresome way: each lady and each man had to come up to them and bow – this pleasure lasted for two hours.'

It took another year and another family wedding to arrange matters between Nicky and Alix. Alix's brother Ernie was marrying Ducky, Uncle Alfred and Aunt Marie's daughter, in Coburg. All the previous year Alix and Nicky had been writing to each other. So had Alix and Ella. So had Alix and Xenia, Nicky's sister. But still Alix held out. Like her mother, Princess Alice, she was almost mystically devoted to the Protestant religion. She explained that she had been brought up with it and loved it, and without it she would never find peace of mind. To convert to the Russian Orthodox religion was an impossibility.

No one seems to have mentioned the fact that Alix's brother had been a haemophiliac, and had died as a consequence. On 15 April 1894 Nicky was in the Imperial train, on the way to Coburg. 'It was very hot in the compartment,' he wrote in his diary. 'I sweated and read a lot. At 6.30 we arrived at the border and flew ahead at full steam in three sleeping cars. Uncle Vladimir and Aunt Michen, Uncle Sergei and Aunt Ella, Uncle Pavel and I, all with our adjutants and staff.' There was a guard of honour waiting for them at Coburg station the following afternoon. Everyone was coming to the wedding, including Uncle Bertie, and Willy, the Kaiser. Queen Victoria herself was attending, mainly, fond as she was of Ernie, to keep an eye on Alix and Nicky. 'My God! What a day!' Nicky wrote two days later. 'After coffee at about 10 o'clock Ernie and Alix came to Aunt Ella's rooms. She has grown noticeably prettier, but looked extremely sad. They left us alone together, and then we began the conversation which I have so longed for and yet so feared. We talked until 12 o'clock, but without success, she is still against changing her religion. She cried a lot, poor thing.'

The wedding took place on 19 April, followed by a family luncheon. In the afternoon Nicky went for a walk with Uncle Vladimir, arriving back just before a storm broke. It poured all night. That evening they dined with Aunt Marie 'in uniform because of the Emperor, who never wears civilian clothes'. The night before, Willy had sat talking to Nicky until one in the morning, determined to steer him into marriage with Alix, seeing it as a most useful alliance between Germany and Russia. His relationship with Alexander III had, despite his best efforts, remained on polite but formal terms. But once Nicky, married to his cousin Alix, became Tsar, there would be fewer obstacles, and things could be more easily arranged 'between colleagues' who shared the same views about the dangers of the liberal and democratic system practised in England, where the monarch, even one as formidable as Queen Victoria, was entirely subservient to Parliament. Once the Queen died Uncle Bertie, 'the Old Peacock', would inherit the throne, and the monarchy in England would become weaker and weaker, thought Willy.

'A wonderful, unforgettable day in my life – the day of my betrothal to my dear beloved Alix,' Nicky wrote in his diary on 20 April. 'She came to Aunt Michen after 10 o'clock, and after they had talked, she and I had our discussion. God, what a mountain has fallen from my shoulders . . . Wilhelm sat in the next room with the uncles and aunts and waited for the outcome of our talk.' Indeed he did, and ever after took credit for the marriage, claiming that it was he alone who had been able to reassure Alix about changing her religion. 'I cried like a child and she did too,' Nicky wrote to his mother about the moment of decision, 'but her expression had changed; her face was lit by a quiet content.' It was as if Alix, in giving her consent, had found a new religion, vested in Nicky. Likewise, Nicky now vested his life in Alix. 'The whole world is changed for me,' he told his mother in the same letter, 'nature, mankind, everything.' That very day there was a thanksgiving service, and a pile of telegrams of congratulation began to arrive. In the evening there was a Court concert at which the Bavarian regimental string band played. The following morning Queen Victoria's Dragoon Guards, not to be outdone, played a whole programme under Nicky's windows. Later Uncle Bertie insisted on a group photograph in the garden. In the evening they dined with the Queen. Happily, Nicky was now able to wear evening dress: Wilhelm, his task completed, had already left.

'My dear old Nicky!' wrote happily married Georgie from York Cottage on 21 April, 'I wish you and Alix every possible joy and happiness, now and in the future.' Nicky's mother, reconciled to the inevitable but struggling to express enthusiasm, wrote from their 'prison' at Gatchina: 'My dear sweet Nicky! Words cannot express with what DELIGHT and GREAT joy I received this happy news! I almost felt FAINT I was so overjoyed!' She wished to be called 'Motherdear' by Alix, just like her sister the Princess of Wales in England. Nicky's father wrote, his sister Xenia wrote, his brother Georgei, ill as he was with tuberculosis, wrote. Nicky and Alix spent many hours answering the letters and telegrams, and in between they walked and talked, Alix relaxed and happy now that the decision had been made. At the end of the twelve-day stay Nicky returned to Russia. 'My sweet darling beloved Alix! Oh it was too awful saying goodbye like that, with a lot of people looking on from all sides!' That same day Alix, back at Darmstadt, replied, in English as always: 'My own precious Nicky darling, I am lying in bed, but cannot go to sleep before I have written to you, as speak, alas, we cannot. Oh, how I miss you, it is not to be described and I long for the two hours all alone with you. No goodnight kiss and blessing, it is hard. But our thoughts will meet won't they?' It was the start of a passionate affair which would last for the rest of their lives.

At the end of April Alix was in England, staying with her grandmother at Windsor Castle. She sat down to write to Nicky straight after breakfast with Granny. She had moved back into her old room, she told him, arranging all her photographs, mostly of Nicky with his 'beautiful big eyes', and now she was off to play the piano which she had neglected so shamefully of late, due to all the other excitements. She signed herself his 'Ever deeply devoted little girl, Alix', adding as a postscript, 'Your bride – how funny it sounds. Sweet one I cannot stop thinking of you.' Nicky wrote back: 'Good morning my own precious one! I am just aroused from my slumber, which had been disturbed at 3 in the night by an insolent bat.'

He told Alix how boring life was at Gatchina, playing the piano with Xenia, reading *The Times*, and refusing to play that 'detestable patience' with the others. 'I see my sweet little girly-dear looking back at me, sometimes with a sly look, which makes me think of a certain house on the road from Coburg to Ketchendorf on the left!!!' he wrote from the privacy of his own room. 'You naughty thing,' Alix replied,

'how dare you say that about the sly look and the house on the left!!!'
Not for them the shyness of Georgie and May's relationship. On
another day Alix wrote showing off her newly acquired Russian –
'*Dorogoy mili Nicky*' – but soon reverting to English and more practical matters: 'That foolish Georgie says I am to insist upon you
wearing high heels and that I am to have quite low ones. May, he says,
won't change hers, but he wears much higher ones.'

In mid June 1894 Nicky was embarked for England aboard the new
Imperial Yacht *Polar Star*, lent to him by Papa. With him he took Fr
Yanisheff, a Russian Orthodox priest who was to prepare Alix for her
conversion. By 20 June they were cruising up the Thames estuary,
saluted by the destroyer *Thunderer*, on which cousin Georgie had served
in his Navy days. The royal train was at Gravesend to carry him to
Walton-on-Thames, where Alix waited in her sister Victoria's house.
Nicky found his betrothed looking 'more lovely and more beautiful
than ever'. On the 22nd they were with Granny at Windsor. There
were trips to London and Sandringham to stay with uncle Bertie, who
shocked Nicky by the company he kept, which included Baron Hirsch,
a railway magnate and a Jew, who buttonholed Nicky on the need to
help the oppressed Jews of Russia. At Windsor Nicky received a delegation from Russian trading houses, and the following day attended a
service with Granny and Alix in Prince Albert's mausoleum. Finally, on
9 July, he remembered to write to his mother. They had been to see
Georgie and May's new baby, he wrote, adding that he planned to leave
for Russia on 9 July, a month and a day after his arrival. It is a short
letter, affectionate as always, but Nicky's emotional shift from his
mother to his future wife is unmistakable.

Georgie meanwhile was leading the life of a contented married
man. He and May had given their first dinner party on 4 March at
York House, just for the family. The menu included oysters, thick
soup and clear soup, soles and turbot, mutton, chicken, quails, asparagus, a soufflé, apricot tart and ices. A few days later there was another
dinner party, formal this time, attended by both Lord Rosebery and
Mr Gladstone, the new Prime Minister and the old, lately retired. The
Yorks' first child was born in June. Queen Victoria was quick to ask
that her great-grandson and future heir be called Albert. Georgie was
ready, armed with capitals: 'Long before our dear child was born, both
May and I settled that if it was a boy we should call him Edward after
darling EDDY. THIS IS THE DEAREST WISH OF OUR

HEARTS, dearest Grandmama, for Edward is indeed a SACRED name to us,' he wrote on 1 July. Queen Victoria replied the very next day, 'Of course if you wish Edward to be the first name I shall not object, only I think you write as if EDWARD was the REAL name of dear Eddy, while it was ALBERT VICTOR.'

Unperturbed, Georgie made his accustomed entry in his diary that evening, 2 July, describing a typically satisfactory day. 'Got up at 8,' he wrote. 'Saw May and baby.' Then at nine he drove up to York House, where he had breakfast before attending a Requiem service 'in uniform' with Papa and Uncle Affie. This was followed by a family luncheon at Marlborough House, thirty-four people he noted with his usual interest in exact numbers, including Nicky and Alix. After lunch, 'Talked to Nicky and Alicky in sister's room.' Whether in Copenhagen, Coburg or London, the two cousins always found time to talk. By the evening Georgie was back home, dining with May. This was followed by a spot of patience before 'bed at 12'. If he did not play cards after dinner, Georgie liked to read the newspapers while May did some knitting, or smoked a cigarette. Best of all Georgie liked to attend to his growing stamp collection, an interest fostered by Uncle Affie, who had finally inherited his 'dear small country', Coburg, in 1893.

A week after his talk with Georgie in Toria's room at Marlborough House, Nicky left for St Petersburg, stopping off to visit Amama and Apapa in Denmark. As soon as he arrived home he wrote to Alix. 'You have got me entirely and for ever, soul and spirit, body and heart, everything is yours, yours.' Alix in turn wrote, 'Oh, lovy, had I but got you with me, I want you too badly – a mad longing takes hold of me, and I don't know how to keep quiet.' Preparations for the wedding, planned provisionally for January, quickly got under way. Queen Victoria was still not happy, in spite of 'charming' Nicky's successful visit to England. 'All my fears about her future marriage now show themselves so strongly and my blood runs cold when I think of her so young,' she wrote to Princess Victoria at Walton-on-Thames, 'most likely placed on that very unsafe throne, her dear life and above all her husband's constantly threatened and unable to see her but rarely. It is a great additional anxiety in my declining years! Oh! how I wish it was not to be that I should lose my sweet Alicky.' Not for Queen Victoria the idea that an autocratic monarchy was the safe and secure way to a stable future.

In October the Tsar, famed for his physical strength, unexpectedly became seriously ill. He had been suffering from a kidney condition for some months, and medical specialists had been called in, but none could solve the problem. Now, as the condition worsened, and it became clear to everyone that he was dying, he called for Alix to join them at the palace of Livadia, near Yalta in the Crimea. Nicky was already there. There had never been a new Tsar who was a bachelor. Alix arrived on 10 October, accompanied by Ella. Nicky went to meet her at the station and together they drove to Livadia in an open carriage, villagers along the way welcoming them by throwing flowers and bunches of grapes. Ten days later the Tsar was dead.

'My God, my God, what a day!' Nicky wrote in his diary on 1 November. 'The Lord has called unto him our adored, dearly beloved Papa. My head is going round, I simply cannot believe it – it seems inconceivable, a terrible reality.' No one could believe it. The Tsar was only forty-nine. 'Emperor Alexander III died as he had lived,' wrote Sergei Witte, profoundly upset, 'a true Christian, a devoted son of the Orthodox church, a simple, strong, honourable man. The entire world recognised that it had enjoyed peace during his reign only because of his great love of peace, a love not expressed in words – he did not prattle about peace or initiate international peace conferences – but through action, by his firmness and devotion to peace.' Nicky, the new Emperor, slight of build and completely unprepared for the task, could hardly take it in. His cousin Sandro, married to Nicky's sister Xenia, saw the matter clearly. 'He [Nicky] took me by the arm and led me downstairs into his room. We embraced and cried and cried together. He could not collect his thoughts. He knew he was the Emperor now, and the weight of this terrifying fact crushed him. "Sandro, what am I going to do?" he exclaimed pathetically. "I am not prepared to be a Tsar. I never wanted to become one. I know nothing of the business of ruling. I have no idea of even how to talk to ministers."'

IO

Nicky and Willy

~

THE PRINCE AND Princess of Wales left London for Livadia at short
notice on 30 October 1894 to be with Minny in her hour of
need. By the following evening they had reached Vienna, where they
heard that the Tsar had died. They arrived at Livadia on 4 November,
and the following day the Prince of Wales wrote to Georgie, urging
him to join them for the State Funeral in St Petersburg 'out of respect
for poor dear Uncle Sasha's memory', but also because 'the opportunity to see the great capital of Russia is not one to be missed.' He
added, 'Poor Mama is terribly upset . . . this is indeed the most trying
and sad journey I have ever undertaken.' The two sisters shared a
bedroom in the palace of Livadia while Bertie was allotted his own
suite of rooms, overlooking the sea.

On 10 November the funeral train began its long journey via
Sebastopol and Moscow to St Petersburg, bearing the embalmed Tsar
in his coffin, attended by his royal relations. The train stopped at all the
larger stations, where huge crowds gathered and the local clergy
chanted prayers for the repose of the dead Tsar's soul. Nicky took
comfort from Alix's presence and rarely left her side. Among the throng
of royalties, courtiers and officials waiting when the funeral train
reached St Petersburg stood Sergei Witte. 'Emperor Nicholas II, still a
young man, left the train, followed by two women. Naturally, I was
eager to see our future Empress, whom I had never seen before, and
mistakenly thought the prettier of the two was she. I was astonished
when I was told that the prettier one was her aunt, Princess Alexandra,
wife of Edward, Prince of Wales. The young lady who turned out to
be our future Empress seemed not only less good-looking, but also less
sympathetic than her aunt. Of course, she too was pretty then, and still
is, but her mouth always seems to be set in anger.'

The funeral procession made its way from the station to the
Cathedral of St Peter and Paul, where for two days and two nights

the Tsar's subjects filed solemnly past his open coffin. By now
Georgie had arrived from England, as had his grandparents the King
and Queen of Denmark, and the Kings of Greece, Romania and
Serbia. The Kaiser could not find time in his busy schedule to come,
sending his brother Prince Heinrich and a letter instead. 'My dear
Nicky, the heavy and responsible task for which Providence had destined you has come upon you with the suddenness of a surprise,
through the so unexpected and untimely death of your dear lamented
father.' His elaborate English soon moved from the personal to the
political. Now that Nicky was Tsar, 'I only can repeat the expression
of absolute trust in you and the assurance that I shall always cultivate
the old relations of mutual friendship with your House.' With pre-
dictable misjudgement, Willy failed to realise that actions speak
louder than words. His own presence in St Petersburg would have
served him much better.

The Prince of Wales meanwhile attended all the long and elaborate ceremonies, never once complaining, not even when he had to
kiss the dead Tsar in his open coffin. He knew too well how important it was to remain on the best of terms with his nephew the new
Tsar and his niece the future Tsarina, who was by good fortune also
his goddaughter. He went everywhere and got on with everyone. He
even managed a bit of diplomacy, having a long conversation about
Anglo-Russian relations with the Foreign Minister, Nicholas Griers.
He also managed to persuade Queen Victoria to appoint Nicky
Honorary Colonel of the Scots Guards; Nicky in return appointed
him Honorary Colonel of the 27th Dragoon Guards of Kiev. 'Nicky
does everything so well and quietly, but is naturally shy and timid,' he
wrote to his mother on 11 November. 'There is no doubt that the
greatest loyalty and affection for the Emperor and his family exists
among the people, but they only wish to be trusted by him; and if
Nicky is liberal in his views, and tolerant to his subjects, a more
popular Ruler of this country could not possibly exist,' he added with
uncanny foresight.

Georgie had been enjoying a peaceful summer before his father
requested his presence in St Petersburg. On 6 August he had written
to May from Cowes, 'William arrived here in his Yacht this afternoon,
& I have just seen him, he is looking very well, he asked a great deal
after you & Baby . . . I am just off now with Papa to pay William a
visit on board the *Hohenzollern* but I hope he will be out . . .' William

was never too busy to go to Cowes. The next day Georgie wrote again to tell May that William had come second in the sailing-yacht race with his *Meteor*, he and Papa beating him by seventeen minutes. On 8 August he wrote to 'my own sweet little wife' again – every day a letter. Summing the matter up with unexpected candour, he told her, 'I know I am, at least I am vain enough to think that I am capable of loving anybody (who returns my love) with all my heart and soul, and I am sure I have found that person in my sweet little May. You know by this time that I never do anything by halves, when I asked you to marry me, I was very fond of you, but not very much in love with you, but I saw in YOU the person I was capable of loving most deeply, if only you returned that love . . . I have tried to understand you and to know you, and with the happy result that I know now that I do LOVE you darling girl with all my heart, and am simply DEVOTED to you . . . I ADORE YOU SWEET MAY, I can't say more than that.'

When the news of his uncle the Tsar's death came, Georgie was profoundly shocked. 'It is a terrible calamity for the whole world, a more honest, generous and kind-hearted man never lived,' he wrote in his diary, setting off for St Petersburg with Lord Carrington, Queen Victoria's Lord Chamberlain. In St Petersburg he was lodged at the Anitchkoff Palace along with all the other royals. The funeral service on 19 November lasted four hours. 'Dear Aunt Minny is quite won-derful, she is so calm, resigned and brave, it is quite touching to see Nicky with her, so different to the way someone else we know behaves to his mother,' Georgie found time to write to his mother-in-law. He kept the menu of 21 November, to paste in his diary when he got home. It was all in French: *Sterlet à la Moscovite, Foie Gras, Canetons Nontais, Asperges Hollandaise, Mazarin aux fruits*, and finishing, humorously, *with Bombe à la Napolitaine*. On 25 Novem-ber he noted, 'Nicky's last dinner as a Bachelor. Talked with Nicky, Georgie and Waldemar. Bed at 12.30.' The English, Russian, Greek and Danish cousins, 'the Club' as Georgie called them, were together again.

'The day of my wedding!' Nicky wrote in his diary on 26 November. 'Everyone had coffee together, and then went off to dress: I put on the Hussar uniform and at 11.30 drove with Misha to the Winter Palace.' Misha was his brother the Grand Duke Michael; his brother Georgei was so ill with tuberculosis that he had had to stay at

Livadia for both the funeral and the wedding. 'The whole Nevsky was lined with troops waiting for Mama to drive past with Alix. While she was being dressed in the Malachite Hall, we all waited in the Arabian Room. At ten to one the procession set off for the big church where I returned a married man!' Lord Carrington, who well knew the keen interest his Sovereign took in detail, 'ventured to put down a few things concerning the Imperial marriage which may not have appeared in the papers.' The weather, dull; the ladies, in Russian costume with some fine diamonds but hardly a pretty face; the pages, in red and gold with white breeches and long boots; the carriage servants, in red cloaks and laced cocked hats; the halls of the Winter Palace, so crowded with some 10,000 people that 'threading through them was not easy'; the seventy maids-of-honour, all dressed alike with scarlet sleeves, long trains and head circlets, one so old she needed to be propped up against a wall; the Marshal of the Court, Prince Troubetskoi, carrying a gold staff seven feet high with a diamond crown on the top; the Imperial procession, led by the King of Denmark and the Empress Marie – Minny – 'who was dressed in white, looking very pale and sad'; and finally the Imperial couple themselves, the Emperor in a very plain uniform walking with the bride, Queen Victoria's favourite granddaughter, who 'moved along quite simply and with great dignity' looking 'simply magnificent' in her crown of diamonds and 'enormous mantle of cloth of gold lined with ermine.'

From his position outside the palace the foreign correspondent of the *Daily Telegraph* was able to inform his readers in England over their breakfasts: 'So impenetrable was that living hedge all along the route that persons who set out for the Winter Palace a quarter of an hour after me never reached their destination at all. Peasants, hucksters, officers of reserve, petty tshinovnicks, old men, women, and young children, all braved the raw wintry blast, which grew gradually colder as the hours passed on. Some carried chairs, others bore ladders, many of the most enterprising constructed platforms of beams and boxes, whence to snatch a glimpse of the historic pageant; but the crowds were extremely orderly, and the police had very rarely to interfere.' Georgie, in the Anitchkoff Palace, noted that it had been 'a beautiful service but sad'. He and Papa had dined with the Lascelles at the British Embassy, and later played some billiards. The following day they lunched with Aunt Minny and Nicky and Alix. At this early stage in the extended period of Court mourning, the Dowger Empress had not permitted the royal couple to go on even the briefest honeymoon. The Prince of Wales told Carrington that Nicky and Alix had come down to breakfast the next morning 'as if nothing had happened.' For the time being Nicky was still very much under his mother's influence, though not for much longer.

When Lord Carrington left for England he took with him three letters for Queen Victoria, one from Nicky, one from Alix, and one from dutiful Georgie. 'Nicky has been kindness itself to me,' he told her, knowing as well as anyone how important good family relations were. 'He is the same dear boy he has always been to me, and talks to me quite openly on every subject.' When the Prince of Wales reached England, Lord Rosebery, Gladstone's successor as Prime Minister, congratulated him on his 'good and patriotic' work in Russia, which had been a 'signal service to your country as well as to Russia and the peace of the world.' Princess Alexandra stayed on in St Petersburg for another month, to be with Minny. 'I cannot think how the Empress would have got through these terrible days without her,' wrote Charlotte Knollys, Alexandra's Lady-in-Waiting and sister of Francis Knollys, to Queen Victoria from St Petersburg. On 1 December it was Princess Alexandra's fiftieth birthday. Nicky gave her a beautiful Fabergé diamond-centred crystal flower in a gold pot. 'All the family came,' wrote Georgie in his diary. 'She got half Fabergé's shop.' Three days later he himself was making for home, stopping off in Berlin, where he had tea with Aunt Vicky. The next day he saw William and then left for England, dining on the train. At Calais the following morning they washed and had breakfast in a hotel before crossing the Channel in thick fog. From London Georgie made his way swiftly to Windsor, where he found Grandmama, darling May and Baby waiting for him.

At first Nicky and Alix lived with the Dowager Tsarina at the Anitchkoff Palace, until their apartments in the Winter Palace were ready. Nicky's day began with breakfast at nine, seeing ministers and officials till eleven, a half-hour turn in the garden, then more audiences before receiving guests for luncheon, after which he and Alix made a *cercle* lasting till a quarter to three. A short drive or walk was followed by more work until tea, which was often taken with members of the Imperial family. Dinner was usually taken with the Dowager Tsarina, after which Nicky once more retired to his study, while Alix sat with her mother-in-law.

Whenever possible they escaped to the smaller Alexander Palace at Tsarskoe Selo, fifteen miles from St Petersburg. 'We have come here for four days and enjoy the quiet and beautiful air,' Alix wrote to Queen Victoria, 'poor Nicky has so much to do, that this rest here is very good for him and having him all to myself is such utter happiness. I can never thank God enough for having given me such a husband – and his love to You touches me also so deeply, for have You not been as a mother to me, since beloved Mama died . . . I always wear Your pretty ring. But now I must say goodbye, beloved Grandmama. Kissing Your dear hand most tenderly, I remain, Yr very loving devoted Child, Alix.' Alix, half-German, half-English, now tied herself to Nicky, becoming half-Russian as well. Nicky was not only her husband and lover but her life, a replacement for everything she had lost. She demanded to read his diary daily and took to adding comments, her English hand mixing with his Russian one. As early as 28 October, when Alexander III lay dying in Livadia, she wrote: 'Darling boysy, me loves you, oh, so very tenderly and deeply. Be firm and make the doctors come alone to you every day and tell you how they find him . . . Don't let others be put first and you left out. You are Father dear's own son and must be told all and be asked about everything. Show your own mind and don't let others forget WHO YOU ARE! Forgive me, lovy.' The words 'be firm' appear as a leit-motif in her letters to him, echoing all the way down through history.

Firmness was to prove a problem for Nicky for the rest of his life. 'Undoubtedly the new Emperor had loved his father very much and was consequently very grieved by his death; but, in addition, he was distressed at the thought of his new responsibilities, for which he was totally unprepared. Moreover, he was very much in love with his bride-to-be. Thus he was subject to various and strong impressions,' wrote clever Sergei Witte. Equally telling was the comment later sent by Sir George Buchanan, the urbane British Ambassador in St Petersburg, to his masters in England: 'The gentle but uneducated Tsar is afflicted with the misfortune of being weak on every point except his own autocracy.' Count Mossolov, a long-serving courtier who became head of the Court Chancellery, agreed. 'When he became Tsar, Nicholas II made it a fixed rule that he was in no way bound by his position as monarch to do anything that he did not want to do. In this his natural timidity played a part. He hated to have to investigate anything, to "stand up" to anybody.' Nicky's uncle

Bertie already knew this. 'Weak as water' was how he described his nephew.

This poses the question whether anyone could have been strong enough to rule Russia single-handedly. Even Alexander III had not managed to stem the growing tide of revolutionary activity; certainly it was beyond Nicky, who like his royal cousin in England was happiest living the life of a country gentleman, surrounded by his family. 'I am up to my neck in work, but thank God I am able to deal with it fairly easily,' he wrote to his brother Georgei, still immured at Livadia. 'There are receptions on Wednesdays and Fridays only – I am fed up with them! I remember how dear Papa could not bear them – how I understand him now!' The day before he had endured the *baisemain* reception, when 550 ladies came to Court to kiss the Tsar's hand. But he also managed to go skating most days, and on drives with Alix, and to read aloud from *Le Journal de la Duchesse D'Angoulême* to his mother in the evenings.

'Even those who were least partial to Nicholas II never denied his charm,' wrote Alexander Isvolsky, who later became Nicky's Foreign Minister. 'Personally I confess to have fallen under the spell of his attractive nature, and never more than when I saw him together with the Kaiser, whose loud exuberance and theatrical bearing were in direct contrast with the simple and unaffected behaviour of Nicholas II.' Nicky might not have been as well-educated as Willy but he was quite as clever as his German cousin, and a great deal more hardworking. On the other hand, even an admirer like Isvolsky had to admit that Nicholas was too easily influenced by the last person he had been talking to. He also lacked presence. Unlike his powerfully-built father, who had only to enter a room to be the centre of attention, Nicky was small and slight and, being shy, too inclined to slip into a room, almost unnoticed.

On 29 January 1895 he was 'in a terrible state' because he had to go to the Nikolayevsky Hall and deliver a speech to representatives of the nobility, the *zemstvos* (local councils) and the town committees. He was nervous, as so often before an important State event. Nevertheless, he stated his position clearly. 'I am aware that recently in some *zemstvos* there have arisen the voices of people carried away by senseless dreams of taking part in the business of government. Let everyone know that I will retain the principles of autocracy as firmly and unbendingly as my unforgettable late father.' The phrase 'senseless dreams' was particularly badly received: one can almost hear the voice of Pobednostsev. 'It was Pobednostsev who drew up the address which the Emperor received at his hands at the last moment before entering the hall of the audience,' wrote Isvolsky. 'When one thinks of the wide circulation of this unfortunate speech, taken back by the representatives of the Zemstvos to their constituents in the uttermost corners of Russia, one will understand my assertion that this first contact of Nicholas II with his people marks the beginning of a misunderstanding which from that day never ceased to prevail between the Sovereign and the Russian nation.'

The new Tsar was not helped by his family. His uncles the Grand Dukes, who all towered over him, were loth to give up the positions they held to this young and inexperienced nephew with so little of a real Tsar about him. Nicky's cousin Sandro, married to Xenia, put his finger on it: 'The uncles always wanted something. Nikolai fancied himself a Great Warrior. Alexei ruled the waves. Sergei tried to turn Moscow into his private domain. Vladimir advocated the cause of the Arts. They all had their favourite generals and admirals who were supposed to be promoted ahead of a long waiting list; their ballerinas desirous of organising a "Russian Season" in Paris; their wonderful preachers anxious to redeem the Emperor's soul; their miraculous physicians soliciting a Court appointment; their clairvoyant peasants with a divine message.' Sandro and Xenia's son-in-law, Felix Yusupov, left an unforgettable portrait of one of the uncles, Ella's husband Sergei, who had, as Queen Victoria rightly supposed, played an important part in bringing Alix and Nicky together. 'I adored the Grand Duchess,' wrote Yusupov, 'but had little liking for the Grand Duke. His manners seemed strange to me and I hated the way he stared at me. He wore corsets, and when he was in his summer uniform the bones could be clearly seen through his white linen tunic. As a child, it always amused me to touch them, and this of course annoyed him intensely.' Sergei was an unpleasant bully and, as most people at the Russian Court knew, a homosexual.

The Kaiser meanwhile began to bombard the new Tsar with long telegrams, crammed with advice. He thought Nicky would be malleable, unlike his father Alexander III who, right to the last, and encouraged by his Danish wife, had retained his dislike and distrust of Prussia and Prussians. Willy's main aim was to detach Nicky from France. Ever since the Franco-Prussian war Germany had been concerned to avoid a *revanche* war with France, still smarting from the loss of Alsace-Lorraine. In the event of such a war, France's alliance with Russia would mean fighting on two fronts. 'Encirclement' became Willy's obsession and eventually developed into a full-blown paranoia, fanned by his warmongering military, that he was being attacked on all sides, France, England and Russia ganging up on him like schoolboys in a playground. To an extent, he was right. One of Alexander III's last acts before he died had been to form a secret defensive alliance with France. Willy's mistake was to feel that the solution to this was military, rather than political.

In January he wrote to wish Nicky and Alix a happy New Year, adding a few words of advice about Nicky's choice of new Russian Ambassador for Berlin. In February he wrote a few words of warning about France and her republican government. 'The impulse given to the Democrats and the Revolutionary party is also to be felt here. My Reichstag behaves as badly as it can, swinging backwards and forwards between the Socialists egged on by Jews, and the ultramontane Catholiks [*sic*]; both parties being soon fit to be hung all of them as far as I can see. In England the ministry is toddling on to its fall amidst universal derision! In short everywhere the *principe de la Monarchie* is called upon to show itself strong.' In April he was writing to introduce Prince Radolin, his personal choice for Ambassador to St Petersburg, taking the opportunity to reassure Nicky that he would do all in his power to 'keep Europe quiet and also guard the rear of Russia so that nobody shall hamper your action towards the Far East! For that is clearly the great task of the future for Russia, to cultivate the Asian Continent and to defend Europe from the inroads of the great Yellow Race.' Privately Willy thought that a war in the East would conveniently exhaust Russia, making a war on two fronts less likely. He assured Nicky that he would gladly help him settle the question of eventual annexations of territory for Russia, if he would kindly in return see that Germany acquired a port somewhere useful. When he next wrote he wished his cousins 'a quiet summer and a nice little boy to come', Alix being by now pregnant with their first child. By July he was back to his favourite subject, the Far East, describing it as Nicky's great mission, for which Heaven had shaped him, as sure as 'Amen in Church!' He took the opportunity of telling Nicky that two Russian engineers had been caught spying on some of his battleships and fortifications at the opening to the Kiel Canal in June. Nicky had been invited to attend but had unaccountably refused, sending his uncle Grand Duke Alexei instead.

Cousin Georgie in England was not given any choice. It was thought diplomatically expedient that he should attend, especially as the Canal clearly had a strategic as well as a peaceful purpose. On June 18 he embarked on the Royal Yacht *Osborne*, steaming from Sheerness to Hamburg. During the day he sat on deck and read or played piquet; by the evening they were cruising up the river Elbe, having dinner. 'Very pretty,' Georgie noted. They arrived at Hamburg at 9.15. 'A great many ships here, crowds of people and boats. Bed at 12.' The following day William arrived on *Hohenzollern*. That evening there was a banquet for 600, followed by a trip to an island in the middle of a lake, built for the occasion; it had cost 500,000 Marks, and was to be removed again on 1 July. No expense was too great to mark the achievement which gave Germany access to the Baltic Sea, as planned by Bismarck and Willy's grandfather right from the start of their three wars of German unification. After a firework display the party set off for the entrance to the Canal. 'Very pretty sight going thro' Canal, all the banks lined with people & troops.' At Kiel were some eighty ships dressed overall, and the Channel Squadron, looking 'magnificent'. After dinner on the *Hohenzollern* there was a ball – 'Awful crowd'. The next day Georgie and his wife presented themselves 'in full dress (in German uniform)' to attend as Willy and Dona laid a foundation stone. In the evening there was another banquet, this time for 1000, in a house built to look like a ship, and William made an 'excellent' speech. 'Beautiful night. Fireworks and illuminations. Bed at 12' wrote Georgie, the nice, simple and straightforward cousin. By Monday 24 June he was back at York House where he found his 'darling beloved May and sweet Baby' waiting for him. They lunched with Papa, Motherdear and sisters. But that evening they dined alone.

'I received the German Emperor's Aide-de-camp, Moltke. He brought me a letter and an engraving from that bore, Herr Wilhelm,' wrote Nicky in his diary on 11 September 1895, evidently not impressed. The subject of the engraving was Russia's glorious fight against the Yellow Peril which Willy had commissioned one of his artists to produce. Based on a sketch by his own hand, it showed the Powers of Europe, artfully represented by Genii, being called together by the Archangel Michael to unite and resist 'the inroad of Buddism, heathenism and barbarism for the Defence of the Cross'. Later, on a new tack, Willy wrote to warn Nicky that he had just received information that England was after the Dardanelles. He expressed himself stupefied at the news, adding that 'since Salisbury's *avénément* England's foreign policy has become most mysterious and unintelligible, and the quaint way in which the Fleet sulks around the Dardanelles indicates that it means something there.' Knowing how susceptible the Russians were on this subject he was highly pleased with his effort, offered privately, as one royal colleague to another. His ministers, on the other hand, were appalled by this further example of the Kaiser's autocratic behaviour, bypassing all normal channels of Government. Eulenburg had meanwhile floated to Holstein the idea of a pre-emptive war against Russia. Holstein worded his reply carefully. 'In *one* point I share your opinion, namely that a *successful war* would have a very salutary effect. But as a precondition of this a *righteous* cause, as in 1870, would be necessary. You will agree that if we undertook a war of *aggression* we would have to be prepared for strange surprises,' he wrote. 'There is little prospect now of a defensive war, however, because no one wants to do anything to us.'

The main issue in foreign affairs remained the 'Eastern Question', as the Great Powers busily carved up the disintegrating Ottoman Empire. Everyone knew that Russia wanted Constantinople and the Dardanelle Straits in order to gain access to the Mediterranean. This did not please Britain, who foresaw that it might in time threaten her control of Suez and, eventually, India. For its part, the Hapsburg Empire was concerned to have control of the Balkans. Willy meanwhile was warning Nicky not to support the French, who had been spotted moving their troops along the border. 'God knows I have done all in my power to preserve the European Peace, but if France goes on openly or secretly encouraged like this to violate all rules of international courtesy and Peace in peace times, one fine day, my dearest Nicky, you will find yourself nolens volens suddenly embroiled in the most horrible of wars Europe ever saw!'

In mid September Nicky and Alix had moved to their new apartments in the Alexander Palace at Tsarskoe Selo. 'We settled ourselves in these marvellous rooms; sometimes we simply sit in silence wherever we happen to be and admire the walls, the fireplace, the furniture,' Nicky wrote to his mother. 'The mauve room (Alix's boudoir) is delightful – one wonders when it looks better, in the evening or by daylight? Alix's first room, the Chippendale drawing room, is also attractive, all in pale green.' The Tsarina was 'a lover of flowers and nature, and her rooms were always a mass of white lilac and every kind of beautiful orchids', recalled Baroness Buxhoeveden, her Lady-in-Waiting. 'These throve, for the Empress's rooms were always extremely cold, a trial to those unaccustomed to it. Like her grandmother Queen Victoria, she could not stand a temperature that was even moderately warm. The bedrooms and nurseries were all simply upholstered in bright chintzes. The Empress kept faithfully to the English ideas that had been her mother's, and these rooms were like those of a comfortable English house.' Half-English, half-German – whichever way you looked at it, the new Tsarina was unmistakably foreign.

Minny, the Dowager Tsarina and Alix's mother-in-law, had been cleverer, taking on many Russian ways, and charming people at Court with her attractive manner, showing an interest in everyone while nevertheless maintaining her dignity. Alix, shy and prickly, could not do this. Instead she immersed herself in family life. 'Twice we went up to the future nursery,' Nicky wrote to his mother. 'The other day part of the baby's trousseau arrived from England and a cot – the same as Xenia had.' Queen Victoria also sent out an English nurse. And of course there was Orchie, Miss Orchard, who had been Princess Alice's nurse all those years ago in England, then Alix's own in Germany, and now followed Alix to Russia to have overall supervision of the nursery. In November 1895 their first child was born. Nicky and Alix had already chosen the name, Paul. When the baby turned out to be a girl, they called her Olga.

In England Queen Victoria was once again vexed by William, who had taken it upon himself to interfere in Britain's business in South Africa. On 30 December Leander Starr Jameson, a close friend of Cecil Rhodes, Prime Minister of the Cape Colony, had crossed the border into the Boer Republic of the Transvaal with 470 mercenaries of the British South Africa Company and eight machine-guns, attempting a lightening raid on Johannesburg as part of a revolt organised by Rhodes to bring the Transvaal into a federation owing allegiance to the British Crown. Led by their President Paul Kruger the Boer Republic, rich in diamonds and recently-discovered gold, naturally resisted. The revolt failed through lack of support, and Jameson and his men were forced to surrender on 2 January 1896.

Officially, Britain denied any involvement. On the following day the Kaiser sent a telegram of congratulation to Kruger, verbosely offering 'most sincere congratulations that you and your people have been successful, by your own strength and without appealing for help of friendly powers, against the armed band that broke into your land as destroyers of peace and restored peace and defended the independence of the country against attacks from without. Wilhelm IR.' German businessmen had traded for years and invested millions of Marks in Kruger's republic, and there was no doubt in the Kaiser's mind which side he was on. 'After all,' he wrote in February to Sir Edward Sullivan, an English yachting friend, 'the commandment "Thou shalt not steal" is also written for Britons as well as for other people?!'

In this he was surely right, but it was not clever to send the telegram. The English press had a field day. Queen Victoria was furious. 'As your Grandmother to whom you have always shown so much affection and of whose example you have always spoken with so much respect, I feel I cannot refrain from expressing my deep regret at the telegram you sent President Kruger,' she wrote on 5 January 1896. 'It is considered very unfriendly towards this country, which I feel sure it is not intended to be, and has, I grieve to say, made a very painful impression here. The action of Dr Jameson was of course very wrong and totally unwarranted, but considering the very peculiar position in which the Transvaal stands towards Great Britain, I think it would have been far better to have said nothing.' The Prince of Wales, outraged, called William's behaviour 'a most gratuitous act of unfriendliness'. Georgie felt much the same. He had been talking to one of Willy's ADCs who was visiting Osborne, and wrote to tell May: 'He assured me that W. would NOT come to Cowes this summer, at which I am mightily pleased,' he added.

The Prince of Wales was soon bucked up. By March an outstanding young soldier, Herbert Kitchener, was advancing from Egypt to the Sudan on the first stage of a further colonial expansion. 'I hope, as you do, that the Force will be large enough, as any reverses would be disastrous to our interests,' he wrote to Georgie. 'The French are mad with rage with us about it; but, as we never do right in their eyes, it is useless paying any attention to their abuse.' June was even better: he won the Derby with Persimmon, beating his friend Leopold de Rothschild's St Frusquin by a head to deafening cheers from the patriotic crowd, and earning a total of £28,734 in stake money that year.

But in Germany the incident of the Jameson Raid caused the Kaiser to think ahead. He realised he had been powerless to act in a situation in which war between Germany and Britain threatened, however briefly. South Africa was simply too far away: only a navy as powerful as the Royal Navy could enable Germany to act so far from Europe, and from then on the Kaiser had his sights firmly set on his Big Navy. Year after year he insisted on swingeing increases to the Naval budget which the Reichstag was forced to accept.

By the mid 1890s there was regular, if veiled, criticism in the press of the Kaiser's increasingly autocratic behaviour, and of his powerful entourage and the way it acted unconstitutionally, without recourse to Parliament. In 1894 the journalist Ludwig Quidde published a pamphlet, 'Caligula, a study in megalomania'. No one was in any doubt about Caligula's identity. In the same year the satirical magazine *Kladderadatsch* ('Jibberish Gossip') launched an attack on the men advising the Kaiser, seen at that time to be Eulenburg, Holstein and an ally of Holstein's in the Foreign Office, Alfred von Kiderlen-Waechter. The three were not named, but again everyone knew who was meant, especially Eulenburg, aptly dubbed 'Count Troubadour'. It was noted that Count Troubadour was manipulating all his friends into positions of influence. The three men were just waiting for the fourth player to join them at their card game of Skat. For those in the know, the fourth player was Eulenburg's old friend Axel Varnbüler. That year Eulenburg had managed to get Varnbüler the post of Württemberg's envoy to Berlin. 'Axel is first and foremost your Majesty's servant,' Eulenburg wrote to the Kaiser. 'I have briefed him exactly and explained the task he must fulfil.' Most people assumed that all this inside information could be traced straight back to the Bismarcks.

For the time being Holstein was part of Eulenburg's plan, but not for much longer, since he had never shared Eulenburg's advocacy of absolute monarchy. In March 1894 Eulenburg wrote the Kaiser one of his secret memos, coolly setting out the agenda for the next three years, in preparation for the instigation of the Kaiser's 'Personal Rule'. First Caprivi was to be dismissed and replaced by Botho zu Eulenburg, the reactionary Minister of Interior and Philipp zu Eulenburg's cousin, 'the most important statesman Your Majesty possesses.' Next Marschall, the Secretary of State at the Foreign Office, was to be replaced by Bernhard von Bülow, as a last stage before Bülow took over the Chancellorship from Botho. Finally, Holstein should be dismissed if he objected to these moves. By October Caprivi had resigned, worn out by the Kaiser's refusal to accept any constraints from his Chancellor or the Reichstag. August zu Eulenburg, usually so discreet, now for once showed his true colours, speaking out in favour of his brother Botho. But Holstein resisted so strongly that a compromise candidate was found: Prince Chlodwig zu Hohenlohe-Schillingsfürst, currently viceroy of Alsace-Lorraine. Hohenlohe was old and frail, a Bavarian aristocrat and a Catholic – certainly not an obvious choice for Imperial Chancellor and Minister-President of Prussia. It was soon apparent that he was acceptable to the Eulenburg circle because he would mostly do as he was told.

This left Marschall and General Walter Bronsart von Schellendorf, Minister of War and another Holstein man. 'The position of Ministers is becoming utterly impossible,' Bronsart noted in February 1895. 'One wears oneself out trying to achieve something, and then anonymous advisers come along and ruin everything. Things cannot go on like this.' Marschall felt the same. 'It is a fine thing to have to deal not only with foreign states, but with HM and his irresponsible advisers into the bargain,' he wrote in his diary on 17 February 1895.

The issue which brought matters to a head was the reform of the military code, in particular the system of courts martial, which were held in secret, effectively placing the military above the law. Bronsart, supported by Marschall and Holstein, introduced a Bill to the Reichstag. The Kaiser was beside himself. 'The army is subject, both in war and peace, exclusively to My orders,' he proclaimed in a speech in 1895. Nevertheless, initially it looked as though the Reichstag would prevail, Hohenlohe having for once made a stand, pushed to it by Holstein. Throughout December 1895 Holstein was writing to Eulenburg, urging him to find a way of controlling the Kaiser. 'Apply yourself seriously to this,' he warned on 26 December, 'and bear in mind that without this bitter medicine, the Kaiser and the Vaterland, both, will find themselves in deep trouble.' He reminded Eulenburg that 'a Kaiser as his own Imperial Chancellor would be questionable under any circumstances, but most particularly with this impulsive and unfortunately totally superficial Master, who has absolutely no idea about constitutional law, political precedent, the history of diplomacy, or how to handle people. Am I right? So please, don't bury your head in the sand.' He signed himself 'your worried Holstein' and advised him to consult Bernhard von Bülow before taking any action.

Holstein did not know that Eulenburg was sending copies of his letters straight to Bülow. 'Be careful that History does not some day picture you as the dark horseman who was at the side of the imperial wanderer when he turned into the false path,' he warned Eulenburg again, still thinking he might prevent disaster. Like Bismarck before him, he tried to use a political crisis to force the Kaiser into line but, like Bismarck, he failed, because the *camarilla* surrounding the Kaiser were determined to resist any move towards constitutional reform and democracy. By May 1896 Eulenburg and Bülow were winning, Hohenlohe was slipping back into the shadows of appeasement. Some said it was because he was too old and too weak; some thought that in spite of his grand name he was too poor, and needed money to sustain a large family in suitable fashion. He was in fact awarded a huge bonus of 20,000 Marks per annum, which it is hard not to construe as a bribe. By August 1896 Bronsart was gone, replaced by a man entirely to Eulenburg and the Kaiser's liking. It took another year to get rid of Marschall, just long enough to arrange for Bernhard von Bülow to take his place. The chance of forcing the Kaiser to some constitutional reform, a chance which might have changed the course of both German and world history, was now finally lost.

Eulenburg and Bülow's fateful relationship had its beginnings as far back as 1881, when they were both diplomats at the German Embassy in Paris. In January 1886 Eulenburg described a visit to Bülow, now posted to Vienna and conveniently married to his divorcée, the Countess von Dönhoff, Wilhelm's confidante of many years past. 'It was, as ever, the greatest pleasure to see Bernhard,' he wrote to his mother. 'We share absolutely the same political views, and are so attached to one another both personally and through our working relationship that we can tell each a thousand things which we can't tell anyone else, or not easily, and that does one good.'

The following month Bülow was moved to St Petersburg. He did not write to Eulenburg until 29 May 1886, just a few days after Eulenburg's first meeting with Prince Wilhelm at Prokelwitz, an event he most certainly had heard about from his colleague Holstein. 'How delightful it would be if we could see each other!! Spending time with you, my dearest friend, is such a joy for me,' he wrote, after making his excuses for not having written for so long. 'I have a real longing to talk with you. Although yours is an essentially aesthetic nature, and mine essentially a political one, we have so much in common. I pay myself a great compliment in saying this. Always your loyal friend, Bernhard B.' Bülow, known as 'the eel' for his impressive powers of flattery and manipulation, was planning ahead.

Eulenburg certainly believed in his friend's sincerity. By the time of the Bismarck crisis in 1890 he could write to Bülow in full confidence: 'How often I think of you when questions and decisions of a serious nature crop up and how I wish I had your experience at my side . . . Write me what you advise . . . If only *you* were in Berlin.' Bülow was quick to take up the role of political adviser, sending Eulenburg outrageously flattering letters written in an emotional style like Eulenburg's own, and quite unlike the style in which he wrote to others. 'As sisters our souls once arose from the mysterious spring of Being,' he wrote in March 1893, 'we were simply given different shells and differently coloured wings. As the heavenly beings have granted you the magic gift of a rich and brilliant artistic talent . . . I, by inclination and upbringing more dependent on historical, legal, economic studies, may be able to pass over to you from the storeroom which I am slowly stocking up, many a piece for the edifice which you, having been thrown into the political struggle against your own inclinations, are nevertheless constructing with a felicitous and certain touch for the benefit of our Kaiser and country.' In another letter he assured Eulenburg that the Kaiser's ideas were almost always right, and often brilliant, but 'It is another question whether the All-Highest's intentions are always efficiently carried out.' He might as well have written 'Bülow for Chancellor' in red letters all over the page.

Eulenburg needed no convincing. 'Bernhard is the most valuable servant Your Majesty possesses, the predestined Reich Chancellor of the future,' he wrote to the Kaiser as early as February 1895. He himself continued to have no wish for official political power, still preferring to exercise his influence at a distance from Vienna, by letter or through his regular private meetings with the Kaiser in the intimate safety of the Liebenberg Circle. He had the loyal and devoted Lucanus in place at Court as Chief of the Civil Cabinet, and his cousin August zu Eulenburg quietly supporting him in his key position as Marshal of the Court. But the Reichstag remained a problem. Eulenburg despised the parliamentary process, nursing a particular loathing for the Social Democrats and the social reformers who were threatening everything he believed in. He needed Bülow as Chancellor – Bülow, who shared not only Eulenburg's views, but his soul.

'I would be a different kind of Chancellor from my predecessors,' Bülow assured Eulenburg on 23 July 1896. 'I would regard myself as the executive tool of His Majesty, so to speak his political Chief of Staff. With me, personal rule – in the good sense – would really begin.' Hohenlohe was kept on until 1900, merely as a 'façade', to use his own word. Impetuous Wilhelm could hardly wait. 'Bülow will be my Bismarck' he announced, long before the event and on the clear understanding that Bülow would be his 'executive tool'. Holstein, finally understanding the situation, held tenaciously to his job, but he never spoke or wrote to Eulenburg again.

I I

Turn of the Century

~

GEORGIE WAS MOST upset at not being allowed to attend Nicky's Coronation in May 1896. 'My dear old Nicky,' he wrote from Copenhagen, where he was staying with Amama and Apapa, on 17 April. 'I want to tell you how disappointed both May and I are that we are not coming to the Coronation. I regret it most deeply. Of course it was impossible for you to do anything after Grandmama had told you she was going to send Uncle Arthur. Everybody in England expected that we were going and when at last it was settled that the Connaughts were going I must say I was furious, but there was nothing to be done.' Willy in Germany could have attended, but did not care to: again, he sent his brother instead. 'Your Embassy has enquired about my being represented at the Coronation at Moskau [sic] and I have named Henry as my representant,' he wrote to Nicky in a mixture of German and English. 'I should be very thankful if you would kindly see that the question of his rank is made out clearly, as I heard that your Master of Ceremonies has hinted to Radolin that he would have to follow all the Hereditary German Granddukes and Princes, even the son of the Prince of Montenegro.' Precedence was a matter on the importance of which all three royal cousins could agree.

'A great solemn day for Alix, Mama and myself,' Nicky wrote in his diary in Moscow on 26 May, the day of his Coronation. 'We were on our feet from 8 o'clock in the morning; though our procession did not move off till 9.30. Luckily the weather was heavenly. The Grand Staircase presented a glittering sight. Everything took place in the Uspensky Cathedral, and although it seems like a dream, I will remember it all my life!' Those waiting inside the cathedral could hear the distant cheers of the crowd massed in the square as their Majesties' procession approached. The Dowager Tsarina, clad in a heavy purple mantle, waited on a throne to the right of the thrones of the Tsar and the new Tsarina. The priests went out onto the steps of the cathedral to greet their Majesties, blessing them with holy water. Entering the cathedral, their Majesties bowed to the icons. At the altar the Tsar recited the Credo in a clear voice, then donned his purple mantle, raised the crown onto his own head, and took the orb and sceptre, at which everyone sank to their knees before him. That evening, as darkness fell, all the towers and walls of the Kremlin were lit up with electric illuminations.

Four days later, by tradition, food and gifts of tankards and china were distributed to the people in the new Tsar's name in celebration of the Coronation in a field on the outskirts of Moscow known as the Khodinka meadow. In anticipation thousands had gathered the night before, and by the time the gifts were distributed early the following afternoon, the crush was so great that more than nine hundred people, including many children, were trampled to death. 'My blood froze. I felt sick. Yet I still stared on,' wrote Olga, another of Nicky's sisters. 'Those carts carried the dead – mangled out of all recognition.' By the time the Tsar and Tsarina arrived all the bodies had been cleared away, and everything was back to normal. But they were both extremely distressed, and intended to cancel their appearance at a ball given by the French Ambassador that evening. Nicky's uncle, Ella's husband, Grand Duke Sergei, by now Governor-General of Moscow, objected strongly, on the grounds that it would be an insult to the French, and insisted they attend. Nicky, uncertain and vacillating, finally gave way. His sister Xenia and her husband Sandro were appalled. 'My brothers could not control their indignation,' wrote Sandro, 'and we four demanded the immediate dismissal of Grand Duke Sergei and the calling off of all festivities. A painful scene ensued. The elder Grand Dukes rallied around Uncle Sergei.' They all had to go to the ball, where Sandro noted that Sergei was greeting everyone with a broad smile as though nothing had happened, causing foreigners there to think the Romanovs, including the Tsar and Tsarina, were out of their minds. Sandro and his brothers left as soon as the dancing began, causing Uncle Alexei to remark, 'There go the four imperial followers of Robespierre.'

This was the crux of the matter, and remained so for the rest of Nicky's reign. Were you for the Romanovs, or for Robespierre? Would Russia be ruled by a repressive autocratic regime, or a progressive, proto-democratic one? Even Russia herself could not decide: her people and her politicians were divided. All through the 1880s and

1890s the Ministry of Internal Affairs, worried by the constant threat of social unrest and revolution, argued for more money to be invested in education and agriculture, railway construction and industrial development, and gave moderate support to the emerging trade union movement, but also brought in draconian measures to curb striking workers and combat revolutionaries. The Ministry of Finance meanwhile was arguing for fewer restrictions, to allow the natural development of trade and capitalism, the only solution in the long run for a country as vast as Russia, with a hundred million peasants and smallholders and an ineffective tax system. The War Ministry argued that Russia, so much poorer than England, France or Germany, needed to spend hugely on her Army and Navy in order to maintain her position in world affairs. The War Ministry won, putting the Russian economy under even greater pressure.

Count Sergei Witte, appointed Minister of Finance in 1893, tried to bring in legislation to improve the Russian economy and argued for the improvement of workers' conditions, particularly in the fast-growing factories. For this he gained a reputation as a dangerous liberal, although he was in fact a monarchist with a certain respect for the English model, believing a monarch needed to be surrounded by good advisers. 'When Tsar Nicholas II ascended the throne, he had, if one may put it this way, an aura of resplendent good will. He truly desired happiness and a peaceful life for Russia, for all his subjects, whatever nationality they might belong to. There is no question that he has a thoroughly good, kind heart,' wrote Witte in his memoirs, finished in 1912. 'If he displayed other characteristics in later years it is because he experienced many tribulations. Perhaps he brought on some of these tribulations by placing his faith in unsuitable people, but he acted as he did in the belief that he was doing the right thing.' This is Witte's way of saying Nicky was good, but not that good.

'This year seems to be a year of hard labour, with Alix and me as the martyrs,' Nicky wrote to his brother Georgei, still immured in the Crimea, on 10 August. 'Moscow in the Spring, and now soon these intolerable foreign visits. First of all we go to Austria, then Kiev, Germany, Denmark, England, France and finally Darmstadt; there at least we can hope for a complete rest. An attractive prospect, don't you think? On top of it, we shall have to drag our poor little daughter with us, as all the relatives want to see her.' This would not be everyone's idea of 'hard labour', travelling in Imperial trains and on Imperial yachts in the greatest luxury attended by dozens of servants, courtiers and officials, but for Nicky, the man who loved the simple home life, it seemed so. The two royal cousins Nicky and Georgie not only looked alike, but were alike in their tastes. On that 29 July Nicky had been out all day duck-shooting, killing 72 birds, only coming home to have tea with his sister Xenia and Sandro, who were visiting. In England, at his beloved Sandringham, Georgie was the proud possessor of a pair of 12-bore Purdeys, given to him as a wedding present by the people of Kings Lynn, with which he slaughtered thousands of pheasants, partridges and woodcock.

In September Nicky and Alix were in Scotland, visiting Grandmama. They arrived at Leith on board their new Imperial Yacht *Standart* and were met by uncle Bertie and uncle Arthur, both in their Russian uniforms. Nicky was wearing the uniform of the Royal Scots Greys, bearskin and all. After a reception hosted by the mayors of Leith and Edinburgh the royal party proceeded to the royal train. The Prince of Wales had cut short his annual holiday at Homburg to supervise every detail of the Tsar's visit. There were torchlight processions along the route and bonfires on all the hills as they proceeded from Leith to Ballater. At Ballater station, decorated and lit by electric light, Georgie and May awaited them. Georgie wore the kilt. The royal procession continued by carriage to Balmoral. 'Heard of Nicky and Alicky's disembarkation, and of their departure from Leith,' wrote Queen Victoria in her Journal at Balmoral on 22 September 1896. 'Went down soon after half-past seven into the visitors' rooms and waited there till we heard the church bells ringing and the pipers playing. Punctually at eight, the procession reached the door. The escort of Scots Greys came first, then the pipers and torch bearers, and finally the carriage containing Nicky, Alicky, Bertie and Arthur. I was standing at the door. Nicky got out first, whom I embraced, and then darling Alicky, all in white, looking so well, whom I likewise embraced most tenderly.'

They all dined with Grandmama at 8.45. 'Family dinner, only 12,' Georgie noted in his diary. After dinner he 'had a talk with dear Nicky. He is just the same dear boy he always was.' The next day they went deer-stalking, and later the younger set all hung around in Alix's room talking and smoking before playing a game of billiards. The day after, Motherdear and Toria, who remained unmarried, arrived from their usual summer holiday in Denmark. On 26 September Lord

Salisbury arrived from London, hoping for some informal chats with the Tsar on matters of international importance.

Salisbury was chiefly preoccupied with the Middle Eastern question. He thought the best solution was to dethrone Abdul Hamid II, the Sultan of Turkey, and agree the division of Turkey 'before dinner at Balmoral'. In August he had written to his friend Canon Gordon about the strangeness of the fact that the future of Europe, 'for good or evil', depended on the will of three men, the Kaiser, the Tsar and the Sultan of Turkey, in spite of the progress of democratic ideas. His own sovereign, Queen Victoria, was not included because, as a constitutional monarch, she reigned but did not rule.

Salisbury and the Tsar met informally at seven in the evening – before dinner – on the following day, Sunday 27 September 1896. In a memo headed VERY SECRET Salisbury reported the conclusions of their meeting to his Cabinet. The Tsar did not object to Britain being in Egypt but refused to discuss Turkey, insisting that the Straits should be open to Russian warships and the Dardanelles in Russian hands; otherwise, he said, Russia was like a man who did not own the key to a room in which he lived. As for his royal cousin the Kaiser, the Tsar made it quite plain that he disliked him, finding him 'nervous and ill-mannered', with an awful habit of poking him in the ribs, or slapping him on the back like a schoolboy.

Nicky was expected to go out shooting with uncle Bertie and cousin Georgie every day, regardless of the weather. Luckily uncle Bertie soon tired of Balmoral, where his mother never included him in any of the more serious conversations held between herself, the Tsar, Lord Salisbury and various other ministers who turned up. On 29 September he was at the races at Newmarket where, gratifyingly, one of his horses won a race. 'After he left I had an easier time, because I could at least do what I wanted to, and was not *obliged* to go out shooting every day in the cold and rain,' Nicky later wrote to his mother, adding, 'Granny was kinder and more amiable than ever. She sent Lord Salisbury to see me, and I had two very serious talks with him. It's good at least for him to learn from the source what the opinions and views of Russia are.' He had been glad of cousin Georgie's company on the shoots, he said. 'We can at least talk over the good times we've just had in Denmark.'

On the way home the Tsar and Tsarina paid a State Visit to France, Russia's ally despite all the Kaiser's threats and warnings. Nicky began with his usual little 'fit of nerves', but they were quickly overcome when he saw their enthusiastic reception. 'Wherever we went huge crowds lined the streets with policemen about every twenty yards apart in front, and the people stood absolutely still, everybody keeping his place in the most orderly manner while cheering as loud as they could, and frantically waving hats and handkerchiefs.' So much for Willy's warnings about dangerous Republics. The Tsar and Tsarina left France four days later with regret, arriving at the frontier in the Imperial train at eleven at night. 'There, for the last time, we saw the little *pioux-pioux* [term of endearment for French soldiers] and heard the strains of our national anthem,' Nicky wrote to his mother. 'After this began German helmets, and it was unpleasant to look out of the window. At every station in France one heard "Hurrah" and saw kind and jolly faces, but here everything was black and dark and boring! Happily it was time to go to bed.'

The following July Nicky had to put up with Willy's company whether he liked it or not. The Kaiser went to Russia on a State Visit, with his usual retinue of officers, courtiers, and a clutch of personal servants to care for his comfort and his appearance. 'The wardrobe of the Kaiser was a comprehensive one, and under a large and efficient staff of attendants,' recalled the Court official, still hard at work in the service of his third Kaiser. 'Uniforms were naturally innumerable; gala uniforms of his own and every other important nation were kept in readiness for a visit to be paid or for a visitor to be received in; uniforms of every one of His Majesty's regiments; interim uniforms for house wear; naval uniforms for the sea or the river. For ordinary repairs several tailors had their quarters in the Schloss, the making of uniforms being entrusted to the Court firms. The Kaiser's civilian dress was very limited. Whenever he went to London he ordered a good quality of clothing; England was the only country where he wore mufti-suits.' In all, the Kaiser possessed some four hundred uniforms, and he had himself photographed in most of them, posing in haughty military fashion or in more relaxed naval mode, moustaches twirling gaily upwards, always artfully lit, like something out of a German operetta. Now Willy was thrilled to acquire a new Russian uniform. 'I'm sorry to tell you we shall have to give Wilhelm the rank of Admiral in our Navy,' Nicky wrote apologetically to his mother, who had made a hasty retreat to Denmark. 'Uncle Alexei reminded me of it; and, I think, no matter how disagreeable it may be, we are obliged to let him wear our naval uniform, particularly as he made me last year a captain in his own navy and, what's much worse, I'll have to greet him as such at Kronstadt. *C'est à vomir!* (It makes you sick!)'

For once the Kaiserin accompanied the Kaiser, attended by her usual set of ladies-in-waiting, the Hallelujah Aunts, led by the Countess von Benckendorff. 'On the whole Wilhelm was very cheerful, calm and courteous,' Nicky wrote to his mother, 'while she tried to be charming and looked very ugly in rich clothes chosen without taste; the hats she wore in the evenings and at the performance at Olgino were particularly impossible.' He went on to describe a ridiculous incident concerning the performance of Offenbach's *La Vie Parisienne*. Strict orders had been given to leave out all 'improper passages' so as not to give offence to the Kaiserin and her Hallelujah Aunts. But the following day it became known that 'that idiot Countess B' had nevertheless disapproved of the play, deciding that it was a deliberate parody on the Germans and the character of the Swiss admiral an allusion to the German Kaiser who had just been appointed Admiral of the Russian fleet. Grand Duke Konstantin Konstantinovich, Nicky's cousin, known as Kostia, observing the German Kaiser, noted: 'I do not really like the Emperor despite all his affection and kindness to me. Although he's a good fellow in many ways, and has much enthusiasm and strength of will, yet he is too much a child and a buffoon. His familiarity is shocking.'

In June 1897 the Tsarina had given birth to their second child, another girl, Tatiana. Although Nicky called it 'the second bright day in our family life', his cousin Kostia recalled that when he received a telephone call with the news just before going in to luncheon at the officers' mess, 'everyone was very disappointed as they had been hoping for a boy'. It was the old problem of producing an heir, and this second failure did nothing to help the Tsarina, already awkward in Russian society, become more confident. 'She is not very talkative,' Kostia noted. 'She is very shy. The necessity of talking to a group of schoolgirls is torture for her, she has difficulty overcoming her fear in crowded gatherings. It's noticeable she does not have her mother-in-law's charm, and still does not, therefore, inspire general adulation.' Not only had Alix produced a second girl, but she could never forget that her brother Frittie had died because he was a haemophiliac. From now on Alix was often ill, staying in bed till late in the morning and going out in society as little as possible, though insisting on every formality when she did. Nicky was meanwhile still trying to come to terms with his life of burdensome responsibility. 'I rejoice at the cancellation of an audience,' he confessed to his brother Georgei, 'and have now become such a keen hunter, that I use every free moment to fly to the woods, like a lazy schoolboy who enjoys skipping lessons!'

That summer of 1897 was a turning-point in German affairs, the moment Eulenburg and Bülow had been working towards for many years. In October Bülow replaced Marschall as Secretary of State at the Foreign Office, his last move on the way to becoming Chancellor. That same summer the Kaiser appointed Admiral Alfred von Tirpitz State Secretary of the Imperial Naval Office. Tirpitz was an advocate of a Big Navy, including a battle fleet powerful enough to challenge Britain's age-old supremacy at sea. The Reichstag, that 'imperial monkey house' as Willy called it, was soon up in arms against the astronomical naval budgets. But the Kaiser and Tirpitz persisted in their grandiose plans. Never again would Wilhelm feel impotent to act, as he had at the time of the Kruger telegram. The fact that his grandmother, irritated by all his interference, had refused to allow him to attend her Diamond Jubilee celebrations in June did not help. 'I feel', he wrote to her, objecting to his omission in startling language, 'like a charger chained in the stables who hears the bugle sounding, stomps and chomps his bit, because he cannot follow his regiment.' As Sir Frank Lascelles, the British Ambassador to Berlin, warned Salisbury, the Kaiser was extremely sensitive to snubs, especially from his English relations.

For Queen Victoria the Jubilee was another 'never-to-be-forgotten day', the crowds 'indescribable', the cheering 'quite deafening'. She went in the State Landau, drawn by eight creams, with dear Alexandra sitting opposite 'looking very pretty in lilac'. Behind them came Vicky, the absent Kaiser's mother, in a separate carriage drawn by four blacks, 'not being able to go in mine, as her rank as Empress prevented her sitting with her back against the horses, for I had to sit alone.' Electricity being quite the latest thing, the Queen celebrated the day by pressing an electric button which telegraphed a message throughout her Empire. 'From my heart I thank my beloved people,' it read. 'May God bless them!' Georgie and May were despatched to the other side of the world for the opening of the first Parliament of the Commonwealth of Australia. 'Took leave with much regret of

Georgie and May,' she noted in her Journal on 30 September 1897.
'Every time I see them I love and like them more and respect them
greatly. Thank God! Georgie has got such an excellent, useful and
good wife!'

If only she could say the same of Willy. 'William's fortieth birthday. I wish he were more prudent and less impulsive at such an age!'
the Queen confided to her Journal in January 1899. In March she was
obliged to write to the other royal cousin, Nicky: 'I feel I must write
and tell you SOMETHING which you OUGHT to know and
perhaps do NOT. It is, I am sorry to say, that William takes every
opportunity of impressing upon Sir F. Lascelles that Russia is doing all
in her power to work AGAINST US; that she offers alliances to other
Powers, and has made one with the Ameer of Afghanistan against us.
I need not say that I do NOT believe a word of this, and neither do
Lord Salisbury nor Sir F. Lascelles. But I am afraid William may go
and tell things against us to you, just as he does about you to us.' Nicky
was neither surprised nor perturbed. 'Dearest Grandmama,' he wrote
from St Petersburg to the Queen, who was spending some days on the
French Riviera incognito, as the Countess of Lancaster, 'I am so happy
you told me in that open way about William. Now I fully understand
what he is up to – it is a dangerous game he is playing at . . . I am very
glad you did not believe the story of the alleged alliance between us
and the Amir of Afghanistan, for there is not a syllable of truth in it.'
Hoping that the Riviera weather was good and promising a private,
not state, visit to Balmoral with Alix and the babies that autumn, he
signed himself 'your ever devoted and loving grandson, Nicky'.

Wilhelm was up to no good, as events subsequently confirmed, but
he had one point in mitigation. It was simply this: whatever Willy did,
whether within the family or on the international stage, he was always
the odd one out, always the one who, as Kostia had spotted, no one
really liked. Handicapped at birth, emotionally confused by an odd
and unhappy childhood, and badly advised both by his military
entourage and by Eulenburg, he lived increasingly in an unreal world
of grandiose gestures, jumping first this way then that, hardly knowing
who he was or what he felt. England was the main focus of his confusion and his resentment, but England was not disposed to make any
concessions or offer any understanding. On the contrary, Lord
Salisbury smoothly rejected all Willy's advances, and English society
laughed behind the Kaiser's back as he paraded about the country in

his various uniforms – or, worse still, in mufti, looking as one unkind observer remarked 'like a Bank Holiday tripper to Margate'. The Kaiser complained endlessly to Queen Victoria that his efforts to be Britain's 'best friend' were constantly rejected. Half-English, half-German, William/Wilhelm felt snubbed, and this played right into the hands of the Anglophobes at the Berlin Court. Lord Salisbury's air of effortless superiority, in particular, became an obsession with Wilhelm. 'The pain and shame I have suffered by the high-handed or disdainful treatment of ministers who have never come over to stay here,' Willy complained to his grandmother on 27 May 1899. 'Lord Salisbury's government must learn to respect and treat us as equals.'

For this Willy earned another snub. His letter 'greatly astonished' his grandmother, who felt it was 'most irregular' of him. 'The tone in which you write about Lord Salisbury I can only attribute to a temporary irritation on your part, as I do not think you would otherwise have written in such a manner, and I doubt whether any Sovereign ever wrote in such terms to another Sovereign, and that Sovereign his own Grandmother, about their Prime Minister.' The cumulative snubs had the ultimately disastrous effect of making Willy even more determined to build up his Big Navy, and then, once it was large enough but not before, to show Britain who was master. As Wilhelm told Eulenburg, the problem with Salisbury was that 'he does not fear us'. Throwing caution to the winds, the Kaiser told Sir Frank Lascelles that the day Germany had a proper fleet Britain would have to show her proper respect. Lascelles promptly wrote to tell Salisbury, but the Prime Minister of the greatest nation on earth took little notice. Tapping his forehead, he put it down, not for the first time, to the Kaiser being mentally unstable. He did not understand that the Kaiser and Tirpitz, together with the rampant Anglophobes in Berlin, were ready to embark on a naval race and follow it to its disastrous conclusion. For the time being Salisbury was more concerned with another crisis.

On 12 October 1899 Britain went to war with the Boers in the Republics of South Africa and the Orange Free State. Perhaps Salisbury had genuinely known nothing of the Jameson Raid; he was certainly involved in the subsequent Government cover-up. The great aristocrat had something of the buccaneer about him. His style might not be to 'occupy, fortify, grab and brag', in Lord Derby's memorable description of Disraeli, but when British interests were at stake Salisbury was not inclined to back down. Ten years earlier, in dispute with France over Egypt, he had explained his preference for 'informal' empire: 'The only form of control we have is that which is called moral influence, which in practice is a combination of nonsense, objuration and worry.' On that occasion he had agreed to 'share' Egypt with France under a dual Anglo-French authority, thus avoiding the risk of war. With the Boers in South Africa there was no such option. On 19 October Queen Victoria inspected the Gordon Highlanders before they embarked for the Cape. As the kilted Highlanders marched through the streets, pipes playing, the crowds wildly cheered them on. 'I sincerely hope that the increased taxation, necessary to meet the expenses of the war, will not fall upon the working classes,' the Queen wrote to Salisbury later that day. 'but I fear they will be most affected by the extra sixpence on beer.'

'I am wholly preoccupied with the war between England and the Transvaal,' Nicky wrote to his sister Xenia at the outbreak of the Boer War. 'Every day I read the news in the British newspapers from the first to the last line . . . I cannot conceal my joy at yesterday's news that during General White's sally two full British battalions and a mountain battery were captured by the Boers!' Nicky was not the only one to be pleased. All the Great Powers were up in arms at this latest example of British aggression, the gold and diamonds of the Transvaal being a rich prize most of them would have been only too happy to acquire. Russia's ambitions were already blocked by the British in Central Asia and the Far East, and now British Imperialism was making a claim on the Transvaal as well. There was an outpouring of support for the Boers from the Russian public. Orchestras played 'Transvaal, Transvaal, My Country' as though it were their own anthem, books and pamphlets were published, plays were written and prayers offered for a speedy Boer victory against the perfidious English. Tolstoy, the pacifist, found himself caught up in the fever, reading the papers every morning just like the Tsar, hoping for a Boer victory. Lenin, the young revolutionary, felt the same, supporting the Boers' struggle against Imperialism. Putting on the pressure, Russia built up her Mediterranean and Atlantic fleets and moved her troops to the borders of Afghanistan and India.

Nicky meanwhile decided to have a chat with Willy. Willy, it seems, was not the only cousin to feel that international crises might best be handled privately, between 'royal colleagues'. 'I intend to set the Emperor on the British, reminding him of his famous telegram to

Kruger!' he told his sister Xenia. If Nicky had known that Willy routinely referred to him as a 'ninny' and a 'whimperer' who was dominated by women and 'only fit to live in a country house and raise turnips', he might not have been quite so confident. As it was, he and Alix visited Willy at Potsdam for two days on their way home from Wolfsgarten, one of the Hesse family's summer homes. He quite enjoyed the visit, he told his mother on 9 November 1899, having first apologised for the long delay in answering her letters. Willy, keen to please and impress, had shown them round all the historical sights of Berlin and Potsdam, which Nicky found interesting. The only problem had been the overheated rooms, which gave him a headache and made the evening banquet harder work than usual. 'On the whole everything went off all right,' he wrote, adding, 'The Anglo-Boer War interests me terribly; I wish all possible success to those poor people in this unequal and unjust war. Almost unbelievable sympathy is shown all over Europe to the Boers, even ordinary folk take the greatest interest in their fate.' To Queen Victoria in England he naturally put it rather differently: 'I cannot tell you how much my thoughts are with you as I know how distressed you must be about the war in the Transvaal and the terrible losses already sustained by your troops. God grant it may come to a speedy conclusion!'

The royal colleagues Nicky and Willy never could accept the power belonging to ministers and Parliament in a constitutional monarchy. After the Relief of Mafeking they might well have expected the British to seek a peace settlement. Not Lord Salisbury. On 29 May 1900, in a speech at a banquet in the City of London, he told his audience that there could be no long-term security for the British in South Africa 'so long as we leave a shred of real independent government to either republic.' After the toast he was able to stand up again and make a timely announcement. He had just been told that Lord Roberts, the Commander-in-Chief, had taken Johannesburg. The audience burst into applause and the band struck up the National Anthem. By the end of the year the war was beginning to turn in Britain's favour, Salisbury having decided to commit half a million troops to making sure not a shred of independent government was left to the Boers.

Nicky had miscalculated on many points. 'You know, my dear, that I am not arrogant, but it is pleasant for me to know that I and I ONLY possess the ultimate means of deciding the course of the war in South

Africa,' he had written to his sister at the beginning of hostilities. 'It is very simple – just a telegraphic order to all the troops in Turkestan to mobilise and advance towards the [Indian] border. Not even the strongest fleet in the world can keep us from striking England at this her most vulnerable point.' But Russia could not in fact manage on her own, hence Nicky's courting of cousin Willy in Potsdam. At the same time Lamsdorff, the Russian Foreign Minister, tried to interest France in an anti-British alliance. Neither initiative bore fruit. France might have been pro-Boer but she had no wish to antagonise Britain, her neighbour and the only Great Power who could protect her from her belligerent neighbour Germany, on her other side. Geography, the background to so many alliances, played its part in this, as on other occasions in French history.

In Germany the matter was more complicated. The public and the greater part of the ruling elite were thoroughly anti-British. But the Kaiser remained adamantly neutral throughout the war, incurring a great deal of criticism in his own country, a fact of which he was keen to remind his English cousins on many later occasions. To an extent Wilhelm's neutrality rested on the knowledge that his Navy was not yet large enough or powerful enough for war, but there was a strong suspicion in Germany that the Kaiser had once again been seduced by his English relations. William not Wilhelm. At the beginning of hostilities the British Government had thought it expedient to invite the Kaiser on a State Visit. Cousin Georgie was enlisted to help his reluctant father with the entertaining. 'We left London with Papa by special at 11.45 for Windsor,' he recorded in his diary on 20 November 1899. 'Saw Grandmama. Changed into German uniform. Motherdear and Toria arrived. We all went to the station at 1.30 and received William, Dona and two sons. I drove in the carriage with William, Papa and Uncle Arthur, the streets were decorated and he got a very good reception.' The Kaiser was warmly welcomed back into the fold by his grandmother. 'William came to tea,' she recorded in her Journal for 22 November. 'I had a long interesting conversation with him on many subjects. We first spoke about his dear Mama's health, which is not satisfactory, then of the shocking tone of the German press and the shameful attacks on England, as well as monstrous misrepresentations and lies about the war, which he greatly deplores.'

The Prince of Wales outdid himself, cordially entertaining his nephew at Sandringham for three entire days. There William had bacon and eggs for breakfast, and porridge too if he so wished. Many interesting guests were invited to meet him, and his uncle could hardly have been more genial. Even the Princess of Wales managed to disguise her dislike, though she was heard to mutter '*Ach*, the fool!' when she found he had brought three valets, a hairdresser, and a barber for the special task of curling the Imperial moustache. At Sandringham Georgie was again on call to help entertain Willy and Dona, showing them round the gardens and the stud and the farm. Then he took them to York Cottage where they were delighted with the children, who by now numbered three, but made no comment about the size of the house, though they must have been surprised. In the evenings, after dinner, the Kaiser and the Duke of York played bowls. On the Sunday they all went to church, and on the Monday they went to Wolferton Wood, where they shot, as Georgie carefully noted, 1891 birds, adding, 'William shot remarkably well considering he has only got one arm.' Everyone was pleased to report a most satisfactory visit. But they failed to notice the significance of the fact that the Kaiser was accompanied by Eulenburg, on his single visit to England, and his friend Bernhard von Bülow, now only weeks away from achieving his goal of becoming Chancellor of the German Reich. Seeing the uncle talking to the nephew, Bülow noted, was like watching 'a fat malicious tom-cat, playing with a shrewmouse'.

Once back in Germany Willy, responding to his warm reception in England, began to bombard his uncle with friendly pieces of advice about South Africa, suggesting that Britain accept defeat, as in cricket, 'with chivalrous acknowledgement of her opponent.' His uncle wrote politely in reply, 'I am unable to share your opinion, in which you liken our conflict with the Boers to our Cricket Matches with the Australians.' In 1900 the French press was so hostile that the Prince of Wales decided to forgo his usual spring holiday on the Riviera, joining his wife in Denmark instead. This was a shrewd move in another respect. He had been spending too much time in the company of his new favourite, Alice Keppel, behaviour which, though tolerated by the Princess of Wales, could never be counted upon to put her in a good humour. 'How are things going on in general?' May wrote to Georgie, at Cowes later in the year with his parents. 'I mean, does peace reign or have you had a difficult time?' To which Georgie replied, 'Alas, Mrs K. arrives tomorrow and stops here in a yacht, I am afraid that peace and quiet will not remain.'

In Russia Nicky had other things on his mind. The previous June their third child had been born, another daughter, the Grand Duchess Maria Nicolaevna. 'And so, there's no Heir. The whole of Russia will be disappointed by this news,' Nicky's cousin Kostia noted in his diary. Queen Victoria wrote in congratulation, but did not beat about the bush. 'I am so thankful that dear Alicky has recovered well, but I regret the 3rd girl for the country.' Only two weeks later Nicky's brother Georgei, still at Livadia with tuberculosis, died from a fall while out riding his bicycle. At the funeral the Dowager Empress Minny, whose mother, the cheerful Queen Louise of Denmark so frowned upon by Queen Victoria, had died the previous September, collapsed in grief and had to be carried away by Nicky, Xenia and her husband Sandro. Now, with the birth of a third girl to Nicky and the death of Georgei, Minny's third son, Misha, the Grand Duke Mikhail, was proclaimed as having 'the next right of succession to the throne of All the Russias'. To Nicholas the Tsar it was a profound setback. To Nicky the husband it made little difference. 'My own sweet little Wify dear,' he wrote to Alix on 10 July 1899, before setting off on one of his journeys the following day. 'It seems strange to write to you, while I'm sitting downstairs in my room and I know that you are quietly on your balcony. But tomorrow I shall be far away and I do not want to let a day pass without your hearing from your husband, either from his lips or on paper – how he loves you and the three little ones!' He ended, 'Goodnight my sweet darling Alix, my own wife, my joy, my happiness, my one and all!'

Beyond the family circle there were great problems in Russia. The Nihilists and student revolutionaries were increasingly active, and Nicky disliked ordering the usual repressive measures, which were anyway not having a great effect. He could not 'bring himself to admit that he could put a stop to it all,' wrote Kostia in his diary. 'In Xenia's words, Nicky's attitude to all this is that of a spectator!! If only he had more strength and self-confidence!' Sergei Witte, still Minister of Finance, saw nothing but trouble ahead. His assessment of the situation, gained from his broad experience as a man of business, was that the Russian Government needed to introduce labour legislation to improve the lot of the workers, much as was happening in other industrialised countries, or risk an increase in social unrest. Under Bunge, the previous Finance Minister, and particularly under Witte himself, Russia had seen a rapid industrial growth. Witte had greatly improved the railway network, and reduced the national debt by attracting foreign investment. Now he was concerned to raise the productivity of the work force, whether in the urban factories or in the peasant village economies. Reforms were urgently needed. His list included length of the work day, workers' associations, insurance and compensation for workers and workers' medical care, and in the villages, a shift from the collective to individual endeavour and reward. But he met with strong opposition in all these from the reactionary circles which dominated political life under Nicholas II and only managed to get a workmen's compensation bill approved. 'Because we lagged in such matters, relations between workers and capitalists became embittered,' he later wrote about that period. 'A socialist, even revolutionary, view began to gain support among our workers.'

Few people listened to Witte, the dangerous liberal. In foreign affairs he was no more successful. In November 1897 the Germans had landed troops at Kiaochow Bay in China. Instead of joining the international pressure on the Germans to remove themselves, the Russian Foreign Minister, Count Muravev, saw an ideal opportunity for Russia to acquire a much-needed port in Chinese waters, under the pretext of helping the Chinese. Port Arthur in the Liaotung Peninsula was his choice. Witte argued strongly that this would turn China into an enemy, especially since Russia already had an agreement to protect China from Japan. It would have the added effect, he warned, of aligning England and Japan against Russia. During his next audience of the Tsar at Tsarskoe Selo, Witte mentioned the matter and found to his dismay that Nicholas fully supported Muravev. As he was leaving the Tsar's study he bumped into Grand Duke Alexander Mikhailovich, Commander-in-Chief of the Russian Navy. 'Remember this day, Your Highness,' Witte warned. 'It is one that will be remembered for the terrible consequences it will have for Russia.' History proved Witte right. War with Japan was the inevitable outcome, sooner or later.

Witte was disturbed to deduce from the Grand Duke's reaction that he had known in advance about Port Arthur. It turned out that the Kaiser and the Tsar had cooked the whole thing up privately, between 'royal colleagues', so that each country could gain a foothold in China. Next time Witte reported to the Tsar, he offered his resignation. Nicholas refused it, pointing out that Witte's job was as Finance Minister, and in this his opinion of him was high. Witte, writing just before the outbreak of the First World War, knew who the real culprit was. 'There is no doubt that he [the Kaiser] and his diplomats sought by all possible means to involve us in Far Eastern affairs, to which we would devote all our strength, thus providing him with security on the Russo-German border. In this he succeeded completely.' The Tsar saw things differently. In March 1899 he wrote to Queen Victoria: 'As you know dearest Grandmama all I am striving at now is for the longest possible prolongation of peace in this world. The latest events in China must have clearly proved this . . . All that Russia wants is to be left quiet and to develop her position in the sphere of interest which concerns her being so close to Siberia. Our possession of Port Arthur and the Manchurian railway are of vital importance to us and can in no way affect any other European power's interest.'

Weddings, funerals, birthdays, christenings fill the royal calendar with events which mark out the years of family life while at the same time marking out the years of history. On Friday 4 May 1900 Georgie set off from London for Berlin to attend the coming-of-age birthday celebrations of the Crown Prince, the Kaiser's eldest son. He was by no means pleased. 'I hate going of course,' he wrote to Knollys, his father's Private Secretary, 'but am always ready to do what the Queen wishes or anything that may in any way benefit my country.' That fairly sums up Georgie's general attitude to his life of duty and service, though it has to be admitted that not many of his days were particularly onerous. In the train he read, slept and wrote to Mama and Papa, who were happily excused from attending. Then he dressed in full uniform, 'German' as he carefully noted in his diary, and arrived in Berlin at 7 p.m., to be received by the Kaiser, all the princes and a Guard of Honour. There followed the usual succession of banquets, luncheons at embassies, inspections of regiments, speeches and toasts. The coming-of-age ceremony was conducted in full dress uniform. 'The Service lasted over an hour. It was very hot, many of the soldiers of the Guard standing round the Chapel fainted & fell down, rather dangerous as they all had fixed bayonets.'

Two days later he went to visit Aunt Vicky at Friedrichshof, her 'lovely house' at Cronberg. By now Vicky, once her parents' greatest pride and hope, was a bitter and disappointed woman, her letters to her mother filled with complaints about the son who neglected her, and who was bringing ruin to his country. In the matter of the Boer War, she had no doubts where her loyalty lay. 'I cannot say how thankful I feel for you, for Lord Roberts and Lord Kitchener – for the Army in general and for all England,' she had written to her mother as Great Britain's fortunes in South Africa began to turn. Surrounded by Anglophobes, Vicky, the Dowager Empress of Germany, remained 'the English Princess' to the last. By the time of Georgie's visit she was already seriously ill with cancer. They had a long talk, but Georgie noted that his aunt was in a great deal of pain. The following day he was on his way home. 'Found darling May and the children very flourishing. Had a little lunch. Went over to MH and saw Papa and Motherdear.'

In July Georgie's cousin Alix, the Tsarina, wrote to her friend Princess Bariatinsky. 'My grandmother invites us to come to England, but now is certainly not the moment to be out of the country. How intensely I long to see her dear old face, you can imagine, never have we been separated so long, 4 whole years, and I have the feeling as tho' I should never see her any more. Were it not so far away, I should have gone off all alone for a few days to see her and left the children and my husband, as she has been a mother to me, ever since Mama's death 22 years ago.' Alix was Queen Victoria's favourite grandchild, the one who loved her best. Now aged 81, the Queen found everything bleak and difficult. 'Already thirty-eight years since the dreadful catastrophe which crushed and changed my life, and deprived me of my guardian angel, the best of husbands and most noble of men!' she wrote in her Journal.

On 31 July there was more bad news. Poor darling Affie, who had finally inherited the 'dear small country' of Coburg in 1893, had died suddenly in his sleep. He had been suffering from cancer for some time. 'It is heartrending,' the Queen wrote. 'Recollections of dear Affie's childhood and youth, and nowhere more vivid than here, crowded in on me.' The news of Vicky in Germany was also a constant worry. 'Darling Vicky's sixtieth birthday,' she noted in her Journal on 21 November 1900. 'To think of her, who was so wonderfully active and strong, now so ill and suffering, is heartbreaking.' The Queen herself had not been feeling well for many weeks. She could not sleep and her appetite was completely gone. She found it most trying, sitting through meals, eating nothing. Not sleeping was 'too provoking'. She was often in pain. The doctors could find no remedy. Lord Salisbury came to tea and urged her to go abroad for a change and some rest. Occasionally she took a short drive with Beatrice. On 2 January 1901 Lord Roberts went to

Osborne, and she bestowed the Garter on him. Two days later she noted, 'From not having been well, I see so badly, which is very tiresome.' She made her last entry in her Journal on 12 January. She died on the 22nd in the early evening, surrounded by her children and her grandchildren, ending a reign of 63 years.

Willy had arrived two days earlier, having sent an uncoded, open telegram to announce his intention. This annoyed the Queen's Household but had the desired effect of informing the British public of his devotion to his grandmother, and they promptly responded by showering him with praise and affection. His uncle the Prince of Wales was obliged to leave Osborne and his mother's side to go to London to meet him, stopping first at Marlborough House to change into his Prussian uniform. Early the following morning they travelled down to Osborne together. That day the Queen uttered her last word, 'Bertie!', after which she became unconscious. Willy remembered it differently. In his memoirs he described one of the doctors asking the dying Queen if she was pleased that her grandson had arrived from Germany, to which she replied, 'Yes, very glad, for I love him very much.' William remained at his grandmother's side all day, together with the rest of his English family, propping up her pillows, and holding her when she died.

The following day he despatched an Army Order to Germany from Osborne. 'The decease of my beloved, highly-honoured, ever lamented grandmother, Victoria, Queen of Great Britain and Ireland, and Empress of India, has plunged me and my House in the profoundest grief. I am well aware that My army condoles with me sincerely in the painful loss I have sustained, and accordingly, I hereby order all the officers of My army to wear mourning for a fortnight.' The First Regiment of Dragoon Guards, his grandmother's regiment, were ordered three weeks of mourning. All flags on military buildings were to be flown at half-mast for three days, and no musical instruments were to be played.

The Prince of Wales, now Edward VII, sensibly praised William for all his kindness and help, and put him in charge at Osborne when he travelled to St James's Palace to attend the Accession Council. Georgie accompanied his father to London, and was the first to swear allegiance to the new monarch. The Archbishop of Canterbury administered the oath, and then Edward VII delivered a short speech, from the heart and using no notes. It was a typical gesture, showing his sure touch when it came to the British public. 'Papa made a beautiful speech in which he said he wished to be called Edward VII,' was the way Georgie recorded it that evening in his diary.

The State Funeral did not take place until 4 February, but William refused to return to Germany in the interim, declaring that he remained in England as a bereaved family member, not as the Kaiser of Germany. Like his orders to the Army, this was not well received in Germany. 'I am anxious when I think of our beloved Kaiser in Osborne,' Eulenburg wrote to his old friend Bülow. 'I think of all the things he will say! He will be like a child amidst these people who are crude despite their mourning. Amongst them he forgets all his shrewdness. A sort of truthful embarrassment takes possession of him and any one of them could easily get at the secrets of his soul (and our state secrets).' The Kaiser made bad worse by an act that might have been designed to alienate him from his ministers and his subjects. Carried away by his English family's warm embrace, he quite forgot that he was Wilhelm not William, and impetuously conferred the Order of the Black Eagle on Lord Roberts. It was the very height of the Boer War, and the German people were appalled. The British were enchanted. On the day of the State Funeral it was the German Kaiser who gained the greatest admiration from the massed crowds standing for hours in silence along the funeral route, uniformly dressed in black. When he finally left England for Germany two days later *The Times* ran the headline, in German, '*Es lebe Der Kaiser*', 'Long Live the Kaiser', and the *Morning Post* wrote that 'one heard on all sides expressions of friendliness and admiration for his Imperial Majesty. Hats were waved in the air, handkerchiefs were fluttered to and fro, and there was a splendid scene of enthusiasm.'

12

Uncle Bertie and his Two Nephews

~

THE NEWSPAPERS WERE extravagant in their praise of the new
King, all but *The Times*, which took a high moral tone, reminding its readers that although Edward VII's public life had always been
conducted well and he had never failed in his duty to the nation, 'we
shall not pretend that there is nothing in his long career which those
who respect and admire him would wish otherwise.' In case the reader
could not pick up the inference, it was spelled out: the King had been
'importuned by temptation in its most seductive forms.'

If this bothered Edward, he did not show it. He embarked on his
reign with all the energy and enthusiasm of someone who had been
waiting too long in the wings. At his side stood the faithful, hard-
working Francis Knollys, who made it his duty to see that his sovereign would be fully consulted on all matters by his ministers, but most
particularly by the Prime Minister, Lord Salisbury. Edward VII himself
was not particularly keen on Lord Salisbury, or Arthur Balfour who
soon succeeded his uncle as Prime Minister. They were altogether too
intellectual for the King, who preferred horse-racing and gambling
to literature and art. But he was particularly not keen on Lord
Lansdowne, the Foreign Secretary. Edward VII considered foreign
affairs to be *his* province, the province of monarchs, and one in which
he preferred to operate with minimal interference from any
Government minister. But at the same time the King acknowledged
the constraints of a constitutional monarchy, and only occasionally
acted unconstitutionally, and without first consulting his ministers.

Within those constraints, Edward VII nevertheless retained a certain
amount of power. Early in his reign he gathered around him a small
group of friends who were able to influence the Government, by the
back stairs, into conformity with some of the King's own wishes and
opinions. Politically these friends tended towards a moderate liberalism,
though all were monarchists, believing in gradual evolution, certainly

not in revolution. At the centre was Francis Knollys. Others were Sir Charles Hardinge, a long-standing friend of the King's and a diplomat at the Foreign Office, who later became Viceroy of India; Sir John Fisher who became First Sea Lord in 1904, dedicated to reforming and modernising the Royal Navy; and the brilliant financier Sir Ernest Cassel, who had taken charge of Edward VII's private investments and made a quick impact on his mounting debts. Born in Germany, the son of a modest Jewish family, Cassel left school at fourteen. He arrived in Liverpool aged twenty-two with nothing but a violin and a bag of clothes, and made his way to London, where he was soon the manager of an international financial house, earning five thousand pounds a year. Additional to this group, in more minor roles, were Luis de Soveral, the entertaining and cosmopolitan Portuguese Minister in London, who became a personal friend of the King and was known to hate the Germans, and Alice Keppel, Mrs George Keppel, Edward's clever and charming favourite, who knew how to be discreet and how to charm the politicians who came to her house. She was received and accepted by everyone, even the Princess of Wales, now Queen Alexandra.

But perhaps the most active member of the group was Lord Esher, an old Etonian of many talents but no clear direction until his old school friend Lord Rosebery made him Permanent Secretary at the Office of Works in 1895. Esher already knew the Prince of Wales slightly, but they became firm friends after he organised the Diamond Jubilee celebrations in 1897. Esher liked to shape political events behind the scenes, free from the responsibility of public office. After Edward came to the throne Esher refused numerous Government posts, becoming instead Lieutenant and Deputy Constable of Windsor Castle, in which position he had regular but informal contact with the King. He also took on the chairmanship of committees, most notably the Defence Committee, always cleverly serving the interests of his sovereign. 'Although you are not exactly a public servant,' the King wrote to him in March 1905, 'yet I always think you are the most valuable public servant I have.' Esher spent his days criss-crossing the square mile between Buckingham Palace, Downing Street and the Foreign Office, pressuring one person here, confiding in another there. This did not always endear him to politicians, who saw it as an infringement of the rules of a constitutional monarchy, but his advice was usually sound, and his influence mostly good. He amused the

King with a rich fund of anecdotes and gossip, which a variety of politicians found useful at different times.

In fact, Esher's role in England was not unlike Eulenburg's in Germany, with this difference: Esher was very much cleverer than Eulenburg, and operated within a very different political system and climate. Esher, Francis Knollys and Fisher dined regularly at Brooks's in St James's, within the square mile, not a stone's throw from Buckingham Palace, exchanging views and information, keeping the ship of state afloat. Like Edward VII, Esher left his finances in the capable hands of Sir Ernest Cassel.

Once he was King, Edward VII's income was raised by Parliament to £470,000 a year, not including the upkeep of palaces and royal yachts. Georgie, now the Prince of Wales, was voted an annual income of £100,000, and his sisters a joint annual income of £18,000. This was at a time when a farm labourer earned no more than forty pounds a year, and a domestic servant half that. Georgie and May moved from York House to Marlborough House, vacated by the King and Queen when they moved to Buckingham Palace, and at Windsor they moved into Frogmore House, a charming William and Mary building, a mile from Windsor Castle. But at Sandringham Georgie refused to move from York Cottage, even though his father, accompanied by Lord Esher, had taken the trouble to motor all round Norfolk looking for something more suitable.

As King, the pattern of Edward VII's year did not change noticeably. He spent Christmas and New Year at Sandringham, followed by a week's shooting with friends. By the end of January the King was back in London, at Buckingham Palace, to attend the State Opening of Parliament. The winter Season with its balls, dinners and theatres lasted till the beginning of March, when the King went abroad for two months, always including a visit to Paris, and to Marienbad, where he took the waters for his 'cure'. Here he liked to be incognito, living in some luxury at the Weimar Hotel. Each year when he left the hotel sold the furniture from his suite of rooms for double what it had cost, proving, like the crowds who followed him everywhere he went, that he was not as incognito as he liked to think.

He was back in London in time for the Season, which began in May and included the Derby and Royal Ascot in June. In July the King always made an official tour of one of the provinces, during which he unveiled plaques, opened hospitals, made speeches to local business communities and shook hundreds of hands, charming everyone with his easy manner and his sure sense of public opinion. September was divided between Buckingham Palace and visiting friends about the country. In October he went to Balmoral for the grouse- and deer-shooting, and to Newmarket Races by the royal train. November was spent between Buckingham Palace, Windsor and Sandringham, followed by theatres, supper parties and balls in London, leading up to Christmas at Sandringham. In between, or along the way, Edward VII performed his tasks as King. He saw his ministers on matters of state, usually through the medium of Francis Knollys. He gave audiences, received foreign ambassadors, went to military reviews, made speeches, laid foundation stones, proceeded to town halls, opened schools, held Courts, attended charity balls, inaugurated institutes and exhibitions, and awarded many medals. He signed endless Government papers, always giving special attention to military and naval commissions. And on occasion he attended the House of Lords, when a debate was of particular interest to him.

If Francis Knollys attended to matters at home, Frederick Ponsonby, the King's Assistant Private Secretary and equerry, mostly attended to matters abroad. Ponsonby was a courtier to his fingertips. After Eton and the Guards, for over forty years he served first Queen Victoria, then Edward VII, and lastly George V. He left one of the best available accounts of Court life. His work as an equerry he perfectly described as 'keeping the ball rolling' – keeping the conversation going, keeping the arrangements of a royal visit going, keeping the correct etiquette going, keeping the King going. Ponsonby was brilliant at keeping things going. He was a fine linguist, a perfect authority on matters of ceremonial and etiquette, an entertaining companion, and a good bridge player. In short, he was indispensable.

On 23 February 1901 Ponsonby accompanied Edward VII on a visit to the King's sister Vicky in Germany. Vicky was by now so ill with cancer that she had not been able to attend her mother's funeral. On the third day of their visit the Dowager Empress called for Ponsonby. He was shown into her sitting room, where he found her propped up on cushions. She had just had another shot of morphine, enabling her to talk for a few minutes. 'There is something I want you to do for me,' she said. 'I want you to take charge of my letters and take them with you back to England . . . Willie must not have them, nor must

Above left: 'That beloved and promising child,' wrote Queen Victoria of her first grandchild, Willy, who, aged eight, was already doing ten hours of study a day, as well as learning to cope with his withered arm, damaged at birth

Above right: Nicky, aged five, on an early trip from Russia to England where he visited cousin Georgie and his family at Marlborough House

Right: Georgie and his mother, Princess Alexandra, were extremely close. 'With a great big kiss for your lovely little face,' she later wrote to Georgie, by then a twenty-five-year-old naval officer

The family of the future Tsar Alexander III (known as Sasha), *c*.1877. *From left*: Nicky, Alexander III, Xenia, Marie Feodorovna (known as Minny) and Georgei. Due to the constant threat of assassination, the children were overprotected, shut away from normal life in vast, heavily guarded palaces

BUCKINGHAM PALACE

To
Major-General Sir John Hanbury Williams.

"Please give following message to Emperor from King".

STAMFORDHAM.

BEGINS.

"EVENTS OF LAST WEEK HAVE DEEPLY DISTRESSED ME. MY
THOUGHTS ARE CONSTANTLY WITH YOU AND I SHALL ALWAYS
REMAIN YOUR TRUE AND DEVOTED FRIEND AS YOU KNOW I
HAVE BEEN IN THE PAST."

ENDS.

19th.March 1917.

Above: By 1917 Russia was in turmoil. The troops were demoralised, deserting in their thousands. There was mutiny in the Russian Navy. The people in the cities were starving. There were strikes and demonstrations, and full-scale revolution was again threatening. Georgie sent Nicky a telegram of commiseration, but it wasn't long before Nicky's 'devoted friend and cousin', fearful for his own crown, refused him asylum in England

Left: 'I cannot share your hardships, but my heart is with you every hour of the day,' George V told troops on the Western Front with typical simplicity and sincerity. During the course of the war he personally conferred 50,000 awards for gallantry, and visited, with Queen Mary, some 300 hospitals and a further 300 munitions factories and shipyards. He shut down most of the royal palaces and banned the consumption of alcohol at Buckingham Palace

Nicky was forced to abdicate in March 1917 and the Imperial family was kept under arrest at Tsarskoe Selo, outside St Petersburg, until 1918, when they were moved to Tobolsk and thence to Ekaterinburg in Western Siberia. Here, during the night of 17 July, they were shot by local Bolsheviks

Willy too was forced to abdicate. In November 1918 he fled to Holland where he remained in exile, a sad and disillusioned old man, until his death in 1941. Hitler sent a wreath of lilies to his funeral

Georgie, alone of the three royal cousins, emerged triumphant from the war. As he stood on the balcony of Buckingham Palace in November 1918 saluting the wildly cheering crowds below, he may have spared a thought for Willy and Nicky. They and their autocratic monarchies were gone; his own monarchy, less powerful but more constitutional, had never been more popular

he ever know you have got them.' They would be taken to his room at one o'clock that night, in two large black boxes. Ponsonby pondered how to get the boxes out of a palace full of secret police. He wrote 'Books with Care' on one and 'China with Care' on the other, and hoped for the best. The following morning, as soldiers carried everything to a wagon outside, Ponsonby stood nervously beside the Kaiser. Luckily he was 'holding forth on some subject which interested him, and naturally everyone, including myself, listened attentively.' The Kaiser noticed nothing. When they got back to England Ponsonby locked up the two boxes in his own home at Old Windsor, where they remained. He was just keeping the ball rolling.

Vicky, the Dowager Empress, died a few months later, on 5 August 1901. The King and Queen travelled to Germany for the funeral, again attended by Ponsonby. Queen Alexandra brought a wreath of flowers from Windsor, the childhood home Vicky had missed so much when she went to Prussia. English Princess to the last, Vicky had left instructions that her body was to be laid in an English coffin and buried according to Anglican rites. Willy followed his mother's instructions to the letter, only later ordering that her coffin be encased in a German one, and buried a second time, according to German rites.

Edward VII chose Sir Arthur Bigge, later Lord Stamfordham, to become Georgie's Private Secretary. Stamfordham had an unusual background for a courtier. He was the son of a Northumbrian parson and first came to Queen Victoria's notice in 1879, as a young officer in the Royal Artillery recently returned from the Zulu Wars. Queen Victoria liked spotting people, and in 1880 she appointed him Assistant Private Secretary under Sir Henry Ponsonby, Frederick Ponsonby's father. Stamfordham learnt everything he knew about being a courtier from Sir Henry, describing him as 'One of, if not the greatest gentleman I have known: the entire effacement of SELF: the absolute non-existence of conceit, side or pose: the charming courtesy to strangers old, young, high, low, rich, poor.' When Sir Henry died in 1895, Stamfordham stepped almost imperceptibly into his master's shoes, serving the Queen with the same devotion until her death in 1901. Now, as Private Secretary to the Prince of Wales, he took on his biggest task: that of moulding the future sovereign. He remained with his master for thirty years, until his own death in 1931.

In March 1901 Georgie and May took up their new responsibilities as Prince and Princess of Wales, setting off to represent the King on a royal tour to Australia, New Zealand and Canada. They were gone for eight months, leaving their children behind in the care of nannies and governesses. At first Edward VII had resisted such a long absence, less for the children's sake than his own. He and Alexandra hated to be parted from Georgie for more than a week at a time. Georgie was not much better. After the family farewells at Portsmouth he wrote to his parents, 'May and I came down to our cabins and had a good cry and tried to comfort each other.' With them on the steamship *Ophir* went Georgie's old tutor, now Canon Dalton, and Lord Stamfordham. Together, as Georgie carefully noted, they covered 45,000 miles, laid 21 foundation stones, received 544 addresses, presented 4,329 medals, reviewed 62,000 troops, and shook hands with 24,855 people at official receptions. The royal tour was an important aspect of the job because, as Arthur Balfour explained to Edward VII, he was 'the greatest constitutional bond uniting together in a single Empire communities of free men separated by half the circumference of the Globe. All the patriotic sentiment which makes such an Empire possible centres in him or centres chiefly in him; and everything which emphasises his personality to our kinsmen across the seas must be a gain to the Monarchy and the Empire.' The Prince of Wales added a note of his own. 'The Old Country must wake up if she intends to maintain her old position of pre-eminence in her colonial trade against foreign competitors,' he told an audience of City men at the Guildhall on his return, no doubt with Stamfordham's help.

In January 1902 Georgie was in Berlin for Willy's birthday celebrations. Feelings between Germany and Britain were still running high – peace in South Africa was not declared until May of that year. As a result, Edward VII first wrote a letter warning the Kaiser: 'In sending my son George to Berlin to spend the anniversary of your birthday with you, I intended it as a personal mark of affection & friendship towards you, but I must confess since reading the violent speeches in the Reichstag against England, & especially against my Colonial Minister and my Army, which shows such a strong feeling of animosity towards my Country, I think that under the circumstances it would be better for him not to go where he is liable to be insulted.' Willy responded by making Georgie Colonel of the 8th Cuirassier Regiment. 'Tried some of the uniform on but it was not much of a success, especially the boots which hurt abominably!' wrote Georgie in his diary. He had a long talk with Count von Bülow, now

Chancellor. On 28 January he made a detailed note of the menu, which was in chef's French as usual and amusingly included Roastbeef à l'Anglaise. By early Monday, 30 January, Georgie was happily on his way back home again to his familiar routine. 'Found darling May quite well,' he wrote that evening. 'Lunched at 1.45. Bigge brought me a lot of letters.' Then he went to see Motherdear, Papa and sisters and told them all about Berlin. 'Sat with May all the evening & talked.'

In Russia the early years of the twentieth century were filled with turmoil, in both domestic and foreign affairs. The Tsar and Tsarina's private life also had its troubles. When Alix heard of her grandmother Queen Victoria's death she wanted to start for Windsor immediately, but was dissuaded from it because she was pregnant with a fourth child, perhaps the long-awaited son and heir. It was five years since she had seen her grandmother; she broke down at the funeral service held for Queen Victoria in the English Church at St Petersburg. The baby was born on 5 June. It was a girl. 'My God! What a disappointment! . . . a fourth girl,' wrote Nicky's sister Xenia in her diary that evening. 'They have named her Anastasia. Mama sent me a telegram about it, and writes, "Alix has again given birth to a daughter!"' Kostia, Nicky's cousin, was more circumspect. 'The new Grand Duchess Anastasia entered this world at 6 in the morning; the birth was normal and lasted three hours, the baby is quite big. Forgive us Lord, if we all felt disappointment instead of joy; we were so hoping for a boy, and it's a fourth daughter.' Nicky left a factual account of the birth in his diary, only adding 'Luckily Alix felt quite cheerful.'

By July the Tsar and Tsarina had made the acquaintance of M. Philippe. Described as a mystic and faith-healer by some and a charlatan by others, Philippe was a Frenchman from Lyons who had been introduced to them by the Montenegrin princess, Grand Duchess Militsa, who was deeply involved in the occult. Philippe had twice been prosecuted in France for practising medicine without a licence. By 1901 he was in St Petersburg, holding séances, and curing nervous diseases through hypnosis; most critically, he claimed to be able to determine the sex of an unborn child. On 10 July he arrived at Tsarskoe Selo. 'M. Philippe talked and instructed us,' wrote Nicky in his diary. 'What a wonderful few hours.' The following day Nicky and Alix were referring to him as 'our friend', introducing him to their four daughters and praying with him in their bedroom. When Nicky had to go to Danzig that August, to attend the Kaiser's naval display, Alix wrote: 'My own precious One, I want you to find these lines when we are separated so as that you may feel that Wify is near to you. My thoughts and earnest prayers will follow you all the time. Mr Philippe's too I know and that is ONE comfort to ME, as otherwise our parting would be too awful.' She ended, 'I love you, I love you and cover your precious face with tenderest burning kisses. God bless and protect you and keep you from all harm. Oh, how hard to part – fare well, sweety, my Nicky, my very own Boy, to whom I cling with every fibre. I kiss you, kiss you ever your own old Wify.'

Being religious by temperament as well as conviction, both Nicky and Alix were susceptible to mystics. The sacred festivities of the Russian Orthodox church were some of the high points of Nicky's year, times when he felt in communion with all his subjects but in particular the peasants with their simple faith. Alix had inherited her religious temperament from her mother Princess Alice. Having converted to the Russian Orthodox Church after her initial reluctance to give up her Protestant faith, she transferred all her fervour to it. M. Philippe was soon seeing them on a regular basis. 'He is a man of about fifty, small, with black hair and a black moustache, very unsightly in appearance, with an ugly southern-French accent,' wrote Kostia in his diary. Nicky and Alix often went to Militsa's house, where they prayed with Philippe, spending long evenings there 'from which they return in an exalted state, as if in ecstasy, with radiant faces and shining eyes.' In England, May wrote to Georgie that she had had a long chat with Motherdear. 'We talked about the spiritualist's influence in Russia and she told me it was more Alicky who is under this horrid man's influence than Nicky. Aunt Minny is in despair.'

In 1902 Anne Topham arrived at the Berlin Court as English governess to the Kaiser's youngest child and only daughter, Victoria Louise. She came from a small village in Derbyshire, and it was her first brush with the strange world of Court life. 'Towards the middle of August 1902, on a very hot, dusty, suffocating day, I was travelling, the prey of various apprehensions, to the town of Homberg-von-der-Hohe, where the Prussian Court was at that time in temporary residence,' she wrote in her memoirs, published in 1914, before the events which led to outbreak of the First World War. Anne Topham was a sensible young Englishwoman with a lively sense of humour, and a sharp eye for detail. After a stormy eight-hour night passage across the North Sea and a long train journey she arrived at the palace of Homburg, where she was met by a stately gentleman wearing a black frock-coat and a tall silk hat, one of the many minor officials who saw to the smooth running of the Court.

A servant led Anne down a long, cool passage and up a small winding staircase into a pleasant, shady room looking out over the red roofs of Homburg. Everything was spotlessly clean. There were flowers on the writing-table, and an old-fashioned chair covered in blue spotted chintz. A small bedroom led off the sitting room. The bedstead had deep wooden sides. Soon a man dressed in the plain dark livery of all male royal servants above the rank of footman entered the room and bowed. She was expecting coffee, having been assured many times over that only coffee was drunk in Germany. Instead it was tea, direct from a big London warehouse – Anne Topham's first experience of the Kaiser's dual identity. Another knock on the door revealed a tall, middle-aged, smiling person, Countess von Kessel, one of the Kaiserin's three ladies-in-waiting, the Hallelujah Aunts. She greeted Anne warmly and told her to change into a 'high' dress, because she was to dine with Her Majesty at half-past seven that evening. His Majesty was, as usual, away. Anne Topham worried that she had no 'high' dress, only a low-necked one. She worried too that she might not have the right length of train. By seven o'clock she was being conducted through the long passages to Her Majesty's apartments, wearing only one long kid glove, as instructed, and clutching the other in her free hand.

An elderly footman ushered them into an ante-room furnished in brilliant yellow satin, and Countess von Kessel whispered that Anne should kiss Her Majesty's hand. Soon she was talking surprisingly easily to the Kaiserin, whose English was good. It was the usual talk of an indulgent mother about her favoured daughter. At seven-thirty the Kaiserin rose and walked through several rooms, preceded by a footman, to a large dining room lit with many wax candles, where the subdued conversation of the waiting company instantly ceased as they entered, everyone dropping in a curtsey or bowing 'like a field of corn when the wind passes over it.' She met Victoria Louise the next day, a highly-strung child, but engaging, always talking about 'Papa', and always quarrelling violently with Prince Joachim, the youngest of her six brothers. Sissy, as she was known, was soon calling Anne Topham 'Topsy'.

A few days later the Kaiser returned from his travels, and Anne Topham was presented to him. The occasion was a picnic. As she stood waiting, slightly nervous, she made the first of her sharp observations: His Majesty was talking volubly to the group of uniformed men who as always surrounded him. The Kaiser was not as she had expected from his fierce reputation and posed photographs. 'I had imagined him tall and slender,' she wrote, 'whereas he was barely medium height and rather thick-set, his harsh eyes bulging in an exaggerated and rather unpleasant stare, as he talked emphatically and shook his forefinger incessantly at the person he was addressed. "How d'ye do?" said the Emperor, and held out his hand. His powerful grip made me wince perceptibly. "Ha-ha! The mailed fist! What?" he said jocularly.' She was lucky she wasn't a man. With men, the Kaiser liked to turn his rings to the inside before grasping their hands in his iron grip. It was his idea of a joke.

Over the following weeks Anne Topham's keen eye noticed several other revealing details about the Kaiser. She noticed that he was often away, and that as soon as he returned to Court there was a tension in the air, with everyone ready at all times to leave on a sudden trip, a visit to a museum, a ride, a picnic, anything to amuse a restless man who could never sit still for one moment. Luncheon, when the ladies had to wear 'something in silk or satin, with a long train completed by the inevitable fan and white lace gloves', had to be bolted down. The Kaiser never took more than half an hour over his food. His plate arrived with the meat already discreetly cut up, since his withered arm and hand were quite useless. A footman stood behind each chair, except for the Kaiser. He had his own *Jaeger* huntsman, in green uniform. His Majesty never drank alcohol, and talked non-stop. On the rare occasions when he wore mufti, he looked odd. 'The ordinary easy lounge tweed suit, which many Englishmen wear with advantage, is distinctly unflattering to him,' Anne Topham noted perceptively, adding, 'Civil dress has with him something of the baffling nature of a disguise, he never appears quite himself.'

There was a great deal of waiting about at Court, and a lot of hand-shaking: 'presumably it helps to pass the time away.' Dress was an endless trial. There were often seven changes in a day. For luncheon it was a high neck, for formal evening wear a low one and a long train, and a bodice with painful whale-bones at the waist. The ladies-in-waiting had maids to help them out; Anne Topham had none, and her evening gowns had dozens of tiny pearl buttons down the back. 'However many fastenings by a feat of super-dexterity one managed to close by one's own contorted efforts, there were always two or three in the middle of the back that remained entirely out of reach.' The Court was constantly on the move from one palace to another, and Anne Topham was forever packing and unpacking her suitcases.

When the Court left Homburg for Potsdam, the royal waiting room at the station was decorated with flags and evergreens. At every wayside station and crossing there was 'a palpitating crowd' of little girls wearing wreaths of wilted flowers and boys waving flags, officials in dress suits and tall chimney-pot hats and, on the platforms, station-masters in military-style blue uniforms, who remained saluting as the train passed through. 'The German waves patriotic flags on the least provocation, puts his small son of six into a complete miniature Hussar uniform, lets him swagger about the streets wearing it,' she wrote with distinct disapproval, adding, right on the mark: 'That patriotism finds its chief centre in the personality of their Emperor.' Kaiser and country, country and Kaiser – the two reflected one another perfectly.

More even than the Kaiser in Germany, the Russian Tsar enjoyed limitless power. In practice, however, each monarch was susceptible to the influence of others, unofficial advisers who were answerable to no one. In Germany Phili zu Eulenburg remained the Kaiser's best friend. In Russia the Grand Dukes and various Court favourites still wielded great influence. But increasingly it was Alix, the Tsarina, who wielded the most. Nicky was bound to her in an intense relationship which frequently excluded all others. Through Alix's influence Nicky became more and more convinced that only God could tell the Tsar what to do. But not even God could make the Tsar less vacillating, and it was his vacillation that made his ministers' lives almost as difficult as those of the Kaiser's. Alix was neither very clever nor, since she spoke only basic Russian, was she very well informed. As a German she had little real understanding of Russia, though she thought she had. Again and again she exhorted her husband to be firm, not so much for the sake of the matter in hand as for that of his autocracy. And Alix in turn listened increasingly to the faith healer Philippe, who had quickly gained a position of influence with the Tsar and Tsarina.

'My own beloved One,' Alix wrote to Nicky on 4 July 1902, when Nicky was playing host to the Kaiser at an inspection of the Russian fleet at Reval (now Tallin), a return visit following Nicky's inspection of the German fleet at Danzig the previous year, 'It is terrible to have to let you go off all ALONE, knowing that worries are awaiting you.

But our dear friend [Philippe] will be near you and help you answering William's questions. Be friendly and severe, that HE realises HE dare not joke with you and that he learns to RESPECT you and be afraid of you – that is the CHIEF thing. HOW I wish I were with you.' The granddaughter of Queen Victoria knew at first hand what it was to be a powerful and respected monarch. Writing in an English peppered with capitals she referred, as her grandmother always had, to William, not Wilhelm. The next day she wrote again. Her sister Ella and husband Sergei were staying. After breakfast Sergei went to visit aunt Marie, back in Russia after uncle Affie's death in Coburg, while she and Ella went for a drive round the park at Tsarskoe Selo. Ella quizzed her about 'our Friend', but Alix remained quiet and gave deliberately dull answers. Ella had heard many very unfavourable things about 'Him' and that 'He' was not to be trusted. 'I explained that all came from jealousy and inquisitiveness. She said such secrecy had been spun around it. I said no, that we did everything openly and that in our position there never can be anything hidden, as we live under the eyes of the whole world.'

The Kaiser continued to court the Tsar, mostly by letter, and often without the knowledge of his ministers. The letters were rambling affairs, an odd mixture of family gossip, unwanted advice, pious moralising, and political intrigue. The Tsar also wrote to the Kaiser, but his letters were fewer and shorter. Although Nicky had little sympathy for Willy personally, as Tsar and Kaiser they had much in common. Each rejected the English system of constitutional monarchy. Each was concerned to deal firmly with the socialists and Nihilists. Nicky was outraged by the Boer War, and by being once again blocked by Great Britain in his territorial ambitions. Willy repeatedly told Nicky that they together were the defenders of the Christian faith. 'Clearly it is the great task of the future for Russia to cultivate the Asian Continent and to defend Europe from the inroads of the Great Yellow Race,' he wrote again. 'You have well understood the call of providence in the Defence of the Cross and the old Christian European culture against the inroads of the Mongols and Buddhism.' After the Reval visit he wrote to warn Nicky about Japan, which seemed to him to be becoming 'a rather restless customer'. He suggested they could maintain 'the Peace of the World' by sharing their naval secrets. He signed himself 'Your devoted friend and cousin Willy, Admiral of the Atlantic.'

Sergei Witte noted that the Kaiser exerted a marked influence on the Tsar, 'directed toward undermining our relations with other powers.' He learned this principally from Count Lamsdorff, the Russian Ambassador to Berlin, who was always trying to counter the Kaiser's influence and was consequently hated by him. 'The Count told me that if the secret papers in his possession were ever published, they would create a sensation.' By the end of 1903 Willy was writing to Nicky to warn him about the 'Arch plotter', their uncle Edward VII. England was planning to bring 'freedom' to the suppressed Balkan races, he said, by which (he explained) she meant Parliaments and Republics. It was further proof that England was working against Russian interests. In the next letter he warned that 'the Japs' were clandestinely arming the Chinese behind Russia's back. 'I hope the Admiral of the Pacific will not be angry with the Admiral of the Atlantic's signals, who is always on the look out!' He signed himself 'Ta ta, best love to Alix from Your devoted friend and cousin *toujours en vedette*! Willy'.

Nicky's correspondence with his other, English, cousin was much less complicated. In January 1902 he wrote to thank Georgie for the Christmas present of a 'delightful' walking stick. The winter, he told him, was cold and clear, with any amount of snow. He had shot twenty stags that autumn in Poland. They were in the midst of a boisterous Season, with endless balls and parties, and Archduke Franz Ferdinand was staying. He sent his love to May, signing himself 'ever your loving and devoted cousin and friend' as usual, having avoided all mention of the Boer War. Georgie's reply to this letter, not written until March, mentioned that he and May might be in Denmark the following month for Apapa's birthday celebrations, and wished Nicky and Alicky might be there too. He complained that they were much busier these days, having to go to a function in Bristol one week and another in Manchester the next. He and May were in London; the children were still in Sandringham with Mama and Toria, where they were much happier 'as we still have the fogs in London.' Like Nicky, Georgie avoided all mention of politics, other than to commiserate with him about the students, who were again 'kicking up a row' in different universities. Georgie knew this would be a great worry to Nicky.

The students were always 'kicking up a row' in Russia, but they were not the only ones. The workers and many sections of the middle and upper classes were increasingly opposed to the Government, demanding constitutional reform and threatening revolution. Vyacheslav Plehve, the Minister of Internal Affairs, reacted with repressive measures which appeared to have little effect. 'After the students' disorders there have followed strikes and factory workers' battles with the police. Next the peasant mass will rise up with a demand for land,' wrote Polovtsov, a member of the State Council. The revolutionary socialist parties were growing at an alarming rate. The Marxists, who split into the Bolsheviks and the Mensheviks in 1903, believed that the urban worker, arising out of the capitalist system, would lead the revolution. The Socialist Revolutionary Party believed that it would be led by the peasants and lower middle classes along with some members of the intelligentsia, and they were prepared to use terror tactics against the ruling elite: they assassinated three ministers between 1901 and 1904. Russia's liberal parties, peopled largely by professionals and intellectuals, were relatively new and not yet a powerful force in the political scene.

Witte, as Finance Minister, continued to argue that only a successful market economy could save the country, which was in a parlous financial state in spite of rapid industrial expansion, largely in consequence of excessive spending on defence and an ineffective tax system. But the ministers could not agree among themselves and wasted hours and days arguing this way and that, with no one able to take firm control. The Tsar insisted on making all final decisions, but then frequently changed his mind. He also consulted unofficial advisers, often friends from his own familiar aristocratic background. They were quite possibly intelligent, but they were amateurs, and they enraged the ministers, who were professional politicians.

The Tsar had perfected the art of playing off one minister against another to maintain his own authority and autocracy, handed to him by God and his ancestors. 'He has a naturally good brain [and] analytical skills and he grasps what he is told. But he only grasps the significance of a fact in isolation without its relationship to other facts, events, currents and phenomena,' wrote his old tutor Pobednostsev. 'Wide general ideas worked out by an exchange of views, argument or discussions are lacking. This is shown by the fact that not long ago he said to one of his entourage: "Why are you always quarrelling? I always agree with everyone about everything and then do things my own way." ' The system was frighteningly out of date, and Nicky was not the one to modernise it. He might be 'weak as water', as his uncle

Bertie put it, but he remained strong on this one point: he was the Autocrat of All the Russias, and no one but God could change that.

On 18 September 1903 Kostia noted in his diary that many felt the present situation in Russia to be fatal, adding, 'The reason for our mood is the weakness of the Emperor, who is unconsciously influenced by other opinions, first one, then the other, the last one expressed is always right.' The following year, on 28 July 1904, Plehve was assassinated in St Petersburg by a young Socialist Revolutionary who threw a bomb at his passing carriage. Now Nicky had to choose a new Minister of Internal Affairs. The obvious choice, the man he preferred, was General von Wahl, Plehve's assistant minister and of much the same persuasions as Plehve. But once again Nicky was swayed by someone else's opinion, this time his mother's.

Although the Dowager Tsarina's political influence was not as powerful as it had been when her husband was alive and in the early years of Nicky's reign, she still stepped in forcibly from time to time and, with her Danish background, usually on the liberal side. The scene was well described by Count Paul Benckendorff, the Grand Marshal of the Court, in a letter to his brother Count Alexander Benckendorff, Russian Ambassador in London. 'Wahl was going to be appointed Minister of Internal Affairs. A *scène de famille* ensued during which she [the Dowager Tsarina] almost threw herself at his [the Tsar's] feet in order to get this nomination stopped,' he wrote, adding, 'One cannot absolutely change one's political colour just to give one's mother pleasure.' Prince Svyatopolk-Mirsky, who held an entirely different point of view from Plehve, was appointed instead. Mirsky presented the Tsar with a programme of reform which included civil rights, religious tolerance, and the need for an elected body of local representatives to be consulted on policy and legislation. To this Nicky replied that he could not agree to a representative form of government 'because I consider it harmful to the people whom God has entrusted to me.' Alix agreed, writing in early 1905 to her sister Victoria in England, 'the Minister of Internal Affairs is doing the greatest harm. He proclaims grand things without having prepared them. It's like a horse that has been held very tight in hand, and then suddenly one lets the reins go. It bolts, falls and it is more than difficult to pull it up again before it has dragged others with it into the ditch.' She added, 'St Petersburg is a rotten town, not an atom Russian. The Russian people are deeply and truly devoted to their Sovereign.'

According to Paul Benckendorff, who saw the Tsarina daily, her role in domestic politics was growing, and she remained 'ferocious' in her defence of her husband's autocracy.

That summer the Tsar and Tsarina, accompanied by various members of the family, travelled by Imperial train to the monastery at Sarov to seek the protection of St Serafim, who, their friend Philippe assured them, would grant them a son. 'We were welcomed in a marquee on the platform by the nobility, the *zemostvo*, the towns and peasants of Nizhegorodsky province,' wrote Nicky in his diary on the evening of 30 July. 'We got into carriages and set off along a good, dusty road. We went through large villages, where we were greeted by peasants outside buildings along the road. We had tea some 40 miles from Arzamas. At 6 o'clock we arrived at the Sarov monastery. There was something very special about going into the cathedral of the Assumption and then into the church of St Zosima and St Savvaty, where we were able to pray to the relics of the holy father Serafim.' There were long processions and incense-laden requiem services lasting three hours, with crowds of pilgrims queuing to kiss Serafim's casket and cripples hoping to be cured by a miracle. Nicky and Alix heard of many people who had been cured. At night and in the dark, they walked down to the holy river to bathe in its icy waters and pray. Later, Nicholas ordered the Holy Synod to canonise Serafim. Pobedonostsev, who was still the Procurator of the Synod, had to explain to the Tsar that a saint could not be proclaimed by Imperial order. But the Tsarina informed him otherwise. 'The Tsar can do anything,' she said, and Serafim was canonised.

Whatever the unbelievers might think, by the following year Alix was pregnant again, and this time it was a son. 'A great and unforgettable day for us, during which we were clearly visited by the Grace of God,' wrote Nicky in his diary on 12 August 1904. 'At 1.15 in the afternoon Alix gave birth to a son, whom we named Alexei as we prayed. Everything happened remarkably quickly – at least for me. In the morning I went to visit Mama as usual, after which I went to find Alix for lunch. She was already upstairs, and half an hour afterwards the happy event occurred. There are no words to thank God enough for sending us this comfort in a time of sore trials!' Mama came in the afternoon, and Nicky sat down to write a mass of telegrams. He and Alix dined that evening in the bedroom. There is no mention of the haemophilia which had hastened the death of Alix's brother Frittie and her uncle Leopold, Queen Victoria's son, as well as her small nephew, her sister Irene's son, who had died in February that year when his bleeding could not be stopped after a fall.

'God has sent their Majesties a son. What a joy!' cousin Kostia wrote in his diary. 'Russia has waited 10 years for an Heir, and now it has happened. Soon we heard the cannons being fired from the fort – a 301-gun salute. The Heir has been named Alexei. The Te Deum had just finished when we reached the gothic church. The Tsar emerged from inside and, together with his mother and his elder daughters Olga, Tatiana and Maria, started to go round the assembly receiving congratulations.' Three days later Kostia and his wife were having tea with the Dowager Tsarina when her son Misha joined them, Nicky's appointed successor until Alexei's birth. 'He is radiant with happiness at no longer being Heir,' noted Kostia.

Who would have wanted to be the Heir to the Russian throne in 1904? There had already been a general strike in Odessa in 1903. Throughout 1904 the threat of revolution hung in the air. Nicky wavered first this way then that. 'Nothing is definite, the same matter will be viewed in one way today, and in quite another tomorrow,' wrote Kostia in his diary. 'The disturbance is increasing, and one senses ahead something unknown, inescapable and terrible.' Members of the council of *zemstvo* workers were meeting daily to discuss the conditions necessary for progress to be made in the social and political life of the country. On 4 December Kostia wrote, 'It is as if a dam has been broken: in the space of two or three months Russia has been seized with a thirst for change. It is talked about loudly. The Dumas of Kaluga, Moscow and now Petersburg have unanimously adopted motions in which they respectfully ask for every freedom. Revolution is banging at the door. A constitution is being openly discussed. How shameful and how terrifying.'

At 9 a.m. on 6 January 1905 Nicky and Alix left Tsarskoe Selo under heavy guard for the annual religious ceremony of the Blessing of the Waters of the Neva in St Petersburg. They went to the Winter Palace where they changed, surrounded by attendants, into Court dress. The Dowager Tsarina was already there, wearing a long train which hung from the shoulders, the high Russian head-dress of stiff white silk studded with pearls, and the blue ribbon of the order of St Andrew across her brocade bodice, the star of diamonds pinned on the left side. Her necklaces and earrings were heavy with pearls and diamonds. Once the rest of the Imperial family had assembled, the Arab door-keepers, draped in Cashmir shawls, opened the great double doors which led into the hall where all the dignitaries of the Empire were gathered. The chamberlains in gold uniforms banged the floor with their staves for silence. Then the Imperial procession made its way slowly to the palace church through the halls of the palace, each hall lined with regiments of the Guards in magnificent uniforms, gold and silver cuirasses, helmets with double-headed eagles, Imperial eagles on their silk standards. Behind them stood the throng of courtiers and ladies of the Court, several thousand nobility and people of rank, the ladies in Court dress, heavily jewelled, the men in colourful uniforms or frock-coats and silk stockings. Nicky, by contrast, was dressed in the simple uniform of his Rifle Regiment. As the Imperial procession passed, the ladies made low curtsies and the men bowed. The service, lasting an hour and a half, proceeded as it had for centuries: the priests of the Russian Orthodox Church in their heavy vestments chanting, the choir singing, the air heavy with incense. 'We put on our coats to go out to the Jordan,' Nicky wrote that night in his diary. 'While the salute was being given, one of the guns of my first battery of mounted artillery discharged shrapnel from the Vassili Island, sweeping with it the Jordan very closely, and hitting a part of the Palace. One policeman was wounded, bullets found on the platform and the banner of the Marines was torn.' It was the first shot of the 1905 Revolution.

Soon full-scale revolution had broken out in most parts of Russia. The unions in St Petersburg organised a demonstration, demanding a list of radical reforms, both political and economic, including an elected assembly. There were not enough police to contain the crowd, so the army was brought in. It was a fatal mistake. On 22 January, Bloody Sunday, they opened fire on the unarmed demonstrators, killing more than a hundred. For Lenin, expelled from the University of Kazan for his involvement in radical student politics and by now featuring heavily in the Tsarist police files, it marked the beginning of the end of the old regime. In the cities there were more strikes and demonstrations, in the countryside more riots and arson attacks. In October Nicky was forced to issue an Imperial Manifesto guaranteeing freedom of speech, conscience and association, and the creation of an elected assembly, the State Duma, with Count Witte as Chairman of the Council of Ministers.

On 27 April 1906 Nicholas II opened the first State Duma with the greatest ceremony. He walked alone in the Imperial procession, and mounted the steps to the throne in the St George Hall, where all the Court and dignitaries were assembled. The American Ambassador described the scene: people in every conceivable costume, peasants in rough clothes and long boots, merchants and tradespeople in frockcoats, lawyers in dress suits, priests in long robes and long hair, courtiers covered in decorations, generals in brilliant uniforms, even a Catholic bishop in violet vestments. Xenia, Nicky's sister, who was also present, saw the scene in a different light: 'Directly opposite us were the members of Council and the high officials. To the left the members of the Duma, who included several men with repulsive faces and insolent disdainful expressions! They neither crossed themselves nor bowed, but stood with their hands behind their backs or in their pockets, looking sombrely at everyone and everything.' The Tsar read out his speech in a loud steady voice, only his shaking hands betraying his feelings to those standing near him. 'We all experienced an indescribable emotion,' admitted Kostia, 'it's difficult to convey what we felt. It was a great historic moment, unforgettable to those who witnessed it.'

The first Imperial Duma assembled on 10 May 1906. It was dominated by the Constitutional Democratic Party, the Kadets, which came into immediate conflict with the Crown by demanding a general amnesty for the many thousands of political activists languishing in prison. They also demanded universal suffrage, a responsible Cabinet, suppression of the Imperial Council, equality of all classes before the law, abolition of discrimination on grounds of race, class or religion, reforms in the administration of local government, education and public finances, abolition of capital punishment, and redistribution of the land in favour of the peasantry. On 22 July the Duma was dissolved by Imperial Edict, 5 March 1907 having been selected as the date for assembling the new Duma, to be elected on a restricted franchise, firmly rejecting the demand for universal suffrage.

With the dissolution of the first Duma, mutiny broke out in the port of Kronstadt. Isvolsky, now Minister for Foreign Affairs, had gone to Peterhof, only ten miles from Kronstadt, for his weekly audience of the Tsar. He could not resist asking Nicholas how he managed to remain so calm at a moment when the fate of his dynasty hung in the balance. '*Si vous me voyez si peu troublé,*' the Tsar answered in his excellent Court French, '*c'est que j'ai la ferme, l'absolue croyance que le sort de la Russie, que mon propre sort et celui de ma famille, est entre les mains de Dieu, qui m'a placé là où je suis. Quoi qu'il arrive, je m'inclinerai devant sa volonté, avec la conscience de n'avoir jamais eu d'autre pensée que celle de servir le pays qui'il m'a confié.'* (If you see me so little concerned, it is because I have the firm, absolute belief that the fate of Russia, my own fate and that of my family, lie in the hands of God, who has placed me where I am. Whatever happens, I will bow before His Will, always aware that I have had no other thought than to serve the country He entrusted to me.) God and the Tsar, the Tsar and God. There was nothing in between and, '*quoi qu'il arrive*', the Tsar would bow to his ordained fate. But he refused to concede any but the most minor reforms to his autocratic power, which might have averted that fate in the first place.

13

Willy and Nicky in Trouble

~

'WHAT A VERY kind thought that was of yours to ask me to be Godfather to your little boy!' Willy had written to Nicky on 16 August 1904. 'You can well imagine what our joy was when we read your telegram announcing his birth! "*Was longe wahrt, wird gut!*" says an old German proverb, so may it be with this little dear one! May he grow to be a brave soldier and a wise and powerful statesman; and may God's blessing always rest on him and preserve him from all harm of body and soul. May he always be as a ray of sunshine to you both during your life!' The letter was delivered by Prince Henry, as Willy persisted in calling his brother, along with a golden goblet for 'my little Godchild', because 'a man's thirst cannot be quenched by milk only!'

His comment about preserving the child from all harm, in body as well as soul, would have been understood by every one. On 20 September Nicky wrote in his diary, 'Alix and I were very worried because little Alexei started bleeding from the navel, and it continued on and off until the evening! We had to send for Korovin and the surgeon Fedorov; at about 7 o'clock they applied a bandage. The little one was remarkably calm and gay! How painful it is to live through such moments of anxiety.' Relief came two days later. 'Thank God, dear Alexei has had no more bleeding now for 48 hours! How much lighter my heart feels!' But everyone in the family knew that things would never be the same. 'Even in our house a certain melancholy reigned,' remembered Maria Pavlovna, Nicky and Alix's cousin. 'There is no doubt that the parents were quickly advised as to the nature of their son's illness. Nobody ever knew what emotions were aroused in them by this horrible certainty, but from that moment, troubled and apprehensive, the Empress's character underwent a change, and her health, physical as well as moral, altered.' For Alix, who had passed on the disease inherited through her mother and grandmother, it became a source of insurmountable guilt, making her even more vulnerable to the promises of faith healers.

When Nicky had to go away for a few days the following week, Alix wrote as soon as he had left. 'Sweetest One, It was horrid seeing you drive off and I know what it costs you leaving our treasure – but thank God it was not last week, which would have been unbearable . . . baby dear's shoe and glove are to give you a nice warm feeling in your heart when you go to bed. Your beloved big sad eyes, I see them always before me. Our dear Friend I am sure is watching over you, as He did over tiny last week – oh, what anguish it was, and not to let others see the knife digging in one. Thank God he is so well now!' She signed herself 'ever and ever your very own old Wify, Sunny.' 'Sunny' was the nickname given her as a child, in those carefree years before her mother died. 'My own beloved Sunny,' Nicky replied the very next day from the Imperial train, and in his good English learnt over many years with the genial Mr Heath, 'What a joy your sweet letter gave me. Thank you ever so many times, darling, for the kind forethoughts that touched me so. Only Wify could have such ideas to give pleasure to Huzy when he is away. Your telegrams are a great comfort, one feels nearer hearing twice a day.' He ended with a familiar refrain. 'Duty, duty, there is nothing to be done. Now goodbye, and bless you my sunshine and love, and our sweet children. Kiss my son very tenderly for me. Your own Huzy, Nicky.'

Nicky's devotion to his wife did not entirely exclude his mother. He was in almost daily contact with her when she was in St Petersburg, remaining attached to her in much the same way as his cousin Georgie in England remained attached to his own 'Motherdear'. When the Dowager Tsarina was at Gatchina or in Denmark he wrote to her regularly, and she in turn wrote him long letters filled with family news, laced with careful advice, though it was clear to everyone that her political influence over her son was waning. Everyone went to visit the Dowager Empress at the Anitchkoff Palace – ministers, governors of provinces, courtiers, high officials, diplomats, writers, artists, and foreign statesmen. 'If anyone is curious enough to ask the question as to who is the most popular lady in Russia,' reported an English journalist, 'there is little doubt that the answer would be the Dowager Empress. For the grace and winning tact she always displays towards her subjects have won all hearts. The Empress takes a personal interest in everything and everybody.'

In Denmark the two sisters Minny and Alexandra now built Hvidore, a holiday villa on the coast near Copenhagen. 'I have never seen a more ghastly property,' wrote Edward VII's friend Charles Hardinge, 'there being no privacy, owing to the road passing close by to the house, so that those on the road could look straight into the windows, whilst access to the sea could be obtained only by crossing the road.' It could hardly have been in greater contrast to their usual vast palaces, but Minny and Alix loved it, and used it to keep the Danish link alive as they worked steadily towards a lasting friendship between England and Russia, and against Germany. Isvolsky, for some years the Russian Minister in attendance at the Danish Court, wrote later in his memoirs, 'The aversion of the Empress Dowager of Russia for Germany and everything German was so pronounced that, when she came to see her father, she arrived always on her yacht, in order not to have to cross Germany. When bad weather or the season of the year obliged her to return by land through Germany, she refused to cross the narrow straits between the Danish isles and the German coast in a steamer flying the German colours, and, instead, took a Danish boat to Warnemunde, where a special train of Russian railway carriages awaited her and transported her to the Russian frontier with as few stops as possible.'

Three years later the Kaiser paid his first visit to Denmark since the bitterness of the Prussian–Danish war, King Christian's birthday celebrations the pretext. He sent Nicky a telegram to show how well he got on with everyone. 'Just leaving,' he wrote, 'having spent a few delightful days with the whole family in Copenhagen. Your dear grandfather was kindness itself. Your beloved mother and Aunt Alix quite spoilt me, both still looking so young, everybody of the royal family tried their utmost to make me feel at home, so that I have no words for thanking them.' Nicky promptly sent a copy of the telegram to his mother, adding a note of his own, because he knew too well what lay behind their smiles of welcome. 'Deeply moved – isn't he?' wrote Nicky in sarcastic vein. 'That is because his dearest wish to get into the Danish family circle has at last been fulfilled, so there is no end to his delight!' But he conceded, 'We have read his speech in reply to Apapa's – rather clever and well put.' Alix had her own way of summing up cousin Willy: 'He thinks himself a superman, and he's really nothing but a clown!'

Willy was always the odd man out in the family circle. Even decent Georgie was reluctant to pay him visits. 'My dear Francis,' he wrote to Knollys in 1905, after reading a letter from the British Ambassador to Berlin, 'Many thanks for letting me see Lascelles' letter. I do not call it a very satisfactory letter & what he says at the end, about my reluctance to go to Berlin & that I have not yet paid a visit to my Regiment, although I have already been Colonel of it for three years, is BOSH. It is a pity that the Emperor should always go out of his way to find fault & make complaints. I had no wish whatever to become Col of a German Regt, that was forced upon me, & because I have not yet had an opportunity of seeing it, it is continually rammed down one's throat.'

But family was family, and politics were politics. And as far as politics were concerned, Nicky currently had more in common with Willy than with Georgie or Georgie's father the 'Arch plotter' Edward VII. On 3 January 1904 Willy had sent Nicky a cheery Christmas message: 'Dearest Nicky, These lines are meant to reach you on your Xmas eve and will I hope find you well and happy with Alix at your side and the merry little company romping around you in the glimmer of the light of the Xmas tree.' He hoped their lives would run 'softly as a rippling brook' if the times were peaceful, or, if not peaceful, then 'victorious and enwreathed with fresh laurels.' He enclosed a couple of articles which might interest Nicky, including one from an English penny news-paper which, he said, was read daily by thousands in the streets of London and elsewhere in England. 'It is to show you with what stuff and in what a tone this Press is feeding its readers for many weeks already, and how they are blowing flames where they can. To us here on the Continent this hypocrisy and hatred is utterly odious and incompre-hensible.' On this occasion the subject was Russia's ambitions in Korea, but the real purpose of each letter was always the same: to attack his uncle Bertie, who was busy negotiating a further alliance with France.

From the moment he became King, and once the Boer War was successfully concluded, Edward VII had planned to visit France, cloaking a political purpose beneath a visit described as one purely for personal pleasure. To make the deception all the more convincing, he had planned the visit to Paris as part of an extensive European tour. The tour was undertaken in April 1903 and Ponsonby, who formed part of the extensive suite, was interested to note that the King made all the arrangements himself, down to the last detail. The more serious point, which did not escape Ponsonby, was that he informed no one. The real purpose of the journey became clear to Ponsonby as he helped with the itinerary: to prepare the way for an Entente Cordiale with France, even though the outcome was bound to be an *entente* non*cordiale* with Germany.

Edward VII meant to get his own back. He had suffered too long under his nephew William's arrogant behaviour, too often aimed at himself. He kept his arrangements so secret that even some members of his suite did not know where they were going. The itinerary included Portugal, Gibraltar, Malta, Italy and France. Germany was left out entirely. 'I soon was convinced that Paris was the King's real objective,' Ponsonby noted. Edward refused to take a Cabinet Minister with him, insisting on his friend Charles Hardinge instead. Since Hardinge was not the senior man at the Foreign Office, this was extremely unconventional; but the King continued to insist that it was nothing but an informal tour, with no official status. 'This visit seemed to me to strain the limitations of constitutional monarchy to breaking point,' noted Ponsonby. It was the single deliberately unconstitutional act of Edward VII's reign, and certainly had serious political consequences.

When the royal party arrived in Paris, shouts of '*Vive les Boers!*' could be heard from the crowd. Edward VII smiled and waved, genially showing that he took it all in good part. The next day there was a speech in which he stressed his 'old and happy ties with Parisians', and in the evening, at the theatre, he made a point of greeting the great actress Mlle Jeanne Garnier, kissing her hand and reminding her of the time in London when he went to see her perform and she 'represented all the grace and spirit of France'. The remark quickly reached the streets of Paris, and by the time the royal party was making its way to the Hôtel de Ville the following morning, the atmosphere had noticeably changed. At the Hôtel de Ville Edward VII made another impromptu speech, telling his audience that he would never forget their beautiful city '*où je me trouve comme si j'étais chez moi.*' This had the authentic ring of truth, since everyone knew how much Edward enjoyed his visits to Paris. After an appearance at Longchamps races and another speech at the State Banquet at the Élysée Palace that evening, again in French, the crowds were completely won over, greeting the King with deafening cheers, chanting 'Good old Teddy!' and '*Vive Édouard!*' The British Ambassador reported that the visit had been 'a success more complete than the most sanguine optimist could have foreseen.'

With his sure touch when it came to popular opinion, the King had almost single-handedly prepared the ground for the Entente Cordiale which was formally signed on 8 April 1904. It was Edward VII's greatest political achievement, allying England firmly with France, already in a fully-fledged defensive alliance with Russia, that last act of Edward's brother-in-law Alexander III before his death in 1894. The link between England and Russia so keenly fostered by the two Danish princesses Minny and Alexandra, the wives of Tsar Alexander III and King Edward VII, now finally appeared to come to fruition.

But the Entente Cordiale created a serious problem in its turn. England and France had cosily agreed to support one another in North Africa: England could keep Egypt, France could have Morocco in her sphere of influence. In the forked tongue of diplomacy, 'it appertains to France, more particularly as a Power whose dominions are coterminous for a great distance with those of Morocco, to preserve order in that country and to provide assistance for the purpose of all administrative, economic, financial and military reforms which it may require.' Germany, with rapidly growing trade interests in North Africa, had been pointedly left out. And although Edward VII had tried to put matters right with an official visit to Kiel in June 1904, this time with Lord Selborne, the First Lord of the Admiralty, as Minister in Attendance, the damage had been done. Long-held family animosities had moved from the private to the public arena and were soon to affect world events. From April 1904 onwards Germany felt herself to be encircled by Russia, France and England. The obsession that this was so, fanned by the Kaiser's paranoia, played a critical part in the lead-up to the First World War.

Japan, meanwhile, was demanding that Russia withdraw her troops from the left bank of the Yalu river, Russia having more or less taken over Manchuria, which bordered Korea, after leasing Port Arthur from the Chinese in 1898. As Sergei Witte had warned the Tsar at the time, war with Japan was the likely outcome of this provocative act. Witte was keen for trade with China, and especially Korea, and keen to complete the Trans-Siberian Railway, but he was not keen for war. The Russian economy was in an extremely bad state and they could not possibly afford a war, least of all at such a distance. Witte did not share the Interior Minister Plehve's view that 'a small victorious war' would solve Russia's internal problems and the threat of revolution. The Japanese might accept Russia in Manchuria, but not in Korea, where they had their own territorial ambitions. Nor was it certain that the war would be small, and victorious. Witte found that the Dowager Tsarina shared his misgivings. 'As I had not lost all hope yet of preventing the war against Japan, I saw the need of warning the Dowager Empress that if the policy were not altered a conflict was inevitable,' wrote Witte. 'I advised her to send for Count Lamsdorff [Minister of Foreign Affairs]. She did so immediately, and he confirmed my warning.' She also sent for General Kouropatkin, the Minister of War, who told her the same thing. Nicky, influenced first this way then that, prevaricated. 'I am still in good hopes about a calm and peaceful understanding,' he wrote to Willy. Willy thought otherwise. 'Nicholas is doing himself a lot of harm by his flabby way of going on,' he told Bülow, showing him the letter and noting that Nicky was 'compromising all Sovereigns' by his weakness.

Russia repeatedly promised to withdraw from the Yalu, but repeatedly failed to do so. 'Despite the fact that the Japanese actions were far from provocative, and despite the fact that their demands were considered essentially acceptable by the chief ministers in St Petersburg,' wrote Witte, 'negotiations did not lead to a successful outcome. For no good reason these negotiations dragged on. Failing to receive any reply to their final proposals, the Japanese decided finally on a rupture.' Without further warning, on 9 February 1904 the Japanese attacked the Russian squadron anchored off Port Arthur, sinking two battleships and a cruiser. In Witte's mind there was no doubt where the failure to negotiate lay. 'The degree to which the Sovereign Emperor did not expect this rupture can be seen from the fact that in September he left for Darmstadt and did not return to Petersburg until the late autumn.' By then Nicholas II had dismissed Witte and, without consulting any of his ministers, appointed Admiral Alekseev as Viceroy of the Far East. In so doing, and typically, he passed on the responsibility for the situation to someone else; but everyone, including the Japanese, knew that all decisions had in fact to be ratified by the Tsar himself.

'Dearest Nicky,' Willy had written from peaceful Potsdam in January 1904, 'Only a line to tell you how my thoughts are occupied with you in this serious time. May God grant that everything will come off smoothly and that the Japs may listen to reason, notwithstanding the frantic efforts of the vile press of a certain country.' He signed himself, 'Ever Yours most affectionally, Willy', adding as a post-script: 'Forgive me if I trouble you so often with telegrams, but at Wolfsgarten, you kindly said that you were thankful for any news worth while which I was able to communicate to you; of course *I rely on your secrecy*, as they are only for you. Admiral of the Atlantic.'

The war with Japan was a disaster for Russia. The great distances involved meant that initially only the few Russian troops already in the area could be deployed to fight; the rest took months to arrive. The single-track Trans-Siberian Railway, bringing guns, munitions, food and reinforcements, was four thousand miles long. The Japanese had to cover only a few hundred miles by sea. The Russian Baltic Fleet had to steam half-way round the world to go to the aid of the Pacific Fleet. After the years of peace achieved by Alexander III, Russia's senior commanders, both military and naval, were unprepared for war. The Russians had spent more than they could afford on defence – but, paradoxically, not enough to sustain a far-distant war. Through ignorance and prejudice, the Russians seriously underestimated the Japanese. Willy came to Nicky's aid, coaling the Baltic Fleet with his merchant fleet in home waters and in German South West Africa as the Russian fleet steamed from Kronstadt, the port by St Petersburg, all the way to Vladivostok, Russia's port on the Pacific. It suited the Kaiser perfectly. Now he could extract a formal alliance from Russia, to be used against England and France and help nullify his *bête noire*, the Entente Cordiale, ratified that April. 'But as the Chinaman says in pigeon English,' he wrote delightedly to Bülow, 'If no have coal, how can do?' Before enough coal was provided by his devoted cousin and friend for the Russian fleet to travel on, Nicky had to agree to enter into negotiations. 'Dearest Nicky,' Willy wrote, 'The outbreak of hostilities has had sad consequences for your brave Navy, which have deeply moved me! How could it be otherwise seeing that I am Russian Admiral and proud of this rank too!'

In October England and Russia almost came to blows in a good example of the 'cock-up' theory of history. In the early stages of its lengthy journey to the Far East, off the Dogger Bank the Russian Baltic Fleet mistook some Hull fishing trawlers for Japanese torpedo boats and opened fire, sinking one boat. 'If it were not for the loss of life,' wrote Edward VII to Georgie on 24 October 1904, 'one would laugh at the Russians for being such damned fools.' The British public, egged on by an indignant British press, was outraged. 'The English are very angry and near boiling point. They are even said to be getting their fleet ready for action,' wrote Nicky to his mother. 'Yesterday I sent a telegram to Uncle Bertie, expressing my regret, but I did not apologise.' The matter only died down when the incident had been referred to the Tribunal at The Hague, and Russia had agreed to pay a large sum in compensation. The British Admiralty, however, preferring to err on the safe side until the Russian fleet was well out of the way, detached some warships to shadow them. The Tsar took this very badly, complaining to the Kaiser about English arrogance and insolence. In England Edward VII's great friend and unofficial adviser Lord Esher, always alert to any political developments which might be unfavourable to England, noted that there was no doubt that Russia and Germany now had a 'secret and very intimate understanding.' By Russia and Germany he meant Nicky and Willy. The Tsar and the Kaiser were doing what they liked best, acting off their own bats, unfettered by the caution exercised by ministers. Esher knew this because Queen Alexandra had told him, and Queen Alexandra knew because her sister, the Dowager Tsarina, had told her.

Russia's war with Japan went from bad to worse. The Japanese, having control of the sea, landed troops in Korea and Manchuria, and laid siege to Port Arthur. On 13 April 1904 the Russian flagship, the battleship *Petropavlovsk*, hit a mine and sank, with the loss of seven hundred men, including Admiral Makarov, Commander of the fleet. On 2 January 1905 Port Arthur finally fell. 'I have been struck, as if by lightning, by the news of the fall of Port Arthur,' wrote Kostia in his diary. 'The defenders had run out of ammunition, they were all suffering from scurvy and typhoid, there were endless wounded, the Japanese shells kept falling on the hospital and wounding those who were already injured.' In February the Russians fought a major battle against the Japanese over control of the city of Mukden in Manchuria: 330,000 Russian troops faced 270,000 Japanese. After losing 89,000 men, the Russians fled.

The war, disastrous and disastrously managed, was creating support for the revolutionaries at home. On 16 February 1905 Grand Duke Sergei, Ella's husband, the notoriously repressive Governor of Moscow, was assassinated by a bomb as he was driving through the city in his carriage. 'A terrible crime was perpetrated in Moscow: Uncle Sergei was killed at the Nikolsky gates,' wrote Nicky in his diary. 'Poor Ella, bless her and help her, Lord!' Ella later told Kostia that Sergei had been extremely happy that day, having just received a miniature portrait of Alexander III from Nicky 'without diamonds, surrounded by a laurel wreath of gold.' Shortly after luncheon she heard a loud noise 'as when snow falls from the roof, only louder', and she could see people running into the square. She quickly put on her hat and coat and ran out in the direction of the noise, pushing her way through the crowd which had gathered. There she found the remains of Sergei lying about, 'part of the torso and a leg, a blown off hand, pieces of the body and clothes.' Not everyone was sad. 'Uncle Sergei, Grand Duke Sergei Alexandrovich, played a fatal part in the downfall of the Empire,' wrote Sandro, Xenia's husband.'Try as I will, I cannot find a single redeeming feature in his character.'

The Baltic Fleet had been making its way to Port Arthur by way of the Cape of Good Hope and Madagascar, shadowed all the way by Japanese spies. By the time it neared Japanese waters the enemy was lying in wait, fully prepared. At two o'clock on the afternoon of 27 May 1905 the fleet appeared in the Straits of Tsushima between Japan and Korea, its eight battleships steaming ahead in a long column. Admiral Togo, the Japanese commander, had them in his sights at a range of seven thousand yards, and gave the order to open fire. Within forty-five minutes all eight battleships had been sunk, along with seven out of twelve Russian cruisers and six out of nine destroyers. Two weeks later the Black Sea Fleet was facing mutiny. 'The most unbelievable news has arrived, simply disgraceful, it makes you feel ashamed!' wrote Kostia on 28 June. 'There has been a mutiny on the *Potemkin*, the commander and several officers have been killed. They arrived in Odessa yesterday evening, and this morning the body of a sailor was brought ashore, with a placard on his chest, saying that he had been killed by the officers for complaining about the bad food.' The *Potemkin*, commanded by her rank-and-file, put out to sea, ready for battle with the rest of the squadron, and some further mutinies occurred. But the authorities refused to coal the *Potemkin*, or provide them with food. Martial law was imposed, and the *Potemkin* was forced to give herself up. 'I feel so depressed, it's impossible,' wrote Xenia in her diary on 8 June. 'It's terrible what's happening – strikes, murders, discontent, a general lack of authority! I read a memorandum issued by the nobility – it's strong and cruel, but unfortunately true.'

The war with Japan was effectively over. At first Nicholas held out, reluctant to accept defeat, especially at the hands of the Yellow Race.

But by September a peace had been brokered. Reluctantly the Tsar had sent for Witte, his only really capable statesman, to represent him at a peace conference presided over by President Theodore Roosevelt in Portsmouth, New Hampshire. 'When a sewer has to be cleaned, they send for Witte,' said Witte, accepting with no enthusiasm. The Japanese proved happy to reach a compromise. Korea was to be left to the Japanese and Russia was to evacuate Southern Manchuria, but no indemnity was to be paid. Alexander Isvolsky, soon to be Russia's Foreign Minister, knew they had Witte's great powers of negotiation and persuasion to thank: 'No diplomat by profession could have done it.' Nicholas too was prepared to show his gratitude, within limits. 'Witte came to see us,' he wrote to his mother. 'He was very charming and interesting. After a long talk, I told him of his new honour. I am creating him a Count. He went quite stiff with emotion and tried three times to kiss my hand!'

The Kaiser had his own take on the matter. On 11 March 1905 he wrote to Bülow: 'News just received via "Wolff" in reference to the peace negotiations through the Gallo-English group on behalf of the Tsar indicates that the Rothschilds are no longer prepared to go on paying for the war. These negotiations may be the chief reason for the sudden cancellation of King Edward VII's journey. He will want to finish off the Gallo-Brit-Japanese Alliance now that he has got Afghanistan and Tibet in his pocket . . . It is monstrous that we, who have loyally stood by the Tsar with "Counsel", should again be completely excluded now.' Willy was convinced that the Danish link was once again joining forces against him. Incensed by England's treatment of Germany as a '*quantité négligeable*', he now became increasingly paranoid about the encirclement of Germany by her enemies, and redoubled his efforts at Weltpolitik.

In Russia there was chaos as demoralised troops made their way back home along the Trans-Siberian Railway. The expense of the war, the humiliation of defeat and the disaffection of the returning troops all increased social unrest and the threat of revolution. Renewed violence and strikes broke out all over Russia. Bakers, plumbers, locksmiths, tram conductors, print workers, all went on strike. Newspapers ceased to be published. Chemists' shops closed. The law courts ceased to work. In the cities, gas and electricity supplies were cut. A railway strike paralysed the country. 'As for the state of things in Russia,' wrote Edward VII to Georgie in October of that year, 'it is simply too awful & anarchy seems to reign everywhere! There are now railway strikes throughout the Country & nobody is able to travel!' His friend Charles Hardinge, despatched to do a short stint as British Ambassador in St Petersburg, had to make a dash for it, hastily returning by sea to the safety of home.

At home, Edward VII was back from Doncaster Races, where he had stayed with Lady Savile at Rufford Abbey, taking with him a valet, a sergeant-footman, a brusher, two equerries each with their own valets, two telephonists, two chauffeurs, and an Arab boy to prepare coffee the way he liked it. In Russia the Tsar was finally forced to create a new Council of Ministers and reluctantly called for Witte to take on the role of Chairman. 'The news from Russia has lately been rather more favourable & that the insurrection is being put down,' wrote Edward VII to Georgie on 12 January 1906. 'If only a Constitution may be acceptable to the people now, and may Nicky remain firm and stick to his promises.' By April 1906 Russia had its first Duma.

In Germany the Kaiser had serious troubles of his own, troubles so secret that they eventually exposed him to the threat of blackmail. The first rumblings had been felt as early as 1897. In that year Friedrich zu Eulenburg, Phili's brother, was sued for divorce by his wife Klara von Schaffer-Voit. They had been unhappily married for twenty years, but she now cited 'unnatural passions' as the grounds, and Fredi was called before a military court martial. Believing that everything could be fixed, Fredi asked Phili to ask the Kaiser to dismiss the proceedings. 'I would like to ask Your Majesty to keep all of this information, which are *military secrets*, secret,' wrote Phili to Willy, the Liebling, on 8 October, evidently under the same illusion as Fredi that he, who was the Kaiser's best friend, would be able to pull off this small favour for his brother. But when Phili approached Wilhelm he got a severe shock and a frightening foretaste of things to come. Instead of being understanding, Wilhelm declared himself outraged, and insisted that Fredi clear his name. Both Phili and Wilhelm knew this to be disingenuous, but the Kaiser, in a panic so great that he came close to a nervous breakdown, would not budge. Fredi, quite unable to do as Wilhelm demanded, was forced to resign from his regiment. The Kaiser now further insisted that Phili break off all contact with his brother. Eulenburg, at the very height of his power and influence, could not accept the charade which Wilhelm was playing. 'I saw no reason to turn away from my poor brother,' he wrote to his old friend Bülow.

Bülow, of course, knew all about the Liebenberg Circle, since his brother Alfred was an intimate member of it, though he himself took care never to join them. The three at the heart of the circle remained Eulenburg, Kuno Moltke, and Varnbüler, the only one who failed to burn his letters as the scandal subsequently unfolded in all its baroque horror. Added to these were Edgard von Wedel and Eberhard Dohna-Schlobitten, Eulenburg's close friends from boyhood. Edgard had become Wilhelm's *Kammerherr* or Gentleman of the Bedchamber, and Eberhard was the one who had brought Phili and Wilhelm together in 1886 at Prokelwitz. Karl von Dornberg, a gifted diplomat, was another close friend, from Eulenburg's days in the Guards regiment. When Karl, known as 'Chacha' or 'the little one' within the Liebenberg Circle, died in unspecified circumstances in St Petersburg in 1891 Kuno Moltke wrote to Varnbüler, 'I long for the old Philine. I must chat and gossip with *her* about our little one. I must see *her* out of the feeling that we must hold each other doubly tightly after this tear in our intimate circle.' Another less regular member of the circle was Georg von Hülsen, the theatrical friend to whom Phili persuaded Wilhelm to offer the post of Director, first at the Royal Theatre at Wiesbaden and then at the Court Theatre in Berlin, resulting in the usual accusations of political manipulation. Hulsen was twice accused of homosexuality, and twice escaped prosecution. Jan Baron von Wendelstadt, the artist of the group, was also accused, drawn into the whirlpool of scandal against his will. He committed suicide in 1909.

Not all the Liebenberg friends were necessarily practising homosexuals, but most were, and all were in the know. August zu Eulenburg, Wilhelm's Marshal of the Court, always present at the Liebenberg hunt and the Nordlandreise, the North Sea Cruises, was certainly in the know. So were Gustav von Kessel, Wilhelm's long-serving ADC, and Walter Baron von Esebeck, Deputy Master of the Imperial Stables. All three were cousins of Eulenburg; Esebeck, notorious for his lack of discretion, was among those forced to resign when the scandals eventually became public. As in the England of Oscar Wilde, it was permissible to be homosexual, but it was not permissible to be found out.

Bülow also knew all about Kuno von Moltke, who became the main focus of the scandal. In August 1897 Wilhelm had appointed Kuno as military attaché to Vienna where Eulenburg was the German Ambassador. Eulenburg wrote to his mother that he was 'in bliss' about it, and hoped to persuade Moltke to leave his wife Lily behind for the first year – suggesting that Eulenburg's mother knew very well what his inclinations were. 'This marriage was extremely *gruesome* to me,' Eulenburg had written at the time of Kuno's marriage, 'Kuno looked like a man *in despair* – and that was for me the most painful experience on this wide earth.' But Lily, unlike Eulenburg's wife who stayed at Liebenberg looking after the children, insisted on going to Vienna with her husband. It subsequently emerged that Vienna had been the scene of towering rows between husband and wife and jealous battles between Lily and Eulenburg for Kuno's love, with Eulenburg begging Lily to 'Release my friend, give me back my friend.' The marriage soon ended in divorce, and Kuno was immediately moved back to Berlin, where he became one of Wilhelm's ADCs. 'I know now, through Phili, what I saw coming for a long time,' wrote Varnbüler to Kuno. 'If you had succeeded in truly carrying it through, in trans- forming yourself so completely inside, in denying the ideals which you've held all your life, in climbing down from these pure heights and feeling at home in the oppressive atmosphere of the normal, then, *mein Dachs*, and only then would you have lost yourself, and I, you.'

The homosexual scandals at the Berlin Court would almost cer- tainly have been hushed up and dealt with in secret, but for one man. His name was Maximilian Harden. Harden was the son of a Berlin silk merchant, one of the well-to-do, assimilated Jewish families belong- ing to the intellectual middle class who emerged in the rapid economic growth which followed German unification. Harden attended the most elite secondary school in Berlin, the Französische Gymnasium, where the language of instruction was French. There was nothing specifically Jewish in his upbringing, and he, along with most of his family, later became Christian, possibly because opportunities for advancement for Jews in the Germany of Kaiser Wilhelm II were few.

When he left school Harden, a brilliant student, first tried his hand at acting, later switching to journalism, for which he proved to have a natural talent and which became his life's work. He began in a general capacity on the *Berliner Tagesblatt* but soon moved to liberal weekly magazines like *Die Nation* and *Die Gegenwart*, where he wrote book and theatre reviews as well as articles on literature and politics. Harden possessed an outstanding intellect and a superb memory. He despised the reactionary tastes of the Kaiser's Court which, in antici- pation of Hitler, rejected everything modern as degenerate, preferring works of art like the Siegesallee, an avenue of massive sculptures of

Germanic heroes standing on towering pedestals, in the Classical style. From the moment Wilhelm II ascended the Imperial throne in 1888, Harden hated the empty swagger, the flashy uniforms, the bombastic speeches, and the endless military parades with their loud, flag-waving music.

In July 1890 Harden wrote his first article in *Die Gegenwart* under the signature 'Apostata', and with it moved decisively from the cultural to the political. Before he had mostly criticised the style of Wilhelm's Court, dominated by the sentimental and reactionary tastes of the Liebenberg Circle. Now it was their reactionary political views which became his target. It is likely that the step was a consequence of Bismarck's dismissal in April of that year. The 'Apostata' articles were pro-Bismarck and anti the new royal entourage made up exclusively of mediocre military on the one hand, and Eulenburg and his friends on the other. Soon everyone was reading 'Apostata', including Bismarck. But it was not till January 1892 that Bismarck discovered who 'Apostata' was, when Harden decided to send him a New Year card. 'I was gladdened by the warm expression of good will in your friendly New Year's greeting,' Bismarck wrote back. 'Should you happen to find yourself in this vicinity, I would be pleased to repeat my thanks to you personally.' Harden happened to find himself in the vicinity of Friedrichsruh, Bismarck's estate near Hanover, shortly afterwards, and the association that grew between the two men continued fruitfully till Bismarck's death in 1898.

In 1898 Harden founded his own weekly periodical, *Die Zukunft*, The Future, which became his personal vehicle for criticising the Kaiser and his entourage. He campaigned fearlessly for political change, eventually bringing down the whole system of Personal Rule which Eulenburg had been busy setting up during the 1890s with his old friend Bülow. 'The German capital is not poor in intellects and talents,' Harden wrote in an early edition. 'But a vulgar, ostentatious minority rules here.' He dubbed the Kaiser the 'Filmhelm', a nice play on 'matinée idol', and laughed at his posing and his bravado speeches. But it was the flattering Liebenberg Circle that remained the real target of his criticisms. 'You have been lied to for years,' he wrote in an open letter to the Kaiser in *Die Zukunft* on 25 June 1898. 'The lying sycophants have now convinced you that the magic of your glorious personality, before which all the world bows in admiration, has long overcome the malice [of others] . . . All of this is untrue.' Sometimes,

for greater amusement and greater safety, he thinly disguised his pro-
tagonists. The Kaiser might be Louis XVI, Eulenburg was again
'Count Troubadour' and Kuno Moltke 'the Sweet One'. He invented
a fictitious correspondence between Moritz and Rena, a brother and
sister from an old Prussian family, to comment on the intrigues at
Court. The ruse did not always work. Issues of *Die Zukunft* were often
confiscated, and on three occasions Harden was arrested and sentenced to some months in prison.

As Eulenburg's grip on the Kaiser tightened, Harden began to think
of ways to rid the country of his malign influence. He knew there
were people keen to help him, because as Eulenburg manipulated his
friends into positions of power and influence, he made many enemies.
One by one they contacted Harden, always wishing to remain anonymous. The most unexpected of these was a man Harden had often
attacked in the past: Friedrich von Holstein. Eulenburg and Holstein
had by now fallen out so completely that from 1897 onwards they had
ceased to have any contact. Holstein could only watch from the
Foreign Office in the Wilhelmstrasse as the Kaiser, encouraged by
Eulenburg and various reactionary members of his military entourage,
became less and less inclined to listen to his ministers, and openly
disdained the Reichstag. 'I alone am Master of the Reich, I will suffer
no other,' he announced in one of his typically bombastic speeches,
way out of touch with reality. Wilhelm kept his greatest fury for the
Socialists and Social Democrats. 'Until the leaders of the Social
Democrats are dragged out of the Reichstag and shot, nothing will
improve,' he told Eulenburg, apparently in all seriousness, in July 1899.
After a tram workers' strike he said he expected his troops to shoot at
least five hundred of them.

It was clear to everyone who came into contact with the Kaiser that
his behaviour was becoming increasingly erratic. There had been
many rumours about his moods, his nerves, his constant travelling,
his megalomania, even his sanity. In private people had begun to
comment that his outbursts reminded them of mad Ludwig of
Bavaria. Count Anton Monts, the Prussian envoy to Bavaria, wrote to
Eulenburg on 20 March 1897 that in Catholic South Germany 'many
are saying secretly that HM is insane. Already there are hints of this in
the press . . . What I think of HM I don't even dare to say, but I fear
he is completely finished here in the South . . . they are talking very
seriously about a *coup d'état* in the Reich.' Bismarck let it be known

that he held on to office for so long only because of the Kaiser's mental state. As early as 1888 he was already convinced that the Kaiser 'suffered from a condition inherited from his English and Russian ancestors'. In England Lord Salisbury, hearing the rumours and recalling the medical report of 1879 stating that the damage caused at birth to Wilhelm's inner right ear, with its growths and discharges, could in time infect the brain, tapped his forehead as he had before and muttered 'Erichson'.

In the event, the Kaiser never had a complete mental breakdown. But he suffered a series of nervous collapses, the first in 1893, followed by others in 1900 and 1903 and another in 1908. Frail and vulnerable beneath all the bravado, he was more than ever in need of clever, wise and diplomatic advisers. Instead he had Eulenburg, a rabid monarchist and reactionary with a deep-seated hatred of parliaments. Worse still, Eulenburg was a second-class mind, as Bismarck had noted many years earlier. Or, as Harden put it in *Die Zukunft* in November 1901, 'he belongs to those people of whom Goethe has said: it is in the nature of dilettantes that they do not realise the difficulties that lie in a thing, and that they are always undertaking something beyond their powers.' The combination of the Kaiser and Eulenburg was extremely dangerous, all the more so since Eulenburg seemed to operate from conviction and ideology as much as from opportunism.

After tendering his resignation on various occasions in an attempt to bring the Kaiser into line and force him into a modicum of constitutional government, Holstein finally left his post on 6 April 1906, a worried and bitter man. *Die Zukunft* noted that the news would be causing jubilation in Liebenberg since 'the Austernfreund [Holstein] would no longer pose a danger to the Troubadour and his Kuno.' It was not long before Holstein contacted Harden.

Paradoxically, ever since 1897, when the Kaiser informed him so harshly that he would not protect Eulenburg's brother Fredi from the homosexual scandal enveloping him, Eulenburg had been trying to extricate himself from his position at Court. He knew too well what damage a public scandal could do to him personally, to the political system he had so carefully constructed, and perhaps even to the Kaiser himself. Now, disillusioned by the Kaiser's faithlessness, he became sharply critical of Wilhelm, seeing unpleasant traits which he had, strangely, never spotted before. On 21 August 1899 he had written to Bülow that Wilhelm was 'unchanged in his explosive nature. He is even harder and more impulsive in a self-reliance upon his mature experience – which is no experience.' By the following year, from aboard the *Hohenzollern* on the annual North Sea Cruise, he was writing that he felt as if he were sitting on a powder keg. He warned Bülow not to send Wilhelm any political news which might upset him and cause another outbreak. 'HM *no longer has himself under control.*' No amount of distraction of the usual sort – musical turns, crude sketches, fun and games on deck – made any difference. No one, not even the Kaiser's personal physician, could think of a solution. Everyone had to pray to God that nothing would provoke another drama which might lead to a complete nervous breakdown. Lulled for years into a false sense of security by his flattering entourage, Wilhelm only had his public persona to fall back on. And now that he had caught the whiff of public scandal, it terrified him.

Harden's veiled attacks on Eulenburg and the Liebenberg Circle in *Die Zukunft* continued, and Eulenburg repeatedly tried to find excuses to resign. But Bülow, Chancellor since 1900, would not let him go. He still needed Eulenburg to help control the Kaiser, for the time being at least. Shrewd Count Witte had this to say after a meeting with the German Chancellor: 'My impression of Bülow was that he is not a bad sort, is not particularly industrious or clever, but is able to speak well. His chief trait as a diplomatist is his slyness, in the good sense of the word, if you will, and the chief use he makes of it is in dealing with his Emperor. Knowing his Sovereign's weaknesses, he makes good use of them, but in the process he often pockets not only his personal pride, but also the dignity befitting a first minister. Obviously he is no Bismarck, nor can he even be compared to the straightforward and honourable Caprivi. All in all, I consider Bülow to be a second-rate political figure.'

By 1902 Eulenburg had become too much of a liability, and Bülow was no longer determined to keep him. Eulenburg resigned in August. 'Certain people must be told that my health requires a life in the South, far from Berlin and its social intercourse,' he wrote to Bülow on 14 January 1902, in a clear reference to Harden. Harden's critics have tried to suggest that his campaign was motivated by a hatred of homosexuals. If this were so, Eulenburg's resignation would not have sufficed to stop his attacks in *Die Zukunft*. But the attacks did stop, and were only revived three years later when Eulenburg tried to make a comeback. Harden's concern was for Germany, and he used the homosexuality of the Liebenberg Circle as the only means at his disposal to remove them from their position of power, and to force an end to the Kaiser's Personal Rule.

Now it was Bülow's turn to try to rein in the Kaiser's autocratic behaviour. But it was too late. The fictitious in the Kaiser's life, fed by a constant diet of flattery, had long since replaced any sense of reality the young Wilhelm might have possessed. When, aged four, he went to stay with his grandmother at Osborne, she had described him as 'dear little William, a darling, promising child.' At school the promise was still in evidence. With good guidance the promising boy might have grown into a promising man, or at least have had his worst excesses contained. As it was, by 1902 Willy, the German Kaiser, was heading straight for disaster.

14

Dangerous Disagreements

~

THE LATER YEARS of his short reign were felicitous for Edward
VII. His personal finances were now in good order thanks to the
astute management of his friend Ernest Cassel. His family relationships were harmonious. Alix had accepted the presence of Mrs Keppel
with diplomatic grace, even inviting her to Court, and the King
remained on excellent terms with his son Georgie, telling him, 'We
are more like brothers than father and son.' Their lives overlapped at
Sandringham, London, Balmoral, and Windsor, where Edward VII
arranged to have Georgie's desk placed next to his own so they could
work side by side. He was determined not to make the same mistake
as his mother Queen Victoria, and kept the heir to the throne well
informed about matters of State, showing him Cabinet papers and
Foreign Office reports and making sure he was acquainted with all the
leading statesmen of the day. After the success of the Entente Cordiale,
which was seen as his personal triumph, the King's popularity in the
country could hardly have been higher. To Georgie he wrote happily
that the Anglo–French agreement was a splendid thing. 'We have
really the best of the bargain and, as regards the concessions in
Morocco, if we had not made them they would have taken them; and
our position in Egypt is more assured than ever!'

In October 1905 Georgie and May set off on another royal tour, this
time to India. They were away for five months, leaving behind their
now complete family of six children. In Calcutta the Viceroy and his
wife, Lord and Lady Minto, were preparing Government House for
their arrival. Seven hundred men were employed painting and clean-
ing, and fifty large carpeted tents, with bedrooms, sitting rooms and
bathrooms, were put up in the grounds to house the extra staff and servants. 'By luncheon time bullock wagons by the score piled with Royal
luggage were to be seen at the back premises stretching as far as the eye
could see,' wrote Lady Minto in her journal. 'Five hundred coolies

have been engaged to handle the luggage.' Throughout the royal tour the Prince of Wales prepared notes on India for his father. 'No doubt the Natives are better treated by us than in the past, but I could not help being struck by the way in which all salutations by the Natives were disregarded by the persons to whom they were given. Evidently we are too much inclined to look upon them as a conquered & down-trodden race & the Native, who is becoming more and more educated, realises this. I could not help noticing that the general bearing of the European towards the native was to say the least unsympathetic. In fact not the same as that of superiors to inferiors at home.' He discovered that no Indian, whatever his background, could be a member of a European club, and was not convinced by the explanation that the clubs would otherwise become overcrowded.

Although the Prince of Wales benefited from the advice of various India specialists throughout the tour, and had Stamfordham's help in formulating his ideas, the feelings he expressed were clearly based on his own observations, and shared by the Princess of Wales. Together Georgie and May undertook to strengthen the ties of the Common-wealth, and together they shared the wave of popularity for the monarchy which was the result. 'Somehow I can't tell you, so I take the first opportunity of writing to say how deeply I am indebted to you darling for the splendid way in which you supported and helped me during our long Tour. It was you who made it a success,' he wrote to her on their return to England. 'Although I have often told you before, I repeat it once more, that I love you darling child, with my whole heart and soul, and thank God every day that I have such a wife as you, who is such a great help and support to me and I believe loves me too.'

But Georgie preferred to stay at home, performing his public duties, looking through Government papers, serving on Royal Commissions, and occasionally attending debates in the House of Lords. His only problem was his nerves. To cover his shyness, he was inclined to talk too much and much too loudly, and sometimes indis-creetly. And he always hated making speeches, trying to get out of them whenever possible. Lord Esher, looking ahead, was worried. 'However much HRH may dislike it he will have to give way, or the monarchy will be doomed!'

Edward VII still had his small group of intimate friends who protected his interests and, where necessary, kept him *au fait* in more informal ways. Knollys and Esher, still meeting regularly at Brooks's Club, were the main keepers at the gate, together with Sir John Fisher, and, from time to time, Charles Hardinge, de Soveral and Alice Keppel. On 28 August 1905 Esher wrote to Knollys about 'the remissness of the King's present advisers in not keeping His Majesty informed, and in not sending their written reasons or seeking the King's authority *before* action is taken.' The King's anxiety was perhaps heightened by the prospect of a Liberal Government. 'The days of our Govt are numbered. A. Balfour has determined to resign before Christmas, which I think is unnecessary and a mistake,' Edward VII wrote to Georgie. 'The formation of a new Government will give much trouble in many ways, and I presume I will have to send for Sir H. C-B.'

Knollys busied himself trying to ensure that Campbell-Bannerman's Cabinet would contain people like Asquith, Grey and Haldane, who were less radical than some of the party. Bowing to the inevitable, the King fell back on his own good sense, writing to Georgie on 15 December: 'It is certainly a strong Government with considerable brain-power. Let us hope that they will work for the good of the Country and, indeed, the Empire. Sir E. Grey will, I hope, follow in the footsteps of Lord Lansdowne in every respect. Lord Tweedmouth should make a good "1st Lord" and takes the greatest interest in his appointment. Mr Haldane, with sound common sense and great power of organisation, ought to make an excellent War Minister, which is much needed as his predecessor was hopeless.' Asquith became Chancellor of the Exchequer; Lloyd George, President of the Board of Trade; Lord Carrington, who was the King's good friend, President of the Board of Agriculture. All in all, it wasn't a bad show. If nothing else, most of them were friends or at least acquaintances of his devoted Private Secretary Francis Knollys, and his equally devoted friend Lord Esher.

The greatest matter facing Edward VII's friends was the reform of the Navy and the War Office. Esher was most concerned to bring Britain's defences up to date so that they were ready, if necessary, for war. Like Eulenburg in Germany, Esher continued to offer his Sovereign unofficial advice, and advice to certain others as to how to gain his Sovereign's favour. Also like Eulenburg, Esher was homosexual. But Esher operated within a system of constitutional monarchy, always open to the scrutiny of Parliament; and he himself was a forward-looking man of liberal instincts, and infinitely cleverer than Eulenburg, the reactionary.

Esher's whole instinct was anti-German. As he watched the Russians becoming more and more embroiled in their disastrous war with Japan he was already considering the wider implications. 'The future does not look very bright,' he noted in his journal on 7 September 1904. 'A prolonged war, for now it is bound to go on, and a secret and very intimate understanding between Russia and Germany. Of this there is no doubt in the world.' In March 1905 he wrote to his son Maurice about the war in Russia: 'Was there ever so great an object lesson in the value of careful and scientific preparation, or so heavy a blow dealt to the policy of muddling?' On 6 June, with the war effectively lost, he noted that 'the crushing defeat of Russia redresses the balance in favour of Germany'. The next day he wrote again, on a happier note: 'The party last night at Buckingham Palace was very well done. Melba and Caruso first rate. The Queen had on her Russian tiara with the Imperial crown behind it, and looked a fitting leader of about 12 Duchesses, one smarter than the other.' Alexandra, always good at wardrobe politics, was showing solidarity with her sister, the Dowager Tsarina.

'My dear Esher,' wrote the King from HM Yacht *Victoria and Albert*, anchored off Corfu on 14 April 1906, 'Many thanks for your interesting letter of 6th. Pray write to me fully and confidentially about anything that you think will interest me and I think you know of old that I take interest in most things . . . Believe me, Yours very sincerely, EDWARD R.' Esher was spending most of his time at the head of the Committee for Imperial Defence, having already chaired the War Office Reconstruction Committee and the Committee to organise the Territorial Army. 'L'allemagne c'est l'Ennemi,' he wrote to Maurice in September, not for the first time. 'There is no doubt that within measurable distance there looms a titanic struggle between Germany and Europe for mastery. Germany has 70,000,000 of people and is determined to have commercial pre-eminence. To do this England has got to be crippled and the Low Countries added to the German Empire. France contains 40,000,000 of people. England about the same. So even combined, the struggle is by no means a certainty.' A good eight years before the outbreak of hostilities, the talk was already of war.

The origins of the problem lay as far back as 1897 when Germany took a sharp swing to the right, masterminded by Eulenburg and Bülow, now in Berlin to head the Foreign Office. In that same year the Kaiser, heady with the success of Eulenburg's plan, had appointed Admiral Alfred von Tirpitz as Secretary of State for the Imperial Naval Office. Tirpitz advocated a massive German navy, entirely echoing Wilhelm's own determination, ever since events in the Transvaal, to have a Navy large enough and powerful enough to take on the Royal Navy anywhere in the world. Eulenburg noted that the Kaiser had told him the only way to protect Germany's colonial interests was to have a sufficiently powerful Navy. Germany would have to prepare itself, if necessary, for an *offensive* action against Britain. Modest naval budgets were no longer acceptable.

Tirpitz had developed a 'risk theory' by which the Royal Navy – pinpointed as a future threat to Germany – would not, because of its commitments elsewhere in the world, risk a war with Germany in the North Sea once Germany's ships were in a ratio of 2 to 3 with the Royal Navy's. Tirpitz envisaged this build-up of the German fleet taking about twenty years. Opponents of the plan, including Holstein, pointed out early on that a powerful German battle fleet was bound to upset the British, who traditionally had mastery of the sea. The Germans had the most powerful Army in the world, the British the most powerful Navy. To upset that balance of power would be to court disaster. But Kaiser Wilhelm, strongly encouraged by his reactionary military entourage and Tirpitz, took no notice.

In the teeth of opposition from the liberal factions the First Naval Law was passed in the Reichstag on 8 March 1898. Over the next seven years, and with a huge budget of 408 million Marks, nineteen battleships and thirty-two cruisers were to be built, the first stage in the construction of a German battle fleet. Wilhelm was jubilant. On the occasion of his next dispute with Lord Salisbury, in July 1898 over the disintegrating Portuguese Empire in Africa, in a marginal note to Eulenburg, he wrote: 'One can see once again how the noble Lord plays with us and shifts around, merely because he does not fear us since we have no fleet – which has been continually refused me in ten years of government by that donkey Reichstag.' He warned Lascelles, the British Ambassador, that the day would come, once they had a real fleet, when Britain would have to show Germany proper respect. But the outcome of his decision was not so simple. Edward VII lost no time: he courted France, culminating in the Entente Cordiale, then set about trying to negotiate something similar with

Russia. But this would take time. Nicky in Russia was angry about Britain's alliance with Japan during the Russo-Japanese war.

The contents of a coded telegram from the Tsar on 28 October 1904 put the Kaiser in a distinctly buoyant frame of mind. 'I have no words to express my indignation with England's conduct,' Nicky wrote, still smarting over the Dogger Bank incident. 'I agree fully with your complaints about England's behaviour concerning the coaling of our ships by German steamers, whereas she understands the rules of keeping neutrality in her own fashion. It is certainly high time to put a stop to this. The only way, as you say, would be that Germany, Russia and France should at once unite upon an arrangement to abolish Anglo-Japanese arrogance and insolence. Would you like to lay down and frame the outlines of such a treaty and let me know it? As soon as accepted by us, France is bound to join her ally. This combination has often come to my mind; it will mean peace and rest for the world. Best love from Alix. Nicky.'

Willy could not have been more delighted and, with Bülow's help, began at once to frame the terms of a treaty. It went off 'by Imperial Fieldjaeger' the following evening. In the accompanying letter Willy described the treaty as a 'purely defensive alliance', like a 'mutual fire insurance against incendiarism'. He had some misgivings about France, however. 'As for France we both know that the Radicals and antichristian parties, which for the moment are the stronger ones, incline towards England.' He added that the draft treaty was so secret that 'nobody knows anything about it, not even my Foreign Office; the work was done by Bülow and me personally.' It took Nicky ten days to reply, and when he did he insisted that France, Russia's ally, must be shown the draft before he could sign it. 'Therefore I ask your agreement to acquaint the government of France with this project and upon getting their answer shall at once let you know by telegraph. Nicky.' This did not suit Willy at all. He telegraphed back: 'Best thanks for telegram. You have given me new proof of your perfect loyalty by deciding not to inform France without my agreement. Nevertheless, it is my firm conviction that it would be absolutely dangerous to inform France before we have both signed the treaty.' A *fait accompli* was the only way to force France onto their side, argued Willy. 'Should however France know that a Russian–German treaty is only projected, but still unsigned, she will immediately give short notice to her friend (if not secret ally) England, with whom she is bound by "entente cordiale", and inform her immediately.' For Willy it all led back to the Entente Cordiale. He ended on a thinly veiled threat: 'Should you, notwithstanding, think it impossible for you to conclude a treaty with me without the previous consent of France, then it would be a far safer alternative to abstain from concluding any treaty at all.'

Nicky prevaricated, promising to send his 'explanations on the matter'. Willy, impatient for action, wrote again two days later, signing himself with a flourish: 'God grant that we may have found the right way to hem in the horrors of war and give His blessings in our plan. Believe me dearest Nicky, with best love to Alix, yr most affate cousin and friend Willy.' Three weeks later he wrote again: 'It is far from my intention to hurry you in your answer to my last remarks about your proposal about our defensive treaty,' he began politely, but ended with another threat. Should Nicky be unprepared to fight 'shoulder to shoulder' beside him, 'I regret to assert to be under the necessity of immediately forbidding German steamers to continue to coal your fleet.' But by July of the following year nothing had yet been achieved. As Bülow recorded it in his not entirely reliable memoirs, Willy now took matters into his own hands, relying on the 'compelling powers of his own personality'. The Kaiser was off on his summer cruise to the Baltic, hoping to see the Tsar, but he preferred to go alone, without Bülow or any other interfering minister. From the Imperial Yacht *Hohenzollern* Willy sent a telegram to Nicky, also on a cruise in his Imperial Yacht. 'I shall shortly be on my return journey and cannot pass across entrance of the Finnish Sea without sending you best love and wishes. Should it give you any pleasure to see me – either on shore or your yacht – of course am always at your disposal. I would come as simple tourist, without any fêtes.'

'Delighted with your proposition,' replied Nicky. 'Would it suit you to meet at Björkesmund, near Viborg, a pleasant, quiet place, living on board our yachts?' Russia had effectively lost the war with Japan. Full-scale revolution was threatening. Nicky was in need of support. 'Looking forward with intense pleasure to see you, Nicky.' Willy was quick to pick up on the suggestion of secrecy. Only his Captain knew their real destination, he told Nicky in his next eager message. 'All my guests under impression of going to Visby in Gothland. Am overjoyed at seeing you again. Have most important news for you. The faces of my guests will be worth seeing when they suddenly behold your yacht. A fine lark. Tableau. Which dress for the meeting? Willy.'

On 23 July 1905 the two imperial yachts dropped anchor off the island of Björkö in the Gulf of Finland. The first night Nicky went to have dinner with Willy. He stayed until 3 a.m. The next morning at 9 a.m. Willy boarded the Russian Imperial Yacht with the draft treaty, hand-written by him in French, in his pocket. It was substantially the same as before: if either empire were attacked, the other would come to her aid by land and by sea with all her forces. Nicholas was to inform the French and get their signature once Russia had concluded peace with Japan. But without consulting Nicholas, or anyone else, Willy had added the words '*en Europe*' specifying the area of attack. The Kaiser had no wish to become involved in the Far East, but he needed Russia's help with England. They signed the treaty in Nicky's cabin with no one official present except Nicky's malleable naval minister, Admiral Birilev, who later claimed that Willy had placed his hand over the offending phrase.

Willy, beside himself with triumph, wrote like a happy child to Bülow: 'It was deathly quiet; the only sound was that of the waves and the sun shone bright and clear in the cosy cabin. I could see the *Hohenzollern* glistening white with its imperial standard fluttering in the breeze . . .' He described the Tsar reading the treaty through and seeming to agree. 'Should you like to sign it?' the Kaiser asked the Tsar 'with every appearance of casualness', opening the inkstand. They both signed, Willy with tears of pure joy in his eyes, thinking all the while of his grandfather and Frederick the Great. According to Willy at least, the Tsar said, 'You are Russia's only real friend in the whole world. I have felt that through the whole war and I know it.' Willy for his part decided that 'God has ordained and willed it.'

But when Bülow read the full text of the treaty, including the phrase '*en Europe*', he was appalled. 'What has Germany at stake? A fine navy, flourishing trade, rich coastal cities, her colonies. And what does Russia offer? A navy that scarcely any longer exists, very little commerce, insignificant towns on the coast, no colonial possessions.' Bülow had to threaten to resign before Wilhelm came down from the clouds, to fall swiftly into a decline. 'For the best and most intimate friend I have to treat me in this way without offering any adequate reason has given me such a terrible blow that I am quite broken down,' he wrote. 'I have taken immediate steps to induce Nicholas to get these two words weakened or left out,' he wrote, adding, close to desperation: '*I could not survive this* . . . I appeal to your friendship for me. Do not let us hear any more about resigning. Wire "all right" when you get this letter and I shall know you are going to stay. For the day after your request for release arrived there *would no longer be a Kaiser alive*! Think of my poor wife and children!'

Luckily for Willy, Nicky in Russia was also encountering difficulties. Count Lamsdorff, now the Foreign Minister, only learnt of the treaty's existence two weeks after it had been signed. It was incompatible with the alliance Nicky's father Alexander III had signed with France in 1894, and France, Lamsdorff was obliged to remind the Tsar, would never join an alliance with Germany. 'During my stay at Björkö I did not have with me the documents signed by my father which clearly define the principles of our alliance with France,' Nicky wrote lamely to Willy. But Lamsdorff soon found himself replaced by Isvolsky.

Over the next few months Willy tried to salvage something of the treaty, reminding Nicky in a letter of 22 August of their uncle Edward VII's 'net of secret information . . . cast over Europe and over you', via Copenhagen, and the Danish link. But the thing was essentially dead and buried. 'Tsar Nicholas, from the beginning of his reign, regarded our Kaiser with mixed feelings,' wrote Bülow. 'At one time he was friendly and confidential, at another irritable and ill-humoured. The Kaiser had upset the Tsar by too frequent and unasked advice and visits, and by his almost naively displayed superiority.' After Björkö, things were never the same between Willy and Nicky.

Germany remained extremely concerned by the high-handed manner in which Morocco had been dished up for the French under the terms of the Entente Cordiale. In January 1905 a French diplomatic mission had arrived in Fez and presented the Sultan with a comprehensive programme of reforms, removing from him virtually all independent power. Addressing the Reichstag in March, Bülow insisted that Germany had many economic interests in the Sultanate of Morocco which Germany 'must and would protect'. The fact that the French, in particular their Minister for Foreign Affairs, Théophile Delcassé, had not consulted Germany before signing the Entente, was unacceptable. Germany decided to make a stand. The Kaiser would signal her claims by stopping off at Tangiers during his forthcoming Mediterranean cruise at the end of March 1905 for a short, informal visit lasting no more than a few hours. The Kaiser himself was unsure about this, fearful of the risks to his person at such a volatile time, but

Bülow was adamant, keen to use the visit as a signal to remind the French of Germany's rightful commercial interests in Morocco.

Knowing Wilhelm's impetuous and irrational character well by now, Bülow gave him detailed instructions as to how to behave: with whom to speak, and whom not, what to say and what not to say – and above all, to avoid his usual verbosity. Wilhelm dithered until the last minute, then finally decided to land. Unsurprisingly, he quickly forgot Bülow's careful advice and gave Count Chérissey, the French Chargé d'Affaires, to whom he had been told not to speak, a piece of his royal mind. The visit of the All-Highest, he told the Count, was an indication that His Majesty demanded 'free trade for Germany and complete equality of rights with other nations.' When this point was politely conceded, the Kaiser pushed on. 'His Majesty remarked that he would come to an understanding with the Sultan as a free and equal ruler of an independent country,' reported von Schoen, a member of the German Foreign Office, adding that the Count went pale but, luckily, was curtly dismissed by the Kaiser without having to reply. Otherwise the visit went off splendidly, reported von Schoen. 'Our ships, as is the custom of the country, were exceedingly and richly loaded with products of the country.'

News of the visit soon got out, and the English and French press were instantly up in arms, describing it as a premeditated and provocative act. Edward VII, also cruising in the Mediterranean, called it 'the most mischievous and uncalled for event which the German Emperor has ever been engaged in since he came to the Throne. It was also a political fiasco, and if he thinks he has done himself good in the eyes of the world he is very much mistaken.' The Sultan, meanwhile, strongly backed by Germany, insisted on an international conference to decide Morocco's future. When France refused to attend, Germany threatened war and demanded Delcassé's resignation. Finally, on 6 June, the French backed down, agreed to a conference, and Delcassé was forced to resign.

The Kaiser, cock-a-hoop, promptly created Bülow a prince. This infuriated Edward VII, who refused to send Georgie to attend the German Crown Prince's wedding that summer. He himself refused to meet the Kaiser on his way to Marienbad that August, although the Kaiser, in high good humour, had invited him to Homburg for a reconciliation. Instead, Edward VII invited the Crown Prince and his new wife to Windsor. Now it was Willy's turn to be furious. Still caught up in his love–hate relationship with England, he himself had hoped for an invitation to Windsor that autumn. 'Perhaps *next year*,' wrote Knollys in answer to a letter from Sir Frank Lascelles, the British Ambassador in Berlin, 'unless the Emperor continues to trump up imaginary grievances against the King and to intrigue, whenever he has an opportunity, against this country, a meeting might be arranged.'

Sir John Fisher, First Sea Lord, had written to Lansdowne on 22 April, three weeks after the Kaiser's visit: 'This seems a golden opportunity for fighting the Germans in alliance with the French, so I earnestly hope you may be able to bring this about. Of course I don't pretend to be a diplomat, but it strikes me that the German Emperor will greatly injure the splendid and growing Anglo-French Entente if he is allowed to score now in *any way* – even if it is only getting rid of Delcassé . . . We could have the German Fleet, the Kiel Canal, and Schleswig-Holstein within a fortnight.' Schleswig-Holstein was a giveaway: Fisher and Queen Alexandra were the best of friends, happily sharing a hearty dislike of Germans. Fisher liked to refer to 'Blessed Queen Alexandra'. The Queen addressed him as her 'dear Admiral Fisher'.

Fisher was busy modernising the British Fleet in response to Tirpitz's massive battle fleet. The determination was to maintain a ratio of 2:1 ships with the Germans. By 1906 *Dreadnought* and three equally large battleships were in commission. These were big-gun ships, so revolutionary in design that they made all others obsolete. *Dreadnought* herself was named after one of Sir Francis Drake's ships involved in defeating the Spanish Armada; she could fire an 8-gun broadside, turn at 21 knots, and burn both coal and oil. Following events in Morocco and bowing to public opinion, the new Liberal Government was prepared to fund this huge enterprise, but wished to limit the expenditure to three ships. 'Yes with pleasure I will give you a seat on my train if you will give us a fourth Dreadnought,' the Queen merrily telegraphed Fisher that July after he had requested a seat on the royal train. 'Humbly beg to inform Your Majesty that four Dreadnoughts will be built and building on Your Majesty's next birth-day,' Fisher replied, 'so therefore humbly hope to be allowed the seat so graciously offered on Your Majesty's train.'

Edward VII meanwhile busied himself trying to mend relations with Russia. Sergei Witte, returning from the peace conference in America in September, stopped off in Paris for talks with the French premier. While he was there he received a visit from Poklewski-Koziell, Secretary at the Russian Embassy in London. He told Witte he came on his own initiative, but Witte, knowing him to be a good friend of Edward VII, quickly realised who had sent him. Poklewski-Koziell told Witte that the King and his people wanted Witte to visit England. Witte replied that this would be impossible without the Tsar's permission, which was unlikely to be forthcoming: 'even if King Edward had addressed himself directly to our Emperor he would have been refused,' he later wrote, 'because Emperor Nicholas II still considered England our sworn enemy and more than once had said in my presence that there was no difference between "kikes" and Englishmen.' When Poklewski-Koziell said it was time for England and Russia to end their senseless quarrels over Persia, Afghanistan 'and other matters', Witte responded: 'I favoured good relations with England, but not at the expense of good relations with the continental powers. Undoubtedly, the entente we subsequently established with England demonstrated the influence of King Edward on Poklewski-Koziell, and the latter's influence on his friend Isvolsky, the Foreign Minister.'

Georgie followed the political developments from the sidelines, happy to leave the action to his father the King, and concentrated instead on his agreeable and regular home life, his shooting, his fishing, his stamp collecting, and his not-too-onerous public engagements. Lord Esher called him a '*garçon éternel*', partly because the Prince of Wales still expressed his views like a young sailor rather than a forty-four-year-old Heir to the Throne – in loud and not always discreet language. 'Bosh!' was a favourite term of disapproval, short and to the point. When his cousin Princess Ena of Battenberg changed her religion before marrying King Alfonso of Spain in the spring of 1906, a dinner guest noted, 'The Prince and King are *very* angry about Ena Battenberg marrying the King of Spain and turning Roman Catholic. The Prince's language wasn't even Parliamentary and the Princess had to say "George!!!" more than once.' Georgie was not at all pleased when the Liberals swept to power in 1906. At one dinner party he leant across the table to tell the Permanent Secretary of the Treasury, 'I can't think, Sir George, how you can go on serving that damned fellow Lloyd George.' At another he indiscreetly told Winston Churchill that although he trusted Asquith, who was about to take over from Campbell-Bannerman as Prime

Minister, he thought him 'not quite a gentleman'. But the good thing about the Prince of Wales was that he could admit his mistakes and learn from them. 'I ought not to have said it, and it was a damned stupid thing to say,' he admitted in 1914, 'but Winston repeated it to Asquith, which was a monstrous thing to do, and made great mischief.'

The man who had more to do with preparing the Prince of Wales for the responsibilities of monarchy than anyone was his Private Secretary, Lord Stamfordham. 'Fancy, how quickly time flies, it is nearly seven years already since you came to me,' the Prince of Wales wrote punctually on Christmas Day 1907 from Sandringham in answer to Stamfordham's Christmas wishes. 'You have nothing to thank us for, it is all the other way and we have indeed much to thank you for. As for myself during these seven years you have made my life comparatively an easy one, by your kind help and assistance and entire devotion to work connected with me. What would have happened to me if you had not been there to prepare and help me with my speeches, I can hardly write a letter of any importance without your assistance. I fear sometimes I have lost my temper with you and often been very rude, but I am sure you know me well enough by now to know that I did not mean it . . . I offer you my thanks from the bottom of my heart. I am a bad hand at saying what I feel, but I thank God that I have a friend like you, in whom I have the fullest confidence and from whom I know on all occasions I shall get the best and soundest advice whenever I seek it.' Of the three royal cousins, Georgie was the most modest, always prepared to listen to advice, even if he indulged in a certain amount of effing and blinding before acting on it.

It was rare that Georgie disagreed with his father on anything. One occasion was when the King decided to replace the bowling alley at Sandringham with a library. A more serious disagreement arose over John Fisher. Fisher's plans to modernise and reform the Royal Navy were greeted with great enthusiasm by his supporters and equally great disapproval by his detractors, led by his rival Admiral Lord Charles Beresford, Commander-in-Chief of the Channel Fleet. Beresford, a wealthy patrician, was opposed at virtually every step to the reforms proposed by Fisher, whom he viewed as an upstart. The first was a new system of common entry for officers, Esher and Fisher having been struck by the inferior quality of the officer class in both the Army and the Royal Navy. There was to be rapid promotion based on merit rather than seniority, and proper technical training for senior officers. Fisher then proceeded to scrap a large number of beloved but obsolete warships, replacing them by an efficient Reserve Fleet with a nucleus of specialist crews and a much enlarged Home Fleet which kept three-quarters of the nation's battleships in readiness for war in Europe – that is, against Germany – rather than in the Mediterranean or somewhere the Empire. To the same purpose Fisher introduced his big-gun battleships and cruisers, sending the naval estimates rocketing to over £31 million in 1907. Beresford and his supporters, flying the flag for tradition and Empire, were appalled. Fisher, whose language was always colourful, minded not a jot. 'Their wives should be widows, their children fatherless, their homes a dunghill,' he said cheerfully of his critics. Georgie, an old Royal Navy man himself, was ranged firmly on the Beresford side.

The conference to decide Morocco's future opened on 16 January 1906 in the Town Hall at Algeciras in southern Spain. For the next three months the delegates battled it out, and the result was a complete diplomatic defeat for Germany. One after another the European powers, including Russia, lined up behind France and against Germany. The Pact of Algeciras, signed on 2 April 1906, allowed for foreign commerce in Morocco, but only under France's supervision. Bülow's initiative of the previous year had come to nothing, and Germany found herself isolated. 'All the wretched, degenerate Latin peoples have become instruments in England's hands in order to combat German trade in the Mediterranean,' ranted Wilhelm. 'Not only do we no longer have any friends, but this race of eunuchs descended from the farrago of peoples assembled by Rome hates us with all its heart!' Germany's only supporters had been the Austro-Hungarians, and that half-heartedly. As for Russia, Willy raged against cousin Nicky, so recently his friend and colleague, for being weak and vacillating and, above all, ungrateful. After all the help Germany had extended to Russia during the Russo-Japanese war, her value to Germany turned out to be 'absolutely nil'.

It was clear to everyone that the Moroccan crisis was not really about Morocco, but about alliances between the Great Powers. Germany's construction of a massive battle fleet under Tirpitz was seen for what it was, a threat to the balance of power, if necessary by means of war, and England, Russia and France were not prepared to give Germany a place at the table. At the time of the Moroccan crisis

Lord Lansdowne had authorised the preparation of a secret Anglo-French plan of naval and military action against Germany, should it prove necessary, and Sir Edward Grey took it over when he became Foreign Secretary. Now Russia was turning her back on Germany. As A.J.P. Taylor noted, Germany's defeat at Algeciras marked a turning-point because, for the first time in thirty-five years, there was a real threat of war, which 'shattered the long Bismarckian peace'. By April 1906 the Great Powers were ranged in the alignments that propelled them all into the First World War.

In Germany Bülow tried to put a good face on the Pact, describing it as 'equally satisfactory to Germany and France and useful to all nations.' In private he blamed Wilhelm for Germany's friendless condition. He felt the Kaiser's dithering before his disembarkation at Tangier had signalled Germany's ambivalence, and undermined the later negotiations at Algeciras. After six years of trying to rein in the Kaiser's autocratic and unpredictable behaviour Bülow, like all his predecessors, was facing defeat. He had tried all the tricks he knew. In the early years he had used his famed powers of flattery. Later he had threatened resignation. Lastly he had tried engineering a political crisis to force Wilhelm to subject himself to the rule of Parliament. But if he had hoped that the crisis provoked in Germany by the failure of the Algeciras Conference would have the effect of forcing the Kaiser into line, he soon found that it did not.

Bülow's disenchantment with the Kaiser was made infinitely worse by a fact known to only very few intimates at the Berlin Court: Phili zu Eulenburg, after a nervous collapse and three years of virtual exile, had in the past year made a comeback, not in public but, as usual, in private. 'How I long to see Your Majesty again!' Eulenburg had written to the Kaiser in August. 'I hope that my health is now recovered so that I am not a gloomy companion.' He was soon fully reinstated, albeit in secret, once again happy in the Kaiser's warm embrace. In October 1905 Wilhelm was a guest at Liebenberg for the annual Kaiser Hunt. In November Wilhelm invited Eulenburg back to Rominten, even assigning him an informal diplomatic role: to have talks with the Russian Minister-President, Sergei Witte, who was on the next lap of his return from America.

'I was met at the Rominten station by Prince Philipp Eulenburg, an elderly man reputedly very close to the Emperor and one of the chief figures in the court camarilla,' wrote Witte. When they arrived at Rominten he was greeted 'very kindly' by the Kaiser, who was dressed in his hunting outfit. Count August zu Eulenburg was on hand to show Witte to his rooms, where Philipp zu Eulenburg soon came to talk about 'the international situation, including Russo-German relations.' He assured Witte that in future, 'because his Emperor had complete confidence in him, I could communicate with his Master through him concerning matters of great confidentiality. I could be certain, he said, that whatever I sent would be given immediately to Emperor Wilhelm and he would then send the reply directly to me.' The following day, the Kaiser and Witte sat down to talk. Witte told the Kaiser that a *rapprochement* between Germany and France was critical for a unified Europe. Wilhelm's response was to complain that France was continually behaving badly towards him – as though the French hatred of Germany had nothing to do with him. He offered Witte some words of advice on Russia's problems with the revolutionaries, and spoke sarcastically of Count Benckendorff, Russia's Ambassador in London, ascribing his importance solely to the fact that Edward VII liked him because he was a good bridge player.

'I was particularly struck by the Emperor's attitude toward Prince Eulenburg,' Witte disingenuously observed. 'He sat on the arm of the Prince's chair, his right hand on Eulenburg's shoulder, almost as if he were putting his arm round him. The prince was the most relaxed person there. Had a stranger been asked to point out who in that company was the Emperor, he would have been amazed by the question, but, upon being assured that one of those present was in fact the monarch, he would probably have pointed to Prince Eulenburg.' Before he left Witte was presented with a gold-framed portrait of the Kaiser, personally inscribed with the words 'Portsmouth–Björkö–Rominten. Wilhelm Rex'.

Ominously, after the failure of the Algeciras Conference, Eulenburg, confident once again of his place in Wilhelm's affections, had advised Bülow to resign. The Kaiser now felt that Bülow was to blame and, in case Wilhelm did not fully realise it, Eulenburg lost no time telling him that the whole débâcle was an attempt by Bülow to create another political crisis as a means of forcing him into line. Rumours soon appeared in the press that the Kaiser was looking for a replacement for his Chancellor. The Kaiser's Personal Rule was firmly back on the agenda, and Bülow's position became increasingly insecure now that he was no longer trusted to play his appointed role as his Master's 'executive tool'.

In May 1906 Holstein, still working at the Foreign Office, discovered Eulenburg's intentions and again threatened to resign if the Kaiser did not submit himself to a modicum of parliamentary restraint. It was his fourteenth attempt at resignation, and this time it was accepted. 'Your aim of many years, my removal, has now at last been achieved,' Holstein wrote to Eulenburg on 1 May. 'I am now free, I need exercise no restraint, and can treat you as one treats a contemptible person with your characteristics. I do so herewith and expect to do more.' It was the first letter he had written Eulenburg in years. The threat was unmistakable. Holstein made straight for Maximilian Harden. With suspicious convenience, Bülow had fainted in the Reichstag on 5 April, just two days after Holstein told him what he intended to do, enabling him to disappear from the political scene for the next six months, pleading ill health. He knew too well what scandals would become public if Eulenburg did not heed Holstein's threat, and Holstein and Harden got together.

Harden had not known of Eulenburg's return to favour till Holstein contacted him. On 18 August an open letter from Holstein published in *Die Zukunft* caused a sensation. In it Holstein refuted accusations that he had had anything to do with the Kruger telegram, or with the Kaiser's anti-British speeches in the Reichstag, both of which were seen to have contributed to the Franco-British Entente Cordiale and Germany's resultant encirclement by her enemies. 'In each case I found myself before either a *fait accompli* or an action that had already begun,' he wrote, in a clear indictment of the Kaiser's Personal Rule, and of the advisers, the 'camarilla' as they were known, who surrounded him.

Eulenburg instantly knew what Holstein's letter denoted: 'I see in it not only the revenge he intends to take upon me,' he wrote in his diary, 'but I see more, something much more critical, and cannot hide my worry.' Harden now also found out that Raymond Lecomte, a French diplomat friend of Eulenburg since their days in Munich, had been a guest at Liebenberg when the Kaiser was there in 1905, and again in 1906. Lecomte was listed as a suspected homosexual in the Berlin police files, as was Eulenburg himself. The allegation was that Lecomte had gained inside information that the Kaiser would not go to war over Morocco, knowledge which enabled the French to maintain a hard line in the negotiations at the Algeciras Conference. For Harden it was the final straw. This time he would not hold back.

Edward VII was highly satisfied with the outcome of the Conference. Not only had the Germans been unable to damage the Entente Cordiale, but Sir Arthur Nicolson, who had been one of the British delegates at the conference, was now despatched as British Ambassador to St Petersburg, to continue talks with Russia for an Anglo-Russian understanding. But the King was also concerned, now that Britain had won the contest, to remain on good terms with the German Emperor. He was still of the opinion that foreign affairs were best arranged between 'royal colleagues', the trade union of kings, who shared views on many matters, including the press and even, on occasion, Parliament.

'We are, my dear William, such old friends and near relations,' he had already written in January, on the occasion of William's forty-seventh birthday, 'that I feel sure that the affectionate feelings which have always existed may continue. Most deeply do I deplore the uncalled-for expressions made use of by the Press concerning our two Countries.' The King may have verged on hypocrisy – but he may indeed have felt a certain sympathy for his beleaguered nephew. William expressed himself deeply touched. 'The whole letter breathed such an atmosphere of kindness and warm sympathetic friendship that it constitutes the most cherished gift among my presents,' he replied, going on to recall the warm moment they had shared when Queen Victoria died. 'The silent hours when we watched and prayed at her bedside, and when the spirit of that great Sovereign-Lady passed away as she drew her last breath in my arms. I feel sure that from the home of Eternal Light she is now looking down upon us, and will rejoice when she sees our hands clasped in loyal and cordial friendship.' It was agreed that Edward VII would pay the Kaiser a short visit in August, on his way to Marienbad.

At Marienbad the King relaxed and played croquet and golf, always taking care to be dressed appropriately. For casual wear he liked a blue jacket and white trousers, which might be creased either in front or sideways. Sometimes he replaced his hard grey felt hat with the local soft, plumed, green model. When Haldane, the War Minister, came to visit on his way to Berlin for talks with Bülow, the King indulged his penchant for going about incognito. He suggested they motor into the countryside, wearing plain clothes, and have coffee somewhere.

But first Haldane was instructed to buy an Austrian hat, to look the part. The purpose of Haldane's visit was to discuss his forthcoming Berlin talks with the King, and to get him to sign an Army Order which he had conveniently brought with him. Like Fisher with the Navy, Haldane was busy reforming the Army into an efficient modern fighting machine, consisting of the Regular Army plus a Territorial Army, both voluntary. Kitchener, the Commander-in-Chief, favoured conscription for the Territorials. Esher had his opinion on this as on everything else. 'As you know,' he wrote to Knollys on 30 September 1906, 'I am a confirmed believer in *compulsion*, but until a final experiment has been tried to get the *youth* of the Nation to *volunteer* for what is called Home Defence . . . and until the experiment has proved a failure, there is not much hope of getting Parliament or the country to agree to the compulsory principle.' He quickly set about convincing the King of his views. The King might be attempting a *rapprochement* with his nephew the Kaiser, but that did not mean that Britain could let up on her preparations for war.

15

Scandals and Rivalries

~

IN FEBRUARY 1907 Edward VII took Queen Alexandra on a private
visit to Paris for a week, to cheer her up. Over the years her deafness had worsened, and although she became an excellent lip-reader,
it increasingly cut her off from the kind of social life and chatter she
so enjoyed, with the result that she spent more and more time alone
at Sandringham. Her much-loved father King Christian had died the
previous year and now she was feeling so low and unwell that Edward,
who normally went to Paris *en garçon*, decided to take her with him.
In March her sister arrived from Russia for a stay of several weeks. It
was Minny's first visit in thirty-four years, political considerations
having always intervened in the past. The two sisters visited galleries,
orphanages, hospitals, West End theatres, and West End shops. 'How
happily we are living together!' Minny wrote to Nicky on 13 March.
'We spent Sunday at Windsor. It was the 44th anniversary of Aunt
Alex's wedding! We went by car. After lunch we went over the
Castle – I have no words to describe *how magnificent* it all is. Aunt
Alex's rooms are remarkably beautiful and cosy – I must say, they are
the same here at Buckingham Palace. Everything is so tastefully and
artistically arranged – it makes one's mouth water to see all this
magnificence! I do wish you, too, could come over here a little, to
breathe another air . . . How *good* for you that would be! I myself feel
as if I were a different person – and *twenty years* younger!' The
Denmark link was at work again, busily promoting Anglo-Russian
relations against hated Germany.

But the Dowager Tsarina's influence over her son was rapidly
diminishing, and not just because of the Tsarina. A new holy man had
made his appearance at Court and quickly taken the place of the
Frenchman Philippe, who had mysteriously disappeared, some said in
fear of his life. 'A few days ago I received a peasant from the Tobolsk
district, Grigory Rasputin, who brought me an icon of St Simon

Verkhoturie,' wrote the Tsar to Stolypin, the Minister-President, on 16 October 1906. 'He made a remarkably strong impression both on Her Majesty and on myself, so that instead of five minutes our conversation went on for more than an hour.' Stolypin's daughter had been injured in a bomb attack and Rasputin wished to see her, claiming to be a healer. He also claimed to be able to stem the flow of blood. The Tsar and Tsarina, vulnerable to any promise of help for their only son and heir, were soon convinced, and it was not long before Rasputin had gained a strong position at the Russian Court.

In mid April Edward VII and Queen Alexandra were embarked on a Mediterranean cruise. The royal party met King Alfonso of Spain at Cartagena, and under cover of a private rendezvous some political manoeuvring took place, England, France and Spain secretly agreeing to guarantee each other's possessions in the Mediterranean. It was not long before the news leaked out, causing another furore in the German press. 'In Germany they have imputed to His Majesty the most sinister motives, and accused him of deep-laid plots against Germany,' wrote Ponsonby, also on the cruise, to 'keep the ball rolling' as usual. 'The *Neue Freie Press* has indeed written d—d nonsense about our cruize & attributed to me political intrigues which I was certainly most ignorant & innocent of,' wrote the King disingenuously to Georgie on 25 April. 'They seem to object to me having a quiet cruize in the Mediterranean & meeting the Kings of Spain & Italy in small harbours on their coasts. However, I suppose it amuses the Foreign Press & it certainly does not harm *me*.'

The Prince of Wales, safely at home, had just written what Esher described as 'an excellent Memo on the policing of the seas' – something the Fisher policy had neglected – making suggestions which the Admiralty accepted. He gave a dinner at Marlborough House to discuss it. It was the usual off-the-record affair, attended by Fisher, Esher and Knollys. Everyone, it seemed, was determined to keep Germany in her place. When the high navy estimates caused lively discussion in Parliament and the press, Esher remained unruffled. 'It is the discussions which keep alive popular fears and popular interest,' he wrote to Fisher. 'A nation that believes itself secure, all history teaches, is doomed. Anxiety, not a sense of security, lies at the root of readiness for war.'

But it was clear that the Germans required appeasing. It was therefore decided that the King should invite the Kaiser to spend five days at Windsor the following November. First, the King visited his nephew in Germany, again on his way to Marienbad. 'We got to Wilhelmshohe at about 1 in lovely summer weather,' he wrote to Georgie. 'Nothing could have been kinder than William and Donna were – & the visit though short was a success in every respect – & will I hope lead to more satisfying results than the Hague Conference will . . .' The Hague Conference on disarmament and the humanisation of war was something the two royal colleagues could agree on: it was tiresome and futile. The King left Cassel and made for Gmunden, where he met Emperor Franz-Joseph, by now eighty years old. 'Although the King was outwardly on the best of terms with the German Emperor, and laughed and joked with him,' reported Hardinge to his superiors at the Foreign Office, 'I could not help noticing that there was no real intimacy between them.' This was in contrast to the Austrian Emperor, with whom Edward VII got on delightfully.

'Meeting with Uncle Bertie satisfactory,' telegraphed Willy to Nicky on 2 August 1907. 'Uncle in good humour and peacefully disposed . . . When asked by the King about the actual state of Russia I was happy to inform him that I heard from you that all went well, the dismissal of the Duma by you being the same act as the dismissal of the Portuguese Parliament by his cousin Carlos. After several rainy days we have since yesterday beautiful weather, and made yesterday auto drive through the silent woods of the neighbourhood. Hope so much you found Alix in good health. Best love to her. Willy.' The comparison with Portugal proved an unhappy one. There were constant strikes, peasant uprisings and mutinies there. The King and Crown Prince were assassinated on 1 February 1908. The second son, as Manoel II, was deposed in October 1910 and a republic established.

Nicky and Willy had met only two weeks earlier, at Swinemünde off the Baltic coast, each in his Imperial Yacht. Nicky, accompanied by Isvolsky as the Minister in Attendance, so dreaded a recurrence of the Kaiser's bullying that he made Isvolsky forewarn Bülow, who was also present, along with Admiral Tirpitz and Prince Heinrich, that there could be no further discussion about the Björkö treaty. 'The Emperor is not false but he is weak!' the Kaiser noted, adding with sharp insight, 'Weakness is not treachery, but it fulfils all the same functions.' The three days were filled with naval manoeuvres and displays, brass bands and grand banquets on the *Hohenzollern* and the

Standart, the Tsar's yacht. 'In his youthful manner, he is most pleasing,' wrote Hopman, one of the Kaiser's suite, about the Tsar. 'After the first impression of shyness there is a deal of seriousness, thoughtfulness and tact. His expression is benevolent and, for a man, somewhat soft. But inside he is much stronger and more determined than he appears to the world.' Hopman's opinion of his own Master was not as favourable. In his leaving speech on the *Standart* the Kaiser, filled with pride at the splendour of his fleet, expressed the hope that the Tsar would soon manage to achieve something similar. 'The only thing missing was a slap round the head,' wrote Hopman.

'It is not easy letting you go – I do not like bidding you goodbye, my Own One,' Alix had written to Nicky when he set off for Swinemünde, 'tho' distance makes nothing really, when one loves. The souls and hearts are together and nothing can part them ever . . . So I hope everything will go smoothly and with no hitches or unpleasant talks – Gr[igory] watches over this journey and all will be well . . . Lovy mine I shall look after your Sunbeam [Alexei] and guard him for you carefully. Goodbye my husband, my One and all. Holy angels hover around you. God's blessing be upon you. Tenderly and fondly with an aching heart – I kiss you – every sweet little spot I love so passionately. For ever your very own Wify.' Nicky wrote back from the *Standart*, 'My own beloved Darling, I thank you from all my heart for your sweet letter. It touched me deeply, I read it before going to bed and it did me such good. I feel quite lonely by myself down in the cabins. The doors to yours are open and I look into them often, always thinking I will find my Wify. I miss you and the children frightfully, so do all the officers!'

On 5 September 1907, the day before he left Marienbad for England, Edward VII entertained the Russian Foreign Minister, Isvolsky, to luncheon. A week earlier, in St Petersburg, Isvolsky and Sir Arthur Nicolson had signed the Anglo-Russian Convention and this, combined with Russia's alliance to France, established the Triple Entente. Over luncheon Edward VII and Isvolsky again discussed the Central Asian question. Isvolsky told the King about the difficulties with which he had to contend from the reactionary party and, to a certain extent, from the military party, though the latter had lost much of their influence, for Russia could not afford another war. Edward VII praised Isvolsky for his services to peace and suggested that all future differences between England and Russia would be solved in a spirit of give and take, now that the ice had been broken. Three weeks later Edward VII in England and Tsar Nicholas II in Russia signed the agreement.

The Kaiser's State Visit to England was scheduled for 11 November 1907. But on 31 October a telegram arrived from the Kaiser saying that he was tired and weak after a virulent attack of influenza, and would not now be coming after all. Sir Edward Grey thought it was a diplomatic illness brought on by the Foreign Office's suggestion that the Kaiser's planned escort of numerous German battleships would not be welcome. Bülow knew better. Maximilian Harden had been working hard for Eulenburg's downfall ever since Holstein's defection, and the case of Kuno von Moltke *v.* Harden had just come to trial, with Harden accused of defamation of character for suggesting Moltke was homosexual. The German public was scandalised. Edward VII, strongly supported by the Foreign Offices of both countries, insisted that the visit must take place as planned, and finally the Kaiser backed down. He duly arrived with the Kaiserin on 11 November, both looking, as Edward VII was pleased to point out, 'in splendid health'.

Georgie was despatched to meet Willy and Dona at Portsmouth, wearing his German Admiral's uniform, and accompanied by the German Ambassador and his suite. In the train to Windsor Georgie had a long talk with Willy and, unaware of his relief at being away from the impending scandals, found him in excellent spirits. 'Papa, Mama, May and the family received them at station. Drove in state procession to the Castle. Had tea in their rooms.' Then Georgie and May returned to Frogmore to change for a family dinner at the Castle at 8.30.

The next day turned out bright and sunny. The royal party went out shooting, bagging more than 1500 pheasant. By 4.10 Georgie was back at Frogmore, where he read for a while and then sat, a point he always carefully noted, with May. By 8.30 they were back at the Castle, in St George's Hall, for a State Banquet. Georgie wore his German Curassier's uniform. 'We sat down 161, a fine sight, both Papa and William made excellent speeches.' Georgie, the decent, straightforward royal cousin, was happy to give credit where it was due. After dinner there was more than an hour of the usual hanging about. 'Rather tired standing so long. Bed at 12.' The next day was fine and bright again, 'but strongish winds, not cold.' William and Dona visited the City, with Georgie driving ahead of their procession from Paddington to Guildhall. 'There were great crowds in the streets and they got a splendid reception.' In those more innocent times a State Visit was enough to affect the mood of public opinion. The Lord Mayor gave a luncheon for 900, and William made another excellent speech, again well received. Back at Frogmore that evening, Georgie dined with his old tutor Canon Dalton before bed at 11.45.

Two days later there was more shooting, and another State Banquet in the evening, this time mostly for admirals, generals and their wives. And Lord Esher. 'Our King makes a better show than William II,' he noted in his journal. 'He has more graciousness and dignity. William is ungraceful, nervous and plain. There is no "atmosphere" about him. He has not impressed Grey or Morley. Grey had two long talks with him. At the first he declaimed vehemently against Jews. "There are far too many of them in my country. They want stamping out." Morley, watching the Kaiser closely, "noticed the convulsive movements and *wondered*." ' There was more shooting, a spot of golf, some theatre at the Castle and lots more standing about before Willy and Dona finally left, in the pouring rain, on Sunday, 17 November. While Dona returned direct to Germany, Willy went off for a three-week stay with Colonel Edward Montagu-Stuart-Wortley, a Germanophile, at Highcliffe Castle near Bournmouth.

On 15 December 1907 Georgie wrote to Nicky to wish the family a Happy Christmas. He ended, 'I trust now that your Duma will work better than the last two and that the country will gradually quiet down and give you less trouble and anxiety than it has during these last few years. What do you say to Georgie [of Greece] at last being married [to Olga of Russia], now all the members the Club are married. Your devoted cousin and friend, Georgie.' That was the 'Club' that went back many years, to happy summers in Denmark and family visits in England, Russia and Greece, and it did not include Willy.

Although 1908 started well for relationships between the royal cousins, they did not last. By February a crisis had arisen which encouraged Willy's paranoia to flourish. In defence of his friend Fisher and the high naval estimates, Lord Esher had written an open and injudicious letter to the Navy League which included the sentence 'every German from the Emperor down to the last man wished for the downfall of Sir John Fisher'. The Kaiser responded furiously with a nine-page letter, all in his own hand, addressed to Lord Tweedmouth, as First Lord of the Admiralty, in which he called Esher's statement 'a piece of unmitigated balderdash' and ventured to suggest 'that such things ought not to be written by people who are highly placed, as they are liable to hurt public feelings over here.' It was a fair point to make.

The crisis propelled Edward VII into one of his rages, firstly with Esher, then with the Kaiser. Esher was not in the least bothered. 'It is a most extraordinary proceeding for the Emperor to write to one of the King's Ministers at all,' he noted in his journal. 'As the Prince of Wales said to me this evening, "What would *he* say if the King wrote to von Tirpitz a letter of this kind!"' He wrote the King a letter of apology, and got a friendly reply from Buckingham Palace the same day: Fisher had pleaded his cause and Francis Knollys had been 'like a trump, as he always is'. On March 25 Esher wrote to Fisher, 'I shall never, and never have, regretted that letter. It was well worth all the bother (not very much of that) to have done anything however little for the Navy. I shall always believe that we were then at the parting of the ways. The Nation was on its trial. The struggle is far from over yet. You see that Bülow again tries to lull our people to slumber. Next year there will be a bitter fight. I hope to heaven that Asquith will *make terms* with Lloyd George, before absolutely making him Ch.of the Ex. Terms which will fix the total of Naval Estimates for the next 2 years.'

Esher was making sure that the British Government and public remained in a state of alert insecurity. He knew that the Reichstag were voting to approve Tirpitz's own substantial naval estimates that month; he was not sure the Liberals in England would do the same. But his action had the desired effect. The Prince of Wales was as alarmed as the rest of the country, writing to Hardinge that Britain now had 'no alternative but to build as many battleships . . . as fast as possible.' The English newspapers soon joined in the fray, 'vapouring', as Esher put it, at the Kaiser. And the Germans, hearing of the Kaiser's private letter for the first time, were dismayed. He had not consulted his Chancellor or his Government before writing it. To Tweedmouth he claimed to be writing not in his capacity as German Kaiser but as an Admiral of the British Fleet, a confusion which must have puzzled Tweedmouth. The German Navy was being built not to challenge Britain but to protect German commerce, the Kaiser had assured Tweedmouth, unconvincingly.

In June 1908 Edward VII and Queen Alexandra visited Russia, but without setting foot on Russian soil. They met the Tsar and Tsarina and the Dowager Tsarina at Reval (now Tallin) in the Baltic, each in their royal yachts. All the royal colleagues shared the belief that as long as they remained on water, they could meet informally and discuss matters of international importance without interference. Earlier, Esher had talked to his friend Arthur Balfour about the problems of such a visit. 'I discussed with him the King's Russian visit,' he wrote in his journal on 30 May. 'He sees the constitutional impropriety of the King meeting Isvolsky and Stolypin unaccompanied by Grey. He thought of writing privately to Grey before the debate on Thursday.' The Tsar was extremely unpopular with left-wing supporters of the Government. Keir Hardie made a violent speech against the visit, and Ramsay MacDonald wrote an article describing it as 'hobnobbing with murderers'.

Nevertheless, the King set off for Reval on 5 June 1908, taking his old friend Hardinge as the Minister in Attendance in preference to Grey, saying that the presence of a Government minister would have made him feel like a prisoner handcuffed to a warder while conversing with his relatives through a grille. Sir John Fisher was also part of his suite, along with Sir Arthur Nicolson, the British Ambassador in St Petersburg, and Ponsonby and the King's equerry Seymour-Fortescue to make up a bridge four.

The following night they reached the Kiel Canal, where they were met by the sight of Prince Heinrich, or Henry, of Prussia, together with most of the German Navy and a mass of troops lining the quay, the cavalry making a splendid show as they trotted the length of the Canal on both sides, accompanying the *Victoria and Albert* all the way to Kiel harbour. Willy might not be invited to the party, but he meant to make his presence felt. They anchored off Reval on the morning of 9 June, where they found the two Imperial Yachts *Polar Star* and *Standart* already waiting, along with what remained of the Russian Navy. Edward VII duly donned his uniform of the Kiev Dragoons to greet his nephew the Tsar, his niece the Tsarina, and his sister-in-law the Dowager Tsarina. For the next two days there was the usual round of visits from one Imperial Yacht to the other, with banquets and balls and speeches. 'At the banquet preceding the dance,' recalled John Fisher, 'the Grand Duchess and I, I regret to say, made such a disturbance in our mutual jokes that King Edward called out to me that I must try to remember that I was not in the Midshipmen's Mess.' Undeterred, Fisher later danced the hornpipe on deck. The Russians also provided entertainment. 'A steamer full of some choral society came and sang weird Russian songs,' wrote Ponsonby. At the banquet Edward VII made a speech proposing the Tsar's health and seeking to strengthen 'the many and strong ties which unite our houses', aiming to 'draw our countries together, and of promoting and maintaining the peace of the world.' The two sisters could be forgiven for thinking that they had contributed to a renewal of Anglo-Russian friendship.

Carried away by the success of his diplomatic efforts, on the spur of the moment the King made his nephew an Admiral of the Fleet. Back home in England Esher confided to his journal: 'There has been a great, almost serious, trouble about the appointment of the Tsar as Admiral of the Fleet. The King made the appointment without reference to his Ministers . . . It appears that the King acted beyond his powers. Grey is angry, Asquith grieved.' The Cabinet met and decided to remonstrate with the King. Knollys was obliged to write to Asquith and explain that the King was 'totally unaware of the constitutional point, and that he regretted he had, without knowing it, acted irregularly.' As a constitutional monarch, Edward VII knew how to apologise. But he did not undo his action, and Knollys added a postscript to the letter for good measure: 'The King deplores the attitude taken up by Mr Asquith on the Women's Suffrage Bill.'

The main point held: the visit was a success. As Nicolson put it, the Tsar returned from Reval 'flattered and reassured'. From Björkö and Swinemünde, by contrast, he had returned 'frightened and humiliated'. Metternich, the German Ambassador in London, wrote to reassure Bülow on 25 June: 'The great mass of English people desire peace and this is King Edward's policy.' To which the Kaiser added a marginal note: 'Untrue. He aims at war. I am to begin it, so that he does not get the odium.'

Wilhelm was in one of his paranoid phases, events in Germany having taken a serious turn for the worse. Maximilian Harden had launched his first attack on Eulenburg in *Die Zukunft* on 17 November 1906, naming him openly as the power behind the Kaiser's Personal Rule. 'He has provided for all his friends,' he wrote, and proceeded to describe 'their intercourse, oral and epistolary' as of a 'touching intimacy'. He added what was certainly his own point of view: 'All this would be their private affair if they did not belong to the Kaiser's closest circle and . . . did not spin from visible and invisible positions the little threads that are strangling the Reich . . . Today I say that Philipp Eulenburg is the man who insinuates to Wilhelm II that he was destined to rule alone, that he is incomparably graced and is answerable only to that cloudy seat from whose heights the crown was bequeathed him.' For good measure Harden followed this up, in the next issue, with seven lines inspired by a scene from Goethe's *Faust*: the setting was 'November 1906. Night. Open field in the Ukergebiet.' The two characters, the Harpist and the Sweet One, Eulenburg and Kuno von Moltke, ask one another: 'Did you read it?' 'Already on Friday!' 'Do you think more is coming?' 'We must reckon with the possibility; he seems to be well informed, and if he knows about the letters in which the Liebling is discussed . . .' 'Unthinkable! But it's being reprinted everywhere. They're determined to get our heads.' 'A witches' guild. Begone! Begone!' 'If only He does not learn about it!'

Eulenburg's reaction was to disappear to Switzerland, and Harden for the time being held his peace. But in the spring of 1907 Eulenburg was again spotted in Berlin, and in the April issues of *Die Zukunft* Harden quickly returned to the fight, again implying that several Liebenberg Circle members were homosexual. His main targets were Eulenburg and Kuno von Moltke. He did not go so far as to accuse the Kaiser himself of homosexuality, but he did say that the Kaiser had become the puppet of sexual perverts. It was Harden's only means of bringing the 'camarilla' down, and he meant to use it. At the palace, the Crown Prince was deputed to show the Kaiser the articles, which he did on 2 May 1907. The Kaiser appeared to be surprised and appalled, and in a state of high alarm declared that Eulenburg would have to clear himself of the accusations, or be stoned to death. His ADC was instructed to write to Eulenburg, demanding to know whether he was guiltless of the allegations, and what he intended to do about them. Eulenburg replied immediately. Harden's allegations were entirely false, as the Kaiser who had been his friend all these years should know, and the only reason he had not taken any action against him was for fear of involving the Kaiser in accusations about the nature of his Personal Rule. Wilhelm, pushed by members of his military entourage and also Bülow, responded by telling Eulenburg that he must either institute legal proceedings against Harden, or return the Order of the Black Eagle and leave the country.

Eulenburg retreated to Liebenburg and did nothing. But Kuno von Moltke, in a fatal mixture of stupidity and arrogance, decided to take Harden on. Perhaps he did not realise that Harden had solid evidence against him, Lily von Moltke having handed over the letters Eulenburg and Moltke had written one another at the time of the Moltkes' marriage breakdown. More likely, Moltke simply thought matters could be fixed, as usual.

The case of Moltke *v.* Harden, in which Moltke accused Harden of defamation, opened in October 1907. Eulenburg, and Wilhelm too, must have hoped that the verdict would clear them all, and the scandal be put behind them. In this they seriously underestimated Harden and the strength of the evidence he had collected against them. Eulenburg, pleading ill health, did not testify. The court found for Harden. Faced with uproar in the Reichstag, Bülow tried to play the matter down. No wonder. In November a certain Adolf Brand, a known homosexual, brought a court action against the Chancellor himself, accusing him of homosexuality. Eulenburg appeared this time, to testify that neither he nor Bülow had ever had homosexual relations as defined in Article 175 of the Prussian Civil Code. The case was dismissed within a day. From later statements made by Bülow's nephew and others, however, it is clear that Bülow was indeed homosexual. In this hall of mirrors, it is almost impossible to know for certain what deals were being made behind the scenes, and by whom. But one thing is certain: a month later Kuno von Moltke appealed, and this time Eulenburg came to testify that he too was innocent of offences under the terms of Article 175, adding, in an evasive phrase, that he had 'never done anything dirty'. This time the court decided in Moltke's favour, and Harden was sentenced to four months in prison.

But Harden was not yet done. He had additional information which, had Wilhelm known of it, would have stopped him from assuming the danger was over and taking a fateful step. On 18 December 1907 Count Zedlitz-Truetzschler, the Marshal of the Court, wrote in his diary: 'The Kaiser's plan of rehabilitating Prince Eulenburg and Count von Moltke has taken shape. Even in the earliest stages I did not believe he would let it drop, and now I am convinced he will carry it through. From the human point of view, it is intelligible that he should want this rehabilitation, but as a matter of policy it seems to me the most mischievous of all the mistakes and errors already committed in connection with these scandals.'

Zedlitz-Truetzschler was that rare species, a German Court official whose judgement was clear, fair and reliable. He was married, with two children, and came from the usual background of Prussian nobility,

Guards regiment and the diplomatic, entering the Kaiser's service in 1903. But first he had travelled, to France, England and America, and had early on formed the opinion that the vices of a system so centralised as that of Imperial Germany could not fail to lead to catastrophe sooner or later, and that it must be modernised.

His job put him in charge of Court functions and the royal kitchens, which included three head chefs, twelve chefs, three field cooks, the cellars and wine, the plate, the pantries, linen stores, laundries, and the liveries of 600 men. When the Kaiser travelled, Zedlitz-Truetschler took his turn travelling with him, organising everything. He soon had the measure of his Master. He saw that the Kaiser's personality was, as he put it, a 'dazzling' one, and his intelligence good enough to read a twenty-page report just once and remember all the salient details. But he also saw his restlessness, his moodiness, his inability to judge men, his child-like need for love and praise, and his growing megalomania. 'It is I who dismiss my ministers. Not they me,' he heard him say on more than one occasion. Worst of all, he saw how the Kaiser's entourage, both civil and military, never told him the truth but flattered him, and never interrupted his long lectures and tirades other than to say, 'As Your Majesty commands'. And he saw how Eulenburg and his friends were making sure that the Kaiser's power, 'always quite unlimited, was now developing, step by step, into purely personal and arbitrary rule.' 'When I read over what I have written,' he noted, 'I am often astonished at the pessimism into which I have allowed myself to fall.'

He would have been more pessimistic still had he known what was to come. Harden's additional information came from two men who were outside the usual social circle. They were working men, one a labourer, the other a fisherman, and, unlike those from Eulenburg's own circle, were prepared to testify against him, swearing that they had had sexual relations with him in the late 1880s, at Starnberg in Bavaria where Eulenburg spent his holidays. This was potential political dynamite, not only because it would prove that Eulenburg, hiding behind his officers' Code of Honour, had in fact committed perjury, but because it came very close to threatening the monarch himself – the late 1880s being the very years when Prince Wilhelm, heady with his new friendship, was visiting Eulenburg in Bavaria.

In April 1908 clever Harden set up a libel trial in Munich, beyond the jurisdiction of the Prussian courts, arranging for a journalist friend

to accuse him of not being able to prove that Eulenburg was a homosexual, thus allowing Harden to state all the necessary, irrefutable,
evidence. The inevitable verdict, when it came, meant the end of
Eulenburg. Bülow, safe after his own happily settled court proceedings, ordered him to be arrested, and Liebenberg searched. But he also
took care to order first that all Eulenburg's letters to himself and the
Kaiser be removed from Liebenberg.

The second Moltke–Harden trial was now declared invalid and the
date set for a new trial, in November 1908. Eulenburg's own trial, on
a charge of perjury, was to take place in July 1908. But when the time
came Eulenburg, with suspicious convenience, collapsed and was
declared unfit to continue. After a second false start, the case was postponed indefinitely. Harden attacked again, using another of his
methods: he prepared to address the public at a meeting in a beer hall.
On 10 October 1908 he wrote to Holstein, 'I will say everything
necessary next week in the Brock brewery to loose an even larger
scandal. As long as I have strength I will go through the land to brand
this infamy.'

As Harden told Holstein in a letter of 15 November, his 'even larger
scandal' linked Wilhelm himself to Jacob Ernst, the Starnberg
fisherman. He had already intimated this to Holstein in a letter written
on 16 September, saying it made him shudder just to think of the
'unreserved discussion' which would be provoked about 'the political
strife (Lecomte funditus); Bundesfursten and princes; Kistler-Ernst-
HM; Moltke himself; Kessel-Eberh, etc. etc.' But he was forced to go
ahead because 'this monarch will never change and is simply in the
hands of blackmailers.' If necessary, he added in his November letter,
he would force Wilhelm from the throne by 'privately using the
strongest means (I could say by becoming "earnest").' The play on the
name 'Ernst', which is spelt the same way as the German word for
earnest or serious, was the final threat.

Holstein quickly passed the information on to Bülow, who as
quickly took action. The third Moltke–Harden trial was merely a formality. Bülow, with the help of Albert Ballin, the Kaiser's shipping-
line friend who knew all the players, agreed to a private deal whereby
Harden was fined a sum of 600 Marks, and another 40,000 Marks for
the cost of the three trials. In fact it was Ballin who paid, and he was
later reimbursed by the Reich Chancellery. There were those who
thought Bülow had engineered the whole thing in the first place,

partly to get rid of his one-time friend Eulenburg when he tried to make his come-back in 1902, and partly as a last-ditch attempt to subject the Kaiser to the rule of Parliament – or, if not of Parliament, then at least of the Chancellor.

For Harden to have agreed to the deal he must have been persuaded that Eulenburg would never return. This was indeed the case, Eulenburg remaining effectively in exile at Liebenberg until his death in 1921. He and Wilhelm, the two best friends, never saw each other again. But Harden must also have believed that the Kaiser would now be reined in, and this proved not to be the case. It was too late for that. The Kaiser's reactionary military entourage simply moved into the vacuum left by Eulenburg, and together they marched blindly on to war.

During the autumn of 1908 Wilhelm was as close as he ever came to a full nervous breakdown. He had lost 'Phili' for ever, and discovered for the first time that he, the All-Highest, was not all-powerful but was unable to cover up the scandals unleashed by a mere journalist, and a Jew at that. His faith in Bülow, once destined to be the Chancellor of his Personal Rule, was gone. He felt himself surrounded by enemies, at home and abroad. He railed against the Jews, the Socialists, the English, the French, the ungrateful Russians.

As though to prove his point, another drama unfolded in September, this time concerning Germany's naval race with England. The Kaiser was at his hunting lodge at Rominten with his usual entourage of friends and guests when a letter arrived from Lord Burnham, owner of the *Daily Telegraph*. It enclosed a typed draft of an article based on an interview with Colonel Montagu-Stuart-Wortley, the Kaiser's host at Highcliffe Castle the previous November. At the time London had been agog at rumours of the Kaiser's extravagant table-talk about his repeated attempts at friendship with England and how, he claimed, they were repeatedly spurned. The Kaiser had found a keen supporter in Colonel Stuart-Wortley, whom he had invited to the German Army manoeuvres in Alsace the following August. There they had decided that publicity might be given to the Kaiser's views, with the aim of informing the misguided English public and improving Anglo-German relations. Wilhelm now read the draft interview and showed it to Admiral Tirpitz, a guest at the time, who was not much impressed. Then he sent it to Bülow with a note instructing the Chancellor to 'suggest any desirable alterations on the margin of the existing English text' before sending it back to him, without showing it to anyone at the Foreign Office and 'keeping it as secret from as many others as possible'. Bülow may or may not have read it but, marked 'Confidential' and 'Revise carefully', he sent it off to Berlin, where it was passed from one under-ling to another, gathering a few amendments, before being returned to Bülow, who signed it off and sent it back to the Kaiser – either a classic case of passing the buck, or Bülow making a last-ditch attempt to rid Germany of the Kaiser.

The article duly appeared in the *Daily Telegraph* on 28 October 1908, headed 'From an Unimpeachable Source'. It caused an instant furore both in England and in Germany. The aim had been to allay English fears about Germany's Big Navy plans. 'To be for ever mis-judged, to have my repeated offers of friendship weighed and scrutin-ised with jealous, mistrustful eyes, taxes my patience severely,' the Kaiser was quoted as saying. 'I repeat, I am the friend of England, but you make things difficult for me . . . the prevailing sentiment among large sections of the middle and lower classes of my own people is not friendly to England. I am, therefore, so to speak, in a minority in my own land . . . I strive without ceasing to improve relations, and you retort that I am your arch-enemy. Why is this?' On and on it went. Apparently it had not occurred to the Kaiser that the middle and lower classes in his own country would hear of it soon enough. He was quoted talking of Morocco, of the Boer War, always with himself in the role of peacemaker, and then again of the Big Navy issue which was at the heart of everything. 'But, you will say, what of the German Navy? My answer is clear.' It was clear in the usual way: Germany was rapidly expanding; the Navy was for commerce, not for war. But as the people of England and Germany opened their newspapers and read his assurances, no one believed him. The Kaiser, split as he had always been between England and Germany, and seeking to be loved by both, had managed to outrage both instead.

'Of all the political gaffes which HIM has made,' wrote Edward VII to Hardinge from the Jockey Club on 30 October, 'this is the great-est.' In England the crisis passed soon enough, but not in Germany. The public and the press were up in arms over the Kaiser's indiscre-tion and disloyalty. 'He ruins our political position and makes us the laughing-stock of the world. It makes one wonder whether one is in a madhouse!' wrote Baroness von Spitzenberg in her diary, neatly summing up German public opinion. Bülow, typically, was busy distancing himself from the whole affair. All five parties in the Reichstag were joined in their furious criticism of both the Kaiser and Bülow.

Meanwhile another article was threatening, supposedly based on an interview the Kaiser had given that same summer to a Mr Hale, correspondent of the *New York Times*. The article was so extreme that it was suppressed by the editor of the newspaper, and only appeared in truncated form in one small American publication. In it, the Kaiser was described as saying that Edward VII was corrupt, his Court rotten, and an Anglo-German war inevitable. The Kaiser categorically denied having spoken the words, and in view of the fact that the article was passed on by a series of known Germanophobes, it is likely that it was at least exaggerated. But Edward VII did not think so. 'After your leaving me with [the German Ambassador] Count Metternich's letter, with the German Emperor's emphatic denial, I have, I presume, nothing more to do than to accept it,' he wrote to Knollys on 25 November from Castle Rising in Yorkshire, where he was shooting. 'I am, however, convinced in my mind that the words attributed to G.E. by Mr Hale are perfectly correct. I know the E. *hates* me, and never loses an opportunity of saying so (behind my back) whilst I have always been civil and nice to him.'

Wilhelm, the royal cousin who could never do anything right, was at the end of his tether. He had lost his best friend, his Chancellor had betrayed him, England had rejected him – and now, during an evening of innocent relaxation, General Dietrich von Hülsen-Haeseler, six feet tall and Chief of his Military Cabinet, died of a heart attack on leaving the stage after dancing for the Kaiser and his entourage in a tutu. In late 1908 he was close to a complete nervous breakdown.

But by the beginning of 1909 relations between Germany and England seemed to be on a more even keel again. Edward VII, sensibly advised by his ministers to mend fences, reluctantly agreed to a State Visit to Germany in February, accompanied even more reluctantly by Queen Alexandra. In Germany it was noticed that the King's health was not good. He was suffering from bronchial troubles, wheezing badly, and struggling to climb stairs. After a luncheon at the British Embassy he alarmed everyone by choking over his cigar and collapsing, but he recovered quickly once the Queen had undone the collar of his too-tight Prussian uniform. The visit was a success, and Edward VII genially charmed everyone he met, except Wilhelm's own entourage, who were distinctly unfriendly. Willy told his uncle in confidence that he was planning to get rid of Bülow, whom he no longer trusted. He blamed him for the *Daily Telegraph* affair, and he was certain Bülow was still working hand in glove with Holstein. By July Bülow was gone.

That spring the King and Queen met the Dowager Tsarina on their annual Mediterranean cruise, and when the King returned to England the two sisters travelled on together to visit their brother, the King of Greece. The Balkan states were always giving trouble, and the sisters were in a constant worry on behalf of brother Willi. The previous October Austria had without warning annexed Bosnia and Herzegovina, breaching the Treaty of Berlin and threatening war in the area; everyone waited to see if Russia would intervene on their behalf. Isvolsky meanwhile was trying to negotiate Russia's right of passage through the Dardanelles, which had been closed to warships since the Treaty of Berlin, thus denying the Russian Navy any exit from the Black Sea. Charles Hardinge kept Edward VII informed of developments, and it was suggested that the King write his nephew the Tsar a friendly letter. Nicky wrote back to his 'dear u. B.' that he was happy their two countries were coming to 'several agreements in Asia', assuring him that he would do everything to calm matters in the Balkans, adding: 'Of course you know that Russia needs peace, more than any other country at the moment.' It was clear that, with Germany supporting her ally Austria-Hungary, Russia was not prepared to go to war for Bosnia and Herzegovina.

Willy had written to Nicky in January 1909: 'The annexation of Bosnia and Herzegowina was a genuine surprise for everybody, but particularly for us as we were informed about Austria's intentions even later than you.' Germany had no choice but to support her ally, he told Nicky, but Russia and Germany needed to be as closely united as possible 'for the maintenance of Peace and of monarchical institutions.' It was another of Willy's long missives. 'It is the patent fact that for the last two years Russian Policy has been gradually drawing away from us more and more, evolving always closer toward a combination of powers unfriendly to us. The triple Entente between France–Russia and England is being talked of by the whole world as an accomplished fact. English and French papers miss no opportunity of representing this alleged "Tripleentente" as being directed against Germany, and only too often the Russian Press chimes in joining the chorus.' The Kaiser had a point. But he failed to draw the right conclusion: build fewer battleships.

In England Lloyd George's 1909 People's Budget introduced at the end of April was causing a storm of protest in the House of Lords. Taxes were being raised steeply to provide for old age pensions and education, and also for battleships. The Lords were in the habit of blocking the Liberal Government at every turn and Lloyd George turned his wrath on them, attacking the land-owning dukes with his usual flourish, noting that while 'a fully-equipped Duke cost as much to keep up as two Dreadnoughts', the Duke was less easy to scrap. Happily, in May the King's horse Minoru won the Derby at Epsom at odds of 4 to 1. Racing was a sport for lords and plebs alike. The enthusiastic racing crowd sang 'God Save the King!' again and again, cheering their sovereign with shouts of 'Good old Teddy!', throwing their hats in the air. Unlike the Kaiser, Edward VII was a dab hand at being popular with his public.

On Monday 2 August Georgie, his parents, Toria and uncle Arthur were on board the Royal Yacht *Victoria and Albert*, anchored off Spithead, waiting for the Russian Imperial family, with all five children, who arrived at 12.15 in their yachts *Standart* and *Polar Star*, escorted by two cruisers. The English party boarded the *Standart*, 'then they returned with us to this Yacht & their numerous Suite,' wrote Georgie in his diary that evening. As well as the 'numerous suite', which included Stolypin and Isvolsky, there were dozens of Russian police agents – a contrast to Mr Quinn of Scotland Yard and his small team of detectives, who remained discreetly invisible with the occasional help of a false moustache or beard as disguise.

Asquith and Sir Edward Grey were also present, appearing tall beside the Imperial couple. 'Dear Nicky looking so well & Alicky too, I had not seen him for 12 years.' After luncheon they steamed down the lines of the Fleet to Cowes. 'I was pretty tired after standing about all day and being in full uniform since 10.30. Nicky has most kindly made me an Admiral in the Russian Navy.' It caused no constitutional problems for Nicky, the Autocrat of All The Russias, to create someone an Admiral. That evening there was a large dinner on board *Victoria and Albert*, with the usual toasts and speeches. 'We then talked on deck. The Fleet illuminated. Fine sight. Beautiful night but rather cold. Bed at 11.30.' The next day they all dined 'in full dress' on the *Standart*. On Thursday, 'a heavenly day, very hot sun', the Russians left, but not before the famous photograph had been taken of the two royal cousins, each in his natty yachting outfit and cap, arm-in-arm, again looking so alike that people called them twins.

On Friday Georgie, still on board the *Victoria and Albert*, was in reflective mood. 'Today, 30 years ago, Eddy and I joined the *Bacchante* here at Cowes, it seems like yesterday.' Like everyone else, he was worried about his father's health. It was not helped by the constitutional crisis which threatened because the House of Lords had rejected the Liberal Government's Finance Bill. The Government was now determined to curb the power of the House of Lords by persuading the King to use his Royal Prerogative to create enough new peers to ensure the passage of the Bill. Knollys, the moderate liberal, thought the Lords needed reform, but was worried that the monarchy might appear to be leaning too far to the left. Esher prepared a memo for the King, giving a summary of the dispute. Asquith had visited Balmoral and been very pleasant, which had done some good. In January 1910 the Liberals won the election, but with a much reduced majority.

In March the King's bronchial troubles worsened. His appetite did not seem to be affected: one evening the menu of a great dinner he gave for all his male friends included turtle soup, salmon, grilled chicken, saddle of mutton, snipe stuffed with *foie gras*, asparagus, a fruit dish, an enormous iced concoction, and a savoury. The next day, 7 March 1910, he set off for the Continent. In Paris, he suffered a bout of indigestion and heart pain, but travelled on to Biarritz, where he had a severe attack of bronchitis. Queen Alexandra was cruising in the Mediterranean with Toria. Knowing that Mrs Keppel was with him, she could only write and beg him to leave 'that horrid Biarritz', which Edward resisted, still determined to live life to the full.

When the King returned to England on 27 April he went straight to Sandringham. The next day, in bitter winds, he made his usual inspection of the estate and farm. By the time he returned to London, he was seriously ill. Queen Alexandra was hurriedly sent for. Arriving at Calais, she was handed a letter from Georgie. 'His cough troubles him very much and he has slept very badly the last nights. I cannot disguise the fact that I am anxious about him, as one always must be when he gets one of these attacks and this one following so soon after the one he had in Biarritz. I know Laking [Edward VII's royal physician] is writing to you and I will say no more but thank God you are coming home tomorrow to look after him. God bless you darling

Motherdear.' At Victoria station it was not the King who met her, as he usually did, but the Prince and Princess of Wales with their two eldest children. The next morning, 6 May, the King insisted on donning his frock-coat before receiving first his devoted Knollys and then, lighting a fat cigar, his old friend Ernest Cassel, the man who had done so much to rescue his parlous finances. That afternoon he collapsed. Bertie, who had run up the gangplank to kiss Alexandra in full view of the public when she first arrived in England as the Danish Princess, was dying. The Queen called for the rest of the family and some of his closest friends, including Mrs Keppel. That evening he fell into a coma and, just before midnight, Edward VII, the most popular of kings, loved by his people for his failings as much as for his triumphs, died peacefully at Buckingham Palace.

'At 11.45 beloved Papa passed peacefully away and I have lost my best friend and the best of fathers,' wrote Georgie in his diary. 'I never had a word with him in my life. I am heartbroken and overwhelmed with grief but God will help me in my responsibilities and darling May will be my comfort as she has always been. May God give me strength and guidance in the heavy task which has fallen upon me.'

16

Georgie Inherits the Throne at Last

~

'DEAREST GEORGIE,' wrote Nicky on black-bordered writing paper from Tsarskoe Selo on 8 May 1910, in English as usual, 'Just a few lines to tell you how *deeply* I feel for you the terrible loss you and England have sustained. I know alas! by experience what it costs one. There you are with your heart bleeding and aching, but at the same time duty imposes itself and people & affairs come up and tear you away from your sorrow. It is difficult to realize that your beloved Father has been taken away. The awful rapidity with which it all happened! How I would have liked to have come now & be near you!' The second half of the letter pinpointed the moment when the relationship between the two royal cousins crossed the line from purely personal to purely business, now that Georgie was King. 'I beg you dearest Georgie to continue our old friendship and to show my country the same interest as your dear Father did from the day he came to the throne. No one did so much in trying to bring our two countries closer together than Him. The first steps have brought good results. Let us strive and work in the same direction. From our talks in days past & from your letters I remember your opinion was the same. I assure you that the sad death of your Father has provoked throughout the whole of Russia a feeling of sincere grief & of warmest sympathy towards your people. God bless you my dear old Georgie! My thoughts are always near you. With much love to you & dearest May, ever your devoted friend, Nicky.'

After three days lying in state in Westminster Hall, Edward VII's coffin was drawn on a gun-carriage through the streets of London to Paddington station to be put on a train for the State Funeral at Windsor. Hundreds of thousands of the King's subjects, uniformly dressed in black, stood in silence, heads bowed, as the funeral procession passed by, the only sound the grinding of the carriage wheels, the clang of horses' hooves, and the regular stamp of a slow march. Nine kings, including

Kaiser Wilhelm, were in attendance. The Dowager Tsarina came from Russia to be with her sister the Dowager Queen. Theodore Roosevelt came from America. Princes, ministers, diplomats, racing friends, courtiers, travelling companions, mistresses, all were represented at the passing of one of the most popular monarchs in history. In pride of place behind the gun-carriage walked Edward VII's favourite fox terrier, Caesar, led by a Highland servant. Never before had he been obliged to yield precedence to a dog, quipped the Kaiser.

'Today has been a very long & trying day for me & one I shall never forget as long as I live,' wrote Georgie in his diary. '[A]t 9.5 we started in procession for Westminster Hall, William, all the Kings & Princes riding with me & Motherdear, May & the Princesses driving . . . it was a wonderful & impressive sight . . . the whole route was lined by troops, about 35,000. There was the largest crowd of people there has probably ever been in the world before, the most striking thing was the absolute silence.' The following day the nine kings, splendidly uniformed and festooned with medals, were photographed by Downey, George V sitting in the middle of the front row, cousin William standing behind flanked by King Albert of the Belgians and King Ferdinand of the Bulgarians. The next few days were spent seeing them all off, the last to go being William, who left on 23 May, and wrote even before he had left England's shores to thank Georgie for being allowed to share in his 'grief and sorrow during the laying at rest of my Beloved Uncle Your lamented Father.' In between the farewells there were meetings, audiences, banquets and family dinners, but each day in his diary George noted 'worked with Bigge after breakfast'. Sir Arthur Bigge, Lord Stamfordham, the man who taught George how to be a king, was at his side from first to last.

Immediately after Edward VII's death Stamfordham had suggested that Francis Knollys serve jointly with him as Private Secretary to the new King. It was a fine sentiment in theory, but it worked badly in practice. The two men stood on different sides of the political centre, Stamfordham to the right, Knollys to the left. Edward VII had died in the middle of the constitutional crisis arising from the Liberal Government's determination to reform the House of Lords. George V, at 44, was less mature and experienced than his years might have suggested. He was smaller than his father, both in build and in presence. He had none of his father's flair. He hated making speeches. He was knock-kneed, which did not improve a uniform. He preferred the quiet life of an English country gentleman. But he had a keen sense of duty, a basic decency, and he was willing to learn, if only he could contain his anxieties. 'He told me he cannot sleep,' Esher wrote in his journal on 16 May. 'He wakes about five and finds himself making notes of things which lie before him in his day's work.' Like many others of Edward VII's old entourage, Esher was trying his best to adjust to the new sovereign. 'There never was such a break up,' he wrote to his friend Fisher a week later. 'All the old buoys which marked the channel of our lives seem to have been swept away . . . Francis is behaving so splendidly and is so faithful to his trust. He simply goes on because he knows that it would be the King's wish.' On 3 July Esher was back at Buckingham Palace again, to discuss Edward VII's memorial. 'The King sent for me on Thursday. He was simple, unspoilt, and perfectly open with me. Just a sailor King,' he noted afterwards. 'He is like a really nice boy.'

Knollys and Stamfordham could not agree on the constitutional issue which lay before the King. A conference to settle the matter broke down in November. Before the General Election in December, Asquith asked George V to make a secret pledge to create enough new peers to correct the balance of power in the Lords, should the Liberals be returned. Leaving the King little choice, he said he would resign before the dissolution of Parliament if his request were rejected. Stamfordham advised the King to refuse, saying Asquith should trust him, as King, to act correctly in the event: Knollys advised him to agree. George took Knollys's advice, but regretted it later, particularly once he discovered how it angered the Unionist Party.

The Liberals won the election, and a shift took place in the political life of the country. The Parliament Bill duly ensured that the power of the House of Lords should be subordinated to that of the elected Government. A shift also took place with the King: from then on he put his confidence in Stamfordham more than in Knollys. But Stamfordham's advice had been dubious. A constitutional King is bound to listen to his ministers. After Knollys retired in 1913, the situation between himself and Stamfordham having become untenable, the advice offered to the King by his Private Secretary shifted to the right. 'Everyone lamented the loss of Knollys and the influence of Stamfordham, whose wings the PM earnestly desired should be so clipped,' recorded Sir Charles Hobhouse, Financial Secretary to the Treasury. Everyone but the Tories and the Unionists, that is.

Apart from reform of the Lords, there was another matter which Edward VII's death left unfinished: the memorial to Queen Victoria, celebrating in massive white marble and gilt the greatest Empire on earth, and designed to dominate the wide space in front of Buckingham Palace where it still stands, facing up the Mall. The unveiling was set for May 1911, but first Georgie had to write Nicky an explanatory letter. 'No doubt you will have seen in the newspapers that I have invited William and his Wife to come over to England for the unveiling of Grandmama's statue on May 16th. Papa had always intended to invite William for that ceremony and I know he was very anxious to be present at it. His visit of course will be an absolutely private one, and it has no political significance whatsoever, he is coming as one of the family and the eldest grandson of Grandmama. I wished to tell you this in case the newspapers should invent a lot of rubbish about his visit.' Here was the old problem of the line between private and public in matters between the royal cousins, but it did not stop Georgie, later in his letter, from moving on to politics. 'I rather fear at the present moment that Germany is trying to isolate France, I may be wrong, but that is what I think. No doubt Germany rather resents the friendly understandings which exist between England, Russia and France, but they have not been come to in any way against her but for the benefit of peace and civilisation. I know you don't mind my writing to you quite frankly what I think, as we have always been such good friends, I like to tell you everything.' Earlier he had mentioned the Baghdad Railway, Willy's favourite scheme for a rail link between Berlin and Baghdad, to be financed by Germany, and 'other cognate questions'. 'Cognate' was not cousin Georgie's word. Now that he was King, even his private letters were checked by Stamfordham. Or, to put it another way, once he was King, there was no such thing as a private letter between Georgie and his royal cousins.

Georgie was right about Willy. The Kaiser wrote a long and fulsome letter of acceptance. He was more than pleased that cousin Georgie now sat on the throne instead of uncle Bertie. As he put it, Georgie was just a 'homebody'. The days of the Chief Mischief-maker were over. To Nicky he wrote, 'I go to London for Grandmama's unveiling, at Georgy's invitation,' adding that he meant to find out more about his theory that England was anxious to keep Germany, Austria and Russia apart.

At noon on 15 May Georgie went to Victoria station with May and their two eldest children in barouches to meet 'William and Victoria' who came with their daughter, Victoria Louise, now aged eighteen, for the unveiling. The King had started the day, as he often did, riding in the Park with Charles Cust, his trusted old friend from naval days, now his equerry. In the afternoon he received a deputation from his regiment of Prussian Dragoons, who had come over from Germany for the ceremony. The unveiling took place on the 16th, 'a lovely warm day', at noon. 'William & Victoria & all the family walked in procession to the statue, where Esher as Chairman of the Committee read an address.' George V answered, followed by the Archbishop of Canterbury, after which they all sang a hymn before the King unveiled the statue. The National Anthem was sung, a salute was fired by a battery of The Royal Horse Artillery and, finally, there was a march-past of Grandmama's regiments: 'they looked splendid.'

Dinner that evening was for 57, including Count August zu Eulenburg, Metternich, Asquith, Grey, Haldane, Kitchener, Tweed-mouth, Lascelles and Cust. The next day the King and Queen took the Kaiser and Kaiserin to the theatre at Drury Lane. 'There were enormous crowds in the streets who cheered tremendously.' When they went to Windsor the following day 'there were large crowds of people all the way there and back who cheered'. On Friday evening, after the Military Tournament at Olympia, there was a State Ball at Buckingham Palace in honour of William and Victoria – Willy and Dona – starting at 10 p.m. 'The whole of the family were present. Very full about 2300 people came, a fine sight. I wore my German Dragoon Regts uniform. Saw a great many friends. All over by 1. Bed at 1.30.' On the last day of the visit, Georgie walked in the gardens with Willy for an hour having 'a long talk'. On the way to Victoria station there were large cheering crowds again. 'Their visit I think has been a great success in every way, they certainly got a splendid reception from the people & I think they enjoyed themselves.' The British public were in a mood to like the Kaiser again.

Everything seemed to be looking up for Willy. The scandals surrounding his homosexual friends were finally over, relegated to the dustbin of history. His nerves had calmed down. His new Chancellor, Theobald von Bethmann-Hollweg, though not perfect, appeared malleable enough. Coming from the usual narrow background of Prussian nobility, Bethmann shared the Kaiser's dislike of democracy and especially of Socialism, though as a politician he was concerned to canvass the middle ground in the Reichstag. Kiderlen-Waechter, back from a long stint as Ambassador to Romania following his support of Holstein, became the new Secretary of State at the Foreign Office. Bethmann and Kiderlen were keen to come to some political agreement with Britain, in order to reverse what was perceived as the increasing encirclement of Germany by the Triple Entente. But the Kaiser, as ever, thought matters should be arranged by the two 'royal colleagues', without the interference of politicians and diplomats. Bethmann was already experiencing the usual problems trying to control the Kaiser. Wilhelm for his part soon tired of his somewhat pedantic new Chancellor, preferring to spend his time with his entourage and his familiar unofficial advisers, avoiding Bethmann as much as possible. When Bethmann set about choosing a new ambassador to London, the Kaiser wrote him a sharp reminder: 'I send only *my* ambassador to London, who has *my* confidence, obeys *my* will, fulfils *my* orders with *my* instructions.'

The main issue preventing an agreement between England and Germany was still Tirpitz's rapidly expanding battle fleet, to which was added England's continued support of France in Morocco. In April 1911 France occupied Fez, claiming it was done to protect Europeans from the rebellious Berbers. Germany sent a warship to Agadir to make a stand and protect German business interests. The French took this as a provocative act, but they knew they held the upper hand because while the Kaiser was sending the warship, his Foreign Minister Kiderlen was brokering a deal by which France would cede part of the French Congo to Germany in return for a free hand in Morocco – effectively undermining the Kaiser's warship gesture. Wilhelm, absent from Berlin as usual, accused Kiderlen of bungling things, and threatened to return from his annual North Sea Cruise to take control. The British stood shoulder to shoulder with France. For a time there was talk of war, with the press in all three countries fanning the flames. Germany finally settled for a large but essentially worthless part of the French Congo. The whole episode prompted another upsurge of Anglophobia in Germany, and another outburst of the Kaiser's paranoia. He was certain England had been behind it all along, blocking him at every turn.

In September 1911 Stolypin, Minister-President of Russia since 1906, was assassinated while attending the theatre. He was standing in the front row of the stalls talking to a minister of the Court when a man in a tail-coat came straight up to him and fired twice at point blank. The Tsar and Tsarina were in the Imperial Box only a few feet away. As he fell, Stolypin turned to face the box, making the sign of the cross. His maxim had always been 'order first, reform later'. But however much order he imposed, he could not prevent the Nihilists from pursuing their campaign of violence against figures in prominent positions. Meeting Stolypin at Reval in 1908, Frederick Ponsonby had been impressed by this 'grave, splendid-looking man with a long grey beard'. Stolypin knew the Nihilists had pledged to kill him but went about as if nothing had happened, even though his daughter had already been the victim of a bomb attack, telling Ponsonby that 'if he lived in fear of his life, life would not be worth living.'

Stolypin was replaced by Kokovstev, who asked for Makarov to be appointed as his Minister of Interior. 'No question that the new Premier made the suggestion because Makarov belongs to the extreme right,' commented Witte from the sidelines. 'But Makarov was not the stuff required in a minister of interior at the time, chiefly because he was not and never could be a commanding personality.' On 2 March 1912 Witte wrote the last sentence of his Memoirs: 'Thus I have reached 1912 in my stenographic memoirs,' he noted. 'For the time being I am discontinuing this work . . .' He died three years later, by which time Russia was embroiled in the First World War, and violent political unrest at home was leading to full-scale revolution, as he had predicted.

The constant threat of assassination made the Tsarina's health, never good, very much worse. Every time the Tsar left for St Petersburg or Moscow, always under heavy guard, she was in terror. She spent most of her time with the children at Tsarskoe Selo or one of the other Imperial palaces, shut away from the world. In public she was still shy and awkward, and Court events remained an agony for her. In spite of her romantic attachment to Russia she was still not at home with Russians, and was mocked behind her back for her heavy German accent. Her popular mother-in-law still reigned supreme in St Petersburg society, though these days she spent more time abroad, or at the Imperial palace at Livadia in the Crimea. But Alix's worst problem was her constant fear about the health of their son and heir Alexei. When the family went out he was usually carried by a servant, in case some accident should occur to start the bleeding. Alix became increasingly susceptible to the healer Rasputin, and in this, as in much else, she influenced her husband Nicky.

After a long talk with one of Alix's ladies-in-waiting, Nicky's sister Xenia noted in her diary that she was disturbed by what was going on at Tsarskoe Selo, in particular 'the attitude of Alix and the children to that sinister Grigory (whom they consider to be almost a saint, when in fact he is only a *khlyst*!) He's always there, goes into the nursery, visits Olga and Tatiana while they are getting ready for bed, sits there talking to them and *caressing* them . . . It's quite unbelievable and beyond understanding.' The children, largely cut off from the outside world, were apparently captivated by Rasputin, and fearful of offending their mother. 'My sweet own darling Mama,' wrote Tatiana, now aged thirteen, in English, the language they shared, 'Please forgive me that I have not did what I would last day. I am so sad that I did that, what I knew you would not like. Please forgive me I did not want to do it really Mama dear. I never, never wont do something I know you don't like and I wont [*sic*] do it without asking you my sweet mama. How is your head? I am so afraid that S.I. [the children's governess] can speak to Maria about our friend some thing bad. I hope our nurse will be nice to our friend now.' 'Our friend', Rasputin.

The Dowager Tsarina disliked and mistrusted Rasputin and wanted him to be sent away. But Alix and Nicky would not hear of it. Alix admitted to Olga that anxiety over Alexei's 'illness' had made her ill herself, knowing there could never be a full recovery. She said she believed in Rasputin because she saw that whenever he was near, the child felt better. The slightest accident could cause Alexei internal haemorrhages and the most terrible pain, lasting for days. The boy's cries were often so loud they could be heard along the palace corridors outside his bedroom. During these times Alix never went to bed, hardly even bothered to undress, but just sat in his room, helpless and desperate. Nicky was little better, but because he had to carry on his daily duties he was spared the constant watching and waiting. In public they were careful to hide their anxieties, but in private it dominated their lives.

Pierre Gilliard, Alexei's French tutor, recalled a typical scene. The girls were performing a play one evening in the palace dining room in front of Their Majesties, their suite and several guests. Gilliard was the prompter, concealed behind a screen. By craning his neck he could see the Tsarina smiling and talking gaily to her neighbours.

When the play was over he left and went out into the corridor opposite Alexei's room, from where he heard the distinct sounds of moaning. 'I suddenly noticed the Tsarina running up, holding her long and awkward train in her two hands. I shrunk back against the wall, and she passed me without observing my presence. There was a distracted and terror-stricken look on her face. I returned to the dining room. The scene was of the most animated description. Footmen in livery were handing round refreshments on salvers. Everyone was laughing and exchanging jokes. The evening was at its height. A few minutes later the Tsarina came back. She had resumed the mask and forced herself to smile pleasantly at the guests who crowded round her. But I had noticed the Tsar, even while engaged in conversation, had taken up a position from which he could watch the door, and I caught the despairing glances which the Tsarina threw him as she came in.'

On 3 November 1912 an announcement after the event from the Minister of the Imperial Court appeared in the press: 'The severe and trying period of illness of His Imperial Highness the Tsarevich and Heir Grand Duke Alexei having passed, it is now possible to give a general picture of his illness according to the findings of the doctors of the Imperial patient.' In mid September the Tsarevich had taken 'a very large step whilst jumping into a boat', causing an abdominal haemorrhage. He was just beginning to recover three weeks later, the announcement continued, when, still unsteady on his feet, he fell, causing a new and worse haemorrhage, whereupon his temperature shot up.

On 22 October, four days after the second fall, Nicky wrote, 'I stayed in Alexei's room until 2 o'clock, when he began to quieten down and fall asleep. He had quite a good day in general, and slept frequently, his temperature was back to 39.5. Went for a short walk in the morning with the girls. Played some tennis after lunch. The weather was warm. Took turns with Alix to sit with Alexei.' The next day there was a noticeable improvement in Alexei's condition, and everyone's spirits rose. After Mass the children's religious instructor came to give him Communion, which was a great comfort. In the afternoon Nicky went for a walk with Irene, Alix's sister married to Willy's brother Prince Heinrich, whose own son had died as a consequence of his haemophilia a few years earlier. After tea he sat down to answer the many telegrams of sympathy they had received. By 26 October Alexei was on the mend, his temperature back to normal, and they carried him from his bed to the sofa where he had 'an excellent nap'.

'My dearest Nicky,' wrote Georgie from Sandringham on 16 December, 'I can't tell you how much I have felt for you and dear Alicky in all your anxiety during your dear little boy's illness. I trust he is really better now and does not suffer any more pain. Are you going to send him to the South during the winter. I have also felt for you so much on account of dear Misha. I am so fond of him, that I am in despair that he should have done this foolish thing and I know how miserable you must be about it. What a lot of worries and anxieties there are in this world. Ever, dearest Nicky, your devoted cousin and old friend, Georgie.' Police Agent No. 1638 had reported to His Excellency the Tsar that His Imperial Highness Grand Duke Mikhail, his youngest brother Misha, had married a certain Mme Wulfert, a commoner, on 30 October in Vienna, the couple having first stayed at the Esplanade Hotel in Berlin together.

The unsettled political situation, but mostly Alix's ill-health, had prevented Nicky from attending both Edward VII's funeral and, in June 1911, his cousin George V's Coronation. The Dowager Tsarina went instead to represent the Russian Imperial family. Nicky wrote to her on 18 June: 'I often think of you dear Mama, how happy you must be living peacefully with Aunt Alix at Sandringham. We have followed the details of the coronation with great interest in the papers. Happily for Georgie and May, all these festivities have now come to an end, and, as far as one can judge, very successfully too. It was exhausting even to read the description of all they had to do and go through. It is curious to think that it is already 15 years since we underwent the same thing!'

The newspapers were certainly full of it. Page after page about 'The Historic Spectacle', 'How the King Went Forth To His Crowning', 'Noble Ceremonial in the Abbey', and 'Pageant of Stately Beauty'. Marie Corelli wrote 'An Impression of the Coronation' for the *Daily Mail*. 'Honour, reverence, splendour and stateliness, noble ritual and solemn observance – all these have proclaimed the fact, and grey old Westminster Abbey has seen no more impressive ceremonial than yesterday's brilliant pageant,' she announced before moving on to her main point. 'Why such a frenzy of rapture for a King and Queen? Why? Because England is loyal to the backbone, and Socialism is no more than a ripple of discontent on a stagnant pool!'

'Overcast and cloudy with some showers and a strongish cool breeze, but better for the people than great heat' was how George V began his diary entry that evening, 23 June 1911. Queen Mary, as she now was, agreed. 'Dull but fine – Our Coronation Day. Magnificent reception both going and coming back,' she wrote in her own diary. 'There were hundreds of thousands of people who gave us a magnificent reception,' Georgie's entry continued. 'The Service in the Abbey was most beautiful & impressive but it was a terrible ordeal . . . Darling May looked so lovely & it was indeed a comfort to me to have her by my side as she has been ever to me during these last 18 years.'

Much of Georgie's life was now an ordeal. In February he and May had opened Parliament for the first time. 'I must say that I think opening Parliament the most terrible ordeal I have ever gone through,' he wrote to his mother. 'The House of Lords was crammed with people & so many I knew which made it worse . . . I got your dear telegram just as we were getting into the coach which is not uncomfortable but very high. The cream coloured horses were rather unruly & the leaders shied right across the street every time they came across a band.'

He was happy to have a spell of rest at Balmoral. Esher, again a guest, noted in his journal, 'There is no longer the old atmosphere about the house – that curious electric element which pervaded the surroundings of King Edward. Yet everything is very charming and wholesome and sweet. The house is a home for children – six of them at luncheon – the youngest running round the table all the while. The Queen knits of an evening. Not a sign of bridge.' To his son Maurice he wrote, 'We go to bed early, which I like, and breakfast at nine . . . Last night the French governess sat on the King's right hand at dinner. Imagine the courtiers of Berlin or Vienna if they could have seen.' Lloyd George, also at Balmoral, wrote to his wife, 'The King is a very jolly chap but thank God there's not much in his head. They're simple, very, very ordinary people, and perhaps on the whole that's how it should be.'

The one voyage George V was determined to undertake was to visit India again, this time as King-Emperor, and taking Queen Mary with him, for a Coronation Durbar in Delhi, now replacing Calcutta as the capital. The Government was not keen on such a protracted absence so soon after the King's accession, but Georgie got his way. 'The Great Coronation Durbar, which has occupied the thoughts of India for more than a year, has involved the most elaborate preparation, and has brought a quarter of a million people together from every part of the Indian Empire, was held today on the vast plains beyond Delhi,' wrote *The Times* on 13 December 1911. 'Enthroned on high beneath a golden dome, looking outwards to the far north from whence they came, their Majesties, the King-Emperor and Queen-Empress were acclaimed by over 100,000 of their subjects. The ceremony at its cul- minating point exactly typified the Oriental conception of the ultim- ate repositories of Imperial power. The Monarchs sat alone, remote but beneficent, raised far above the multitude, but visible to all, clad in rich vestments, flanked by radiant emblems of authority, guarded by a glittering army of troops, the cynosure of the proudest Princes of India, the central figures in what was surely the most majestic assemblage ever seen in the East.' Returning to his magnificent silk-lined royal tents in the vast camp set up outside Delhi, Georgie wrote in more sober terms. It had been the most beautiful and won- derful sight he had ever seen, but he was 'rather tired after wearing the Crown for 3½ hours, it hurt my head, as it is pretty heavy.' The new Viceroy, Edward VII's old friend Sir Charles Hardinge, was less convinced than *The Times* of the happy effect of these 'repositories of Imperial power'. Making his own grand State Entry into the new capital a week later, he was slightly wounded by a bomb which killed his personal attendant. George V meanwhile was off to Nepal, where he shot twenty-one tigers, eight rhino and one bear.

'Each year I feel we become more & more necessary to one another & our lives become more and more wrapt up in each others,' Georgie wrote to May from Nepal while she was sightseeing in Jaipur. 'And I am sure that I love you more each year & am simply devoted to you & loathe being separated from you even for a day. Especially now in my present position with the enormous amount I have to do & with all my many responsibilities I feel that I want your kind help & support more than ever. And I must say you invariably give it me, I greatly appreciate it & thank you from the bottom of my heart for all the love & devotion you give me.' This, then, was a letter written without the help of Stamfordham, and none the worse for it. He added that he was 'very proud of being your husband & feel that our coming here to India as the first Emperor and Empress has certainly proved itself to be what I always predicted, a great success.' It was a success in every sense. May became more confident in her new role, and on their return to England the King and Queen were greeted with deafening cheers. They had never been more popular.

Back in London, the effect of the Parliament Act was soon tested. In April 1912 the Government was preparing to introduce its Irish Home Rule Bill. Under the terms of the Act, a Bill need only pass in the Commons three times and need not be passed in the Lords at all before it could be presented to the King for the Royal Assent, a matter taken very seriously by the King but in fact a mere formality in a constitutional monarchy. The Unionists were up in arms; civil war was threatening; Asquith remained unperturbed. The King, strongly supported by Stamfordham, felt the Government had put him in a most difficult position. Whatever he did, half the people of England would object, and all the Protestants or all the Catholics of Northern Ireland. Right-wing Tories were calling for him to dismiss the Government. He wrote Asquith a long memo in which he suggested a conference to be attended by all the relevant parties, to try to find a solution to the problem.

Asquith wrote back, pinpointing the real issue as far as the monarchy was concerned. 'We have now a well-established tradition of 200 years that, in the last resort, the occupant of the Throne accepts and acts upon the advice of his Ministers. The Sovereign may have lost something of his personal power and authority, but the Crown has thereby been removed from the storms and vicissitudes of party politics.' The King wrote back a letter of many pages, mentioning, *inter alia*, the emasculation of the House of Lords, and suggesting that this heavily opposed Bill was being forced through by the Government. 'It behoves us all', he wrote, 'to withhold no efforts to avert those threatening events which would inevitably outrage humanity and lower the British name in the mind of the whole civilised world.' The language was Stamfordham's again, but the sentiments were no doubt the King's own. Asquith remained unruffled, drawing up memos for the 'Royal Eye' to keep the King happy, always hoping to stem the flow of what, writing to his mistress Venetia Stanley, he called 'rather hysterical' letters. But he agreed to a conference, acknowledging the fierce opposition in Parliament and the Lords, and began to look around for a compromise.

'We are lunching today with Georgie and May at Buckingham Palace,' wrote the Dowager Tsarina to Nicky on 29 April, to congratulate him on his forty-seventh birthday. 'They both send you greetings. Last night we saw the film of their journey to India. Kinemacolor is wonderfully interesting and very beautiful and gives one the impression of having seen it all in reality. I went to the theatre once with Toria and Olga.' She ended the letter with 'God guard you! Your loving old Mama.' From the safety of England, the constant threat of assassination and violence in Russia was an almost unimaginable horror.

By October 1912 there was trouble in the Balkans again, this time because Bulgaria, Serbia and Greece, determined to profit from the final disintegration of the Ottoman Empire, had declared war on Turkey. 'Despite Alexei's illness, I am following the war between the Christians and Turks with great attention, and rejoice at their glittering successes against the common enemy,' wrote Nicky to his mother on 2 November. 'The greatest problem will come at the end of the war, when it will be necessary to reconcile the legal rights of the small countries with the interests of what remains of Turkey in Europe, and in effect with the political aims of the larger countries.' The lines of communication between two of the larger countries, England and Russia, had been improved by a visit paid to Britain by Sazonov, the Foreign Minister, in October. 'I cannot say how charmed the Queen & I were with M. Sazonov and how pleased we were that he was able to spend a few days with us in our Highland Home,' Georgie wrote to Nicky from Balmoral, 'and that during this time he had opportunities of several long & most friendly conversations with Sir Edward Grey.'

By November another and more powerful country, Austria, was massing an army on the Russian frontier in response to rumours of Russian troop movements in the area. Germany let it be known that she would go to Austria's aid. In England, anticipating trouble, Haldane had called a meeting of which Esher, informed by his usual network, disapproved. 'Last week Haldane called a very Secret Defence Meeting (not a very wise proceeding) to discuss action to be taken if England joined France in a war against Germany,' he wrote in his journal on 6 September. 'Asquith, Lloyd George, Churchill, and Grey and McKenna were present. Although no decision was taken as to the precise action which might become necessary, they settled to bring five Divisions of Indian troops to take part in the war. Fancy this for a Radical Government.'

The meeting followed an abortive initiative originally brokered 'off the record' by Ernest Cassel and his German friend Albert Ballin, director of the Hamburg-American Line and a friend of the Kaiser. An informal meeting with the Kaiser was agreed and in February Haldane went to Berlin, incognito, as a preliminary to formulating some understanding with Germany. Haldane asked the Kaiser and Bethmann for some 'mutual undertakings' against aggressive attacks. But the Germans wanted something quite different: a pledge of England's neutrality in the event of war, whether aggressive or defensive. This was impossible. Haldane additionally pointed out that if Germany continued to expand her Navy at the current rate, there was no hope of a political agreement. Germany refused to budge, and the Haldane Mission was over. Haldane returned to England with a bronze bust of the Kaiser and a copy of the German naval estimates, both gifts from the Kaiser, but nothing else. The secret Defence Meeting mentioned by Esher in his journal soon followed.

Georgie's royal cousins in Russia and Germany would have deeply disapproved of a meeting of such importance as the Defence Meeting being held in secret, without the sovereign's presence. In Germany, on Sunday 8 December 1912, Admiral Georg von Müller was summoned to the Berlin palace to attend a meeting, also secret, and later described as a *Kriegsrat* or War Council, convened by the Kaiser. Müller had become the Chief of the Naval Cabinet in 1906 and by 1912 had been in the job long enough to know his Master the All-Highest's oddities at first hand. The previous summer he had recorded wearily in his diary from the North Sea Cruise, where he was taking his turn of duty: 'At gymnastics this morning great tomfoolery. HM cuts through General von Scholl's braces with a penknife.' Of the Kaiser's preference for tall, good-looking officers to be his ADCs, he noted that it was 'nothing short of a religious relationship.' He was serving at Court when General von Hülsen-Haeseler, Chief of the Military Cabinet, died of a heart attack after dancing in his tutu, and he was present throughout the Moltke and Eulenburg trials. Unlike most of the courtiers and ADCs, Müller was from a bourgeois background, his father having been a professor of agricultural chemistry. He married a colonel's daughter and joined the German Navy, where intelligence and hard work ensured his swift rise. He supported Tirpitz's Big Navy, not for war but because he realised that Germany's rapidly growing commercial interests needed outlets across the world. His diary, unusually fair and objective, is an important record of events leading to the First World War.

On 8 December the Kaiser returned from one of his hunting trips to find a report of 3 December from Prince Lichnowsky, the German Ambassador to London. The Prince relayed a conversation he had had with Haldane, speaking for Grey, in which Haldane stated that in the event of Germany attacking France, England would 'unconditionally' go to France's aid, 'for England could not let the balance of power in Europe be disturbed.' Accounts vary as to who else attended the War Council which followed, but Tirpitz was certainly one, and Helmuth von Moltke, the Chief of the General Staff, another. Neither the Chancellor nor the Foreign Secretary was invited, making the contrast with the meeting held in England complete. According to Müller's account, the Kaiser opened the proceedings by stating that he welcomed the information as a clarification of the situation. He then set out the following points: Austria had to deal 'energetically' with the 'foreign slavs' – that is, the Serbs – and if Russia supported the Serbs then 'war would be unavoidable for us too'. Germany and Austria could hope to have Bulgaria, Romania, Albania and perhaps Turkey on their side. 'The fleet must naturally prepare itself for the war against England.' Haldane's statement meant that the idea of a war with Russia alone was no longer tenable. Tirpitz was told to speed up the building of his U-boats; submarine warfare and mine warfare were discussed. To this Moltke said, 'I believe a war is unavoidable and the sooner the better.' But they would have to work on the press to make the idea of war more popular with the people. 'Tirpitz', wrote Müller, 'said the navy would prefer to see the postponement of the great fight for one and a half years', as it was not yet ready.

After the meeting Müller was deputed to inform Bethmann about it in writing, and pass on the Kaiser's orders that Bethmann should 'enlighten the people through the press of the great national interests, which would be at stake also for Germany, if a war were to break out over the Austro-Serbian conflict. The people must not be in a position of asking themselves only at the outbreak of a great European war, what are the interests that Germany would be fighting for.'

Preparing the people for the prospect of war would take some doing. By 1912 the Social Democratic Party, supported by the trade unions and fuelled by a discontented working class and increasing social unrest, held a third of the votes. In 1871, at the birth of the Second Reich, two-thirds of the population had lived in rural Germany; now two-thirds lived and worked in the towns. The

Socialists were calling for a republic. Wilhelm was convinced the Jews were behind it. He refused to see their deputies, calling them 'red apes' and 'unpatriotic dogs'.

Had Wilhelm been surrounded by an entourage who calmed him and advised him well, things might have been different. But his entourage was almost exclusively military, almost all from the narrow background of Prussian nobility and with no more understanding of or liking for the Social Democrats and Socialists than Wilhelm himself. Most of them, like General Hans von Plessen, the Commandant of the Kaiser's HQ, were war-mongering reactionaries, completely out of touch with Germany as it had developed since the 1870s – into a thrusting industrial society, much better informed and less deferential than before. The Kaiserin was no better. Although she could comfort Wilhelm like a mother when he was having one of his nervous collapses, she could not influence him, which hardly mattered since her horizons were as narrow and reactionary as the others'. And since Wilhelm rarely saw his ministers, and paid less and less attention to Bethmann, there was literally no one to contain or control him. Yet again the great flaw in Bismarck's constitution revealed itself: it vested so much power in the Kaiser that he did not have to listen to his Chancellor. Without consulting Bethmann, the Kaiser now prepared a new Army Bill and a new Navy Bill demanding even higher budgets. Alarmed, Bethmann could only warn the Kaiser that unless the proposed increases remained secret, there was a risk that Germany would appear to be provoking a war. The Navy Bill was delayed, but in early 1913 an Army Bill with swingeing increases was passed which did indeed prepare the way for war.

'Woke up to a heavenly morning,' wrote Nicky in his diary on 2 June 1913 in Moscow. 'At 10 o'clock we arrived at the landing stage at Kostroma and drove to the cathedral, which was surrounded by lines of troops. I inspected them, then we went inside the cathedral and soon joined the holy procession to the foundation site of the large memorial to the 300th anniversary of the Romanov dynasty. Each of us put a stone with his name. After the foundation ceremony, the troops performed a ceremonial march-past.' Four days later there was another ceremony at the Archangel Cathedral in Moscow, again attended by the entire Imperial family, the Synod and clergy of the Russian church, grand dukes and grand duchesses, ministers, the royal suite, and high officials, all in formal Court dress. Every grand

Imperial event proceeded in the same ritualistic fashion, each section of the ruling elite following the next in strict order of precedence, the massive crowds, held back by hundreds of secret police, standing respectfully by, showing no sign of unrest. 'Rasputin was standing by the entrance, everyone saw him, except for me!' wrote Xenia in her diary that evening. '[He] is once again in evidence all over the place, there is such discontent and protest among the clergy!' Later she went to visit Nicky and Alix to discuss her daughter Irina, who wanted to marry Prince Felix Yusupov, the man who later murdered Rasputin.

The First Balkan War, as it later came to be known, was settled by the Treaty of London at St James's Palace in May 1913, 'greatly due to Sir E. Grey,' noted George V in his diary. 'I trust now that the allies may not fight among themselves.' Turkey lost the war, and with it a large part of her European territories, her prestige, and any lingering respect for her military forces. But little was gained. Before long the Balkan states were quarrelling among themselves over the newly acquired territories, with the Great Powers again pulling the strings in the background. The Second Balkan War soon followed, settled by the Treaty of Bucharest in August 1913, in which Bulgaria lost most of Macedonia to her enemies.

In reporting on the international situation, the press of England, Germany and Russia meanwhile set one royal cousin against the other. The royal cousins themselves had family matters to attend to which they considered equally important. The Kaiser's youngest child and only daughter, Princess Victoria Louise, known as Sissy, was to marry the Duke of Brunswick on 23 May 1913. The Kaiser invited both George V and Tsar Nicholas II to attend. Both accepted, each hoping to meet the other there. Sir Edward Grey was obliged to explain to the French Ambassador that this was purely a family visit, and in no sense a State Visit. But this did not stop the French feeling anxious that England might now be making friendly overtures to Germany.

'We crossed over by day to Flushing in the *Victoria and Albert* and had a wonderfully good crossing. We were all able to sit about the deck and enjoy ourselves,' wrote Ponsonby. It was a splendid jaunt, entirely to the Sailor King's liking. Early archive film of him coming down the gangplank at Flushing, walking along the quay with his courtiers, swinging his furled umbrella, shows a man in high good humour. The party spent the night in the comfort of the Imperial train, sent by Wilhelm, and the following morning found them having coffee, dressed in full uniform, when the train stopped at a station some forty minutes from Berlin to take on board Ambassador Goschen and the German officers who would be attached to the King and Queen for the duration of the visit. The King inspected a Guard of Honour and the German suites were presented. Then everyone went into the restaurant car for coffee and beer, an odd German custom, and Ponsonby found himself occupied in his old role of 'keeping the ball rolling', which was 'hard going' since the Germans spoke little English. Thankfully they soon arrived in Berlin, where the Kaiser and Kaiserin and 'a large number of Princes and Princesses' awaited them. German newsreel shows a great deal of kissing and heel-clicking before the King and the Emperor, Georgie and Willy, together inspected yet another Guard of Honour. Then the band struck up and the Guard marched past doing their 'parade march' – the goose-step or, as Ponsonby put it, 'stepping up to their noses'.

The next day the King insisted on going to the railway station to meet the Tsar, who was arriving with his usual large suite and more than a hundred police agents, but without the Tsarina who stayed at home because of her own ill-health, and Alexei. The Kaiser was 'rather put out', for he had intended to be the only one sitting in the open carriage with the Tsar in the royal procession from station to Neues Palais: he had arranged for it to be filmed, and later coloured by hand. Georgie explained that he had no wish to join the procession and was happy simply to go to the station by the back streets in an automobile, and Willy was appeased. Lunch was tricky for Ponsonby, doing the rounds, because the Russians spoke even less English than the Germans. The next day, in the evening, they went to the Court Theatre to see *Kerkyra*, 'a piece inspired by the Kaiser, giving scenes of Corfu', as Ponsonby wryly described it.

The wedding was on 24 May. 'Copious instructions were issued to everyone, so there was really no excuse for anyone to go wrong.' Everyone duly assembled in the State Rooms at 4.30 to watch the royal procession pass through, led by the bride and her suite, followed by the groom and his suite. The palace chapel was full, with no seats, only standing room. After the ceremony everyone moved into the Weisser Saal to witness the *Defiliercour*, when the entire *Corps Diplomatique* and principal officials filed past the royal couple with their wives, each carrying the train of the woman in front. 'We then all trooped off to dinner and I found my place without the least difficulty,' wrote Ponsonby, referring to the copious instructions. There were 1,200 at dinner, everything arranged by Count Eulenburg as usual, with the help of Zedlitz-Truschler's successor, Zedlitz having retired, with some relief, four years earlier. Then it was back to the Weisser Saal for the famous *Fackeltanz* or Torch Dance, in which the bride proceeded slowly round the room first with her father and father-in-law on either arm, then with the Tsar and King George V, and so on down the royal scale. It was a dance of the most exquisite snobbery. Only Royal Highnesses were allowed to take part. Everyone else was excluded, even Highnesses and Serene Highnesses. It nevertheless took a good hour. 'We were all dead beat by then, standing so long. Except for dinner we had been standing about since 4 o'clock.' Even Ponsonby, used as he was to the trials of Court life, was fed up. 'We retired to our rooms to a well-earned smoke.'

The Tsar left that same evening, but not before he and Georgie had managed a few quiet conversations, alone and out of earshot of Willy. 'Saw Nicky in his room,' wrote Georgie in his diary on 22 May and, of later the same day, 'Went to the Kaiserhof Hotel to see the cousins, found Nicky there & we all had tea together.' 'I had a long & satisfactory talk with dear Nicky,' he wrote the following day, 'he was just the same as always.' Even so, Georgie later complained that it was almost impossible to get away from Willy, who was always spying on them, his ear 'glued to the keyhole', fearful of what his royal cousins might be plotting. On Nicky's last day the two cousins were photographed together, each in their German uniforms. 'May and I sat with dear Nicky until he left at 10.15 for the station on his return to Petersburg.'

It was the last time the three royal cousins, Georgie, Willy and Nicky, ever saw one another. Within fifteen months the First World War had begun and the monarchs of Europe, one after another, began to topple from their once all-powerful thrones. All but Georgie, who was blessed with England's constitutional system, which retained all the pomp of monarchy while divesting it of any real power.

17

Three Cousins go to War

~

'MY DEAREST NICKY,' wrote Georgie from Windsor Castle on 16 June 1914, 'You will remember the many satisfactory conversations we had last year in Berlin, when we both so entirely agreed upon the great importance of maintaining the most friendly relations between our two countries, with a view of securing the peace of Europe. I confess that I feel so anxious upon this subject that I write this private letter to explain what is causing me this anxiety.' Hardly private. In the Royal Archives at Windsor there is another copy of the letter in Stamfordham's hand, and a typed copy, drafted by the Foreign Office. The letter was mainly about the current state of affairs in Persia, but the specific subject hardly mattered. The real point of it was to reaffirm the alliance between Russia and Britain in the event of a threatening war. Georgie told Nicky he would not go into details, since a memo, prepared by 'my Government', had been handed to Count Benckendorff, the Russian Ambassador, and Sir George Buchanan, the English Ambassador in St Petersburg, had received instructions to discuss the points raised in the memo with M. Sazonov, the Russian Foreign Minister.

Sazonov was a willing listener, but Nicky's Minister of Internal Affairs, Peter Durnovo, was not. In February he had presented the Tsar with a memo. A European war was now a real possibility, he said, and, contrary to general opinion, it would not be a short one. Russia was not prepared for war, neither economically nor politically, the country being extremely divided. Full-scale revolution could follow defeat. He urged that Russia should not risk war with Germany, since Germany's main belligerence was aimed at Britain. Durnovo thought the Parliamentary system in Britain too liberal in any case, making Britain hardly a useful ally for Russia.

'It is my great desire to see a friendly feeling towards Russia preserved in British public opinion,' Georgie continued, 'and in both political parties, the conservative as well as the liberal, that makes me most anxious that our two Governments should have a frank and friendly exchange of views on the whole situation in Persia.' Public opinion was critically important, as his father Edward VII had known so well. Many Liberals, and most Socialists, were not in favour of the repressive regime of the Autocrat of All the Russias. There had been a good deal of social unrest and a spate of strikes in England during the past two years, and this alliance had to be handled with great care. The trade unions were joining hands across the seas. At the end of the letter Georgie was able to add a few words of his own. 'I hope you spent a pleasant time at Livadia and that dear Alicky is much better now & stronger from her stay there. Aunt Minny is very well, she and Mama are so happy to be together again. May joins me in sending you & Alicky our best love. I remain always your devoted old friend and cousin, Georgie.'

On the day before, 15 June, in Germany, Willy had celebrated the silver anniversary of his accession as King of Prussia and Kaiser of the Second Reich. There were speeches and dedications, unveilings and military displays. For the people there were parades with bands, local dignitaries, and floats representing all the trades, ending in the beer gardens, eating *Bockwurst*, drinking, singing and dancing. Millions of postcards of the All-Highest were sold, showing him in an array of uniforms, moustaches twirling upwards, eyes glaring, artfully lit. Massive monuments were unveiled throughout the Reich, of granite and bronze, and topped by giant Barbarossas, Hohenzollerns, and various Nordic heroes, dwarfing the people below, in the flamboyant Fascist style, long before the word meant what it means today. In concert halls orchestras belted out Wagner, and in university libraries academics laboured over *Festschrifts* praising Wilhelm II and everything Germanic. In Berlin the crowds flocked to catch a glimpse of their Kaiser riding past on his well-trained horse, his left arm resting on the hilt of his mighty sword, carefully concealing his handicap. Never had the All-Highest been more popular. As for the Socialists, the All-Highest held to his view as expressed to Bülow: 'First shoot the Socialists, behead them, put them out of action, if necessary massacre the lot. And then war abroad! But not before, and not *a tempo*!'

On 28 June Archduke Franz Ferdinand, heir to the Habsburg throne, was assassinated in Sarajevo by a young Bosnian Serb patriot, intent on forcing Austria from his homeland. 'Terrible shock to the dear old Emperor,' wrote Georgie in his diary that evening, not yet realising the full import of the event. The King was once again caught up in the trials and tribulations of the Irish Home Rule crisis, and Bosnia seemed far away. His cousin Henry of Prussia had been staying in England for the past month, and they had had some conversations about the international situation, which Henry had duly, though not necessarily entirely accurately, passed on to his brother Willy. There was Derby Day on 27 May and a Court on 4 June, at which 'One girl, Miss Bloomfield, I suppose a Suffragette, went down on her knees and shouted "For God's sake, Your Majesty." And then she was led away. I don't know what we are coming to.'

On 3 July there was a long and tiring day at the Royal Agricultural Show, and on 6 July the King and Queen set off on a State Visit to Glasgow. By 19 July they were in Portsmouth, steaming between the lines of the British Fleet, which stretched from Spithead to Cowes. Returning to London, the King attended the Conference he had requested of Asquith on Irish Home Rule. Asquith put up with it to appease the King, though he knew there was no point. 'I think he realises Home Rule is inevitable,' he told his daughter Violet. 'He is just in a blue funk. Poor little man, he isn't up to his position.' Everyone knew that Stamfordham was against Home Rule. 'I suppose that old cuttle fish Stamfordham will have been flooding his mind with ink,' commented Violet. Three days later the King was forced to accept defeat, neither side being prepared to compromise for the sake of peace in Ireland. 'I am greatly worried by the political situation [meaning Ireland] which is turning very grave,' wrote the King. It was not until 25 July that the international situation properly impinged on George V's consciousness, following an interview with Sir Edward Grey, who explained Count Benckendorff's assessment of the assassination. 'It looks as though we were on the verge of a European War caused by sending an ultimatum to Servia by Austria,' George V wrote in his diary. The next morning Henry arrived from Cowes to make his farewells before returning to Germany. The King cancelled his visit to Goodwood Races.

Two days earlier the belligerent Austrian Foreign Minister Count Leopold von Berchtold had sent Serbia an ultimatum so worded as to ensure its rejection, giving Austria an excuse to declare war. In Russia the Foreign Minister Sazonov immediately telephoned the Tsar. He assumed that the ultimatum must have been agreed beforehand between Austria and Germany. Nicholas himself found it hard to believe that his royal cousin would wish to start a war. When his Minister of Finance, Peter Bark, came for his audience, the Tsar told him that he thought Sazonov was exaggerating the gravity of the situation and had lost his nerve. 'The German Emperor had frequently assured him of his sincere desire to safeguard the peace of Europe and it had always been possible to come to an agreement with him, even in serious cases,' Bark recorded him as saying. The omnipotent Tsar of All the Russias apparently did not realise that his royal cousin, the All-Highest, surrounded by a belligerent and reactionary military, in fact enjoyed less power than was once the case. Sazonov's analysis was right. Before sending the ultimatum Austria had made sure of Germany's support, in the form of a letter sent from Emperor Franz Joseph to the Kaiser. Wilhelm's drafted reply included the sentence 'His Majesty will under all circumstances faithfully stand by Austria-Hungary.' Bethmann removed the phrase 'under all circumstances', but it was enough for Berchtold: he pushed for war and sent his ultimatum. In fact Serbia accepted all the conditions, save one. They refused to collaborate with Austrian officials, which would have been a violation of their sovereignty.

Reading the text of the Serbian reply, Wilhelm, his moods swinging violently, wrote to Gottlieb von Jagow, his Secretary of State at the Foreign Office: '*No more cause for war exists*; but a *guarantee* that the promises *will be carried out* is probably necessary.' But he also allowed for 'a *temporary* military occupation of a portion of Serbia', offering at the same time to '*mediate for peace*'. Bethmann sent the telegram, which was typical of Wilhelm, who liked to strut about acting the part as he gave the orders during military manoeuvres fixed to make sure his side won, but whose nervous temperament was little suited to the horrors of a real war. Bülow had known this all along. 'It was the Kaiser's own and our misfortune that his words and his gestures never coincided with his real attitude,' he wrote in his memoirs. 'When he boasted or even threatened people in words, it was often because he wanted to allay his own timidity.' Müller noted that the Kaiser appeared to be in a state of 'high anxiety'. On 28 July, Austria declared war on Serbia, bombarding Belgrade, cheered on by Germany's generals and Wilhelm's military entourage, who felt the Kaiser's role should be that not of peacemaker but of *Kriegsherr*, Warlord. The

Army Bill of 1913 had ensured that the military was ready. Tirpitz had had his extra eighteen months to prepare the Imperial Navy. The increasing internal unrest could best be solved by a war. There was nothing to hold Germany back.

Wilhelm was less convinced. Now that it came to it, he wavered at the prospect of war with his 'royal colleagues'. He hoped that negotiations could still take place, with Britain taking the lead, influencing her two allies, Russia and France. His brother Heinrich had told him that Georgie had said, during a private conversation, cousin to cousin, that Britain would try to stay out of a war, and remain neutral. Whether or not this was true, or merely exaggerated, this was not the British position, as Wilhelm should have known. But, confused as ever by his dual identity, he informed Tirpitz: 'I have the word of a King and that is enough for me.' On 29 July Grey informed the Russian Ambassador Prince Lichnowsky that Britain would not become involved, unless the war widened to include France and Germany. Wilhelm saw it as proof of the evils of the English parliamentary system. That 'common cur', Grey, 'that common crew of shopkeepers', the British Government, he told Lichnowsky, who was desperate to avoid war with England, 'has tried to trick us with dinners and speeches.' 'Austria has declared war on Servia,' wrote George V in his diary that evening. 'Where will it end? . . . Winston Churchill came to see me, the Navy is all ready for War, but please God it will not come. These are very anxious days for me to live in.' Two days earlier Churchill, as First Lord of the Admiralty, had directed the Grand Fleet, then on summer manoeuvres, not to disperse to home ports.

The Kaiser was sending off one telegram after another to his royal cousin the Autocrat of All the Russias. On 28 July he assured the Tsar that he was doing everything he could to stop Austria provoking war with Russia. The Tsar replied that Austria's attack on Serbia was 'ignoble' and, on 29 July, mobilised his army along Russia's border with Austria, though not along her border with Germany. Mobilisation was a threat, not war, but Willy warned Nicky in his next telegram that he was provoking 'the most horrible war ever witnessed'. Willy, playing the part of peacemaker, or playing for time, saw it as an act of unimaginable treachery by one 'royal colleague' against another, conveniently ignoring the fact that it was Austria who had taken the first step.

The White Book giving Germany's version of events during the ten days leading up to war, from 23 July to 1 August, is entitled *How Russia and her Ruler Betrayed German Confidence and Thereby Made the European War.* Naturally, Britain's Blue Book, Russia's Orange Book and France's Yellow Book did not agree. At a meeting of the Council of Ministers in St Petersburg on 24 July Sazonov made it clear that, from information at his disposal, he understood that 'Austria-Hungary and Germany were resolved to deal a decisive blow at Russian authority in the Balkans by annihilating Serbia.' The British and the French agreed with their Russian allies: Germany was the aggressor.

But in Germany the people, high and low, echoed their Kaiser in the feeling that they had been blocked for years by Russia and England from their rightful 'place in the sun'. The 'Manifesto of the German Intellectuals', signed by Max Reinhardt, among others, proclaimed: 'As representatives of German Science and Art, we hereby protest to the civilised world against the lies and calumnies with which our enemies are endeavouring to stain the honour of Germany in her hard struggle for existence – in a struggle that has been forced on her.' Gerhardt Hauptmann, winner of the Nobel Prize for Literature in 1912, wrote to his fellow writer Romain Rolland in France: 'Naturally everything you say of our government, our army, our people, is distorted, is false, so false that in this respect your open letter seems to me a blank and empty surface. War is war.' Even the majority of Socialists in the Reichstag now supported the war. 'The sword is drawn, and I will not resheath it without victory and honour,' proclaimed Wilhelm the *Kriegsherr* to his First Foot Guards on the eve of war.

'I am writing to you at a most serious moment. I do not know what may happen in a few days,' Nicky telegraphed Georgie, in cipher as usual, on 29 July. 'Austria has gone off upon a reckless war, which can easily end in a general conflagration. It is awful!' Russia had tried to be patient with Austria, he explained, but to no avail. He was confident of Russia's strength and of her right cause, but they were compelled to take strong measures in case of emergency and for their own defence. 'If a general war broke out I know that we shall have France's and England's full support. As a last resort I have written to William to ask him to bear a strong pressure upon Austria.' 'Foreign telegrams coming in all day,' wrote Georgie in his diary on 30 July. 'We are doing all we can for peace and to prevent a European war, but things look very black.' The debate on the Irish question was postponed indefinitely. On the same day Willy wrote, 'So the celebrated encirclement of Germany has finally become an established fact, and the purely anti-German policy which England has been pursuing all over the world has won the most spectacular victory. Even after his death Edward VII is stronger than I, although I am still alive!'

By the following day, 31 July, the momentum towards war appeared unstoppable. George V saw Asquith in the morning and Kitchener in the afternoon. In the evening he looked through his stamp collection, going to bed, very tired, at 11.30. He was woken by Colin Keppel, his equerry-in-waiting, at 12.45: the Prime Minister wanted to see him. He got up and went to the Audience Room, where Asquith was waiting to show him the draft of a telegram which he wanted the King to send the Tsar as a last-ditch attempt at peace. Unlike the Tsar in Russia or the Kaiser in Germany, in England the King's assent to the Prime Minister's request was a mere formality. He was not required to make any decisions. George V gave his permission for the telegram to be sent to the Tsar in his name, and by 1.40 he was back in bed.

Sir Edward Grey at the Foreign Office sent off the telegram to Sir George Buchanan in St Petersburg. It was dated August 1, 1914, 3.30 a.m., and it read: 'You should at once apply for an audience with His Majesty the Emperor and convey to him the following personal message from the King: "My Government has received the following statement from the German Government: 'On 29 July the Russian Emperor requested the German Emperor by telegraph to mediate between Russia and Austria. The Emperor immediately declared his readiness to do so. He informed the Russian Emperor of this by telegraph, and took the required action at Vienna. Without waiting for the result of this action Russia mobilised against Austria . . . We have therefore informed Russia that, unless she were prepared to suspend within twelve hours the warlike measures against Germany and Austria, we should be obliged to mobilise, and this would mean war. We have asked France if she would remain neutral during a German-Russian war.'"' The telegram continued as from Georgie to Nicky, 'I cannot help thinking that some misunderstanding has produced this deadlock . . . I am most anxious not to miss any possibility of avoiding the terrible calamity which at present threatens the whole world. I therefore make a personal appeal to you, my dear Nicky, to remove the misapprehension which I feel must have occurred, and to leave still open grounds for negotiation and possible peace.'

For good measure the Kaiser sent his cousin the King a personal telegram along the same lines as the official one. It was received at

Buckingham Palace at 1.05 p.m. on 31 July and 'sent out for delivery' to the King at 1.06 p.m. 'Many thanks for kind telegram. Your proposals coincide with my ideas and with the statements I got this night from Vienna which I have had forwarded to London. I just received news from Chancellor that official notification has just reached him that this night Nicky has ordered the mobilisation of his whole army and Fleet. He has not even awaited the results of the mediation I am working at and left me without any news. I am off for Berlin to take measures for ensuring safety of my eastern frontiers where strong Russian troops are already posted. Willy.' Wilhelm had a meeting with Bethmann and General von Moltke, his Chief of General Staff, and at 1.45 they issued a notice that 'a threatening danger of war' existed, and sent the German Ambassador in St Petersburg instructions to inform the Tsar that unless the Russians stopped 'every war measure' against Austria and Germany within twelve hours, Germany would mobilise along her eastern border.

At some point during that day Sir Edward Grey went to Buckingham Palace to try to sort out further 'misapprehensions'. In the Royal Archives there is an undated draft of a telegram written by Grey, to be sent from the King to the Kaiser is an attempt to correct a wrong impression which the Germans, possibly deliberately, were harbouring. 'I think there must be some misunderstanding of a suggestion that passed in friendly conversation between Prince Lichnowsky and Sir Edward Grey this afternoon, when they were discussing how actual fighting between German and French armies might be avoided [the word 'prevented' is crossed out] while there is still a chance of some agreement between Austria and Russia. Sir Edward Grey will arrange to see Prince Lichnowsky early tomorrow morning to ascertain ['ascertain what he understood' is crossed out] whether there is a misunderstanding on his part.'

In any event, the Kaiser sent His Majesty the King another telegram from Berlin on 1 August at 7.05. It was received at Buckingham Palace at 7.14 and sent out for delivery to the King, who had already had his night interrupted by his Prime Minister, at 7.15. 'I just received the communication from your government offering French neutrality under guarantee of Great Britain added to this offer is the enquiry whether under these conditions Germany would refrain from attacking France. On technical grounds my mobilisation which had all ready been proclaimed this afternoon must proceed against two fronts

East & West as prepared. This cannot be countermanded because I am sorry the telegram of your Cabinet came so late,' wrote Willy unconvincingly. 'But if France offers me neutrality which must be guaranteed by the British Fleet and Army I shall of course refrain from attacking France and employ my troops elsewhere. I hope that France will not become nervous. The troops on my frontiers are in the act of being stopped by telegraph and telephone from crossing into France. Willy.' William evidently had decided to ignore the fact of Russia and France's long-standing alliance, not to mention the Entente Cordiale which his uncle Bertie had settled with France all those years ago. The French issued mobilisation orders at 15.55 hours, the Germans at 16.00 hours. At 19.00 hours Germany declared war on Russia.

'Saw Sir Edward Grey. Germany declared war on Russia at 7.30 this evening & German Ambassador left Petersburg,' wrote Georgie in his diary that evening. 'Whether we shall be dragged into it God only knows, but we shall not send Expeditionary Force of the Army now. France is begging us to come to their assistance. At this moment public opinion is dead against our joining in the war but I think it will be impossible to keep out of it as we can not allow France to be smashed.'

In St Petersburg Nicky wrote that same evening, 'After lunch I summoned Nikolasha [his uncle Grand Duke Nicholai] and informed him of his appointment as Commander-in-Chief until such time as I joined the army. Went for walk with the children. At 6.30 we went to church. On our return we learnt that Germany had declared war on us. Olga [his sister] Dmitri and Ioann [son of Kostia] were there for dinner. During the evening the English Ambassador Buchanan arrived with a telegram from Georgie. Spent a long time with him composing a reply.' He later told Maurice Paléologue, the French Ambassador, that as soon as Buchanan left he had gone to the Tsarina's bedroom and stayed with her until two o'clock in the morning, discussing everything with her. Then he went to have a bath, and was just getting in when a servant knocked on the door with a 'very important' telegram from Emperor William. 'I read the telegram, read it again and then repeated it aloud . . . but couldn't understand a word. What on earth does William mean, I thought, pretending that it still depends on me whether war is averted or not! He implores me not to let my troops cross the frontier! Have I suddenly gone mad? Didn't the Minister of the Court, my trusted Fredericks, at least six hours ago bring me the declaration of war the German Ambassador had just handed to Sazonov? I returned to the Tsarina's room and read her William's telegram. She had to read it herself to bring herself to believe it. She said to me immediately: "You're not going to answer it, are you?" "Certainly not!" '

The next day, 2 August, the Tsar signed the manifesto of the declaration of war in the Malachite Hall at the Winter Palace. After the manifesto was proclaimed and a Te Deum celebrated, the Tsar and Tsarina went out onto the balcony overlooking Alexander Square and, in the traditional gesture of devotion, the Tsar bowed his head to the multitude gathered below, at which they fell to their knees, singing the national hymn. Before leaving for St Petersburg that morning the Tsar had gone to kiss Alexei goodbye in his schoolroom. Alexei's tutor Pierre Gilliard remembered that 'he looked even worse than on the previous evening, and his eyes sparkled as if he had the fever. He told me he had just heard that the Germans had entered Luxembourg and attacked French custom houses before war was declared on France.' Bowing to his kneeling subjects, the Tsar was moved to tears. Now Russia was threatened, the people were fervently for war.

That day the telegram from Buchanan arrived at Buckingham Palace: 'At audience which I had with Emperor at 11 o'clock last night, His Majesty wrote following message which he desired me to telegraph to the King: Message begins: "I would gladly have accepted your proposals had not German Ambassador this afternoon presented a Note to my Government declaring war. Ever since presentation of the ultimatum at Belgrade, Russia has devoted all her efforts to finding some pacific solution of the question raised by Austria's action. Object of that action was to crush Servia and make her a vassal of Austria."' This would upset the balance of power, the message continued, and every proposal put forward had been rejected by Germany and Austria. Mediation by Germany was only offered once it was too late. Even then she offered nothing precise. The Tsar had been forced into first a partial and then a general mobilisation by Austria's declaration of war on Serbia, and secret military preparations being made by Germany. That he was right to do so was proved by Germany's sudden declaration of war, which was quite unexpected since he himself had given categorical assurances to the Emperor William that his troops would not move so long as negotiations continued. The message ended, 'In this solemn hour I wish to assure you once more that I have done all in my power to avert war. Now that it has been forced on me, I trust your country will not fail to support France and Russia in fighting to maintain balance of power in Europe. God bless and protect you. Signed Nicky.' Buchanan added: 'In course of conversation His Majesty observed that . . . German Emperor knew perfectly well that Russia wanted peace and that her mobilisation could not be completed for another fortnight at least, but he had declared war with such haste as to render all further discussion impossible and as to throw doubt on Germany's good faith throughout. German statement entirely misrepresents case and its evident object is to persuade His Majesty's Government that responsibility for war rests with Russia in the hope of inducing them to remain neutral.'

By 2 August the mood of the British people, fuelled by the press, was changing. A crowd of some six thousand had gathered outside Buckingham Palace by 10.30 that evening, cheering and singing. When the King and Queen appeared on the balcony, they were given a 'tremendous ovation'. But the Government was divided. Lord Esher, in contact with everyone as usual, summarised the situation in his journal on 3 August: 'There has been a difference of opinion in the Cabinet as to the action which should be taken by England. The question in dispute was the fulfilment of our moral engagements to France and Russia; France, very naturally, asked for an immediate decision; twelve members of the Cabinet were opposed to giving any definite assurance. This was the position up to Sunday night; nothing consequently was decided.' For Esher, the man who had always warned against Germany, the choice was clear. He found Asquith, Haldane and Lloyd George all wavering, though he astutely noted that 'Lloyd George's combative nature and combative instincts will keep him in office and lead him on from battlefield to battlefield. In his heart he hates the German temper, that is so unlike his, and he cares nothing for the Kultur that appeals to some of his colleagues.' One Cabinet member had resigned, and two more were threatening to do so.

But the people had made up their minds. When the King and Queen went for a drive in their Russian carriage the following morning there were large, cheering crowds all the way. 'We were forced to go & show ourselves on the balcony three different times, at 8.15, 9 & 9.45, tremendous cheering. Public opinion since Grey made his statement in the House today, that we should not allow Germany to pass through English Channel & that we should not allow her troops to pass through Belgium, has entirely changed public opinion [*sic*], & now everyone is for war & our helping our friends. Orders for mobilisation of the army will be issued at once.' Grey was not a waverer. 'If we run away from those obligations of honour and interest,' he told Parliament, 'I am quite sure that our moral position would be such as to have lost us all respect.'

The previous evening Lichnowsky had been instructed to inform the British Government that Germany was presenting Belgium with a twelve-hour ultimatum demanding the passage of German troops through her territory in order to invade France. Germany claimed to be forced to this because the French had mobilised their troops along the Belgian border, and fired across it. She promised however to vacate Belgium once the war was over, and compensate her for any damage. Belgium flatly refused, saying she would not 'sacrifice her honour as a nation and at the same time betray her duty to Europe'. The British Government sent Germany an ultimatum to withdraw her ultimatum. The Germans responded by declaring war on France.

'Fairly warm, showers & windy,' noted George V in his diary on 4 August. In the morning he worked with Stamfordham as usual. At lunchtime Churchill came to confirm that the Cabinet had sent Germany the ultimatum, to be answered by midnight. There was no reply. By the evening England was left with no choice. 'I held a Council at 10.45 to declare War with Germany, it is a terrible catastrophy [*sic*] but it is not our fault,' wrote Georgie, making it sound like a nursery quarrel among young cousins. 'An enormous crowd collected outside the Palace, we went on the balcony both before and after dinner. When they heard that War had been declared the excitement increased & it was a never to be forgotten sight when May and I with David [the Prince of Wales] went on to the balcony, the cheering was terrific. Please God it may soon be over & that he will protect dear Bertie's life [Georgie's second son, later George VI]. Bed at 12.' That night German troops crossed the frontier, and so began Belgium's fight for her honour, a fight which, led quietly but bravely by King Albert, lasted for the entire war and made of her one of the great but least-sung heroes of that 'terrible catastrophy'.

'In the morning we heard the good news: *England has declared war on Germany*, because the latter has attacked France and violated the neutrality of Luxembourg and Belgium in the most shameless way,' wrote Nicky in his diary. 'Received all morning and in the afternoon till 4 o'clock. My last interview was with Paléologue, who came to inform me officially of the rift between France and Germany. Went for walk with the children. The evening was free.' The next day Austria declared war on Russia. At 11.30 the Tsar held a meeting of the Council of Ministers. Alix's sister Ella came for luncheon, along with Kostia and his wife who, returning at the last minute from a trip to Germany, had had some difficulty crossing the frontier.

'I have received with much pleasure your kind telegram,' Georgie telegraphed Nicky on 4 August, warmly cementing the alliance between Russia and England, cousin to cousin. 'I perfectly understand and appreciate all that you say and the situation in which you were placed. You will doubtless have received reports of Sir E Grey's statement yesterday afternoon which states clearly the attitude of my country. I am sure you will read the speech with satisfaction . . . We both have serious and grave times before us and my earnest prayer is that both our countries may meet them with calm and with trust in Divine Providence, God bless and protect you, Georgie.'

In Germany Willy felt betrayed. His royal cousins Nicky and Georgie had plotted against him and embroiled them all in war. His years of peace-making had come to nothing. Now he was confronted with the nightmare of a war on two fronts. 'So many enemies!' his daughter Victoria Louise heard him repeat again and again. Disguising his frayed nerves in a series of bombastic speeches, he abandoned his English provenance once and for all, and thundered to the wildly cheering crowds: 'Remember you are a chosen people! The spirit of the Lord has descended upon me, because I am Emperor of the Germans! I am the instrument of the Most High! I am his Sword. His representative. Woe and death to all who resist my will!'

The Kaiser's troops, marching through Belgium, sang their famous *Hasslied*, the Song of Hate: 'A blow for a blow and a shot for a shot; We love them not, we hate them not; We have but one – and only one hate; We love as one, we hate as one; We have one foe and one alone: ENGLAND!' A *News Chronicle* reporter was in Brussels among the silent crowd, watching as the German troops came through. 'Between each line of song they took three steps. At times two thousand men were singing together in absolute rhythm and beat. When the melody gave way the silence was broken only by the stamp of iron-shod boots . . . For seven hours the army passed in such solid column that not once might a taxi-cab or trolley car pass through the city. Like a river of steel it flowed. Then came the cavalry, the guns, the wagons, the cook-stoves, the work horses, more bands, more men, all night long, for 26 hours.'

It is not the purpose of this book to chart the course of the First World War, so extensively and definitively charted elsewhere, but rather to consider the fate of the three royal cousins, Georgie, Willy and Nicky, and the extent to which, in the midst of war, they could still influence events. Or not, as the case may be. For Nicky and Georgie the same held good in time of war as in time of peace: Nicky, the Autocrat of All the Russias, influenced events a great deal; Georgie, the constitutional monarch, hardly at all. Willy, the All-Highest, joined Moltke at the German Headquarters, first in Coblenz, then in Luxemburg, and later still, as the troops advanced on Paris, at Charleville, where he remained for most of the war. By now the power he had held early in his reign was almost entirely dissipated. The humiliation of the Algeciras Conference, the débâcle of the *Daily Telegraph* Affair, the scandal of the Eulenburg trials and the Kaiser's own ambivalence and tendency to nervous collapse had soon led to him being effectively side-lined by his generals, his influence minimalised. He spent most of the war travelling in his Imperial train from one end of the Reich to the other, making his bombastic speeches, patting children in miniature Prussian uniforms or dirndls on the head, opening armament factories owned by his friend Krupp, or visiting the wounded in hospital. When the generals allowed him to the Front he inspected the trenches, pinned medals on war heroes and made more rousing speeches. Müller's diary, kept throughout the war, describes a Kaiser who made few effective decisions, and whose moods swung dramatically from high to low, from shocking blood-lust to abject fear and self-pity. German Wilhelm strutted about showing himself off to his people, most of whom believed in the fiction of the All-Highest almost to the last. English William hovered about feeling betrayed by his royal cousins, the only people in the world who really knew how it felt to be who they were.

'What terrible days we are living through,' Alix wrote to her mother-in-law Minny, who was in England, on 29 July. 'Every moment a telegram, a telephone – nobody knows what the next thing will be. You can only pray and pray that this nightmare will stop. Thank God we have England and France with us. And it also looks as if Denmark and Belgium have mobilised. But I continue to trust that God can and will help. For you who is so far away it must be very unpleasant. How does George see the whole thing? If only one could throw the whole thing in the Hague Conference, which is what they're there for. Sorry about such a short letter, but I'm not in the right frame of mind to write. It is important for me to use all my strength and all my calm to help my beloved Nicky. I send you greetings on your naming day. The parasol handle which we are giving you has been made at our own factory here. I have made a cover, as I don't think you have one. The others are well. Ever your loving child, Alix.'

Alix, half-German, half-English, was writing to her Danish mother-in-law as though they were both Russian – which of course, in a sense, they were. This dual and triple identity, normal for European royals, was manageable in peacetime, but deadly in times of war, as Alix herself was soon to discover.

The outbreak of war found many of the European royals in the wrong place. Heinrich was in England. Victoria, Alix's elder sister who had so pleased their grandmother by marrying handsome Louis Battenberg, was in Russia. Minny, the Dowager Tsarina, was in England with her sister Alexandra. All over Europe nannies and governesses, tutors and businessmen, diplomats and valets, husbands and wives raced for home. Victoria had a terrible journey through Germany, the country of her childhood, which was mad with war fever. Minny was just setting off with Alexandra for Sandringham when Count Benckendorff arrived to confirm that war was now inevitable, and that she must leave immediately.

The two sisters took a tearful leave of one another on 1 August. Minny got as far as Berlin in her Imperial train, which had been waiting for her at Calais, and found she could not proceed to the Russian frontier. She waited for hours, refusing to appeal to Wilhelm for help. The officials, usually so obsequious, were extremely rude. The Germans on the platform were loudly hostile. Her granddaughter Irina with her husband Felix Yusopov managed to reach Berlin and join the train, they too having been caught in the wrong place by the sudden outbreak of war. Various other Russians stranded in Berlin were also found a seat on board. Everyone drew the curtains of their carriages and waited. Finally two officials from the Ministry of Foreign Affairs turned up. The Dowager Tsarina was given the choice of returning to England or proceeding to Russia by way of Denmark,

Sweden and Finland, with the blinds down and all the carriages locked. She chose the latter. Once she was back in Russia Minny dedicated herself to the war effort, helping the inadequate Army Medical Services and the Red Cross Society to organise the evacuation of the wounded from the battlefields to the hospitals. Her daughter Olga was working in a large field hospital close to the eastern front, her son Misha, forgiven at last for his foolish marriage to a commoner, was fighting with a division of the Caucasian cavalry. 'You cannot imagine what a satisfaction it is for me,' she told the President of the Duma, 'after having been obliged to dissimulate my feelings for fifty years, to be able to tell the whole world how I hate the Germans.'

Gilliard, Alexei's tutor, decided not to leave St Petersburg for his native Switzerland but to remain with the Imperial family – as it turned out, almost to the last. He commiserated with the Tsarina, separated from her family both in England and in Germany, with the added horror of knowing that her brother Ernie was fighting on the other side. 'I myself have no news of my brother,' the Tsarina told Gilliard. 'Where is he? In Belgium or on the French front? I shiver to think that the Emperor William may avenge himself against me by sending him to the Russian front. He is quite capable of such monstrous behaviour! What a horrible war this is! What evil and suffering it means! What will become of Germany? What humiliation, what a downfall is in store for her? And all for the sins of the Hohenzollerns – their idiotic pride and insatiable ambition. Whatever has happened to the Germany of my childhood?'

She was right about the ultimate humiliation and downfall awaiting Germany, though it was very much longer in coming than anyone could have imagined. As Lloyd George, who took over from Asquith as Prime Minister in 1916 and led Britain to final victory, later put it: 'As a tribunal for ascertaining the rights and wrongs of a dispute, war is crude, uncertain and costly . . . And the cost is prohibitive.' Almost ten million died in the First World War, with twenty million maimed and mutilated, not to mention those emotionally scarred for life, the wives left without husbands and children without fathers. Of the five Great Powers, the Russians lost 1.7 million, the Germans 1.9 million, the British 1 million, the Austro-Hungarians 1 million, the French 1.5 million. The United States, entering the war at the last minute, nevertheless lost 116,000.

'I heartily congratulate you upon the splendid victory of your gallant troops at Lumberg,' telegraphed Georgie to Nicky on 4 September 1914 of Russia's early success in Galicia, when she got within 150 miles of Berlin. 'My thoughts are continually with you in our united struggle and am confident of our ultimate success. Love from May, Georgie.' On 21 September Nicky wrote back, via his Ambassador, 'I beg Count Benckendorff to assure His Majesty that whatever the difficulties and the losses to be suffered, Russia will pursue the fight against our adversary *to the very end.*' The difficulties and losses had already come, quickly reversing that early success. The Eastern front was a thousand miles long, from coast to coast. The Russian Army, as Peter Durnovo had predicted, was ill-prepared and ill-equipped. The Russian winters were punishing. The railway supply system, bringing food, clothing and armaments, was antiquated. The generals, led by Grand Duke Nicholai, were often incompetent. The Russian Navy had not yet recovered from the humiliations of the war with Japan only nine years earlier. The German counter-attack, led by the unbeatable team of generals Hindenburg and Ludendorff, annihilated the Russians first at Tannenberg and then at the Masurian Lakes. By December the Germans had advanced far enough into Russian Poland to capture the fortress of Lodz.

The Kaiser showered Hindenburg and Ludendorff with honours. He was not so pleased with General von Moltke on the Western front. Moltke had found the Belgian resistance unexpectedly fierce. Liège fell, but only after a fight to the death. Likewise the citadel of Namur, defended by French and British troops alongside the Belgians, which fell only after severe bombardment. Antwerp fell on 9 October, Ghent on 11 October and Lille the next day. Ypres remained, however, and, although it cost the lives of some eighty thousand men, held out for the rest of the war. But General von Moltke's gravest sin was to modify the Schlieffen Plan, devised in 1897 by General Count Alfred von Sclieffen, the then Chief of the General Staff, specifically to fight a war on two fronts, East and West, by means of a lightning attack on France via Belgium, swiftly followed by an attack on Russia. Speed was of the essence. 'Lunch in Paris, dinner in St Petersburg,' as the *Kriegsherr* Kaiser quipped. Moltke amended the plan to invade France – which rested on a two-pronged attack, one north to Calais, the other south to Paris – by deploying troops away from the northern to the southern attack, through the Marne, because he was worried by reports of massed Allied forces blocking the way to Paris. As a result, Paris was lost, and the Kaiser, recently so jubilant, was plunged into anger and nervous depression. Acting as Commander-in-Chief, he replaced Moltke with General von Falkenhayn, the Minister of War.

The Kaiser's one remaining power, to make appointments, he once again exercised on the most unreliable basis of purely personal preference. Falkenhayn had little real experience of war, but he looked the part. He was a tall, handsome man, with a fine military manner and great self-confidence – quite enough to impress the impressionable Kaiser. But Falkenhayn had no more success than Moltke, and in August 1916, as Romania entered the war on the Allied side, the Kaiser, disillusioned, replaced him with Hindenburg and Ludendorff, who remained as joint leaders till the end of the war.

The two generals immediately took an iron hold on all decision-making, removing from the Kaiser the last vestiges of his power. In the mornings he rode, read the newspapers, and lunched with his military entourage; in the afternoons he went for walks, visited places of local interest, and chopped wood. Occasionally he visited the front, when he bestowed medals, made rousing speeches, and inspected the troops. Occasionally he left Headquarters to hunt. Everyone was concerned to keep the Kaiser happy. Old friends like Schönburg-Waldenburg, who had known him since they were schoolboys, were hauled in to join his entourage and lighten his moods. Bad news was rarely passed on. As the war entered its second year, with no sign of victory for either side and stalemate in the trenches, Wilhelm grew increasingly prone to depression and nervous collapse. When news of some small advance on the Western front was reported, he became highly excitable. When he read the lists of the mounting casualties, he was often to be found in tears. Then only Dona, devoted as ever, could comfort him. But Dona was implacably for war, hating England more than ever.

Her comfort was needed when Italy, who had remained neutral in spite of the Triple Alliance, joined the war on the Allied side in April 1915. Jubilant Georgie sent Nicky a telegram via Sir George Buchanan: 'You will have heard that the signature took place today . . . I cannot sufficiently thank you for the great assistance which you have afforded in bringing these delicate negotiations to a successful issue.' It was a critical achievement, since where Italy joined others were expected to follow, but the Tsar, wanting to proceed more slowly, had not noticeably affected the decision. Some days earlier Buchanan had received a cipher telegram from the Foreign Office, marked URGENT and PRIVATE, again enclosing a message from Georgie to Nicky about the Italian negotiations then in progress, but with instructions not to pass on the King's message to the Tsar if he thought it 'at this moment likely to do harm.' In Britain it was the Foreign Office and the politicians who ran the war. Knowing that this was not the case in Russia, they trod with extreme care.

After the early victories, Russia was suffering a series of defeats. Highly successful German offensives resulted in the loss of Poland and Lithuania and a small part of the Ukraine. 'My dear Nicky,' wrote Georgie from the comfort and calm of Windsor Castle on 8 August 1915, 'I feel most deeply for you in the very anxious days through which you are now passing, when your army has been compelled to retire on account of the lack of ammunitions and rifles, in spite of the splendid and most gallant way [they] are fighting against our most powerful enemy . . . I can assure you that in England we are now straining every nerve to produce the required ammunition and guns and also rifles and are sending the troops of our new armies to the front as fast as we possibly can. England has made up her mind to *fight this awful war out to an end*, whatever our sacrifices may be, our very existence is at stake. I am so glad to see by your letter that Russia also means to *fight* to the end and I know France is of the same opinion. God bless you my dear Nicky, Ever your devoted cousin and friend, Georgie.'

That autumn Nicky, encouraged by Alix, made a critical decision. 'In this serious time my country is going through,' he telegraphed from the General Headquarters at Mogilev to Georgie at Windsor Castle, 'I decided to take over the leadership of my Armies in my own hands.' He put his faith in God and 'the combined efforts of the Allies', ending 'love to you and May, Nicky'. Alix had been warning Nicky about his uncle Nicholai for some time. 'Your being charms every single one, but I want you to hold them by your brain and experience,' she wrote in April to her very own Treasure, away at the front. 'Though Nikolasha is so highly placed, yet you are above him. The same thing shocked our Friend, as me too, that Nikolasha words his telegrams, answers to governors, etc., in your style – his ought to be more simple and humble and other things. You think me a meddlesome bore, but a woman feels and sees things sometimes clearer than my too humble sweetheart. Humility is God's greatest gift – but a Sovereign needs to show his will more often.' By May she was enjoining Nicky to 'be firm, Lovy mine, show your own mind, let others feel you know what you wish. Remember you are the Emperor . . . Nikolasha has absolutely no right to give orders without asking your permission first.'

By September 1915 the decision had been taken, and Nicky replaced his uncle Grand Duke Nicholai as Commander-in-Chief of the Imperial Army and the Fleet. He did so without listening to any of his ministers. 'The behaviour of some ministers continues to astonish me!' he wrote to his 'beloved dearest Sunny' from the General Headquarters at Mogilev. 'Well, so much the worse for them! They were afraid of shutting up the Duma – it has been done! I left for here and changed Nikolasha against their advice; the people have taken this step naturally and have understood – as ourselves. The proof – lots of telegrams I get from different parts and in most touching expressions. All this shows us clearly one thing – that the ministers living always in *town* know extremely little of what goes on in the whole country.' No one knew less about the real lives of the people in the whole country than the Tsar and Tsarina, breathing the rarefied air of Court life, but they had a mystical, almost religious, conviction that they and the people, the *narod*, the Russian peasant, shared one and the same soul.

Grand Duke Nicholai had not been especially competent, but at 6'2" and with an imposing manner, he had been a popular leader. Nicky, by contrast, was small and slight, with little 'presence' and no real military experience. But he was convinced that the morale of the troops, mostly illiterate peasants, would improve once they were led by their Tsar, whom they venerated. In the short term it seemed to work. Morale appeared to improve, and Nicky managed to effect some cooperation between the Ministry of War and the industrialists manufacturing arms, so that supplies reached the front more efficiently. General Alekseev, his Chief-of-Staff, was more competent than his predecessors. But in the long term it was a bad mistake. The Russian defeats which soon followed were now all blamed on the Tsar.

At Court, people noticed that the more the Tsar was at Mogilev, the more power at home was left in the Tsarina's hands. 'Will you not come to the assistance of your hubby now that he is absent?' Nicky wrote to Alix on 7 September 1915. 'I know of no more pleasant feeling than to be proud of you, as I have been all these past months, when you urged me on with untiring importunity, exhorting me to be firm and to stick to my own opinion.' Count Paul Benckendorff, Marshal of the Court in St Petersburg since 1904, watched in some alarm, writing to his brother Alexander, still Russian Ambassador in London, that the Tsarina's influence was 'at its peak', an influence born of 'a will of iron linked to not much brain and no knowledge'.

And behind Alix stood Rasputin. Alix's letters to Nicky are filled with references to their 'Friend', who not only watched over Alexei but advised them on politics and warned against enemies. 'Now the Duma is to come together in August, and our Friend begged you several times to do it as late as possible and not now, as they ought all to be working in their own place – and here they will try to mix in and speak about things that do not concern them,' Alix wrote in June 1915. 'Never forget that you are and must remain autocratic Emperor – we are not ready for a constitutional government.' Writing to Nicky on 15 September she reminded him: 'Remember to keep the Image in your hand again and several times to comb your hair with His comb before the sitting of the ministers.'

18

The End

~

'MY DEAREST GEORGIE,' wrote Nicky from General Headquarters on 24 January 1916, in his own hand, 'Let me thank you once more from the depth of my heart for the great honour you have bestowed upon me by appointing me a field marshal of your gallant army. It also gave the greatest satisfaction to my country and to my troops.' One of Britain's generals, General Callwell, had been sent to Russia for talks with the Tsar, and was able to bring the letter back personally. Nicky congratulated Georgie on 'the wonderful manner in which the allied troops left Gallipoly [sic]' and assured him that Russia had had some 'good success' in the Caucasus. He ended, 'I hope you will quickly recover from the results of your accident and not need the help of a stick any more. With my very best love to dear May and your children. I remain, my dear Georgie, ever your devoted cousin & friend, Nicky.' The 'N' of 'Nicky' had its usual flourish.

Georgie's accident had been unfortunate. Arriving at Hesdigneul on the Western Front in a motor-car at the end of October 1915 to inspect the troops, he had then mounted a well-trained and normally placid horse, used to the sounds of big guns and dying men. The horse promptly reared up, throwing the King to the ground. He cracked three ribs and fractured his pelvis, all in front of a cheering detachment of the Royal Flying Corps.

Acute pain then prevented the King visiting the front for some weeks, but by the end of the war he had been 450 times, personally conferring 50,000 awards for gallantry, and had visited, with Queen Mary, some three hundred hospitals and another three hundred munitions factories and shipyards. It was the job of a good constitutional monarch to encourage his troops and his people, and to work as tirelessly as they for victory, albeit without the dangers. Eschewing his cousin Wilhelm's bombastic language, he told his troops, 'I cannot share your hardships, but my heart is with you every hour of the day.'

His simple sincerity was clear for all to see. When he inspected his Indian troops he was worried about their living conditions, especially in winter, and spoke of the matter to Lord Kitchener, the Secretary of State for War, who appointed a Commissioner to look into it. Returning from a visit to the East End of London with Queen Mary, the King instructed Stamfordham to write to Downing Street about food shortages. 'This morning their Majesties in going to and from Deptford saw instances of these queues [for food] and it brings home to the King and Queen the hardship experienced by the poor, while the richer portion of the community do not suffer in this respect.'

Lloyd George, now Prime Minister and trying to think of ways of showing the public that the King and Queen shared their privations, suggested they cut down on luxuries at Buckingham Palace. The King and Queen needed no convincing but were only too pleased to comply. Heating and lighting were kept to a minimum, baths were only allowed a few inches of hot water, menus were limited, wine and spirits were cut out altogether. The napkin-ring was introduced to save on laundry. The King gave away his civilian clothes, his formal frock-coats and tall hats, his informal hand-made suits and black or grey bowlers, and spent the rest of the war in uniform, only occasionally appearing in tweeds and Homburg when he went shooting. He stopped all visits to the theatre, and rarely dined out. Balmoral was closed, and the gardens at Frogmore were given over to potatoes, which their Majesties helped to dig when they had the time.

Guests at Buckingham Palace were appalled. Courtiers were most put out. 'The King and Queen had decided to take the rations very seriously and at breakfast those who were late got nothing,' Frederick Ponsonby, an amused spectator, noted. 'When I say late, the ordinary meaning of the word hardly conveyed the wonderful punctuality of the King and Queen. One was late if the clock sounded when one was on the stairs, even in a small house like York Cottage.' One equerry, coming in late for breakfast, made the unfortunate mistake of ordering a boiled egg. 'If he had ordered a dozen turkeys he could not have made a bigger stir. The King accused him of being a slave to his inside, of unpatriotic behaviour, and even went so far as to hint that we should lose the war on account of his gluttony.' The traditional Derby Day dinner for thirty-two at Buckingham Palace consisted in 1917 of soup, fish, chicken and macaroni, without either red meat or wine. The President of the French Republic, at a dinner in the same year, served caviare, turbot, saddle of lamb, roast partridge and roast pheasant, salad, Neapolitan ice, strawberries, gâteau, grapes, peaches and pears.

George V's chief problem concerned not menus but nationality. As the list of casualties grew, so did the British hatred of all things German. German shops were looted. People bearing German names were attacked. Some were arrested and interned, some even imprisoned without trial. German spies were spotted everywhere. German wines were considered unpatriotic. Prince Louis of Battenberg, that favourite of Queen Victoria, was obliged to give up his job as First Sea Lord, hounded out by the populist press, though he had been in the Royal Navy since first coming to England from Germany to marry Princess Victoria in 1884. 'I feel for him deeply,' wrote George in his diary. 'There is no more loyal man in the country.'

The King's own position was by no means clear. His family name was Saxe-Coburg-Gotha. His wife was a Teck, and had a slight but distinct German accent. His cousin was the Kaiser. St George's Chapel at Windsor was filled with Garter banners belonging to his German relations, who also held honorary commands in various British regiments. 'It is but right and proper for you to have down those hateful German banners in our sacred Church,' wrote his mother, German-hating Alexandra, to Georgie from Sandringham, joining the public outcry. Reluctantly bowing to pressure, the King had the banners of all his German relations removed. Queen Alexandra wrote again, furiously complaining. She had only wanted 'those vile Prussian banners' taken away, not the rest, who were 'simply *soldiers* or *vassals* under that brutal German Emperor's orders.' She and her sister Minny were still fighting the Prussian-Danish war of 1864.

Luckily the King's Russian relations were allies. 'As Field Marshal of the British Army,' wrote Nicky from Headquarters on 16 July 1916, 'I beg you to accept and to transmit to your splendid troops my warm congratulations for the great success they have achieved in France. Best love to May. Nicky.' Ten days later Georgie wrote back from Buckingham Palace, 'My dearest Nicky, William's speech at Kiel about the great Naval victory of the German fleet [at Jutland] made me laugh. I am quite convinced that they lost more ships and more men than we did and we drove them back into their ports. I trust that this action will help your fleet in the Baltic. I am overjoyed at the splendid advance your gallant troops are making in Galicia and in your Western Provinces. It is wonderful the number of prisoners they have taken [300,000] and many guns and machine-guns. The advance of our troops and those of the French have been quite successful on the Somme so far, but our progress must be slow, between us we have taken over 21,000 prisoners and 100 guns. The Germans are very strong in front of us. Ever your most devoted cousin and true friend, Georgie.' Georgie's mother wrote to her sister Minny, 'Thank God we all are doing well in France just now.'

History put it differently. In February 1916 the Germans had begun their attack at Verdun and it lasted, unabated, until October. The Battle of the Somme, beginning on 1 July, has come to epitomise the hell of trench warfare, a mile or two of Flanders mud gained one week only to be lost the next; the villages of northern France flattened; 20,000 dead on the Allied side on the first day alone. Asquith's son Raymond had already been killed and was soon followed by John Bigge, Stamfordham's son. And the losses and setbacks were not confined to France. April saw the beginning of Ireland's unending civil war. In June Lord Kitchener was drowned at sea, on his way to Russia. The Battle of Jutland essentially ended in a stalemate.

The puzzle on the British side is how General Sir Douglas Haig, Commander-in-Chief of the British Army in France since December 1915, managed to outflank the Prime Minister, Lloyd George, who was passionately opposed to Haig's strategy of barrage trench warfare on the Western Front, so wasteful of men's lives. The answer lies, for once, with the King. As a constitutional monarch George V no longer had power, but he retained a great deal of influence. Just like his royal cousins, he deplored any political interference in military matters. War was to be conducted by the professional soldier. General Haig was a long-standing personal friend, married to a former Maid of Honour to Queen Alexandra, one of the charmed circle, and therefore to be trusted. 'Remember that it will always be a pleasure for me to help you in any way I can to carry out your heavy task and important responsibilities,' George V wrote to Haig on his appointment. 'I hope you will from time to time write to me quite freely and tell me how matters are progressing. Naturally I shall consider your letters in the strictest confidence.' This could have been written by any of the three royal cousins, convinced of their freedom to act in the political arena by the back stairs, without informing their ministers.

When Haig threatened to resign following the Calais Conference at which Lloyd George agreed to unity of command with the French without first consulting him, George V persuaded him to stay on. 'Such a step would never have His Majesty's consent,' wrote Stamfordham, expressing at the same time his own view. 'I am to say from His Majesty that you are not to worry: you may be certain that he will do his utmost to protect your interests.' And protect them he did. As the total of casualties grew to almost a million on the British side by the time of Passchendaele, Georgie wrote to May: 'I can't ever sufficiently express my deep gratitude to you darling May for the splendid way in which you are helping me during these terrible, strenuous & anxious times. Very often I feel in despair & if it wasn't for you I should break down.' But General Haig stayed on, backed by the King and the military establishment, and for the time being there was little Lloyd George could do about it.

'Information has reached me from more than one source', runs the draft telegram from the King to the Emperor of Russia dated 23 August 1916, written in Stamfordham's hand, 'that German agents in Russia have recently been making great efforts to sow division between your country and mine by exciting distrust and spreading false reports of the intentions of my Government.' The issue was, once again, Constantinople and the Straits. The agreement of March 1915, that Russia would gain Constantinople in the settlement at the end of the war, had in no sense been modified, assured Georgie. 'So do not allow your people to be misled by the evil workings of our enemies.' But by October Georgie was writing again, to explain that although the agreement stood, the timing of the announcement was something of a problem. 'I know you will also appreciate the necessity for regarding the sentiment of my eighty million Moslem subjects,' he wrote, as one Emperor to another. 'Therefore my Government would also prefer to wait until the final victory of the Allies is evident.' As to Germany trying to detach Russia from England: 'What nonsense. They little know you and your people if they think they can make a separate peace with Russia.' He was awarding Nicky the highest military order at his disposal, creating him a Knight Grand Cross of the Order of the Bath; Buchanan was deputed to hand over the insignia.

Six weeks later there was a distinct note of anxiety in the letter Georgie sent from cosy York Cottage on 6 January 1917, to be delivered to Nicky by the members of a British Government Mission travelling to Russia for urgent talks. There were worrying rumours that Russia might be forced to broker a peace with Germany, her situation having become so precarious. After two and a half years of war, with defeat following defeat, discontent among the troops on the Eastern Front was spreading to the cities back home, causing increasing social unrest. After the usual New Year wishes Georgie wrote: 'I know full well that you will keep your promise to me to fight to the end, as we are prepared to do, whatever difficulties may confront us & whatever sacrifices it may entail.'

The situation in Russia had developed as Peter Durnovo had predicted in February 1914. Although the war had started well enough with a series of victories over the Austrians and the country more unified than it had been for a long time, deterioration had soon set in. Military disasters exacerbated by a chronic shortage of munitions and supplies resulted in the troops at the Eastern Front becoming demoralised, the troops at home unwilling or unable to maintain law and order. Everywhere socialist slogans rallied the masses, and Russia was 'flung into helpless anarchy'. By 1916 the troops at the front, cold, hungry and ill-equipped, were surrendering in their thousands to the Germans.

Like Russia, Alix had started the war well. She helped tend the wounded in her hospital at Tsarskoe Selo, proudly wearing her nurse's uniform, and she toiled with her ladies-in-waiting, sewing amulets for the troops fighting at the front, convinced that each soldier would treasure a personal gift from the Tsarina as a kind of holy protection. Some may have been consoled, but what the troops, mostly illiterate peasants, really wanted was land reform, not pieces of handiwork, however sanctified by the wife of their venerated Tsar. As the war ground on and the list of casualties mounted, Alix became exhausted, both physically and emotionally. Her worst worry remained Alexei, the son and heir. By 1916, Nicky's sister Olga later noted, 'Alicky was indeed a sick woman. Her breath often came in quick, obviously painful gasps. I often saw her lips turn blue. Constant worry over Alexei had completely undermined her health.'

In St Petersburg all but the most reactionary Duma members were demanding reforms. The Progressive Bloc, consisting of some two-thirds of the members, wanted a strong Prime Minister who would have the power to take political decisions and exercise control over his ministers. Although the demands stopped well short of a complete reform of the constitution, Nicky, fiercely backed by Alix, rejected the requests. He remained convinced that the concessions he had made following the 1905 revolution had been a mistake, making the country less, not more, governable. As Tsar he had a God-given task, and he refused to bow to any Prime Minister, which might herald a parliamentary system. Maurice Paléologue, still French Ambassador in St Petersburg, noted on 15 October: 'The Empress is a stronger character than the Emperor, her will is more tenacious, her mind more active, her virtues more positive and her whole spirit more militant and regal. Her idea of saving Tsarism by bringing it back to the traditions of theocratic absolutism is madness, but the proud obstinacy she displays is not without an element of grandeur. The role she has assumed in affairs of state is disastrous, but she certainly plays it like a Tsarina.'

'You have fought this great fight for your country and throne – alone and with bravery and decision. Never have they seen such firmness in you before and it cannot remain without good fruit,' Alix wrote, congratulating Nicky on his rejection of the demands of the Progressive Bloc. 'What the struggle here really is and means – your showing your mastery, proving yourself the Autocrat without which Russia cannot exist. Had you given in now on these different questions, they would have dragged out yet more of you.'

Nicky and Alix liked prime ministers of the old school. 'While I am alive, I will fight for the inviolability of the Tsar's power,' stated Ivan Goremykin, Prime Minister from 1914 to 1916. He was followed in quick succession by three equally malleable men, the last the charming but aging Prince Golitsyn. No better were the ministers of Internal Affairs, one after another weak and ineffective, following the dismissal of the effective but reactionary Nicholas Maklakov in a half-hearted attempt to appease the Duma and an increasingly restive public. The influence of Rasputin could be detected in many of these appointments, including that of Alexander Protopopov in September 1916 as Vice President of the Duma. An industrialist but also a landowner and one-time Cavalry officer, he appeared eminently likely to satisfy a wide spectrum of the Duma and the population at large. He turned out to be a disaster. According to Peter Bark, still Minister of Finance, Protopopov only had one real talent: he was a fine talker. Action was another matter, and his political judgement was nil. 'In his reception room crowds of people gathered waiting the time for their meetings with him, which never took place, and urgent current business fell into a chaotic state.'

By November Nicky had reluctantly accepted that Protopopov would have to go. He wrote to tell Alix the news. Her reaction was extraordinary. 'Darling, remember that it does not lie in the man Protopopov or x,y,z, but it's the question of monarchy and yr prestige now, which must not be shattered in the time of the Duma.' She added: 'Don't think they will stop at him, but they will make all others leave who are devoted to you one by one – and then ourselves,' and exhorted him once again to be firm: 'The Tsar rules, not the Duma.' Then she travelled to Headquarters in person, and Nicky was persuaded to change his mind. Protopopov stayed on, disastrously, until 1917.

Had Nicky been able to make concessions to the Duma in the autumn of 1916 and accepted the necessity of sharing some power with an effective Prime Minister, his fate, which in retrospect seems so inevitable, might have been different. But it was impossible for Nicky, with his upbringing and temperament, to change. Nor could Alix, favourite grand-daughter of Queen Victoria whose empire extended across a quarter of the globe, and wife of the Tsar, ruler of an empire almost as vast. They could not, and would not, make concessions to a Duma. Had Alix been weaker, she might have been forced to give way. Had Nicky been stronger, he might have stood up to Alix and, being more intelligent, might have acted differently. As it was, in the winter of 1916 Russia plunged headlong into 'helpless anarchy'. And the Germans, aware of Russia's plight, now decided to allow Lenin, waiting in exile in Switzerland, to pass through Germany in a sealed carriage on his way to Russia. Chaos and revolution could only help Germany's cause, and should Lenin prevail, he was known to be an appeaser, and would swiftly take Russia out of the war.

'Bad news from Russia,' Georgie wrote in his diary on 13 March 1917. 'Practically a revolution has broken out in Petrograd & some of the Guards regiments have mutinied & killed their officers. This rising is against the Govt not against the war. Nicky is at Headquarters.' The following day he decorated seventy-five officers, received ten Indian officers, inspected six motor-ambulances, walked in the gardens of Buckingham Palace for some exercise, and relaxed in the evening arranging his stamp collection. On 19 March Stamfordham dictated a telegram to Sir John Hanbury Williams, their man in St Petersburg: 'Please give following message to Emperor from King: Begins: Events of last week have deeply distressed me. My thoughts are constantly with you and I shall always remain your true and devoted friend, as you know I have been in the past.' This was one 'royal colleague' speaking to another in the trade union of kings, assuring him of his support. It turned out to be a hollow promise.

Everyone had noticed how altered Nicky was by 1916, his cheeks sunken, his manner nervous and dispirited. 'He can't continue this way much longer,' Benckendorff told the Tsar's doctor. 'His Majesty is a changed man. It is very wrong of him to attempt the impossible. He is no longer seriously interested in anything. Of late, he has become quite apathetic. He goes through his daily routine like an automaton, paying more attention to the hour set for his meals or his walk in the garden, than to affairs of state. One can't rule an empire and command an army in the field in this manner. If he doesn't realise it in time, something catastrophic is bound to happen.' No doubt he wrote in much the same vein to his brother, the Russian Ambassador in London.

As the war went on with no end in sight, rumours began to circulate about the Tsarina's loyalty. She was a German spy, they whispered, with a direct line from her bedroom in the Alexander Palace at Tsarskoe Selo to German Headquarters. Fanciful and untrue as the rumours were, Alix became a scapegoat for Russia's anger and fear. The warring factions at Court now turned on Rasputin, whose power and influence had become too great. The *starets*, the man of the people, confirmed Nicky and Alix in their dangerous belief that the people of Russia, the peasants, loved and venerated their Tsar, and that as long as this was so, the monarchy was safe. 'Many attempts had been made, even by the Tsarina's greatest friends at Court, to open her eyes to the true character of Rasputin. They had all collapsed against the blind faith she had in him,' wrote Pierre Gilliard. Alix's sister Ella arrived from Moscow to make one last effort at persuasion. But each time the subject arose, Alix changed the conversation, and Ella, who had cared for Alix as a girl in Darmstadt when their mother died and had preceded her to Russia, failed like all the rest. At the end of her visit, Alix and her four daughters took Ella to the station. It was the last time the two sisters saw one another.

On 30 December 1916 Rasputin was murdered by a group of young aristocrats led by Felix Yusupov, the husband of Irina, daughter of Nicky's sister Xenia. 'I'll never forget what I felt when I saw the Tsarina again,' wrote Pierre Gilliard. He had been away at Headquarters, tutoring Alexei, whom Nicky liked to have with him from time to time, to show the troops the son and heir, in spite of the dangers to Alexei's health. 'Her agonised features betrayed, in spite of all her efforts, how terribly she was suffering. Her grief was inconsolable. Her idol had been shattered. He who alone could save her son had been slain. Now that he had gone, any misfortune, any catastrophe, was possible.' Maurice Paléologue, walking through the streets of St Petersburg, noticed that there was great rejoicing among the people at the news of Rasputin's death. People kissed one another, and many went to burn candles in the churches. In the unending queues of women waiting in the snow outside butchers' and grocers' shops for their meagre rations of meat, tea and sugar, there was only one topic of conversation.

Nicky returned briefly to Tsarskoe Selo from the front for the burial. 'At 9 o'clock the whole Family went out past the photography building and right into the field, where we witnessed a sad spectacle,' he wrote in his diary on 3 January 1917, 'the coffin with the body of unforgettable Grigory, who was killed by some scum on the night of December 17 [30 December] at Yusupov's house, which had already been lowered into the grave.' In England Queen Alexandra wrote to Georgie: 'The wretched Russian monk caused a tremendous sensation in the world but is only regretted by poor dear Alicky who might have ruined the whole future of Russia through his influence. I am sure she thinks herself like their Empress Catherine.'

On 17 February 1917 Nicky wrote to Georgie, making use of the fact that he could entrust the letter to Lord Milner, the leader of the British Mission, who was returning home. He confided in his cousin that he was worried by the weak state of the Russian railways. They could hardly afford to repair the worn-out engines and carriages – a particularly acute problem in winter, when the rivers and canals were frozen over. 'But I never lose courage,' he reassured Georgie. 'We shall go on with this awful war to the end. Alix and I send May and your children our fond love.'

But by the beginning of March, as Georgie noted, there was nothing but bad news from Russia. Mutiny spread rapidly from the Russian Navy to the troops on the Eastern Front. Thousands abandoned their posts and made their way back to Russia, joining the workers, students and revolutionaries demonstrating in the streets, each trade union marching under its own banner, calling for drastic reforms and the abdication of the Tsar. In the cities food was scarce.

Raging inflation meant that prices were rising fast ahead of wages. In St Petersburg, shops were looted and the factories went on strike. As social unrest gave way to active revolt, Protopopov proved himself powerless to contain it. On 11 March police ordered troops to fire into the demonstrators, killing some and wounding many more. But afterwards one regiment after another mutinied. A total collapse of law and order followed. Revolutionaries, sailors, soldiers, students and workers careered round the streets in stolen trucks, firing rifles stolen from armaments factories into the air. Storming the jails, they released hundreds of political prisoners. Protopopov was finally forced to resign. Nicky, still at Headquarters, decided to return to St Petersburg, believing that his presence would help contain the situation.

'Went over to MH [Marlborough House] and had a talk with Motherdear about Russia and Nicky. She is very much upset about it all,' wrote Georgie in his diary. Five days later, Grand Duke Michel, Sandro's brother, came to visit, '& I told him all about the revolution in Petrograd, he was much upset, I fear Alicky is the cause of it all & Nicky has been weak.' After Michel left, Georgie worked with Stamfordham. 'Heard from Buchanan that the Duma has forced Nicky to sign his abdication & Misha had been appointed Regent, & after he has been 23 years Emperor. I am in despair.'

On Saturday Georgie held an investiture, decorating 130 officers and nurses. Uncle Arthur came for a walk in the palace gardens, 'lovely spring day 52°, the buds are just beginning to show now.' In the evening he again worked with Stamfordham. On Sunday Louis and Victoria Battenberg came to tea, and they talked about the situation in Russia. It was hard to know exactly what was happening. But by the following Saturday it was clear, with no room left for doubt. 'Michel came to see me & we discussed the idea of poor Nicky coming to England,' wrote Georgie. 'Walked in the garden with May, fine & bright but cold.'

At first Nicky had strongly resisted abdication, but when even his generals advised it, he finally acquiesced, agreeing to abdicate in favour of Alexei, determined to uphold the principle of autocracy by passing it on to his son and heir. But once doctors confirmed that Alexei's haemophilia could never be cured, contradicting Rasputin who had promised that the heir would be well by the age of thirteen, Nicky bowed to the inevitable and agreed to his brother Mikhail taking over instead. 'During these decisive days for the life of Russia,

WE consider it a duty of conscience to facilitate OUR people's close unity and the rallying of all popular forces in order to achieve victory as soon as possible, and, in agreement with the State Duma, WE consider it to be for the good to abdicate from the Throne of the Russian State and to surrender supreme power,' decreed the Manifesto signed by the Tsar on 15 March from the town of Pskov, which he had by now reached on his journey home. 'Not wishing to part with OUR beloved son, WE name as our successor OUR Brother, OUR Grand Duke Mikhail Aleksandrovich, and bless his assumption to the Throne of the Russian State. We entrust OUR Brother to conduct state affairs in complete and unshakeable unity with the representatives of the people in the legislative institutions, according to principles they will determine . . .' The Duma delegates insisted he add 'and on this to take an inviolable oath'.

'The essence is that in the name of saving Russia and maintaining calm in the army at the front it is necessary to take this step. I agreed,' wrote Nicky in his diary. 'At 1 in the morning I left Pskov with a heavy heart from suffering over this. All around me is treachery, cowardice, and deceit!' By 21 March he had reached Mogilev, where he signed his farewell statement to the Army and took leave of his Headquarters staff. His mother arrived to be with him in this awful hour, joining him for lunch in the dining car of the train and staying till 4.30, after which Nicky left. Stopping and starting all the way, passing staring crowds on railway stations, some shouting insults, the train of the abdicated Tsar of All the Russias, now plain Nicholas Romanov, travelled slowly on to Tsarskoe Selo. 'Beloved, Soul of my Soul, my own wee one,' Alix wrote to Nicky on 16 March, not knowing whether the letter would ever reach him, 'Ah, how my heart bleeds for you – madning [sic] knowing absolutely nothing except the vilest *rumours* which drive one wild.' It was a long letter filled with passion, capital letters and underlinings, ending, 'You have saved yr son's reign & the country & yr saintly purity & you will be crowned by God on this earth in yr country. I hold you tight, tight in my arms & will never let them touch your shining Soul, I kiss, kiss, kiss & bless you & always understand you. Wifey.' On the same day the Petrograd Soviet had passed a resolution to arrest the Romanov dynasty, the arrest to be carried out jointly by the Provisional Government and the Soviet of Workers' Deputies. The resolution included Mikhail, who was however only to remain under surveillance.

In Germany the Kaiser was strangely unmoved at the news, coolly calling Nicky's abdication 'an irony of world history'. His own take on the event was that Nicky's overthrow had been masterminded by the perfidious British, who feared cousin Nicky was about to make peace with Germany. Sublimely blind to his country's own dramas, he told Chancellor Bethmann to be on the lookout: Britain would try to use the Russian revolution to stir up similar revolutionary sentiments in Germany.

Early in 1917 Willy was on one of his highs, ready to take on the world. But as Rudolf von Valentini, his Chief of Civil Cabinet from 1908 to 1918, noted, the Kaiser's moods could change dramatically, often from day to day. When things were going badly, as when Romania joined the war on the Allied side, he was quickly depressed, collapsing completely, saying the war was lost and there was nothing left but to broker a peace. But on 9 January 1917 he was in a mood of high optimism. The occasion was a meeting at Pless, the German Headquarters on the Eastern Front, chaired by the Kaiser and attended by Hindenburg, Ludendorff and Bethmann, plus Müller, von Lyncker and Valentini, the Chiefs of the Kaiser's three Cabinets, Naval, Military and Civil. It was occasioned by the Allies' refusal to negotiate a peace which the United States had offered to broker at Germany's request following the great losses on the Somme and at Verdun. Such a peace, the Kaiser grandly pointed out, was a moral act. 'Such an act is the province of a ruler, who has a conscience and feels himself responsible to God, who has a heart for his own people and those of the enemy, and the will to free the world from its suffering. I have the courage for this and I will risk it for God's sake.' The trouble was that the Allies were not keen on the idea of a 'peace without victory' for either side, a peace in which Germany insisted on a return to the pre-war status quo plus indemnities for the losses of war, freedom of the seas, and increases in German colonial territories. Moreover France, still bitter from 1871, had no intention of leaving Alsace-Lorraine in German hands.

Wilhelm now felt morally superior, his efforts at peace having been rejected by a vengeful enemy. Thus vindicated, he felt free to pursue all-out war, which was the purpose of the meeting at Pless. Now he finally agreed to unrestricted submarine warfare, which Tirpitz, recently retired but still highly influential, had been urging for months. Bethmann and Valentini were reluctant, fearing, correctly as it turned out, that this would bring the United States into the war. Wilhelm, who had until his moment of moral triumph agreed with Bethmann, now signed the decree to unleash unrestricted submarine warfare, secretly planned for 1 February. He told Müller that if it came to war with the United States, 'so much the better'. Müller went up to the room where Bethmann and Valentini were consoling themselves with a glass of champagne. He found Bethmann very pessimistic, saying the Kaiser had done untold harm to himself and the Hohenzollern dynasty. Valentini agreed. On 3 February America broke off diplomatic relations with Germany.

Over the next few weeks the Kaiser's optimism waxed and waned. On 1 April a strike broke out in the shipyards at Kiel. Müller noted that Bethmann was again 'extremely pessimistic about affairs at home and in particular because much barley and rye has not survived the winter. The Russian Revolution has had a great effect on the masses.' Clearly Bethmann did not share the Kaiser's view that Britain was behind the social unrest in Germany. The masses had sufficient reasons of their own. The troops at the front were war-weary and disillusioned. The workers in the cities were close to starvation, with the bread ration reduced once again and prices soaring. The coal shortage was becoming acute. The situation was not improved by the public's perception that the luxurious standards maintained by the Kaiser and his Court were hardly distinguishable from those of peacetime, added Müller, increasingly disillusioned himself. The Kaiser made a concession by drawing up a proclamation on electoral, though not constitutional, reform. The Kaiserin was not pleased, stating, 'Only the military can deal with democrats.' On 6 April the United States declared war on Germany. The Kaiser went into a decline.

'Nicholas II is in my hands,' announced Aleksander Kerensky in a speech to the Moscow Soviet on 20 March. Kerensky, a lawyer and Socialist Revolutionary, was now the Minister of Justice in the Provisional Government. 'And I'll tell you, comrades: the Russian Revolution happened bloodlessly, and I will not allow anything to overshadow this. I will never be the Marat of the Russian Revolution. But in the shortest time possible, under my personal supervision, Nicholas II will be taken to the harbour and will leave from there for England by ship.' Kerensky later explained that he wanted 'this man' to see that the revolution was magnanimous, even to its enemies.

'I wished that for once in his life he should feel ashamed of the horrors that had been perpetrated in his name.' In its few months of power the Provisional Government freed thousands of political prisoners, proclaimed freedom of speech, the press and assembly, and the right to strike. It abolished flogging, exile to Siberia and the death penalty, and prepared for universal and secret elections. It welcomed thousands of exiles home, including Lenin.

'Made it to Tsarskoe Selo quickly and safely at 11.30. But, God, what a difference, guards are on the street and inside the park surrounding the palace,' wrote Nicky in his diary on 22 March. 'Went upstairs and there saw my darling Alix and the dear children.' The Imperial family was under house arrest behind the locked doors of the Alexander Palace. There were no telephones, and all letters were opened by the palace commandant. The family was only allowed a small area of the palace gardens for exercise. When Nicky first arrived the guards pretended not to know who he was. Loyal Count Benckendorff was there to greet him.

Over the next four months, until their removal for their own safety to Tobolsk in Siberia on 13 August, a monotonous routine was established at Tsarskoe Selo. 'The days followed one another, all alike, divided between lessons and walks,' wrote Pierre Gilliard, who remained with the family almost to the end. In the mornings there were lessons, Nicky and Alix taking turns as teachers with Gilliard and Sydney Gibbes, Alexei's English tutor, who also chose to remain with the family. In the afternoons they walked in the section of the palace park allotted them, taking exercise by chopping down trees or clearing snow or working in a small kitchen garden, always watched over by guards who were often deliberately disrespectful and slovenly in dress and manner. Crowds gathered at the palace railings gaping in fascination at the ex-Imperial family, sometimes politely, often not. In the evenings Alix embroidered while Nicky read aloud. One week it was *The Count of Monte Cristo*, another it was Conan Doyle's *A Study in Scarlet*. Nicky also began to sort through his papers. On 5 April he wrote in his diary, 'I looked through my books and things, and started to put aside everything that I want to take with me, if we have to go to England.' On 21 April he noted: 'Quietly celebrated the 23rd anniversary of our engagement!' Coburg, Queen Victoria, Willy, and Alix's long prevarications about her religion . . . only Nicky's exclamation mark reveals how far away they all now seemed.

Sir George Buchanan, still in St Petersburg, reported to his Government that he had been approached by Pavel Milyukov, Foreign Minister of the Provisional Government, about the Imperial family's asylum in England. Milyukov was 'most anxious to get the Emperor out of Russia as soon as possible, the extremists having excited opinion against His Majesty.' The British Government, led by Lloyd George, was not in principle against such asylum, though they wondered whether Denmark or Switzerland might not be equally possible destinations. As Lloyd George put it, 'a virtuous and well-meaning Sovereign became directly responsible for a regime drenched in corruption, indolence, debauchery, favouritism, jealousy, sycophancy, idolatry, incompetence and treachery – an accumulation of all those vices that make for utter misgovernment and inevitably end in anarchy.' The Sovereign became 'directly responsible' because there was no parliamentary system, along British lines, to direct him or protect him.

Lloyd George invited Stamfordham to Downing Street on 22 March to discuss the matter. It was generally agreed that they could not refuse the request, but Stamfordham wondered how the Tsar and his family would support themselves in exile. It turned out to be not the only matter which worried Stamfordham and the King. A week later Balfour, the Foreign Secretary, received a letter from Stamfordham. 'The King has been thinking much about the Government's proposal that the Emperor Nicholas and his family should come to England. As you are doubtless aware, the King has a strong personal friendship for the Emperor and therefore would be glad to do anything to help him in this crisis. But His Majesty cannot help doubting not only on account of the dangers of the voyage, but on general grounds of expediency, whether it is advisable that the Imperial Family should take up their residency in this country. The King would be glad if you would consult the Prime Minister, as His Majesty understands that no definite decision has yet been come to on the subject by the Russian Government.'

'General grounds of expediency' referred to some protest among certain sections of the public about the residence in Britain of an autocrat like the Tsar. The radical paper *Justice* had published an article condemning the Tsar and all he stood for. On 31 March there had been a rally in the Albert Hall to celebrate the fall of the Autocrat. On 21 April H.G. Wells, moving the debate closer to home, had written a letter to *The Times* declaring it was time for Britain to rid herself of

'the ancient trappings of throne and sceptre.' Elsewhere he referred to
'an alien and uninspiring Court', to which the King retorted, 'I may
be uninspiring, but I'm d—d if I'm alien.' The Socialists were gaining
wide support among the working classes, weary both of war and of
extreme social inequality. The King, strongly influenced by Stamfordham, was frightened for his throne.

Balfour replied that he did not think it was possible for the
Government to withdraw the invitation, which had already been sent.
'Every day the King is becoming more concerned about the question
of the Emperor and Empress of Russia coming to this country,'
Stamfordham countered from Windsor Castle on 6 April. 'His
Majesty receives letters from people in all classes of life, known or
unknown to him, saying how much the matter is being discussed, not
only in Clubs but by working men, and the Labour members in the
House of Commons are expressing adverse opinions to the proposal.
As you know from the first the King has thought the presence of the
Imperial Family (especially of the Empress) in this country would raise
all sorts of difficulties, and I feel sure that you appreciate how awkward
it will be for our Royal Family who are closely connected both with
the Emperor and the Empress. You probably also are aware that the
subject has become more or less public property, and that people are
either assuming that it has been initiated by the King, or deprecating
the very unfair position in which His Majesty will be placed if this
arrangement is carried out. The King desires me to ask you whether
after consulting the Prime Minister, Sir George Buchanan should not
be communicated with with a view to approaching the Russian
Government to make some other plan for the future residence of their
Imperial majesties? Yours very truly, Stamfordham.'

He wrote again that evening, in even more forceful terms. Four
days later he went to Downing Street to persuade Lloyd George. Then
he went back to Balfour. Finally Balfour drafted a telegram to
Buchanan, setting out both sides of the argument, to which Buchanan
replied, on 13 April, that he entirely shared the view that 'if there is
any danger of anti-monarchist movement, it would be far better that
the ex-Emperor should not come to England.' He wondered whether
France was a possibility. And so the deed was done, the British
Government finally agreeing because, after all, they stood in solidarity with the aims of the Russian revolution, and the King and
Stamfordham because there was nothing more important to either of

them than the preservation of the monarchy. Fond as cousin Georgie was of cousin Nicky, his own throne came first. France or Switzerland appeared to be an ideal solution.

But who should take the blame, especially once events in Russia had overtaken the decisions made in Britain? Stamfordham was clear. He wished the Government to take the blame, not the monarchy. And for sixty-five years, until Kenneth Rose published his biography of George V in 1983, the public remained under the impression that it was indeed Lloyd George and his Government who were responsible for the fateful decision. Lloyd George, honourably, did not disabuse them, not even in his Memoirs published in 1934. That secret, as Rose says, was well kept. But one remained: Stamfordham, who had dedicated his life to protecting the monarchy, never rested easy. Some time before he died in 1931 he took the trouble of retrieving his 6 April letter to Balfour from the archives to add, at the bottom and in his own hand, in a deliberate distortion of the truth, 'Most people appear to think the invitation was initiated by the King whereas it was *His Govt* who did so,' signed, 'S'.

'A marvellous day; took a walk with pleasure,' wrote Nicky in his diary on 10 August at Tsarskoe Selo, sounding relieved, as some observed he was, that he no longer bore the responsibility of government. 'After breakfast, we found out from Count Benkendorff that we are to be sent, not to Crimea, but to one of the faraway provincial towns three or four days' journey to the east! But where exactly they don't say – even the commandant doesn't know. We were still counting on a long stay at Livadia! Chopped down and sawed up a large fir by the path at the forest clearing. A short, warm rain fell.' Three days later, at dawn and in a sealed train of the International Wagons-Lits Company, the Imperial family left Tsarskoe Selo, never to return. With them went thirty-nine courtiers, retainers and servants and three hundred guards. The sleeper cars were comfortable and the dining car offered a 'very tasty cuisine', as Nicky noted with his usual relish for food. They were bound, in a nice touch of irony, for Tobolsk in Siberia, the place of Rasputin's birth. For the last part of the journey they sailed pleasantly down the Tobol River in two steamers. Life for the Imperial family appeared to be improving. But appearances can be deceiving. Russia's economy had not improved under the Provisional Government, nor had conditions at the front. By July the Bolshevik party, led by Lenin, were preparing to seize power.

Life in the Governor's mansion at Tobolsk was not uncomfortable. 'Don't forget that this is the former Emperor,' Kerensky, now Minister-President, told Yevgeny Kobylinsky, the head of the guard. 'Neither he nor his family should experience any deprivation.' Although there was a surrounding fence and guards at every entrance, the Tsar and his family were allowed a certain freedom of movement. They could sit in the sun on the balcony, Alix doing her knitting or embroidery, watching the people go by. They could walk in the garden. They were allowed to write letters – Nicky wrote quite regularly to his mother and his sister Xenia, who were at Livadia, keeping away as much as possible from the troubles besetting Russia. They were even permitted to attend some services at the local church. Their suite, including Gilliard and Gibbes, who were housed next door, were allowed to go freely to the town.

On 1 September Vasily Pankratov, sent by Kerensky, arrived to take charge of the Tsar and his family at Toblosk. Pankratov was the son of peasants, with an impressive record of revolutionary activity, including many years of exile in Siberia. He meant to carry out his task nobly, with honesty and decency. Gilliard described him as 'the typical enlightened fanatic'. His deputy Aleksandr Nikolsky was, by contrast, rude, rough and resentful. On 25 October the Bolsheviks seized power. By March 1918 Russia had brokered a peace with Germany at Brest-Litovsk, Lenin and the Bolsheviks aiming to conquer Germany by revolution rather than by war. The fates of Poland, Finland, the Baltic provinces of Lithuania, Latvia and Estonia, and southern Russia were all in Germany's hands. When the possibility of the Baltic becoming independent was discussed, the Kaiser, high as a kite and sublimely detached from reality, announced: 'Nonsense! *I* will be its ruler and will tolerate no resistance. I have *conquered* it and no lawyer is going to take it away from me.' Within nine months the All-Highest was plain Wilhelm Hohenzollern, living in exile in Holland.

At Tobolsk the effect of the Bolshevik revolution was soon felt. Some of the soldiers guarding the Imperial family became more defiant towards their captives, acting, as Nicky put it, 'like hooligans'; the loyal few were sent back to Tsarskoe Selo and replaced by 'a pack of blackguardly-looking young men'. Ten servants were dismissed, and the family's diet was reduced to soldiers' rations, with no butter or coffee. In early 1918 an internal struggle for the control of the Imperial family broke out between the Regional Soviet of

Western Siberia and that of the Urals, based at Ekaterinburg. There were fears of a counter-revolution, and it was considered that the Tsar had been treated with too much leniency. In April orders came from Moscow, now the capital of Russia, that the Imperial family be transferred to Ekaterinburg. Vasily Yakovlev, a keen servant of the revolution, arrived in April from Moscow to oversee the operation. On the long journey to Ekaterinburg Yakovlev had time to form his own opinion of the former Tsar and Tsarina. He was struck by the 'phenomenal narrow-mindedness' of Nicholas Romanov. Alexandra Romanov was quite different: 'She is very wily and proud. She has a strong influence on her husband. The entire trip she kept completely to herself and for whole days did not come out of her compartment. She did not want to accept even a shadow of a favour from us.'

At Ekaterinburg there were no comforts. A fence fourteen feet high had been erected round the house so that no one could see in or out. A chain of sentries policed it day and night. The Imperial family lived in four rooms, a bedroom, a dining room, a bathroom, and what Nicky described in his diary on 30 April as 'a spacious hall with an arch and no doors'. Throughout, these diary entries reveal no self-pity, and he does not complain. Yevgeny Botkin, their doctor, Chemodurvo, Nicky's valet, and Ivan Sednyov, a family servant, who had all devotedly decided to stay with the family to the last, slept in the hall. Everyone else, including Gibbes and Gilliard, had been separated from the family during the transfer to Ekaterinburg. The house, wrote Nicky, was 'nice and clean'. There was a small garden where they were allowed to sit, under heavy guard, for an hour at a time. In the evenings Nicky read to them, or they played bezique. The weather was marvellous throughout. 'The aroma from all the gardens in town is amazing,' Nicky noted, with the sensibility of an exile. They had virtually no news from the outside, learning everything by rumour. On 13 June Botkin heard that they might be being transferred to Moscow, for fear of the actions of some local anarchists; the next day this was proved to be untrue. On 27 June it was Maria's nineteenth birthday; a week earlier Anastasia had turned seventeen, and Tatiana twenty-one a week before that.

On 4 July their new Commandant made a list of all the gold objects in the Imperial family's possession – rings, bracelets, necklaces – which he proceeded to remove. Some things had already been stolen.

But the next day everything was returned by the Commandant, and locked away in a sealed box. Some new guards arrived, who were Latvians. There was a series of thunderstorms during the hot summer days and nights. On 13 July Alexei took his first bath since Tobolsk, where he had injured his knee, but he still could not straighten it. 'The weather is warm and pleasant,' added Nicky. 'We have no news from the outside.' By now Nicky's diary entries were becoming sporadic.

Alix maintained her diary to the last. On 16 July she wrote, in English as usual, 'Grey morning, later lovely sunshine. Baby has a slight cold. All went out half hour in the morning. Olga & I arranged our medicines [code for jewellery]. T[atiana] read *Spiritual Readings 3*.' In the afternoon Alix did her tatting. They had supper at eight. Then she played bezique with Nicky. They went to bed at 10.30.

At 2 a.m. Lenin in Moscow received a telegram from the Ural Regional Soviet: 'In view of the enemy's proximity to Ekaterinburg and the exposure by the Extraordinary Commission of a serious White Russian plot with the goal of abducting the former tsar and his family. The documents are in our hands. Nicholas Romanov was shot on the night of the sixteenth of July by decree of the Presidium of the Ural Regional Soviet. His family have been evacuated to a safe place.' A day later another telegram stated that in fact 'the entire family suffered the same fate as its head'. Nicky, Alix and the five children, together with Botkin and Sednyov, had been woken from their beds in the middle of the night, herded down into the cellar, and shot. When their bodies were stripped for burial, eighteen pounds of diamonds and jewellery were found sewn into their clothing and underwear.

'Held an investiture,' wrote Georgie in his diary at Buckingham Palace on 25 July, at which he decorated 292 officers and nurses. 'At 12.0 May and I attended a Service at the Russian Church in Welbeck Street in memory of dear Nicky who I fear was shot last month by the Bolshevists, we can get no details, it was a foul murder. I was devoted to Nicky, who was the kindest of men, a thorough gentleman, loved his country and his people.' George V had been advised not to attend the service, for fear of inflaming revolutionary sentiments. But this advice he ignored, it being the least he could do for Nicky, his cousin and friend since childhood. By 28 July his information was more accurate. 'Heard from Lockhart (our Agent at Moscow) that dear Nicky was shot by the local Soviet (Bolshevists) at Ekaterinburg on night of July 16th in view of approaching danger of

his capture by Czecs [*sic*]. It was nothing more than a brutal murder.'
By August 31 it was confirmed. 'I hear from Russia that there is every
probability that Alicky and 4 daughters and little boy were murdered
at the same time as Nicky. It is too horrible & shows what fiends these
Bolshevists are. For poor Alicky perhaps it was best so. But those poor
innocent children!' For decent George, it was the fiendish Bolshevists
who were solely responsible. His own small portion of blame appears
not to have crossed his mind.

Willy in Germany could feel a certain moral superiority. When negotiations for the Tsar and his family's asylum in Britain were still taking
place, he had let it be known that he would personally guarantee the
Russian Imperial family's safe passage through Germany. Royal
colleagues were royal colleagues, war or no war. In this moment when
the Tsar faced the worst crime of all, a threat to his crown by an unholy
alliance of revolutionaries and socialists, the Kaiser's judgement was
not clouded by thoughts for the safety of his own throne. With no
advisers like Stamfordham, and effectively cut off from the true state
of affairs at home, Willy grandly offered Nicky something which was
not his to offer: safe passage through a country worn out by war and
seething with social discontent and incipient revolution.

Wilhelm's own nemesis was fast approaching. Since the Russian
revolution, demands for constitutional reform in Imperial Germany
were growing increasingly insistent, as were calls for the Prussian
dominance established by Bismarck over forty years earlier to cease.
The troops and the people, exhausted and demoralised by unending
war, were becoming disillusioned with their Kaiser. 'In the Navy a
certain anxiety is felt with regard to international Socialist activities in
the Fleet and minor mutinies,' noted Müller in his diary on 6 August
1917. Bethmann had been ousted by Hindenburg and Ludendorff for
insisting that a compromise with the Catholic Centre and the
Socialists in the Reichstag was necessary. 'The Reichstag can do what
it likes,' the Kaiser announced grandly, through, as Müller put it, rose-
coloured spectacles. 'I have the nation and the army behind me.' By
the autumn the early success of the Hindenburg Line, designed to
hold back the Allied offensive, was faltering. Unrestricted submarine
warfare, so effective during the summer, was also failing to strike the
final blow, the Allies having developed a successful convoy system to
defend their ships. For those who cared to see it, the end was in sight.

In England George V was having troubles of his own, albeit on a smaller scale. Those family names – Saxe-Coburg-Gotha, Teck and Battenberg – had become an insurmountable embarrassment. Lloyd George advised a change of name, but was no better than anyone else at coming up with a solution. Someone suggested Guelf, someone else Wettin, both ancient family names meaning absolutely nothing to the people of Britain. It was Stamfordham who came up with Windsor, an inspired choice. Though it had no genuine connection to the royal house, being the name of a place and a castle, it immediately struck a chord with the public, who quickly took it to their hearts. The Kaiser, hearing the news, quipped that he would be delighted to attend that well-known operetta, *The Merry Wives of Saxe-Coburg-Gotha*. The Tecks became Cambridge while the Battenbergs, opting for a literal translation, became Mountbattens. All over Britain Schmidts, Brauns and Schwartzes became Smiths, Browns and Blacks.

In January 1918 the Allies declared their conditions for a peace settlement, as summarised in President Woodrow Wilson's Fourteen Points. These included the restitution of all conquered territories, including Alsace-Lorraine, the dissolution of the Hapsburg Empire, and the abdication of the Kaiser in favour of a democratic system. 'There will be no peace conference whatsoever,' declared the Kaiser, way out of touch, in response to a suggestion by Queen Wilhelmina of the Netherlands. 'Our enemies have no desire to do so. We must fight on until we have brought them to their knees and then dictate peace to them.' For his pessimistic attitude to the war, Valentini, Chief of the Civil Cabinet, had already been dismissed from the post he had held since 1906. Later General von Lyncker, Chief of the Military Cabinet, who had lost his two sons in the war, was also dismissed. 'We were all taken today to visit the front to see 40 English guns which had been shelled to pieces in a forest path near Peronne,' wrote Müller on 27 March. 'The trip was particularly interesting on account of the picture we got of the appalling devastation in the zone of Hindenburg's retreat last year. Towns and villages razed, all the fruit trees smashed and miles of shell holes and barbed wire entanglements.' Two days earlier the Kaiser had returned from another visit saying that members of Parliament should be taken there to see what war was actually like. 'This remark was followed by the usual abuse levelled at the Reichstag, that monkey house,' noted Müller wearily.

The following day the Kaiser returned from the front in high spirits, and everyone drank champagne. 'His Majesty declared that if an English delegation came to sue for peace it must kneel before the German standard, for it was a question here of a victory of the monarchy over democracy.'

'I am grateful for your prayers,' wrote Georgie to his mother on 2 June, 'they are a comfort to me & will help me to get through all these anxious days & I fear more lie ahead of us. But we must be courageous & go on to the end, however long it may take, as I shall never submit to those brutal Germans & I am sure the British Nation is of the same opinion.' With casualties approaching one million, not the wounded and the maimed, the British nation was not as steadfast as George V cared to think.

In July Hindenburg and Ludendorff launched their final assault across the Marne, aiming for Paris. But the Allies resisted fiercely, launching a mighty tank attack at Amiens, and driving the German troops back across the Somme. 'At lunch in the train the Kaiser admitted that he had not closed an eye all night,' wrote Müller on 25 July. 'He had seen visions of all the English and Russian relatives and all the ministers and generals of his own reign marching past and mocking him.' On 8 August Hindenburg and Ludendorff informed the Kaiser that the war was lost: it was not simply that the tank battle had definitively proved the Allies' superiority, but their own troops, exhausted and demoralised, could no longer be relied upon to fight.

At their headquarters at Spa in Belgium the two generals and the Kaiser discussed peace negotiations. But on what terms? The Hapsburg Emperor Karl, who had succeeded on the death of Franz Joseph in 1916, wanted to make peace at once, to protect the two monarchies. The Kaiser dismissed this out of hand, then promptly left in the Imperial train for Wilhelmshohe, his favourite palace from student days at Cassel. Here he remained for three weeks, taking trips, walking, riding, and spending time with Dona who, deeply depressed by recent events, had suffered a minor heart attack. In early September, as the reality of defeat finally penetrated the never-never-land encouraged by his entourage, Wilhelm himself suffered a nervous collapse.

By September the Bulgarians had made peace with the Allies, mutinies were threatening at the Naval base at Kiel, and strikes had broken out in the cities. All-out revolution threatened. On 29 September the Kaiser, his nervous crisis over for the time being, had returned to Spa, and now discussed with his latest Chancellor, von Hertling, and Paul von Hintze, his Secretary of State at the Foreign Office, what should be done. Hindenburg and Ludendorff argued that an armistice should be concluded without delay, and peace negotiated along the lines of Wilson's Fourteen Points. Hintze argued for urgent constitutional reform. Hertling, the stolid conservative, disagreed. Neither he nor the Kaiser could even contemplate a parliamentary system. But the Kaiser was finally persuaded by Hintze to begin peace negotiations without delay. Hertling promptly offered his resignation, which the Kaiser accepted with reluctance on 30 September.

Everything was falling apart. The Kaiser broke down in tears, writing to the Kaiserin, still at Wilhelmshohe, 'God has not permitted us to achieve the aim for which we hoped but rather has elected for us the way of suffering and misery.' In times of desperation all three royal cousins tended to turn to God, whose representatives on earth they were. 'I will continue to do my duty towards Him and my Fatherland. so long as he allows me to,' he added, with great fortitude. With fortitude he accepted that Prince Maximilian von Baden, who endorsed the Peace Resolution and promised to introduce democratic reforms, should become the new Chancellor. And with fortitude he agreed that a member of the Social Democratic Party should be part of the new Government. He refused, however, to accept that 'impudent lout' Wilson's terms as regards himself. They were 'unadulterated Bolshevism, a declaration of war against the monarchical principle.' But from now on the power of the Kaiser, and of the German military, was on the wane.

On 30 October Germany's ally Turkey capitulated, and on 4 November Austria signed an armistice. 'Now we stand alone against the entire world!' the Kaiser told Sigurd von Ilsemann, a tall, handsome young officer who had recently been appointed his ADC. 'We have had to endure this war in order not to leave Austria in the lurch, and she has done so to us!' The Kaiser had been to Berlin, and now returned to Spa in the fanciful belief that the presence of their Kaiser would improve the morale of his troops. He never saw Berlin again.

'Rain in the morning,' wrote Georgie at Buckingham Palace on 8 November. 'This morning the German Delegates came in under the white flag & were received by Foch and Rosy Wemyss & the terms of the armistice read to them, they were given 72 hours to refuse or accept them. Apparently revolutions are breaking out at many places in Germany.' A week earlier the Prussian Minister of the Interior, Wilhelm Drews, had arrived at Spa, sent urgently by Max von Baden, to persuade the Kaiser to abdicate. The Kaiser informed Drews that he had no intention of doing so to meet the demands of several hundred Jews and several thousand Socialist workers. Then, like his cousin Nicky, he went back to his preferred work, chopping wood, confident in the knowledge that his troops, ordered back to Berlin from the front and led by himself, would soon have the Jews and the Socialists under control. Later Max von Baden telephoned the Kaiser. The Socialists in the Reichstag were insisting that he abdicate immediately, he told him. Revolution was spreading rapidly in the cities, and if civil authority did not prevail there would be a military dictatorship, with which the Allies would refuse to negotiate. But the Kaiser still refused to renounce his God-given crown.

That day the Kaiser summoned his son, Crown Prince Wilhelm, from his regiment on the Western Front to the Villa Fraineuse, just outside Spa. As the Crown Prince's car jolted through fields of mud it passed 'columns of weary soldiers and troops and groups of men who had once been soldiers and who, now disbanded, trudged their way laden with a medley of odds and ends; it left behind it curses and cries and fists raised in the grey mist.' When he arrived at the villa the following day the Crown Prince found his father in the garden surrounded by a group of officers. 'Never will I forget the picture of that half-score of men in their grey uniforms,' he wrote. 'The Kaiser was passionately excited, and addressing himself to those near him with violently expressive gestures . . . Catching sight of me, my father beckoned me to approach and, himself, came forward a few paces. And now, as I stood opposite him, I saw clearly how distraught were his features – how his emaciated and sallow face twitched and trembled.'

Hindenburg had summoned thirty-nine officers to Spa from various sections of the front and asked them if the Kaiser could count on his troops to fight for him in a civil war. The answer was 'no'. The Kaiser was so informed at a conference hastily convened that morning, and at the same time told that full-scale revolution had broken out in Berlin. Later that morning news came that Berlin was 'flowing with blood': the Kaiser must abdicate instantly, or the troops would desert. One of the few still urging the Kaiser not to abdicate was Count August zu Eulenburg, Wilhelm's devoted Marshal of the Court and Philipp zu Eulenburg's cousin, who had served the Kaiser since 1890 and now revealed himself as the rabid monarchist he had always been. The Crown Prince found the temporary solution: his father could abdicate as Kaiser, but remain as King of Prussia. Now, finally, Kaiser Wilhelm, the All-Highest, gave in. He was ready to abdicate if it would prevent civil war breaking out, he stated, still believing he had some say in the matter; and, as King of Prussia, he would lead his troops home. On this basis he agreed to sign the document, and they all repaired to luncheon. 'That silent meal, in a bright, white room whose table was decked with flowers but surrounded only by bitter anguish and despairing grief, is among the most horrible of my rec-ollections,' wrote the Crown Prince. An hour earlier Max von Baden had handed over the Government to the leader of the Social Democrats, agreeing that the Kaiser would abdicate both crowns.

At five that afternoon Hindenburg came to tell the Kaiser that he was in danger of capture by approaching revolutionaries, and that he must leave immediately for Holland, fifty kilometres away. The Imperial train was prepared, but the Kaiser refused to go. Willy, brought up to rule from the day he was born, could not adjust to this new self. He spent the rest of the afternoon burning his personal papers. In the evening, finally beginning to accept the reality of his situation, he boarded the train, still insisting that he meant to stay with his troops, his officers, those 'kind nice young men' of the regiments where, as a young man himself, he had felt properly happy for the first time in his life, finding there 'my family, my friends, my interests, everything I had previously missed'.

He dined with his entourage, then retired to his sleeping car for a sleepless night. The train left for Holland at 5 the following morning, twenty-five soldiers with machine-guns and grenades guarding the ex-Kaiser's carriage. Not far down the line they were forced to trans-fer to a fleet of automobiles, revolutionaries having blocked the route. Once safely across the border the Kaiser lit a cigarette, and urged his entourage to do the same, saying 'You've deserved it.' When Friedrich Rosen, an old acquaintance, now the German Minister in Holland, arrived several hours later, Wilhelm told him, 'I am a broken man. How can I start again in life? There is no hope left for me and nothing remains for me save despair!'

'We got the news that the German Emperor had abdicated, also the Crown Prince,' wrote Georgie on the same day, 9 November, as though he had never met them in his life. '"How are the mighty fallen." He has been Emperor just over 30 years, he did great things for his country but his ambition was so great that he wished to dominate the world & created his military machine for that object. No man can dominate the world . . . it has been tried before, & now he has utterly ruined his country & himself & I look upon him as the greatest criminal known for having plunged the world into this ghastly war which has lasted over 4 years & 3 months with all its misery.'

Epilogue

~

'WILLIAM ARRIVED in Holland yesterday,' noted Georgie factually in his diary on 11 November 1918. 'Today has indeed been a wonderful day, the greatest in the history of this Country. At dawn the Canadians took Mons which was the place where we first came in contact with the Germans over 4 years ago & from where the retreat began. At 5 this morning the armistice was signed by Foch, Wemyss & the German delegates, & hostilities ceased at 11.'

For Georgie, called again and again onto the balcony of Buckingham Palace by the wildly cheering crowd massed below, waving and singing the National Anthem, it might well have been the greatest day in the history of his country. Britain had triumphed through the long years of attrition, and her monarchy, alone of the major monarchies which ruled Europe before the war, had emerged not only intact but thriving. The King and Queen had never been more popular, all connections to their Russian and German cousins forgiven and forgotten. Nicky was dead, Willy was in exile. Only Georgie, the English royal cousin, stood before his subjects, saluting, in uniform, flanked by his wife and David, his son and heir, accepting their homage. Lloyd George, the true hero of the hour, who had led the country through to the end of the war, hovered in the background. On the sceptred isle, the Republican movement was well and truly dead.

The first thing Wilhelm did when he arrived at Count Bentinck's estate at Amerongen, his destination in Holland, was to ask for 'a cup of real good English tea'. Dona was able to join him at the end of the month, permitted to leave Germany by the new Government. They expected any day to be extradited, and wrote to tell their children that they would never give themselves over into the hands of the enemy. Dona was already seriously ill. The Crown Prince, who had abdicated his right to the throne, was exiled to the small, remote island of

Wieringen, off the coast of Holland, with 'no human sound or sign', only the sea. Prince Joachim, his younger brother, had committed suicide. Another brother, August Wilhelm, was getting divorced. Victoria Louise, the Kaiser's only daughter and favourite child, was permitted to live on quietly in Germany with her husband and children. Prince Heinrich was also permitted to remain in Germany, and went to visit his brother Willy from time to time. Outside the gates of Amerongen Castle a handful of monarchists usually gathered, hoping to catch a glimpse of the German ex-Kaiser on his daily walk, when he liked to feed the ducks, or in his garden, chopping wood. The rest of the Dutch population wanted him gone. His cousin Georgie, with another eighteen years of his reign to be triumphantly lived out before his death in 1936, never saw, spoke or wrote to him again.

Inside the castle Wilhelm filled the long hours and days of exile writing his memoirs. 'My earliest memory, which I can still remember clearly to this day, is of Osborne, on the Isle of Wight,' he began. He wrote at his old desk, which had been sent over from Potsdam, along with his chair in the shape of a saddle. For years he battled for the restitution of his personal fortune and possessions, with considerable success. In due course a large part of the fortune as well as more than 1,500 pieces of table silver, 118 oriental rugs and numerous paintings and pieces of furniture arrived in Holland. It did not stop Wilhelm railing against the Socialists and Bolsheviks, and blaming all his misfortunes on the 'Jewish rabble'. When in 1919 two-thirds of the German people voted for the Weimar 'pig's republic', Wilhelm felt personally betrayed. As Eulenburg had advised Bülow all those years ago, the Kaiser took everything personally.

Willy and Dona were never extradited, but moved to nearby Doorn in May 1920, along with a handful of faithful retainers, including handsome Sigurd von Ilsemann and devoted Countess von Keller, one of the Hallelujah Aunts who had been with the Kaiserin since the day of her marriage. August zu Eulenburg had finally left his Kaiser and returned to Berlin. His cousin Philipp, Willy's best friend, who had shared his soul and instigated the Kaiser's fateful Personal Rule, remained at Liebenberg, shunned by almost all his old friends. Bülow had started to write his memoirs. On his days off at Doorn, Ilsemann began to read them. 'I have now almost finished reading the second volume of the Bülow memoirs,' he wrote in his diary, 'and am struck over and over again by how little the Kaiser has changed since those times. Almost everything that occurred then still happens now, the only difference being that his actions, which then had grave significance and practical consequences, now do no damage. The many good qualities, too, of this strange, peculiar person, of the Kaiser's so very complicated character, are repeatedly stressed by Bülow.' Strange and peculiar was the Kaiser's liking for P. G. Wodehouse, whose books he read at length to his small and baffled entourage in the evenings.

Dona died in April 1921. Her last wish was to be taken back to Germany, and this the new Government sanctioned, allowing her to be buried in the royal mausoleum at Potsdam. Willy accompanied the body to the Dutch frontier, but could go no further. 'My loneliness was indescribable,' he wrote. On 5 November 1922 he remarried. The bride was a minor royal and arch-monarchist, Princess Hermine von Schönaich-Carolath. The marriage began in a state of high romance for Wilhelm but soon degenerated into a relationship filled with friction, for the bride was tough and ambitious, and the couple had very little in common. They agreed on one matter, however: the restitution of the Kaiser's crown, which became Wilhelm's daily preoccupation and obsession. By the time of his death on 4 June 1941, Hitler had come to power and the Second World War had, like some malign twin, followed the First. Wilhelm, the All-Highest, was buried in Holland, not Germany, because he refused to be buried in a country which was not a monarchy. His coffin was covered with the Imperial Ensign. The family arrived from Germany in a special train and Heinrich Himmler's private car. Hitler sent a Nazi-sized wreath of lilies and lilies-of-the-valley. Willy was at rest at last.

After the war Georgie, safe and sound in England, applied himself to helping as many of his remaining Russian relations as possible to escape from a country engulfed in revolution. As well as cousin Nicky and his family, many grand dukes and duchesses had already been murdered, mostly at Alapaevsk in the Urals, where they had been held in prison. Grand Duke Mikhail had been killed, apparently trying to escape. Worst was the fate of Ella, Alix's sister, who had arrived in Russia as a young girl of eighteen to marry Grand Duke Sergei. Having no children, after her husband was murdered she took the veil and founded her own Order of Martha and Mary in Moscow. When the Kaiser offered her safe passage back to Germany in 1917 she refused, not wishing to accept any favours from her German cousin, preferring to stay in her adopted Russia, the country she loved. By

July 1918 she was being held at Alapaevsk with the rest. Xenia's cousin the Grand Duchess Maria Pavlovna, who had escaped to Odessa, wrote in August to Xenia, safe on her estate at Ai Todor in the Crimea with her mother the Dowager Tsarina, offering some information amounting to no more than rumour: 'With them [at Alapaevsk] was Aunt Ella . . . where she is now I absolutely don't know, but all the others disappeared without news.' 'All the others' included Xenia's brothers-in-law, Sandro's three brothers, Sergei, Nicholai, and Georgei, who so many years ago, when they were young, had been accused by Grand Duke Sergei of having Republican sympathies. Ella, it later transpired, had been thrown down an abandoned, half-flooded mine shaft and left to die.

Xenia and her mother waited meanwhile in the Crimea, hoping cousin Georgie could send a gunboat to rescue them. Minny had last seen her son Nicky at General Headquarters at Mogilev in March 1917, after he had signed the Manifesto of his abdication. Responding to his telegram, she had arrived in her Imperial train, accompanied by Sandro, Xenia's husband. 'Nicky's motor-car drew up to the station a minute later', recalled Sandro. 'He walked slowly along the platform, said good morning to the two Cossacks standing at the entrance to his mother's carriage, and went inside. He was pale, but nothing otherwise disclosed his authorship of the horrible manifesto. He remained closeted with the old Empress for two hours. She never told me of the subject of their conversation.' At some point Nicky told his mother he was prepared to go to England, but he preferred to stay in Russia. 'Quarter to four. His train is stationed opposite ours. We get up. He covers his mother's face with kisses. He turns to me and we embrace. He goes out, crosses the platform, and enters his salon car.' They never saw each other again.

Early in April 1919 the Dreadnought *Marlborough* arrived at Yalta, sent by George V to carry the Dowager Tsarina and Xenia and her family out of Russia to England. By now the Red Army was closing in on the Crimea and Minny, who had so far resisted leaving her adopted country, finally accepted that there was no other solution. The Captain of the *Marlborough*, Charles Johnson, arrived with a letter from her sister Alexandra, begging her to leave while there was still time. But Minny refused to go without all her retainers, as well as scores of refugees who had gathered in the desperate hope of escape. Xenia was busy packing her jewels and a 54-piece set of solid gold plate. Sandro was already in Paris, hoping to get some help from the

International community for the many Russian émigrés. The Dowager Tsarina, Xenia and her children arrived at the embarkation jetty carrying their dogs, and their pet canary. Nineteen members of the Imperial family boarded in all, together with their maids, servants, governesses and Court officials, as well as some of the refugees.

George V insisted the party be received with full honours when they docked at Portsmouth on 9 May 1919, after a long journey by way of Constantinople and Malta. Alexandra, waiting at the dockside, was piped aboard, and the two Danish princesses were reunited at last. Together they took the royal train to Victoria station, where Georgie and May awaited them with other members of the British royal family. 'The Dowager Empress Marie of Russia arrives in London today,' announced the Court Circular, 'accompanied by her daughter the Grand Duchess Xenia. The Dowager Empress will go to Marlborough House, while the Grand Duchess and her sons will stay, for the time at least, at Buckingham Palace.' They arrived virtually penniless, and homeless. No doubt remembering his devoted cousin and friend Nicky, Georgie settled an annuity of £10,000 on his aunt the Dowager Tsarina and £2,400 on Xenia, and offered her Frogmore Cottage, a grace-and-favour residence, as her home. He also paid small pensions to the Russian suite and the servants.

'I happened to be in London in November 1919 when the Dowager Empress of Russia's things arrived from Russia,' recalled Frederick Ponsonby. Fifteen huge packing-cases had arrived at Buckingham Palace and were taken up to the Throne Room to be opened, at his insistence, before witnesses who could swear that the seals had not been broken since they left Russia. 'The first one, about four feet high and eight feet long, contained nothing but pokers, shovels and tongs of the commonest description,' he related, with some amusement at the antics of the Bolsheviks. The second contained nothing but harnesses and saddlery, the third a pile of old Russian railway guides . . . and so on to the last packing-case, where 'nothing but worthless trash was found.'

To what extent, then, could Georgie, Willy and Nicky, the King, the Kaiser and the Tsar, be said to have contributed to the events which overtook Europe between 1914 and 1918? Did they themselves, through their own characters and personalities, and through their relationships to one another, bear some responsibility and guilt?

As far as personalities go, Georgie was in no position to make a serious difference, but Nicky and Willy must bear some personal responsibility. 'It was his misfortune to have been born an autocrat, when he was by nature so unfitted for that role,' wrote Buchanan, the British Ambassador, with some sympathy. 'The whole system was out of joint, and he, poor Emperor, was certainly not born to set it right.' In fact Nicky, vacillating on every point except his own autocracy, made many fatal mistakes, not least appointing himself Commander-in-Chief of the Army in the middle of the war.

In Germany it was a similar story. Ilsemann, reading Bülow's memoirs at Doorn, put it nicely: the Kaiser was essentially the same person at Doorn as he had been at Potsdam. The difference was that at Doorn he could 'do no damage', while at Potsdam he could do plenty. 'If Germany had not opted for war in 1914, there would have been no war, because Austria-Hungary would certainly not have dared to risk a war without Germany's support,' concludes John Röhl in his detailed study of the Kaiser and his Court. Nor would Russia, still suffering from the Russo-Japanese war and a constant threat of revolution. Nor would England, having nothing to gain.

Röhl lists at least four moments when things might have been different, all connected to Wilhelm: in 1888, had Kaiser Friedrich, Willy's liberal father, not died prematurely; in 1890, if Bismarck had managed to prevail over the malign influence of Willy's entourage; and again in 1896, if Friedrich von Holstein had managed to persuade Chancellor Hohenlohe to stand firm against the 'personal rule' which Eulenburg and Bülow were busy instigating. The best chance of all, and the last, was in November 1908, after the *Daily Telegraph* affair and during the Eulenburg–Harden trials, when the Reichstag might finally have managed to force through some real constitutional reform. But Bülow himself was compromised by the trials and preferred to do a deal, behind the scenes, and with the usual result: things went on as before.

Could Willy's English and Russian relations have made a difference? 'Certainly the King at one time believed that the Kaiser might, at an earlier stage, have averted disaster,' wrote John Gore in his personal memoir of George V. 'In after years he sometimes, without bitterness, traced the stages of the Kaiser's attitude to England, from admiration to envy, from envy to hatred. He thought him a man of ability with a fatal irresolution in moments of crisis.' This was shrewd of Georgie, who was not rich in insights. But it rather leaves out the part played by the other two cousins, and their families, in Willy's development from admiration to hatred.

Willy's love–hate for England, fostered during his complicated childhood, was perhaps an unavoidable factor. Yet it could have been handled differently. The ease with which Queen Victoria and Edward VII were able to gain Willy's love and even gratitude when it suited them suggests that diplomatic and political solutions might have been found long before the military solution became the only option. As Holstein wrote to Eulenburg as late as 15 October 1895: 'Whatever happens, His Majesty will never give up his grandmother and Cowes week. In these two, Osborne and Cowes, lie the main problem in our politics.' Perhaps it was a small chance, given the Anglophobe belligerence of Willy's entourage, both civil and military. But Bismarck's constitution gave the Kaiser autocratic power, so the chance existed. Instead, Willy was snubbed by his English relations, again and again and often with relish, feeding his paranoia and playing right into the hands of the Anglophobes. The Entente Cordiale, instigated by Edward VII, gave political expression to this family animus, leaving Willy in a state of injured fury, complaining that he had once again been treated as a '*quantité négligeable*'.

His Russian relations were little better. Tsar Alexander III, strongly influenced by his wife Minny, the Danish princess, disliked and distrusted the Prussians, but most especially Willy. It was Alexander III's personal achievement to conclude the secret defensive alliance with France just before he died in 1894, an alliance which eventually flowered into the Triple Entente with England, thus encircling Germany. As for cousin Nicky, although he flirted with Germany at the beginning of his reign, he never liked Willy personally. Sergei Witte soon found that the best way to persuade the Tsar of a particular action was to tell him the Kaiser wanted the opposite. On 11 March 1905, at the time of the Russo-Japanese peace negotiations, Willy wrote to Bülow: 'It is monstrous that we, who have loyally stood by the Tsar with "Counsel", should again be excluded now.' Always excluded, always the odd one out. Willy was in no doubt about who was doing the excluding: it was the Danish princesses and Edward VII at work again. Nicky became England's ally, and Willy's paranoia took another leap.

Once Georgie came to the throne, things might have improved. But by then the friendship between Georgie and Nicky, nurtured through the years by their mothers, was well established, and they did not include Willy in 'the Club'. It was anyway too late. By 1910 the clock was already set for the countdown to war.

Notes

Manuscript Sources

RA: the Royal Archives at Windsor Castle, for the letters of the three royal cousins to one another, as well as for George V's diaries

GARF: the State Archive of the Russian Federation

BA: the Bundesarchiv at Koblenz

Secondary Sources

These are cited in full, with author and title, on first mention, in abbreviated form thereafter: thus, Christopher Hibbert, *Queen Victoria in her Letters and Journals* becomes 'Hibbert' followed by the page number.

INTRODUCTION

1 **'curious to see a real King'**: BFI archive film of 1913 Berlin wedding

1 **'We reached Berlin at 11.30'**: RA GV/GVD1913:21 May. 'Schloss' was how the royal cousins referred to the Kaiser's palaces, in this case the Neues Palais (New Palace) at Potsdam, just outside Berlin. In all, the Kaiser had seventeen palaces large and small, but the two main ones were both in Berlin.

1 **'May and I have accepted'**: RA PS/GV/M 481

2 **'I'll go if you go'**: Maurice Paléologue, *Guillaume ll et Nicolas II*, 155

2 **'However, if the dear child'**: Christopher Hibbert, *Queen Victoria in her letter and journals*, 189

3 **'What a strange spectacle'**: Andrew Roberts, *Salisbury, Victorian Titan*, 643

CHAPTER 1: WILLY'S BAD START

6 **'My precious darling'**: Hibbert, 109

6 **'I am so thankful'**: Sir Frederick Ponsonby, ed., *Letters of the Empress Frederick*, 20

6 **'I am shocked'**: Roger Fulford, ed., *Dearest Child*, 178

6 **'Quite between ourselves'** Lamar Cecil, *Wilhelm II*, Vol. I, *Prince and Emperor*, 12

7 **'I must write down at once'**: Cecil Woodham Smith, *Queen Victoria*, Vol. 1, 363

8 **'Whatever may be the usual practice'**: Ponsonby, *Letters*, 8

8 **'My Beloved Papa'**: *Fulford*, 31

9 **'She shivered from head to foot'**: Anonymous, *Recollections of Three Kaisers*, 49. The anonymous writer of these recollections served all three Kaisers, Wilhelm I, Frederick III and Wilhelm II, in succession, arriving at Court from his village on the Rhine aged seventeen, and remaining in a lowly position from which he was able to observe much. 'I do not think I shall add anything more to my diary – that true companion of my life from early boyhood,' he wrote shortly before he died in 1914. 'The peace that surrounds me seems, as I write, to extend throughout the world. God grant it may continue!'

9 **'You ask me in your letter'**: Ponsonby, *Letters*, 10

9 **'She certainly was a little tyrant'**: Cecil, Vol. I, 11

10 **'Promise me faithfully dear'**: Fulford, 106

10 **'What you say of the pride'**: Ibid., 115

10 **'Medical science was not as advanced'**: Wilhelm II, *Aus Meinem Leben*, 31. The Kaiser's memoirs, written from exile in Holland after the First World War, have been translated in to English in 2 volumes: *My early Life* and *My Memoirs*. For this book I have used my own translations of the original German version. The early years are described with reasonable accuracy, but the later years are less reliable.

10 **'The ARM makes hardly any progress'**: Cecil, Vol. I, 15

11 **'She is 1000 times nicer'**: Ibid.

12 **'Germany does not look'**: John Van Der Kiste, *Wilhelm II*, 11

12 **'These discussions were injudicious'**: Anonymous, 51

13 **'The earliest memories I can recall'**: Wilhelm II, 3

13 **'May your life'**: Ponsonby, *Letters*, 34

13 **'Drove with Alix, Lenchen and Bertie'**: Hibbert, 172

14 **'That beloved and promising child'**: Hibbert, 187

14 **'I shall endeavour'**: Cecil, Vol. I, 15

15 **'It was hard for a seven-year-old'**: Wilhelm II, 25

16 **'The poor arm is no better'**: Ponsonby, *Letters*, 68

16 **'With my arm'**: Schönburg-Waldenburg, *Erinnerungen Aus Kaiserliche Zeit*, 165. Heinrich Prince von Schönburg-Waldenburg came from a long line of courtiers. His memoirs reveal a man blessed with a happy childhood, whose observations are balanced and reliable. His comments about Wilhelm's straightforward attitude to his extremely debilitating handicap are therefore particularly telling.

16 **'In spite of all his begging'**: Wilhelm II, 32

17 **'I wished to answer what you said'**: Hibbert, 201

18 **'A born Berliner'**: Wilhelm II, 4

19 **'My position is not an easy one'**: Daphne Bennett, *Vicky Princess Royal*, 135

19 **'I feel ashamed'**: Ibid., 135

20 **'Your suffering child turns to you'**: Ponsonby, *Letters*, 60

20 **'dull and idle'**: Jerrold M. Packard, *Victoria's Daughters*, 174

20 **'My tenth birthday'**: Wilhelm II, 40

21 **'Poor Willy in his uniform'**: Cecil, Vol. I, 27

22 **'My mother wore the uniform'**: Wilhelm II, 55

CHAPTER 2: GEORGIE, THE SECOND SON

23 **'It seems that IT IS NOT TO BE'**: Georgina Battiscombe, *Queen Alexandra*, 79

24 **'Oh dear, what would happen'**: Philip Magnus, *King Edward the Seventh*, 26

26 **'I went down'**: Hibbert, 172

26 **'At one moment'**: Ibid., 173

26 **'She was trembling'**: Battiscombe, 50

28 **'The dear young couple are here'**: Hibbert, 175

28 **'a little grand'**: Magnus, 74

28 **'Are you aware'**: Hibbert, 176

29 **'I have not the intention'**: Magnus, 86

29 **'his DEEDS OF VALOUR'**: Ibid., 87

29 **'I felt rather annoyed'**: Battiscombe, 63

29 **'As to the names of the young gentleman'**: Kenneth Rose, *King George V*, 1

30 **'I fear I cannot admire'**: Ibid.

30 **'Alix is by no means'**: Battiscombe, 78

30 **'only too happy'**: Magnus, 94

31 **'UPON NO ACCOUNT'**: Ibid., 77

31 **'These are my reasons against it'**: Hibbert, 196

31 **'Dear Alix arrived here yesterday'**: Battiscombe, 81

32 **'Believe me, dearest child'**: Ibid., 74

33 **'She was in her glory'**: John Gore, *King George V, A Personal Memoir*, Vol. I, 9

33 **'With a great big kiss'**: Rose, 4

34 **'A lady may have feelings'**: Magnus, 96

34 **'The Queen trusts that Lord Derby'**: Battiscombe, 91

34 **'a good deal of hissing'**: Hibbert, 197

34 **'Regarding the higher classes'**: Ponsonby, *Letters*, 124

34 **'no intention'**: Magnus, 100

35 **'Alix has made herself nearly quite ill'**: Battiscombe, 99

36 **'If children of their age'**: Magnus, 100

36 **'The dear little children'**: Hibbert, 208

36 **'Now that Ascot Races are approaching'**: Hibbert, 211

37 **'For our time as a Government'**: Magnus, 111

38 **'He has had so much to do for me'**: Ibid., 110

38 **'As regards the studies'**: Rose, 5

39 **'Prince G. this week'**: Harold Nicolson, *King George V*, 7

39 **Excelsior-Regina Hotel**: Hilary Spurling, *Matisse*, 379. Spurling continues the story of this favourite haunt of Queen Victoria's which continued to prosper till the First World War. After the war, no longer popular, it was boarded up until it was converted, some time in the 1930s, into apartments. Matisse bought two adjoining ones there in 1938.

40 **'Because a man has a black face'**: Magnus, 136

CHAPTER 3: NICKY, THE THIRD COUSIN

41 **'my good Mrs Clarke'**: Inger-Lise Klausen, *Dagmar, Tsarina fra Denmark*. I have Klausen to thank for pointing this out to me.

41 **'The mother's family are bad'**: Battiscombe, 12

41 **'I found, as I heard that I should'**: Magnus, 95

42 **'Prussia is hereby empowered'**: Louis Snyder (ed.), *Documents of German History*, 205

43 **'everyone went and we were left alone'**: Klausen, 54

44 **'the Bull'**: E.E.P. Tisdall, *The Dowager Empress*, 29

46 **'My own angel Minny'**: my thanks to Klausen for a copy of this letter of 2 October 1867

46 **'The pangs were stronger and stronger'**: Leppi Publications, *The Romanovs*, 18

49 **'My naughty little man'**: Battiscombe, 110

49 **'The French–German war'**: Klausen, 126

50 **'We had glorious times in Denmark'**: Baroness Sophie Buxhoeveden, *Before the Storm*, 314

50 **'With cautious tenderness'**: Klausen, 125
50 **'It could be interesting'**: Ibid., 125
50 **'Bernsdorff is an ill-conditioned man'**: Magnus, 110
51 **'Heard that the mob at Paris'**: Hibbert, 221
51 **'as though Germany'**: Bennett, 183
51 **'We are called Kaiserliche . . . Hoheit'**: Ponsonby, *Letters*, 119
51 **'I am sure you would be pleased'**: Ibid.
52 **'He has very strong health'**: Ibid., 120
52 **'the constant friend'**: Bennett, 192
53 **'I adored her'**: Wilhelm II, 75
53 **'For this insane militarism'**: Klausen, 130
54 **'The sisters set each other off'**: Battiscombe, 128
55 **'Proud Albion is doing all she can'**: Tisdall, 57
55 **'Wild as hawks'**: Battiscombe, 123
56 **'Too grand for a subject'**: Magnus, 127

CHAPTER 4: THE EDUCATION OF THREE ROYAL COUSINS

59 **'Willy was much pleased'**: Ponsonby, *Letters*, 134
60 **'should equally do so'**: Magnus, 129
60 **'Only after a long dispute'**: Wilhelm II, 123
61 **'I like my life at Cassel very much'**: Cecil, Vol. I, 36
62 **'We were just sitting down for dinner'**: Franz (François) Ayme, *Kaiser Wilhelm II und seine Erziehung*, 113. Ayme is the best and most reliable source we have for Wilhelm's grammar school days. That Wilhelm had potential at this early stage is not in doubt, but Ayme adds the detail, unmentioned by anyone else, that the potential, in some anonymous other person, might have found expression in journalism. This gives a clear indication of the exact nature of that potential, and the type of young man Wilhelm was at that stage in his life. This is the author's own translation.
63 **'Next time we'll do it better'**: Ibid., 145
63 **'In a land'**: Ibid., 161
63 **'If the Crown Prince had lived'**: Ibid., 97
64 **'I have again dreamt about you'**: Packard, 175
64 **'The Christmas fair'**: Anonymous, 63
64 **'Whether commoner or nobleman'**: Ibid., 71
65 **'I hope the cold at St Petersburg'**: Hibbert, 233
65 **'the disgusting Berlin'**: my thanks to Klausen for a copy of this letter of 17 February 1874
65 **'No one wishes more'**: Ponsonby, *Letters*, 139
66 **'My Dearest Eddy and Georgy'**: Gore, Vol. I, 25

66 '. . . climb up your legs and bight you': Magnus, 137

66 'charming, playful': Dominic Lieven, *Nicholas II*, 32

67 'Neither I, nor the Grand Duchess': Leppi, 22

67 'Arm Yourselves with Knives': Tisdall, 61

67 'old Jim Hercules': Lieven, 33

67 'I don't like watching': Lieven, 26

68 'Turkey is in my pocket': Magnus, 154

68 'We don't want to fight': Snyder, 237

68 'I received two high orders': Wilhelm II, 141

68 'Willy would be satisfied': Fulford, *Further Letters*, 174

69 '. . . do anything except ENJOYING': Cecil, Vol. I, 37

69 'It was after Prince Wilhelm became of age': Anonymous, 79

70 'Prince Albert Victor': Rose, 6

70 'Their positions (if they live)': Nicolson, 14

71 'It never did me any good': Ibid., 15

71 'Please give Victoria my very best love': Rose, 7

71 'It is impossible that two lads': Gore, Vol. I, 31

72 'My own darling little Georgie': Ibid., 36

73 'My Darling, Darling Mama': Edward Bing, *The Letters of Tsar Nicholas II and Empress Marie*, 81. It is certainly striking how similar in tone are the letters of the two Danish sisters, Alexandra and Minny, to their sons, Georgie and Nicky. They are extremely, almost excessively, affectionate, and reveal a reluctance to let them go, or grow up. The sons responded in kind, each referring to his mother as 'Motherdear', and keeping in the closest contact, either in person or by letter, for all the years to come.

74 'I hate letting any of you out of my sight': Battiscombe, 155

74 'My darling Motherdear': Nicolson, 24

75 'How I miss you': Battiscombe, 156

75 'Last Saturday we had a very pleasant cruise': Magnus 161

76 'This weakness of the brain': Ibid., 169

76 'Prince George's old enemy': Nicolson, 30

76 'Truthfulness, Obedience, Zest': Ibid., 33

CHAPTER 5: FAMILY DRAMAS

77 'But I didn't only devote my time': Wilhelm II, 162

77 'a very lively person': Cecil, Vol. I, 39

78 'I have very few real friends': Ibid., 41. Wilhelm's letters to Countess Marie von Dönhoff are among the Bülow Papers in the Bundesarchiv, Koblenz, because after divorcing Count Dönhoff she married Bernhard von Bülow.

78 **'something beneath a real man'**: Isabel V. Hull, *The Entourage of Kaiser Wilhelm II, 1888–1918*, 20. Along with John Röhl's study of the Kaiser and his Court, this book offers the most detailed and telling account of the people who surrounded the Kaiser, and the profound effect they had on the political decisions taken during that period.

78 **'One can only imagine'**: Wilhelm II, 177

79 **'So many pretty and charming traits'**: Cecil, Vol. I, 45

79 **'I don't think the Queen realizes'**: Ponsonby, *Letters*, 192

79 **'My shame'**: Wilhelm II, 172

80 **'I never feel happy'**: Hull, 20

81 **'Such a lovely book'**: Nicolson, 39

81 **'The great alarm in the country'**: Hibbert, 260

82 **'I am so delighted'**: Ponsonby, *Letters*, 179

82 **'By then I was Hauptmann'**: Wilhelm II, 125

83 **'I share your horror'**: Hibbert, 268

84 **'This dreadful Radical Government'**: Hibbert, 274

84 **'A frightened servant'**: Andrei Maylunas, *A Lifelong Passion*,

85 **'The Tsar is dead'**: Tisdall, 86

86 **'Never mind, dearest Mama'**: Battiscombe, 160

86 **'We're never letting the boys out'**: Klausen, 162

87 **'They are a set of hogs!'**: Charles Lowe, *Alexander III of Russia*, 326

88 **'After dinner we worked colouring eggs'**: Leppi, 22

88 **'In the morning drank chocolate'**: Ibid., 34

88 **'Today was a march to the fortress'**: Ibid., 36

89 **'After breakfast went to Cinselli's'**: Ibid.

89 **'We had awful fun with Mr Heath'**: Bing, 30

90 **'The voice of God'**: Maylunas, 7

90 **'The new Emperor'**: Battiscombe, 158

90 **'Those who did not know the Tsar'**: Sergei Witte, *Memoirs*, 171

91 **'But how can you expect better'**: Hibbert, 270

91 **'We then passed an ostrich farm'**: Rose, 14

92 **'How could you'**: Ibid., 13

92 **'Weeks and weeks at sea'**: Gore, Vol. I, 47

92 **'It is indeed a bitter disappointment'**: Battiscombe, 162

93 **'My own darling little Georgie'**: Ibid., 164

93 **'It is just a week since you left us'**: Nicolson, 6

CHAPTER 6: FAMILY STRIFE

94 **'from all the Asiatic tribes'**: Lowe, 67

95 **'his tall, stately, knightly figure'**: Klausen, 174

95 **'I am in love with Victoria'**: Leppi, 28

96 **'Still more and more I love Victoria'**: Ibid.

96 **'the AWFUL moment of tearing ourselves away'**: Battiscombe, 165

96 **'Grandeur and loneliness go together'**: Klausen, 178

97 **'We'll see'**: Ibid., 181

97 **'Outside the narrow circle'**: Lowe, 334

97 **'My Darling Darling Mama'**: Bing, 28

98 **'As for Dona'**: Hibbert, 288

99 **'I think him very fascinating'**: Magnus, 186

99 **'With quite unusual cordiality'**: Ibid. (recorded in Rich & Fisher (eds), *The Holstein Papers*, II, 44, since it is Holstein who made the remark)

100 **'Show joy and interest'**: John Röhl, *Wilhelm II*, Vol. I, 426

100 **'Hordes of generals'**: Ibid.

100 **'The Reich has no interests in the Prince'**: Ibid., 429

101 **'It is a true joy'**: Ibid., 427

101 **'That my relationship with my mother'**: Wilhelm II, 317

101 **'I would have given ten years'**: Grand Duke Alexander, *Once a Grand Duke*, 140

102 **'The weather today was wonderful'**: Maylunas, 10

102 **'We jumped about together on the net'**: Ibid., 11

103 **'On seeing you go off by train yesterday'**: Magnus, 194

103 **'You are, I think, rather hard on me'**: Ibid., 197

103 **'I wonder who will have that sweet little room'**: Battiscombe, 143

104 **'I feel that in entrusting my son'**: Rose, 17

104 **'I was sorry to learn'**: Magnus, 197

104 **'You can picture our life here'**: Ibid., 198

104 **'extraordinary impertinence and insolence'**: Hibbert, 288

104 **'As for Willie'**: Cecil, Vol. I, 84

105 **'You have, I hope, got over your disappointment'**: Magnus, 191

105 **'the old hag' . . . 'he was very glad'**: Ibid., 192 (this is also to be found in *The Holstein Papers*, II, 254)

106 **'The day has come, and I am alone'**: Hibbert, 304

107 **'How delightful to be in dear old England again'**: John Gove, *King George V*, Vol. I, 77

107 **'Why on earth should I not?'** Nicolson, 39

108 **'such a pretty, simple, unaffected dear'**: Battiscombe, 172

CHAPTER 7: I BIDE MY TIME

109 **'It is a terrible difficulty'**: Ponsonby, *Letters*, 124

109 **'The Prince has made a brilliant impression'**: Röhl, *Wilhelm II*, Vol. I, 425

109 **'Truly moved'**: Ibid., 427

110 **'You are seeing the Prince'**: Ibid.

110 **'Ella – who is my SPECIAL pet'**: Ibid., 326

111 **'I know too well'**: Packard, 162

112 **'sudden changing of saddle'**: Röhl, *Wilhelm II*, Vol. I, 333

112 **'with soldiers as much as you like'**: Hull, 20

112 **'There sat a youthful man'**: Hull, 17

113 **'Cold as a block of ice'**: Cecil, Vol. I, 41

113 **'The new Hohenzollern Princess'**: Anonymous, 80

114 **'Here I found my family'**: Cecil, Vol. I, 59. These, and further quotes from letters to and from Eulenburg, are taken from John Röhl's collected 3 volumes of Philipp Eulenburg's *Politische Korrespondenz*, a work of definitive scholarship which forms the basis of most of our insights into Eulenburg's relationship with the Kaiser. Author's own translation when not quoted elsewhere.

114 **'Britain must be destroyed'**: Röhl, *Wilhelm II*, Vol. I, 434

114 **'He loves being contrary'**: Cecil, Vol. I, 82

115 **The 'Wales-Copenhagen' link**: Röhl, *Wilhelm II*, Vol. I, 434

115 **'His response ran thus'**: Wilhelm II, 324

116 **'the best defence'**: Cecil, Vol. I, 116

116 **'How badly behaved'**: Röhl, **Wilhelm II**, Vol. I, 577

116 **'The intriguers'**: Ibid., 578

116 **'In general one can say'**: Johannes Haller, *Aus dem Leben*, 82

117 **'This marriage was extremely GRUESOME'**: Hull, 55

117 **'Dearest Axel'**: *Korrespondenz*, Vol. 1, 110f

118 **'My beloved Mama'**: Ibid., 129

118 **'My dearest Herbert'**: Ibid., 163

118 **'Prince Wilhelm is full of friendship'**: Ibid., 163, f4

118 **'Request exact information'**: Ibid., Vol. 1, 170

119 **'My dear Phili'**: Haller, 20

119 **'you must make good use of this'**: Ibid., 21

119 **'I hope you look after the dear man'**: Ibid., 21

120 **'He is so headstrong'**: Cecil, Vol. I, 87

120 **'Got a cipher telegram'**: Hibbert, 303

121 **'one cannot have enough hatred'**: Cecil, Vol. I, 93

122 **'We Brandenburgers'**: Louis Elkind, *The German Emperor's Speeches*, 3

122 **'What I have endured here'**: Röhl, *Court*, 15

123 **'She thinks very badly of him'**: Cecil, Vol. I, 120

123 **'After I had tidied myself up'**: Hibbert, 310

123 **'inexperience'**: Ibid., 311

123 **'Help and do all you can'**: Ibid., 312

124 'if you exercise the power': Van Der Kiste, 57

124 'greatly relieved to hear': Magnus, 202

124 'Instead of William being a comfort': Nicolson, 40

124 'Try, my dear Georgy': Magnus, 202

125 Trade Union membership figures from Harold Kurtz, *The Second Reich*, 82

125 'intolerable insults': Magnus, 205

125 'But as you have not written': Hibbert, 312

125 'How sickening it is': Ibid., 313

126 'We are a most happy family': Battiscombe, 175

126 'Goodbye dear old diary': Nicolson, 41

126 'The scene at Brest': Witte, 92

126 'foppish': Ibid.

CHAPTER 8: WILLY, THE KAISER

128 'It is with deep emotion . . . Army': Elkind, 4

128 'It is with deep emotion . . . Navy': Ibid., 5

128 'and not by a single individual': Lothar Reinermann, *Der Kaiser in England*, 62

128 'jackboot Junkerism': Ibid., 62

129 'sudden accesses of anger': Cecil, Vol. I, 280

129 'It is nevertheless true': Ibid.

129 'I see William is now going': RA GV/AA 36/21

130 'Things began to hum at the palace': Anonymous, 116

130 'The widowed Empress': Ibid., 114

131 'in the political field': Röhl, *Court*, 41

131 'I have known for a long time': Röhl, *Wilhelm II*, Vol. 2, 188; full quote in Bussman

132 'at a moment when matters were': Magnus, 210

132 'as an uncle treats a nephew': Ibid.

132 'Oh he is mad': Rose, 164

132 'a little off his head': Magnus, 202

132 'PERFECT MADNESS': Ibid., 211

132 'The whole thing is fixed': Ibid., 213

133 'almost in ecstasy': Cecil, Vol. I, 269

133 'The visit here is going off': Hibbert, 316

134 'Friday, Oct. 25': RA GV/GVD/1889: 25 October

134 'William brought 67 gentlemen': RA GV/GVD/1889: 26 October

134 'Heil Dir im Siegerkranz': Van Der Kiste, 66

135 *Hohenzollern*: For these details I am grateful to Kevin Brown–

low, with his encyclopaedic knowledge of archive films, for pointing me in the direction of *Majestat*, a German documentary about the Kaiser.

136 **'We were brought in by a Knight'**: RA GV/GVD/1890:22 March
136 **'And so my Georgie boy'**: Nicolson, 42
137 **'When you next write to him'**: Magnus, 217
138 **'I certainly have full trust in you'**: Cecil, Vol. I, 132
138 **'The strike of coal miners'**: Ponsonby, *Letters*, 377
139 **'he wishes himself to govern'**: Cecil, Vol. I, 160
139 **'I am sorry to say'**: Ponsonby, *Letters*, 410
139 **'I see William the Fidgety'**: Rose, 165
140 **'I quite agree with you'**: Nicolson, 43
140 **'People are beginning to ask themselves'**: Magnus, 233
140 **'My dearest Grandmama'**: RA VIC/Z 92/91
141 **'Thank God English George is now better'**: Klausen, 207
141 **'He serves at the same time'**: Hull, 25
142 **'I am tortured'**: Ibid., 47
142 **'How happy it makes me'**: Cecil, Vol. I, 177
142 **'*Eigenart*'**: In *The Entourage of Wilhelm II* Hull offers many other examples of the coded language used by the Liebenberg Circle.
142 **'He lets me say anything'**: Haller, 111 (author's own translation)
144 **'I'll parade you like a clipped poodle!'**: Hull, 69
145 **'There is only one ruler in this Empire'**: Cecil, Vol. I, 219
145 **'The bomb is ready to explode'**: Röhl, *Court*, 42
146 **'William is as good a liar'**: Cecil, Vol. I, 190
146 **'Every day I feel the blessing'**: Hibbert, 333
146 **'In the early years of his reign'**: Anonymous, 184

CHAPTER 9: A WEDDING AND A BETROTHAL

148 **'May has grown quite a tall lady'**: Battiscombe, 157
148 **'I think the preliminaries'**: Magnus, 239
149 **'Poor, poor parents'**: Hibbert, 321
149 **'He is broken down'**: Magnus, 239
149 **'Alas! It is only now'**: Nicolson, 46
149 **'I am glad that you like the title'**: Ibid., 47
149 **'Fancy my Georgie boy'**: Ibid.
150 **'The Flagship'**: Ibid.
150 **'yr whole German uniform'**: RA GV/AA 19/36
150 **'He made a beautiful speech'**: Nicolson, 48

151 **'Have you seen May'**: Rose, 25
151 **'Papa and I are coming to Cannes'**: Ibid., 26
151 **'At 11 she was given her presents'**: James Pope-Hennessy, *Queen Mary*, 244
151 **'Dull, wet day'**: Ibid.
151 **'May is a smart *erscheinung*'**: Ibid., 257
151 **'There is a bond of love'**: Rose, 26
151 **'Received a telegram'**: Hibbert, 324
152 **'I am very sorry'**: Rose, 27
152 **'Thank God'**: Ibid.
152 **'but a portion of the trousseau'**: Pope-Hennessy, 264
152 **'no young lady'**: Ibid., 265
152 **'My darling Mama'**: Bing, 70
153 **'Victoria has got much thinner'**: Maylunas, 27
153 **'The great day'**: Hibbert, 325
154 **'I am indeed lucky'**: RA GV/GVD/1893:6 July
154 **'The young couple'**: Rose, 33
154 **'a glum little villa'**: Nicolson, 51
156 **'I like my bungalow awfully'**: Bing, 34
156 **'Never forget'**: Ibid., 32
156 **'I skated and slid down the hills'**: Maylunas, 15
157 **'We danced till we dropped'**: Ibid., 16
157 **'It was so good of you to write'**: Ibid., 17
157 **'It is about Alicky and N'**: Hibbert, 318
159 **'Any man who saw'**: Lowe, 270
159 **'My more than dearest Nicky'**: Bing, 59
160 **'But he is absolutely a child'**: Leppi, 38
160 **'Inevitably this conversation'**: Maylunas, 20
160 **'What a surprising thing'**: Ibid., 22
161 **'I had to put on'**: Ibid., 26
161 **'It was very hot'**: Ibid., 46
162 **'A wonderful unforgettable day'**: Ibid., 47
163 **'My dear old Nicky'**: Ibid., 48
163 **'My dear sweet Nicky'**: Ibid., 50
163 **'My sweet darling beloved Alix!'**: Ibid., 57
163 **'Ever deeply devoted'**: Ibid., 59
163 **'I see my sweet little girly-dear'**: Ibid., 61
164 **'Long before our dear child was born'**: Rose, 37
165 **'Got up at 8'**: RA GV/GVD/1894:2 July
165 **'You have got me entirely'**: Maylunas, 86
165 **'All my fears about her future'**: Hibbert, 329
166 **'My God, my God, what a day!'**: Maylunas, 99

166 **'Emperor Alexander III died as he had lived'**: Witte, 206
166 **'He took me by the arm'**: Maylunas, 99

CHAPTER 10: NICKY AND WILLY

167 **'out of respect'**: Magnus, 246
167 **'. . . followed by two women'**: Witte, 207
168 **'My dear Nicky'**: Maylunas, 100
168 **'Nicky does everything so well'**: Magnus, 248
168 **'William arrived here in his Yacht'**: RA GV/CC 1/54
169 **'my own sweet little wife'**: Rose, 33
169 **'Dear Aunt Minny'**: RA GV/CC 19/164
169 **'Nicky's last dinner as a Bachelor'**: RA GV/GVD1894: 25 November
169 **'The day of my wedding!'**: Maylunas, 108
170 **'ventured to put down a few things'**: Ibid., 109
170 **'So impenetrable was that living hedge'**: *Daily Telegraph*, 26 Nov. 1894
171 **'Nicky has been kindness itself'**: Maylunas, 112
171 **'Good and patriotic' work**: Magnus, 249
171 **'I cannot think'**: Battiscombe, 206
171 **'All the family came'**: RA GV/GVD 1894: 1 December
172 **'We have come here for four days'**: Maylunas, 115
172 **'Darling Boysy, me loves you'**: Vladimir Poliakoff, *The Empress Marie of Russia and her Times*, 228
172 **'Undoubtedly the new Emperor'**: Witte, 209
172 **'The gentle but uneducated Tsar'**: Sir George Buchanan, *My Mission in Russia*, Vol. 2, 77
172 **'When he became Tsar'**: A.A. Mossolov, *At the Court of the Last Tsar*, 6
172 **'I am up to my neck in work'**: Maylunas, 123
172 **'Even those who were least partial'**: Alexander Isvolsky, *Memoirs*, 247
173 **'I am aware that recently'**: Maylunas, 122
174 **'It was Pobednostsev who drew up the address'**: Isvolsky, 254
174 **'The uncles always wanted something'**: Maylunas, 161
174 **'I adored the Grand Duchess'**: Ibid., 148
175 **'The impulse given to the Democrats'**: Walter Goetz, *Briefe Wilhelm II an den Zaren*, 290
175 **to 'keep Europe quiet'**: Ibid., 291
176 **'Very pretty'**: RA GV/GVD/1895:18 June
176 **'Very pretty sight going thro' Canal'**: RA GV/GVD/1895:20 June

176 'Beautiful night': RA GV/GVD/1895:21 June
176 'I received the German Emperor's Aide-de-camp': Poliakoff, 189
177 'since Salisbury's *avénement*': Goetz, 299
177 'In *one* point I share your opinion': John C.G. Röhl, *Germany without Bismarck*, 125. This letter, written by Holstein to Eulenburg on 17 February 1895, is an early sign of later disagreements between the two men.
177 'God knows I have done all in my power': Goetz, 296
177 'We settled ourselves': Bing, 103
177 'a lover of flowers': Baroness Sophie Buxhoeveden, *Life of Alexandra Fedorovna*, 51
178 'Twice we went up': Bing, 109
179 'most sincere congratulations': Cecil, Vol. I, 287
179 'After all': Ibid., 286
179 'As your Grandmother': Hibbert, 332
179 'a most gratuitous act': Cecil, Vol. I, 288
179 'He assured me': RA GV/CC 1/152
179 'I hope, as you do': Magnus, 254
180 'I have briefed him exactly': Hull, 102
181 'The position of Ministers': Röhl, *Germany without Bismarck*, 136
181 'The army is subject': Cecil, Vol. I, 228
181 'Apply yourself seriously to this': Haller, 184
181 'a Kaiser as his own Imperial Chancellor': Ibid., 185
182 'Be careful that History': Cecil, Vol. I, 238
182 **20,180 Marks**: Röhl, *Germany without Bismarck*, 176
182 'It was, as ever': Röhl, *Korrespondenz*, Vol. 1, 160
182 'How delightful it would be': Ibid., 164
183 'How often I think of you': Hull, 86
183 'As sisters our souls': Röhl, *Court*, 46
183 'It is another question': Hull, 88
183 'Bernhard is the most valuable servant': Röhl, *Germany without Bismarck* 134
184 'I would be a different kind': Ibid., 194

CHAPTER 11: TURN OF THE CENTURY

185 'My dear old Nicky': Maylunas, 140
185 'Your Embassy has enquired': Goetz, 302
185 'A great solemn day': Maylunas, 144
186 'My blood froze': Ibid., 146
186 'My brothers': Ibid.

187 **'When Tsar Nicholas II ascended the throne'**: Witte, 213

187 **'This year seems to be'**: Maylunas, 151

188 **'Went down soon after half-past seven'**: *Royalty Digest*, May 2005, p. 335

187 **'Family dinner, only 12'**: RA GV/GVD/1896:22 September

189 **'before dinner at Balmoral'**: Andrew Roberts *Salisbury, Victorian Titan*, 643

189 **'After he left'**: Bing, 119

190 **'Wherever we went'**: Ibid., 121

190 **'There, for the last time'**: Ibid., 124

190 **'The wardrobe of the Kaiser'**: Anonymous, 169

190 **'I'm sorry to tell you'**: Bing, 128

191 **'On the whole'**: Ibid., 141

191 **'I do not really like'**: Maylunas, 170

191 **'everyone was very disappointed'**: Maylunas, 163

191 **'She is not very talkative'**: Ibid., 172

192 **'I rejoice at the cancellation'**: Ibid., 166

192 **'I feel like a charger'**: Cecil, Vol. 2, 77

192 **'never-to-be-forgotten day'**: Hibbert, 335

192 **'Took leave with much regret'**: Ibid., 336

193 **'William's fortieth birthday'**: Ibid., 337

193 **'I feel I must write'**: Maylunas, 182

193 **'Dearest Grandmama'**: Ibid., 183

194 **'like a Bank Holiday tripper to Margate'**: Cecil, Vol. I, 274

194 **'The pain and shame'**: Ibid., 325

194 **'The tone in which you write'**: Hibbert, 339

194 **'he does not fear us'**: Cecil, Vol. I, 324

194 **Salisbury's cover-up**: Roberts, 636

195 **'The only form of control we have'**: Ibid., 229

195 **'I sincerely hope'**: Hibbert, 340

195 **'I am wholly preoccupied'**: *London Review of Books*, 16/7/98, review of Apollon Davidson's *The Russians and the Anglo Boer War*

195 **'I intend to set the Emperor on the British'**: Ibid.

196 **'ninny'**: Cecil, Vol. 2, 13

196 **'On the whole'**: Bing, 128

196 **'I cannot tell you'**: Maylunas, 191

196 **'so long as we leave a shred'**: Roberts, 767

196 **'You know, my dear'**: *LRB*, 16/7/98

197 **'We left London with Papa'**: RA GV/GVD/1899:20 November

197 **'William came to tea'**: Hibbert, 340

198 **'William shot remarkably well'**: RA GV/GVD/1899:27 November

198 **'a fat malicious tom-cat'**: Magnus, 263

198 'I am unable to share your opinion': Ibid., 264
198 'How are things going': Battiscombe, 209
199 'And so, there's no heir': Maylunas, 185
199 'I am so thankful': Ibid., 186
199 'My own sweet little Wify dear': Ibid., 188
199 'bring himself to admit': Ibid., 184
200 'Because we lagged': Witte, 323
200 'Remember this day, Your Highness': Ibid., 275
201 'There is no doubt': Ibid., 277
201 'As you know dearest Grandmama': Maylunas, 183
201 'I hate going of course': Rose, 43
201 'The Service lasted over an hour': RA/GV/GVD/1900: 6 May
201 'I cannot say how thankful I feel': Ponsonby, *Letters*, 466
202 'Found darling May': RA/GV/GVD/1900: 9 May
202 'My grandmother invites us': Buxhoeveden, 89
202 'Already thirty-eight years': Hibbert, 341
202 'It is heartrending': Ibid., 346
203 'From not having been well': Ibid., 349
203 'Yes, very glad, for I love him': Cecil, Vol. 2, 78
203 'The decease of my beloved': Elkind, 112
204 'Papa made a beautiful speech': Nicolson, 63
204 'I am anxious': Virginia Cowles, *Edward VII and his Circle*, 245
204 'Es Lebe Der Kaiser': Rimmermann, 236
204 'one heard on all sides': Ibid., 239

CHAPTER 12: UNCLE BERTIE AND HIS TWO NEPHEWS

205 'we shall not pretend': Magnus, 271
206 'Although you are not exactly': Ibid., 286
208 'keeping the ball rolling': Frederick Ponsonby, *Recollections of Three Reigns*, 162
208 'There is something': Ponsonby, *Letters*, x
209 'holding forth': Ibid., xiv
209 'One of, if not the greatest gentleman': Rose, 47
210 'May and I came down': Ibid., 45
210 'the greatest constitutional bond': Ibid., 44
210 'The Old Country must wake up': Ibid., 45
210 'In sending my son George': Nicolson, 77
210 'Tried some of the uniform': RA GV/GVD/1902: 26 January
211 'Found darling May quite well': RA GV/GVD/1902: 30 January

211 'My God! What a disappointment': Maylunas, 206

211 'The new Grand Duchess': Ibid.

211 'M. Philippe talked': Ibid.

212 'My own precious One': Ibid., 208

212 'from which they return in an exalted state': Ibid., 219

212 'We talked about the spiritualist's influence': Battiscombe, 254

212 'Towards the middle of August': Anne Topham, *Memories of the Kaiser's Court*, 1

214 'How d'ye do?': Anne Topham, *Chronicles of the Prussian Court*, 15

214 'The ordinary easy lounge tweed': Topham, *Memories*, 20

214 'However many fastenings': Topham, *Chronicles*, 148

215 'The German waves patriotic flags': Topham, *Memories*, 30

215 'My own beloved One': Maylunas, 216

216 'I explained': Ibid.

216 'the Peace of the World': Goetz, 327

217 'The Count told me': Witte, 388

217 'I hope the Admiral of the Pacific': Goetz, 333

217 'kicking up a row': Maylunas, 213

218 'After the student' disorders': Lieven, 80

218 'He has a naturally good brain': Ibid., 106

219 'The reason for our mood': Maylunas, 231

219 'Wahl was going to be appointed': Lieven, 134

219 'because I consider it harmful': Ibid., 136

219 'the Minister of Internal Affairs': Ibid., 137

220 'We were welcomed': Maylunas, 229

220 'At 1.15 in the afternoon': Ibid., 243

220 'God has sent their Majesties': Ibid., 244

220 'It is as if a dam': Ibid., 251

220 'We put on our coats': Poliakoff, 15

220 People in every conceivable costume: Geoffrey Hosking, *Russia*, 414

220 'Directly opposite us': Maylunas, 293

220 '*Si vous me voyez*': Buchanan, Vol. 2, 89

CHAPTER 13: WILLY AND NICKY IN TROUBLE

225 'What a very kind thought': Maylunas, 246

225 'Alix and I were very worried': Ibid., 247

225 'There is no doubt': Ibid., 248

226 'Sweetest One': Ibid., 249

226 'My own beloved Sunny': Ibid., 250

226 'If anyone is curious enough': Poliakoff, 283

227 'I have never seen': Battiscombe, 263

227 'The aversion of the Empress Dowager': Isvolsky, 72

227 'Just leaving': Bing, 172

227 'He thinks himself a superman': Cecil, Vol. 2, 13

228 'My dear Francis': RA VIC/W45/147

228 'Dearest Nicky': Goetz, 333

229 'I soon was convinced': Ponsonby, *Recollections*, 159

229 'This visit seemed to me': Ibid., 173

229 'all the grace and spirit of France': Magnus, 312

229 '*Vive Édouard!*': Ibid., 313

230 'it appertains to France': Ibid., 339

231 'As I had not yet lost all hope': Poliakoff, 239

231 'Nicholas is doing himself a lot of harm': Bulow, 61

231 'Despite the fact that the Japanese': Witte, 349

231 'Dearest Nicky': Goetz, 337

232 'But as the Chinaman says': Cecil, Vol. 2, 91

232 'Dearest Nicky': Goetz,?

232 'If it were not for the loss of life': Magnus, 341

232 'The English are very angry': Bing, 174

233 'secret and very intimate understanding': Esher, *Journals*, Vol. 2, 62

233 'I have been struck, as if by lightning': Maylunas, 251

233 'A terrible crime was perpetrated': Ibid., 261

233 'Uncle Sergei': Ibid., 266

234 'The most unbelievable news': Ibid., 277

234 'I feel so depressed': Ibid., 278

235 'Witte came to see us': Bing, 175

235 'News just received via "Wolff"': *Spectator*, 'Prince Bülow and the Kaiser', 158. This secret letter from Wilhelm to Bülow, taken from the records of the German Foreign Office, was sent from Bremerhaven on 11 March 1905.

235 'As for the state of things in Russia': RA GV/AA 24/24

236 'If only a Constitution': RA GV/AA 24/35

236 'unnatural passions': Hull, 109

236 'I would like to ask Your Majesty': Ibid., 110

237 'I long for the old Philine': Ibid., 55

238 'Kuno looked like a man *in despair*': Ibid.

238 'I know now': Ibid., 56

239 'I was gladdened': Harry Young, *Maximilian Harden*, 39

239 'The German capital': Ibid., 49

239 'You have been lied to': Ibid., 58

240 'Until the leaders of the Social Democrats': Röhl, *Court*, 12

240 'many are saying secretly': Ibid., 22

241 'suffered from a condition': Ibid., 130

241 'he belongs to those people': Young, 89

241 'the Austernfreund': Uwe Weller, *Maximillian Harden und die Zukunft*, 170

241 'Unchanged in his explosive nature': Hull, 111

242 'HM *no longer has himself under control*': Ibid., 112

242 'My impression of Bülow': Witte, 391

242 'Certain people must be told': Hull, 119

243 'dear little William': Hibbert, 186

CHAPTER 14: DANGEROUS DISAGREEMENTS

244 'We are more like brothers': Magnus, 242

244 'We have really the best': Ibid., 337

244 'By luncheon time': Rose, 63

245 'No doubt the Natives': Nicolson, 88

245 'Somehow I can't tell you': Rose, 46

245 'However much HRH may dislike': Ibid., 70

246 'the remissness of the King's': Magnus, 283

246 'The days of our Govt': Ibid., 346

246 'It is certainly': Ibid., 347

247 'The future does not look very bright': Esher, *Journals*, Vol. 2, 62

247 'Was there ever so great': Ibid., 80

247 'the crushing defeat of Russia': Ibid., 90

247 'My dear Esher': Ibid., 159

247 'L'allemagne c'est l'Ennemi': Ibid., 180

248 'One can see once again': Cecil, Vol. I, 324

249 'I have no words to express': Herman Bernstein, *The Willy–Nicky Correspondence*, 74

249 'As for France': Goetz, 346

249 'Therefore I ask your agreement': Bernstein, 19

249 'Best thanks for telegram': Ibid., 21

250 'It is far from my intention': Goetz, 353

250 'I shall shortly be on my return': Bernstein, 104

250 'Delighted with your proposition': Ibid., 105

250 'All my guests': Ibid., 108

251 'It was deathly quiet': Michael Balfour, *The Kaiser and his Times*, 258

251 'What has Germany at stake?': Bernhard von Bülow, *Memoirs*, Vol. 2, 134

251 '*I could not survive this*': Ibid., 140

252 '**During my stay at Björkö**': Hélène D'Encausse, *Nicholas II*, 77

252 '**Tsar Nicholas**': Bülow, Vol. 2, 125

252 '**must and would protect**': Cecil, Vol. 2, 91

253 '**His Majesty remarked**': *Die Grosse Politik der Europaischen Kabinette 1871–1914*, Berlin 1922, XX(1) 6589. Also Snyder, 289.

253 '**the most mischievous**': Magnus, 339

254 '**Perhaps *next year***': Ibid., 345

254 '**This seems a golden opportunity**': Ibid., 340

254 '**Humbly beg to inform**': Battiscombe, 231

255 '**even if King Edward**': Witte, 452

255 '**The Prince and King**': Rose, 68

256 '**I ought not to have said it**': Ibid., 71

256 '**Fancy**': Ibid., 49

257 '**Their wives should be widows**': Ibid., 72

257 '**All the wretched**': Cecil, Vol. 2, 104

257 '**Not only**': Ibid., 106

258 '**shattered**': A.J.P. Taylor. *The Struggle for Mastery of Europe*, 441

258 '**equally satisfactory**': Cecil, Vol. 2, 104

258 '**How I long to see**': Hull, 120

258 '**I was met at the Rominten station**': Witte, 455

259 '**I was particularly struck**': Ibid., 457

260 '**Your aim of many years**': Cecil, Vol. 2, 11

260 '**In each case**': Young, 85

260 '**I see in it**': Haller, 315; Young, 88

261 **trade union of kings**: Magnus, 341

261 '**We are, my dear William**': Ibid., 359

262 '**As you know**': Ibid., 384

CHAPTER 15: SCANDALS AND RIVALRIES

263 '**How happily**': Magnus, 388

263 '**A few days ago**': Maylunas, 296

264 '**The *Neue Freie Press***': RA GV/AA 25/14

264 '**It is the discussions**': Esher, *Journals*, Vol. 2, 249

265 '**We got to Wilhelmshohe**': RA GV/AA 25/18

265 '**Although the King**': Magnus, 395

265 '**Meeting with Uncle Bertie**': Bernstein, 157

265 '**The Emperor is not false**': *Grosse Politik* XXIII, 7877, with thanks to John Röhl for locating this quote for me.

266 **'In his youthful manner'**: Hopman diary, 3 Aug. 07, BA–MA 326/6, also thanks to Röhl.

266 **'It is not easy'**: Maylunas, 304

267 **'Papa, Mama, May'**: RA GV/GVD/1907: 11 November

267 **'We sat down 161'**: RA GV/GVD/1907: 12 November

267 **'There were great crowds'**: RA GV/GVD/1907: 13 November

268 **'Our King'**: Esher, *Journals*, Vol. 2, 255

268 **'I trust now'**: Maylunas, 307

268 **'every German'**: Esher, *Journals*, Vol. 2, 285

269 **'As the Prince of Wales said'**: Ibid., 286

269 **'I shall never'**: Ibid., 298

269 **'no alternative'**: Cecil, Vol. 2, 130

270 **'I discussed with him'**: Esher, *Journals*, Vol. 2, 319

270 **'At the banquet preceding the dance'**: Sir John Fisher, *Records*, 242

270 **'A steamer full'**: Ponsonby, *Recollections*, 196

271 **'There has been a great'**: Esher, *Journals*, Vol. 2, 322

271 **'The King deplores'**: Magnus, 409

271 **'flattered and reassured'**: Ibid., 409

271 **'Untrue'**: *Die Grosse Politik* XXV ii, 479 and Lee, 596

271 **'He has provided'**: Young, 91

273 **Bülow's homosexuality**: Röhl, *Court*, n. 155, p. 227, for this, and the fact that he knew of Eulenburg's inclinations (and activities) from the start.

273 **'never done anything dirty'**: Hull, 138

273 **'The Kaiser's plan'**: Count Robert Zedlitz-Trutzschler (hereafter 'ZT'), *Twelve Years at the Imperial Court*, 210

274 **'It is I who dismiss'**: Ibid., 39

274 **'always quite unlimited'**: Ibid., 28

274 **'When I read over'**: Ibid., 93

275 **Bülow removing Eulenburg's letters**: Rogge, 290

275 **'I will say everything'**: Hull, 136

275 **'this monarch'**: Ibid., 141

277 **'keeping it as secret'**: Snyder, 295

277 **'To be for ever misjudged'**: Ibid., 297

277 **'Of all the political gaffes'**: Magnus, 400

277 **'He ruins our political position'**: Cecil, Vol. 2, 136

278 **Bülow distancing himself**: Bülow, Vol. 2, 350

278 **'I know the E. *hates* me'**: Magnus, 401

279 **Willy to get rid of Bülow**: Cecil, Vol. 2, 142

279 **'dear u. b.'**: Magnus, 417

279 **'The annexation of Bosnia'**: Goetz, 395

280 **'a fully-equipped Duke'**: Magnus, 430

280 **'then they returned with us'**: RA GV/GVD/1909: 2 August
281 **'Today, 30 years ago'**: RA GV/GVD/1909: 6 August
281 **'His cough troubles him'**: Battiscombe, 270
282 **'At 11.45 beloved Papa'**: Rose, 75

CHAPTER 16: GEORGIE INHERITS THE THRONE AT LAST

283 **'Dearest Georgie'**: RA GV/AA43/129
284 **'Today has been a very long day'**: RA GV/GVD/1910: 20 May
285 **'He told me'**: Esher, *Journals*, Vol. 3, 3
285 **'There never was such a break up'**: Ibid., Vol. 3, 4
285 **'The King sent for me'**: Ibid., 8
285 **'Everyone lamented'**: Rose, 141
286 **'No doubt you will have seen'**: Maylunas, 341
286 **'I go to London'**: Goetz, 395
287 **'a lovely warm day'**: RA GV/GVD/1911: 15–16 May
287 **'There were enormous crowds'**: RA GV/GVD/1911: 17–19 May
288 **'I send only *my* ambassador'**: Cecil, Vol. 2, 150
289 **'grave, splendid-looking man'**: Ponsonby, *Recollections*, 196
289 **'No question'**: Witte, 741
290 **'the attitude of Alix'**: Maylunas, 331
290 **'My own sweet darling Mama'**: Ibid., 330
291 **'I suddenly noticed'**: Pierre Gilliard, *Thirteen years at the Russian Court*, 29
291 **'The severe and trying period'**: Maylunas, 359
291 **'I stayed in Alexei's room'**: Ibid., 357
292 **'My dearest Nicky'**: Ibid., 364
292 **'I often think of you'**: Bing, 261
293 **'Overcast and cloudy'**: Rose, 103
293 **'Dull but fine'**: Pope-Hennessy, 440
293 **'I must say'**: Ibid., 436
293 **'There is no longer'**: Esher, *Journals*, Vol. 3, 15
293 **'The King is a very jolly chap'**: Rose, 92
294 **'Enthroned'**: Ibid., 134
294 **'rather tired'**: Ibid., 135
294 **'Each year I feel'**: Pope-Hennessy, 461
295 **'We have now'**: Rose, 148
295 **'It behoves us all'**: Ibid., 150
295 **'We are lunching today'**: Bing, 289
296 **'Despite Alexei's illness'**: Maylunas, 358

296 'I cannot say how charmed': RA/PS/GV/M 456/9

296 'Last week Haldane': Esher, *Journals*, Vol. 3, 58

297 'mutual undertakings': Cecil, Vol. 2, 170

297 'At gymnastics this morning': Röhl, *Court*, 16

297 'Nothing short of a religious': Ibid., 83

298 'I believe a war is unavoidable': Ibid., 162. Müller's diaries are to be found in Walter Görlitz, *Regierte Der Kaiser?* (Did the Kaiser Rule?).

298 'enlighten the people': Röhl, *Court*, 178

299 'Red apes': Cecil, Vol. 2, 182

299 'Woke up to a heavenly morning': Maylunas, 377

300 'Rasputin was standing': Ibid.

300 'greatly due to Sir E. Grey': Gore, 146 (revised edn)

300 'We crossed over by day': Ponsonby, *Recollections*, 293

301 'Copious instructions': Ibid., 294

302 'Went to the Kaiserhof': RA GV/GVD/1913: 22 May

302 'I had a long & satisfying talk': RA/GV/GVD/1913: 23 May

302 'May and I sat' RA/GV/GVD/1913: 24 May

CHAPTER 17: THREE COUSINS GO TO WAR

303 'My dearest Nicky': RA PS/GV/M 624/3. The final version is held in the Russian State Archives, GARF.

304 *Bockwurst*, drinking, dancing: I have Kevin Brownlow to thank, again, for showing me some fine German archive film of the event.

304 'first shoot the Socialists': Bülow, Vol. 2, 191

304 'Terrible shock': Rose, 167

305 'Miss Bloomfield': Gore, 153 (revised edn)

305 'I think he realises': Violet Bonham Carter, *Diaries*, 391

305 'I am greatly worried': Gore, 154 (revised edn)

306 'The German Emperor': Lieven, 200

306 *'No more cause for war exists'*: Snyder, 326

306 'When he boasted': Kiste, 171

306 'high anxiety': Cecil, Vol. 2, 202

307 'that common crew of shopkeepers': Cecil, Vol. 2, 204

307 'Where will it end?': Gore, 156 (revised edn)

307 'the most horrible war': Cecil, Vol. 2, 205

307 *'How Russia and her Ruler'*: Snyder, 312

308 'Austria-Hungary and Germany': Lieven, 201

308 'As representatives': Snyder, 357

308 'Naturally everything you say': Ibid., 347

308 'The sword is drawn': Cecil, Vol. 2, 210

308 **'I am writing to you at this serious moment'**: Van Der Kiste, *Crowns*, 101

308 **'Foreign telegrams'**: Gore, 156 (revised edn)

308 **'So the celebrated encirclement'**: Rose, 162, and Emil Ludwig, *Kaiser Wilhelm II*, 394

309 **'You should at once apply'**: RA PS/GV/Q 1549/11

310 **'Many thanks for kind telegram'**: RA PS/GV/Q 1549/8 and Cecil, Vol. 2, 205

310 **'Some misunderstanding'**: RA PS/GV/Q 1549/7

310 **'I just received'**: RA/PS/GV/Q 1549/12

311 **'Saw Sir Edward Grey'**: Gore, 156 (revised edn)

311 **'After lunch I summoned'**: Maylunas, 394

311 **'I read the telegram'**: Maurice Paléologue, *An Ambassador's Memoirs*, Vol. 1, 196

312 **'he looked even worse'**: Maylunas, 397

312 **'At audience which I had'**: RA/PS/GV/Q 1549/15 and 2551/2

313 **'There has been a difference of opinion'**: Esher, *Journals*, Vol. 3, 174

313 **'We were forced to go & show ourselves'**: Gore, 157 (revised edn)

314 **'If we run away'**: Snyder, 331

314 **'sacrifice her honour as a nation'**: Ibid.

314 **'Fairly warm'**: Robert Lacey, BBC Radio series *The diary of George V, 1914*; with thanks to Robert Lacey for giving me the typescript of his series.

314 **'In the morning we heard'**: Maylunas, 397

315 **'I have received with much pleasure'**: RA PS/GV/Q 1549/23

315 **'Remember you are a chosen people!'**: Snyder, 344

315 **'A blow for a blow'**: Ibid.

315 **'Between each line of song'**: Ibid., 335

316 **'What terrible days'**: Klausen, 288

318 **'You cannot imagine'**: Poliakoff, 106

318 **'I myself have no news'**: Maylunas, 399

318 **'As a tribunal'**: *The Times History*, 278

318 **Statistics**: Ibid.

319 **'I heartily congratulate you'**: RA PS/GV/Q 1550/262

319 **'I beg Count Benckendorff'**: RA PS/GV/Q 1551/264 (the original is in French)

320 **'I cannot sufficiently thank you'**: RA PS/GV/Q 1550/277 and 279

321 **'My dear Nicky'**: Maylunas, 432

321 **'In this serious time'**: RA PS/GV/Q 1550/287

321 **'Your being charms'**: Maylunas, 422

322 **'be firm, Lovy mine'**: Ibid., 424

322 **'The behaviour of some of my ministers'**: Ibid., 439

322 **'I know of no more pleasant feeling'**: Lieven, 226
323 **'a will of iron'**: Ibid., 227
323 **'Now the Duma'**: Maylunas, 429
323 **'Remember to keep the Image'**: Ibid., 439

CHAPTER 18: THE END

324 **'My dearest Georgie'**: RA PS/GV/Q 2551/5
324 **'I cannot share your hardships'**: Rose, 176
325 **'This morning'**: Ibid., 183
325 **'The King and Queen'**: Ponsonby, *Recollections*, 329. My thanks to Kenneth Rose for the details of these menus.
326 **'There is no more loyal man'**: Rose, 172
326 **'It is but right and proper'**: Battiscombe, 285
326 **'As Field Marshal'**: RA PS/GV/Q 1550/312
326 **'My dearest Nicky'**: Maylunas, 470
327 **'Thank God'**: Battiscombe, 283
327 **'Remember that it will always be'**: *Rose*, 193
328 **'Such a step'**: Rose, 202
328 **'I can't ever sufficiently express'**: Pope-Hennessy, 505
328 **'Information has reached me'**: RA PS/GV/Q 1550/313; this is a copy telegram.
328 **'I know you will also appreciate'**: RA PS/GV/Q 1550/314
329 **'I know full well'**: RA PS/GV/Q 1550/317
329 **'Flung into helpless anarchy'**: Lieven, 205
329 **'Alicky was indeed a sick woman'**: Maylunas, 458
330 **'The Empress is a stronger character'**: Ibid., 477
330 **'You have fought this great fight'**: Lieven, 216
330 **'While I am alive'**: Ibid., 217
330 **'In his reception room'**: Ibid., 225
331 **'Darling, remember'**: Ibid.
331 **'Bad news from Russia'**: Maylunas, 541
331 **'Please give following message'**: RA PS/GV/Q 1550/318
332 **'He can't continue this way'**: Ibid., 220
332 **'Many attempts have been made'**: Maylunas, 487
332 **'I'll never forget'**: Ibid., 506
333 **'At 9 o'clock'**: Ibid., 511
333 **'The wretched Russian monk'**: Battiscombe, 290
333 **'But I never lose courage'**: RA PS/GV/Q 2551/8
334 **'Went over to MH'**: Maylunas, 561
334 **'I told him all about the Revolution'**: RA GV/GVD:1917: 15 March

334 'lovely spring day': RA GV/GVD/1917: 17 March

334 'Michel came to see me': RA GV/GVD/1917:24 March

334 'During these decisive days': Mark Steinberg, *The Fall of the Romanovs*, 100

335 'The essence is': Ibid., 107

335 'Beloved, Soul of my Soul': Ibid., 108

336 'an irony of world history': Cecil, Vol. 2, 244

336 Kaiser quickly depressed: Bernhard Schwertfeger, Rudolf von Valentini, *Kaiser und Kabinettschef*, 139

336 'Such an act': Cecil, Vol. 2, 242

337 'extremely pessimistic': Görlitz, 252

337 'Only the military': Ibid., 256

337 'Nicholas II is in my hands': Steinberg, 114

338 'I wished that for once': Ibid., 121

338 'Made it to Tsarskoe Selo': Ibid., 156

338 'The days followed one another': Ibid., 122

338 'I looked through my books and things': Maylunas, 567

338 'Quietly celebrated': Steinberg, 158

339 'most anxious': Maylunas, 563

339 'a virtuous and well-meaning Sovereign': Rose, 209

339 'The King has been thinking': Ibid., 211

340 'I'll be d—d if I'm alien': Nicolson, 308

340 'Every day the King': Rose, 212

341 'Most people appear to think': Lloyd George Papers/F/3/2/19 House of Lords

341 'A marvellous day': Steinberg, 164

342 'Don't forget': Ibid., 171

342 'the typical enlightened fanatic': Ibid., 175

342 'Nonsense!': Cecil, Vol. 2, 266

343 'She is very wily': Steinberg, 258

343 'nice and clean': Maylunas, 617

344 'The weather is warm and pleasant': Steinberg, 331

344 'Grey morning': Ibid., 335

344 'In view of the enemy's proximity': Ibid., 337

344 'the entire family': Ibid., 284

344 'Held an investiture': RA GV/GVD/1918: 25 July

344 'Heard from Lockhart': RA GV/GVD/1918: 28 July

345 'I hear from Russia': RA GV/GVD/1918: 31 August

345 'In the Navy': Görlitz, 292

345 'The Reichstag can do what it likes': Ibid., 305

346 'There will be no peace conference': Cecil, Vol. 2, 269

346 'We were all taken': Görlitz, 345

347 'I am grateful for your prayers': Nicolson, 323
347 'At lunch in the train': Görlitz, 374
348 'God has not permitted': Cecil, Vol. 2, 279
348 'unadulterated Bolshevism': Ibid., 283
348 'We have had to endure': Cecil, Vol. 2, 286
348 'Rain in the morning': RA GV/GVD/1918: 8 November
349 'columns of weary soldiers': *Memoirs of the Crown Prince of Germany*, 232
349 'Never will I forget': Ibid., 240
350 'That silent meal': Ibid., 245
350 'kind, nice young men': Hull, 20
350 'You've deserved it': Cecil, Vol. 2, 294
350 'I am a broken man': Ibid.
350 'We got the news': RA GV/GVD/1918: 9 November

EPILOGUE

352 'William arrived in Holland yesterday': RA GV/GVD/1918: 11 November
352 'a cup of real good English tea': Cecil, Vol. 2, 296
353 'My earliest memory': Wilhelm II, 3
353 'I have now almost finished': Röhl, *Court*, 12
354 'My loneliness was indescribable': Cecil, Vol. 2, 302
355 'With them was Aunt Ella': Van Der Kiste, *Once a Grand Duchess*, 134
355 'He remained': Grand Duke Alexander, *Once a Grand Duke*, 288
355 'Quarter to four': Ibid., 292
356 'The Dowager Empress': Van Der Kiste and Hall, *Once a Grand Duchess*, 154
356 'I happened to be in London': Ponsonby, *Recollections*, 335
357 'The whole system was out of joint': Buchanan, Vol. 2, 86
357 'If Germany had not opted for war in 1914': Röhl, *Court*, 6
358 'In after years': Gore, 175
358 'Whatever happens': Reinermann, *Der Kaiser in England*, 146
358 The Russian family: Mossolov, *At the Court of the Last Tsar*, 203, describes how the Russian family disliked the Kaiser.
358 'It is monstrous': *The Spectator*, Prince Bülow and the Kaiser, with Excerpts from their Private Correspondence, Records of the German Foreign Office, 101

Bibliography

Manuscript Sources

The Royal Archives, Windsor Castle
Bundesarchiv, Koblenz
National Archives
Foreign Office Archives
State Archive of the Russian Federation, Moscow

Secondary Sources

Alexander, Grand Duke, *Once a Grand Duke* (Cassell, 1932)

Anon, *Recollections of Three Kaisers* (1929)

Ascher, Abraham, *The Revolution of 1905* (Stanford University Press, 1992)

Aronson, Theo, *The Kaisers* (Cassell, 1971)

—— *Crowns in Conflict 1910–18* (John Murray, 1986)

Asquith, H.H, *Asquith: Letters to Venetia Stanley*, ed: M. and E. Brock (Oxford, OUP, 1982)

Ayme, François, *Kaiser Wilhelm II und seine Erziehung* (Leipzig, 1898)

Baden, Prince Max von, *Erinnerungen und Dokumente* (Berlin, 1927)

Balfour, Michael, *The Kaiser and his Times* (1964)

Baring, Maurice, *A Year in Russia* (1917)

—— *The Puppet Show of Memory* (1923)

Battiscombe, Georgina, *Queen Alexandra* (Constable, 1969)

Benckendorff, Count Paul, *Last Days at Tsarskoe Selo* (1927)

Bennett, Daphne, *Vicky, Princess Royal of England and German Empress* (Collins, 1971)

Benson, E.F., *The Kaiser and his English Relations* (Longmans, 1936)

Berghahn, Volker, *Germany and the Approach of War in 1914* (1973)

Bernstein, Herman, *The Willy–Nicky Correspondence, Being the Secret Telegrams Exchanged between the Kaiser and the Tsar* (New York, 1918)

Bigelow, Poultney, *Prussian Memories* (New York, 1915)

Bing, Edward, *The Letters of Tsar Nicholas II and Empress Marie* (Nicholson and Watson, 1937)

Bismarck, Otto von, *Gedenken und Erinnerungen*: 3 vols (Stuttgart, 1921)

Bokhanov, Alexander, et al, *The Romanovs* (Leppi Publications, 1993)

Bonham-Carter, Violet, *Lantern Slides, The Diaries and Letters of Violet Bonham-Carter 1904–1914* (Weidenfeld and Nicolson, 1996)

Buchanan, Sir George, *My Mission to Russia*: 2 vols (Cassell, 1923)

Buckle, George, *The Letters of Queen Victoria* (1930)

Bussmann, Walter, *Staatssekretar Graf Herbert von Bismarck* (Gottingen, 1964)

Bülow, Prince Bernhard von, *Memoirs*: 4 vols (Putnam, 1931)

Buxhoeveden, Baroness Sophie, *Before the Storm* (Macmillan, 1938)

—— *The Life and Tragedy of Alexandra Fedorovna, Empress of Russia* (Longmans Green, 1928)

Cecil, Lamar, *Wilhelm II, Vol. I, Prince and Emperor, 1859–1900* (Chapel Hill, 1989)

—— *Wilhelm II, Vol. II, 1900–1941, Emperor and Exile* (Chapel Hill, 1996)

Cowles, Virginia, *Edward VII and his Circle* (Hamish Hamilton, 1956)

—— *The Last Tsar and Tsarina* (Weidenfeld and Nicolson, 1977)

D'Encausse, Hélène Carrère, *Nicholas II, The Interrupted Transition* (Holmes & Meyer, 2000)

Die Grosse Politik der Europaischen Kabinette 1871–1914 (Berlin, 1922)

Dimond, Frances, *Developing the Picture, Queen Alexandra and the Art of Photograpy* (Royal Collection Publications, 2004)

Elkind, Louis, *The German Emperor's Speeches* (1904)

Esher, Viscount (Reginald), *Journals and Letters*: 4 vols (Ivor Nicholson & Watson, 1934)

Esher, Viscount (Reginald), and A.C. Benson, *The Letters of Queen Victoria*, Vol. 1 (vols 2 and 3 ed. George Buckle) (John Murray, 1908)

Figes, Orlando, *A People's Tragedy: The Russian Revolution 1881–1924* (Cape, 1996)

Fischer, Fritz, *War of Illusion: German Policies from 1911–1914* (New York, 1975)

Fisher, Baron (John), *Records by the Admiral of the Fleet, Lord Fisher* (Hodder and Stoughton, 1919)

Fuhrmann, J.T., *The Complete Wartime Correspondence of Tsar Nicholas II and the Empress Alexandra, April 1914–March 1917* (Greenwood Press, 1999)

Fulford, Roger *see* Victoria, Queen

Gilliard, Pierre, *Thirteen years at the Russian Court* (New York, 1921)

Goetz, Walter, *Briefe Wilhelm II an den Zaren 1894–1914* (Berlin, 1920)

Gore, John, *King George V: a Personal Memoir* (John Murray, 1941)

Grabbe, Paul and Beatrice, eds, *The Private World of the Last Tsar* (Collins, 1985)

Haldane, Viscount, *An Autobiography* (New York, 1929)

Haller, Johannes, *Aus dem Leben des Fursten Philipp zu Eulenburg-Hertfeld* (Berlin, 1924)

Hanbury Williams, Major-General Sir John, *The Emperor Nicholas II, As I Knew Him* (1922)

Hardinge of Penshurst, Baron (Charles), *Old Diplomacy*, (1947)

Hibbert, Christopher, *Queen Victoria in her Letters and Journals* (John Murray, 1984)

Hohenlohe-Schillingsfürst, Chlodwig, Prince zu, *Denkwurdigkeiten* (Stuttgart, 1907)

Holstein, Friedrich von, *The Holstein Papers: the Memoirs, Diaries and Correspondence of Friedrich von Holstein*, ed. Norman Rich and M.H. Fisher, 4 vols (Cambridge University Press, 1955–63)

Hosking, Geoffrey, *Russia: People and Empire 1552–1917* (Harper Collins, 1997)

Hull, Isabel V., *The Entourage of Kaiser Wilhelm II 1888–1918* (Cambridge University Press, 1982)

Ilsemann, Sigurd von, *Der Kaiser in Holland* (Munich, 1967)

Isvolsky, Alexander, *The Memoirs of Alexander Isvolsky* (Hutchinson, 1920)

Klausen, Inger-Lise, *Dagmar, Zarina fra Denmark* (Lindhardt & Ringhof, 1997)

Kohut, Thomas, *Kaiser Wilhelm II and his Parents*, in Röhl and Sombart, *New Interpretations* (Cambridge, 1982)

Kurtz, Harold, *The Second Reich* (Macdonald Library, 1970)

Lee, Sir Sidney, *King Edward VII*, 2 vols (Macmillan, 1927)

Lerman, Katherine, *The Decisive Relationship: Kaiser Wilhelm II and Chancellor Bernhard von Bülow 1900–1905*, in Röhl and Stombart, *New Interpretations* (Cambridge, 1982)

Lieven, Dominic, *Russia's Rulers Under the Old Regime* (New Haven, 1989)

—— *Nicholas II, Emperor of All the Russias* (St Martin's Press, NY, 1993)

Lloyd George, David, *War Memoirs*, 6 vols (Ivor Nicholson & Watson, 1936)

Lowe, Charles, *Alexander III of Russia* (Heinemann, 1895)

—— *The Tale of a 'Times' Correspondent* (Hutchinson, 1927)

Ludwig, Emil, *Kaiser Wilhelm II* (Putnam, 1926)

Magnus, Philip, *King Edward The Seventh* (John Murray, 1964)

Mann, Golo, *Wilhelm II* (Scherz Verlag, 1964)

Marie, Queen of Rumania, *The Story of My Life*, 3 vols (Cassell, 1935)

Massie, Robert, *Nicholas and Alexandra* (Victor Gollancz, 1968)

Maylunas, Andrei, and Mironenko, Sergei, *A Lifelong Passion, Nicholas and Alexandra, Their Own Story* (Weidenfeld and Nicholson, 1996)

Monts, Count Anton, *Erinnnerungen* (Berlin, 1932)

Mossolov, A.A., *At the Court of the Last Tsar* (Methuen, 1935)

Morier, Sir Robert, *Memoirs and Letters*, 2 vols (Edward Arnold, 1911)

Müller, Georg von, *The Kaiser and his Court*, ed. Walter Görlitz (Macdonald, 1961) (*Regierte der Kaiser?* [Musterschmidt Verlag, 1959])

Nicolson, Harold, *King George V, His Life and Reign* (Constable, 1952)

Packard, Jerrold, *Victoria's Daughters* (Sutton Publishing, 1999)

Paléologue, Maurice, *Guillaume II et Nicolas II* (Paris, 1934)

—— *An Ambassador's Memoirs*, 3 vols (Hutchinson, 1924)

Pares, Bernard, *My Russian Memoirs* (1931)

—— *The Fall of the Russian Monarchy* (1939)

Pless, Princess Daisy von, *Better Left Unsaid* (New York, 1931)

—— *The Diaries of Daisy, Princess of Pless* (John Murray, 1950)

Poliakoff, Vladimir, *The Empress Marie of Russia and Her Times* (Butterworth, 1926)

Ponsonby, Sir Frederick, *Recollections of Three Reigns* (Eyre & Spottiswoode, 1951)

Ponsonby, Sir Frederick, ed., *The Letters of Empress Frederick* (Macmillan, 1928)

Pope-Hennessy, James, *Queen Mary* (George Allen and Unwin, 1939)

Radzinsky, Edvard, *The Life and Death of Nicholas II* (Doubleday, 1992)

Radziwill, Princess Catherine, *The Intimate Life of the Last Tsarina* (Cassell, 1929)

Reinermann, Lothar, *Der Kaiser in England* (Paderborn: Schöningh, 2001)

Reuss, Martin, 'Bismarck's Dismissal and the Holstein Circle', in *European Studies Review*, vol. 5, no. 1 (1975)

Rich, Norman, and Fisher, M.H., *The Holstein Papers*, 4 vols (Cambridge, 1955–63)

—— *Friedrich von Holstein*, 2 vols (Cambridge, 1965)

Roberts, Andrew, *Salisbury, Victorian Titan* (Weidenfeld & Nicolson, 1999)

Rogge, Helmuth, *Holstein und Harden* (Munich, 1959)

—— ed., *Friedrich von Holstein* (Berlin, 1932)

Röhl, John C.G., *Germany without Bismarck: the crisis of government in the Second Reich* (Batsford, 1967)

—— *Philipp Eulenburgs politische Korrespondenz*, 3 vols (Boppard am Rhein, 1976–83)

—— *Kaiser Wilhelm II: New Interpretations: the Corfu papers* (Cambridge University Press, 1982 (ed. with Nicolaus Sombart))

—— *The Kaiser and his Court: Wilhelm II and the Government of Germany* (Cambridge University Press, 1994)

—— *Young Wilhelm: the Kaiser's early life, 1859–1888* (Munich, 1993)

—— *Wilhelm II: the Kaiser's Personal Monarchy, 1888–1900* (Cambridge University Press, 2005)

Rose, Kenneth, *King George V* (Weidenfeld & Nicolson, 1983)

Rosen, Baron, *Forty Years of Diplomacy*, 2 vols (New York, 1922)

Royalty Digest, ed. Paul Minette (Ticehurst, Sussex)

Sazonov, Sergei, *Fateful Years, 1906–1916* (1928)

Schönburg-Waldenburg, Prinz Heinrich von, *Erinnerungen* (Leipzig, 1929)

Schwering, Count Axel von (pseud.), *The Berlin Court under William II* (Cassell, 1915)

Schwertfeger, Bernhard, ed., *Kaiser und Kabinettschef, Rudolf von Valentini,* (Oldenburg, 1931)

Snyder, Louis, ed., *Documents of German History* (Rutgers University Press, 1958)

Steinberg, Mark, and Khrustalev, Vladimir, *The Fall of the Romanovs, Political Dreams and Personal Struggles in a Time of Revolution* (Yale University Press, 1995)

Swaine, General Leopold, *Camp and Chancery in a Soldier's Life* (John Murray, 1926)

Taylor, A.J.P., *The Struggle for Mastery in Europe 1848–1918* (OUP, 1971)

—— *Bismarck: the Man and the Statesman* (Hamish Hamilton, 1955)

Thimme, Friedrich, ed., *Front Wider Bülow. Staatsmanner, Diplomaten und Forscher zu seinen Denkwurdigketen* (München, 1931)

Tisdall, E.P., *The Dowager Empress* (Stanley Paul, 1957)

Topham, Anne, *Memories of the Kaiser's Court* (Methuen, 1914)

—— *Chronicles of the Prussian Court* (Methuen, 1926)

Van der Kiste, John, *Kaiser Wilhelm II* (Sutton Publishing, 1999)

—— *Crowns in a Changing World* (Sutton, Stroud, 1993)

—— and *Coryne Hall, Once a Grand Duchess, Xenia* (Sutton, Stroud, 2002)

Verner, Andrew, *The Crisis of Russian Autocracy, Nicholas II and the 1905 Revolution* (Princeton University Press, 1990)

Victoria, Queen, *Dearest Child: Letters between Queen Victoria and the Princess Royal* (this and subsequent vols ed. Roger Fulford, Evans Bros, 1971)

—— *Dearest Mama: Letters between Queen Victoria and the Crown Princess of Prussia, 1861–1864*

—— *Your Dear Letter: Private Correspondence between Queen Victoria and the Crown Princess of Prussia, 1865–1871*

—— *Darling Child: Private Correspondence between Queen Victoria and the German Crown Princess, 1871–1878*

Victoria, Princess of Prussia, *My Memoirs* (Eveleigh, Nash, 1929)

Vierhaus, Rudolf, *Aus Dem Tagebuch Der Baronin Spitzemberg* (München, 1979)

Viktoria Luise, Herzogin, *Ein Leben als Tochter des Kaisers* (Göttingen, 1965)

—— *Im Glanz der Krone* (Göttingen, 1967)

Waldersee, Alfred Graf von, *Denkwurdigkeiten*, ed. Heinrich Meisner (Stuttgart, 1923)

Wheeler-Bennett, Sir John, *King George VI, his Life and Reign* (Macmillan, 1958)

—— *Knaves, Fools and Heroes* (Macmillan, 1974)

Weller, Uwe, *Maximilian Harden und Die Zukunft* (Schünemann Universitats Verlag, Bremen, 1970)

Whittle, Tyler, *The Last Kaiser: a Biography of William II* (Heinemann, 1977)

Wilhelm II, *Aus Meinem Leben 1859–1888* (Berlin, 1927) (*My Early Life* [Methuen, 1926])

William, Crown Prince, *The Memoirs of the Crown Prince of Germany* (Thornton Butterworth, 1922)

Williamson, Samuel, *Austria-Hungary and the Origins of the First World War* (New York, 1991)

Witte, Sergei, *The Memoirs of Count Witte*, 3 vols, ed. Sidney Harcave (New York, 1990)

Woodham-Smith, Cecil, *Queen Victoria: her life and times* (Hamish Hamilton, 1972)

Young, Harry, *Maximilian Harden* (The Hague, 1959)

Yusupov, Felix Prince, *Lost Splendour* (Cape, 1953)

Zedlitz-Trutzschler, Count Robert, *Zwolf Jahren am Deutschen Kaiserhof* (Berlin, 1924)

Index